Syntactic Change in Welsh

A Study of the Loss of Verb-Second

DAVID W. E. WILLIS

CLARENDON PRESS · OXFORD
1998

Oxford University Press, Great Clarendon Street, Oxford OX2 6DP
Oxford New York
Athens Auckland Bangkok Bogotá Buenos Aires Calcutta
Cape Town Chennai Dar es Salaam Delhi Florence Hong Kong Istanbul
Karachi Kuala Lumpur Madrid Melbourne Mexico City Mumbai
Nairobi Paris São Paolo Singapore Taipei Tokyo Toronto Warsaw
and associated companies in
Berlin Ibadan

Oxford is a trade mark of Oxford University Press

Published in the United States
by Oxford University Press Inc., New York

British Library Cataloguing in Publication Data
Data available

Library of Congress Cataloging in Publication Data
Syntactic Change in Welsh: a study of the loss of verb-second
David W.E. Willis.
Revision of the author's thesis (Ph. D.)
—University of Oxford, 1996.
Includes bibliographical references and index.
1. Welsh language—Syntax. 2. Linguistic change. I. Title.
PB2171.W55   1998   491.6′6—dc21   98–25545
ISBN 0–19–823759–6

10 9 8 7 6 5 4 3 2 1

Typeset by Peter Kahrel, Lancaster
Printed in Great Britain on acid-free paper by
Biddles Ltd., Guildford and King's Lynn

Preface

This book is a revised version of my 1996 University of Oxford doctoral dissertation. It offers a synchronic analysis of Middle Welsh word order, arguing that a verb-second rule was operative in that language, and traces the changes that have led to the innovation of verb-initial main-clause order in Modern Welsh. In doing this, the work attempts to bring together two traditions of work in linguistics that hitherto have developed separately. Within Celtic linguistics, there has been in recent years a resurgence of interest in questions of word order and word-order change, beginning with pioneering work by T. Arwyn Watkins in the 1970s and continuing to the present day in the work of, amongst others, James Fife and Erich Poppe. This work has in general been conducted in a functionalist framework. At the same time, a tradition of research in Romance and Germanic linguistics has grown up under the banner of 'the New Comparative Syntax' within the Principles and Parameters syntactic paradigm. This research has tried to account for cross-linguistic differences in such areas as clitic placement and word order by comparing geographically or temporally related languages. Related work in historical syntax, particularly that of Ian Roberts and David Lightfoot, has led to the notion of parametric change, the idea that at certain stages in their history languages undergo a period when a change in the setting of a single linguistic 'switch' leads to a number of syntactic changes. These strands of theoretically oriented research have had particular success in the analysis of verb-second phenomena. The central aim of this book is to bring these two major strands of research together. I hope that, in doing so, it has increased our knowledge of the syntactic changes that the Welsh language has undergone, and widened our understanding of the process of syntactic change itself.

With this in mind, I have tried to make the discussion as accessible as possible both to those whose interests lie in theoretical syntax and syntactic change, and to those whose primary interest is in the history of Welsh language and literature. Inevitably this means that the introduction of syntactic theory is gentler than the first group may prefer, and that aspects of Welsh grammar and linguistic history that may seem obvious to the second group are dealt with explicitly. I hope that both groups of readers will be tolerant of any such irritations.

Dates are given in the text and references for Modern Welsh texts (composed after 1450). For most texts, a single date is given, namely that of first publication or that of the earliest extant manuscript as appropriate. Where two dates are given the first indicates the date of first publication or of the earliest extant manuscript, the second, in square brackets, indicates the probable date of composition. Where there is a reasonable possibility that the date of composition was significantly earlier than the manuscript, MS has been added to draw attention to the fact that the date given is that of the earliest extant manuscript.

Texts are cited by page and line number or simply line number as appropriate. *BTy*, is cited by page and column followed by line number. W is cited by folio then line number. Groups of almanacs (AJP, AMW), ballads (BER, BHJ, BJJ) and some letters (Eist., LTE, LUSS) are cited by letters and/or numbers identifying the source text or letter, followed by page and line numbers.

Welsh words are cited in the body of the text using normalized Middle Welsh or standard Modern Welsh forms according to context. In a number of cases the same word (e.g. MW *bot*, ModW *bod*; or MW *y*(*d*), ModW *y*(*r*)) will therefore have two standard forms, according to whether Middle or Modern Welsh is the primary focus of discussion.

There are a number of people whose help and encouragement in the course of my research I would like to acknowledge. Above all, I would like to thank my thesis supervisor, D. Ellis Evans, for his constant support and encouragement. For their willingness to supply native-speaker judgements, I thank Damian Walford Davies, Heather Williams, Alun Jones, Kerstin Hoge, Lars-Erik Cederman, and Judith Pollmann. Much of the data used was collected using the Oxford Concordance Program developed by Oxford University Computing Service. I am also grateful to Thomas Charles-Edwards, Judith Olszowy, Erich Poppe, Gillian Ramchand, Maggie Tallerman, and Matthew Whelpton for their comments on part or all of the draft, and to Anna Morpurgo Davies for her advice and interest in the project. Needless to say, they are not responsible for the ultimate use to which I have put their comments.

For financial support I am grateful to the British Academy, which provided me with a Major State Studentship at St John's College, Oxford, and with a Postdoctoral Research Fellowship at Jesus College. I would also like to acknowledge the support of Somerville College, where I spent three years as Mary Somerville Junior Research Fellow.

Finally, this project would never have been completed without years of love and support from my parents. To them I offer my deepest gratitude for all that they have done.

D. W. E. W.

Contents

Abbreviations

WORKS OF REFERENCE

AJP   Almanacs by John Prys

ALHB   Ellis Roberts (Y Cowper), *Ail Lythyr Hen Bechadur at ei Gyd Frodyr . . .* (Y Mwythig: J. Eddowes, 1772)

AMW   Almanacs by Mathew Williams

AP   *Armes Prydein*, ed. Ifor Williams and Rachel Bromwich (Dublin: Dublin Institute for Advanced Studies, 1972)

BB₁   *Brut y Brenhinedd: Cotton Cleopatra Version*, ed. John Jay Parry (Cambridge, Mass.: Mediaeval Academy of America, 1937)

BB₂   *Brut y Brenhinedd: Llanstephan Ms. 1 Version*, ed. Brynley F. Roberts (Dublin: Dublin Institute for Advanced Studies, 1971)

BD   *Brut Dingestow*, ed. Henry Lewis (Caerdydd: Gwasg Prifysgol Cymru, 1942)

BDGU   Hugh Jones and John Cadwaladr, *Enterlut, neu Ddanghosiad o'r Modd y Darfu i'r Brenhin Dafydd Odinebu efo Gwraig Urias . . .* (Caerlleon: W. Read a T. Huxley, n.d. [*c.*1765])

BER   Ballads by Ellis Roberts (Y Cowper)

BF   'Buchedd Fargred', ed. Melville Richards, *Bulletin of the Board of Celtic Studies*, 9 (1939), 324–34; 10 (1939), 53–9; 13 (1949), 65–71

BHJ   Ballads by Hugh Jones (Llangwm)

BJJ   Ballads by John Jones (Jac Glan-y-gors)

BLl   'Y Brenin Llyr' (National Library of Wales, MS Cwrtmawr 212A, MS *c.*1700–50)

BM   *Breuddwyd Maxen*, ed. Ifor Williams (Bangor: Jarvis a Foster, 1908)

BR   *Breudwyt Ronabwy*, ed. Melville Richards (Caerdydd: Gwasg Prifysgol Cymru, 1948)

Branwen   *Branwen Uerch Lyr*, ed. Derick S. Thomson (Dublin: Dublin Institute for Advanced Studies, 1961)

BSM   *Buchedd Sant Martin* (MS 1488–9), ed. Evan John Jones (Caerdydd: Gwasg Prifysgol Cymru, 1945)

BT   *Facsimile and Text of the Book of Taliessin*, ed. J. Gwenogvryn Evans (Llanbedrog: J. Gwenogvryn Evans, 1910)

BTy₁   *Brut y Tywysogyon: Peniarth Ms. 20*, ed. Thomas Jones (Caerdydd: Gwasg Prifysgol Cymru, 1941)

BTy₂   *Brut y Tywysogyon or The Chronicle of the Princes: Red Book of Hergest Version*, ed. Thomas Jones (Cardiff: University of Wales Press, 1955)

BY   *Y Bibyl Ynghymraec*, ed. Thomas Jones (Caerdydd: Gwasg Prifysgol Cymru, 1940)

CA   *Canu Aneirin*, ed. Ifor Williams (Caerdydd: Gwasg Prifysgol Cymru, 1938)

CC   Oliver Thomas, *Car-wr y Cymru* (orig. pub. 1631); *Gweithiau Oliver Thomas ac Evan Roberts*, ed. Merfyn Morgan (Caerdydd: Gwasg Prifysgol Cymru, 1981)

CD   Edward Thomas (of Rhydwen, Flintshire), *Cwymp Dyn: gwedi ei Osod Allan ar Ddull Interlude, yn Dangos fel y Bu i'r Sarph Temptio y Wraig Yngardd Eden . . .* (Caerlleon: Read a Huxley, n.d. [*c*.1767–8])

CDd   'Catwn a'i Ddehongliad', ed. Ifor Williams, *Bulletin of the Board of Celtic Studies*, 2 (1923), 26–36

CDH   Richard Parry, 'Enterlude neu Chwaryddiaeth ar Destyn Odiaethol, yn Dangos Pa Drigolion a Fu'n Preswylo yn y Deyrnas Hon cyn Dyfod Cymru na Saeson Erioed iw Meddiannu, o Wnaethuriad R P' (National Library of Wales, MS 833A, MS 18th c. (composed 1737))

CF   'The Computus Fragment', ed. Ifor Williams, *Bulletin of the Board of Celtic Studies*, 3 (1927), 245–72

Chad   'The Welsh Marginalia in the Lichfield Gospels Part I', ed. Dafydd Jenkins and Morfydd E. Owen, *Cambridge Medieval Celtic Studies*, 5 (1983), 37–66

ChCC   *Chwedlau Cymraeg Canol*, ed. A. O. H. Jarman (Caerdydd: Gwasg Prifysgol Cymru, 1957)

CHSS   'Cyssegredic Historia Severws Swlpisiws' (MS 1604–12, composed 1574–1604), ed. Thomas Jones, *Bulletin of the Board of Celtic Studies*, 8 (1936), 107–20

CI   Elis Gruffydd, *Castell yr Iechyd* (composed 1540s), ed. S. Minwel Tibbott (Caerdydd: Gwasg Prifysgol Cymru, 1969)

CLlLl   *Cyfranc Lludd a Llefelys*, ed. Brynley F. Roberts (Dublin: Dublin Institute for Advanced Studies, 1975)

CmB   Legh Richmond, *Crefydd mewn Bwthyn; neu, Hanes Jane Bach, yn Dangos y Buddioldeb o Egwyddori Plant* (Bala: R. Saunderson, 1819)

CO   *Culhwch ac Olwen: An Edition and Study of the Oldest Arthurian Tale*, ed. Rachel Bromwich and D. Simon Evans (Cardiff: University of Wales Press, 1992)

CwyC   William Richards (of Lynn), *Cwyn y Cystuddiedig, a Griddfanau y Carcharorion Dieuog; neu, Ychydig o Hanes Dioddefiadau Diweddar Thomas John a Samuel Griffiths, y rhai gwedi Goddef Gorthrymder Tost, a Chaethiwed Caled, Dros Chwech neu Saith o Fisoedd . . . a Gawsant eu Rhyddhau . . .* (Caerfyrddin: Ioan Evans, 1798)

CylC   Morgan John Rhys (ed.). *Cylchgrawn Cynmraeg*, issue 2 (Trefecca: J. Daniel, 1793), 119–20; issue 3 (n.p., 1793), 170–80; issue 4 (Carmarthen, 1794), 234–7; and ed. Gwyn A. Williams, 'Morgan John Rhys and Volney's Ruins of Empires', *Bulletin of the Board of Celtic Studies*, 20 (1962–4), 58–73

DA   Robert Jones (of Rhos-lan), *Drych yr Amseroedd* (orig. pub. 1820), ed. Glyn M. Ashton (Caerdydd: Gwasg Prifysgol Cymru, 1958)

DC   Griffith Robert, *Y Drych Cristianogawl* (orig. pub. 1585), ed. D. M. Rogers (Menston, York.: Scolar Press, 1972)

DE   'Darnau o'r Efengylau' (MS 1550–75), ed. Henry Lewis, *Y Cymmrodor*, 31 (1921), 193–216

DEG   Elis Gruffydd, 'Disgrifiad Elis Gruffudd o'r Cynadleddau a Fu rhwng Harri VIII a'r Ymherodr Siarl V a rhyngddo a Ffranses I, Brenin Ffrainc yn 1520' (composed 1540s), ed. Thomas Jones, *Bulletin of the Board of Celtic Studies*, 18 (1960), 312–37

DFf   Darn o'r Ffestival (Liber Ffestialis), (MS 1550–75), ed. Henry Lewis, *Supplement to the Transactions of the Honourable Society of Cymmrodorion (Session 1923–24)* (Llundain: Cymdeithas y Cymmrodorion, 1925)

DFfEL	Maurice (Morys) Kyffin, *Deffyniad Ffydd Eglwys Loegr* (orig. pub. 1595), ed. William Prichard Williams (Bangor: Jarvis & Foster, 1908)
DGG	*Cywyddau Dafydd ap Gwilym a'i Gyfoeswyr*, ed. Ifor Williams and Thomas Roberts (Caerdydd: Gwasg Prifysgol Cymru, 1935)
DWB	*Dictionary of Welsh Biography down to 1940*, ed. John Edward Lloyd and R. T. Jenkins (London: Honourable Society of Cymmrodorion, 1959)
Eist.	'Llythyrau Ynglŷn ag Eisteddfodau'r Gwyneddigion' (dated 1789), ed. G. J. Williams, *Llên Cymru*, 1 (1950), 29–47, 113–25
EWGT	*Early Welsh Genealogical Tracts*, ed. P. C. Bartrum (Cardiff: University of Wales Press, 1966)
FfBD	'Frederick Brenin Denmark' (National Library of Wales, MS Cwrtmawr 490A, MS *c*.1700–50)
FfBO	*Ffordd y Brawd Odrig*, ed. Stephen J. Williams (Caerdydd: Gwasg Prifysgol Cymru, 1929)
FfM	William Roberts, *Ffrewyll y Methodistiaid neu Buttein-glwm Siencyn ac Ynfydog* (n.p., n.d. [1745])
GA	Thomas Jones, 'Gair yn ei Amser at Drigolion Cymru gan Ewyllysiwr Da i'w Wlad' (orig. pub. 1798), ed. Frank Price Jones, *Transactions of the Denbighshire Historical Society*, 5 (1956), 35–59
GBC	Ellis Wynne, *Gweledigaetheu y Bardd Cwsc* (orig. pub. 1703), ed. John Morris-Jones (Caerdydd: Gwasg Prifysgol Cymru, 1948)
GN	Ellis Roberts, *Llyfr Enterlute Newydd wedi Gosod mewn Dull Ymddiddanion rhwng Gras a Natur* (Warrington: William Eyres, 1769)
GPC	*Geiriadur Prifysgol Cymru*, ed. R. J. Thomas (Caerdydd: Gwasg Prifysgol Cymru, 1950–present)
GWV	'Gwyrthyeu y Wynvydedic Veir', ed. Gwenan Jones, *Bulletin of the Board of Celtic Studies*, 9 (1938), 144–8, 334–41; 10 (1939), 21–33
H.	*Llawysgrif Hendregadredd*, ed. John Morris-Jones and T. H. Parry-Williams (Caerdydd: Gwasg Prifysgol Cymru, 1971)
HG	*Hen Gyflwyniadau* (orig. pub. 1567–1792), ed. Henry Lewis (Caerdydd: Gwasg Prifysgol Cymru, 1948)
HGC	*Casgliad o Hanes-Gerddi Cymraeg* (MSS 17th–18th c.), ed. anon. (Caerdydd: Cymdeithas Llen Cymru, 1903)
HGK	*Historia Gruffud vab Kenan*, ed. D. Simon Evans (Caerdydd: Gwasg Prifysgol Cymru, 1977)
HHGB	Mathew Williams, *Hanes Holl Grefyddau'r Byd, yn Enwedig y Grefydd Grist'nogol etc.* (Caerfyrddin: I. Daniel, 1799)
HTN	Thomas Edwards (Twm o'r Nant), *Hanes Bywyd Twm o'r Nant, yr Hwn yn gyffredin à Elwir Twm o'r Nant, Prydydd . . .* (Aberystwyth: S. Williams, 1814; first published 1805)
ID	*Casgliad o Waith Ieuan Deulwyn*, ed. Ifor Williams (Bangor: Jarvis a Foster, 1909)
IYCA	Thomas Edwards (?), 'Interliwt Ynghylch Cain ac Abel' (composed ?*c*.1758), ed. G. M. Ashton, *Bulletin of the Board of Celtic Studies*, 13 (1949), 78–89
Juv.	'Naw Englyn y Juvencus', ed. Ifor Williams, *Bulletin of the Board of Celtic Studies*, 6 (1932), 205–24; 'Y Creawdwr Hollalluog', in *Blodeugerdd Barddas o Ganu Crefyddol Cynnar*, ed. Marged Haycock (Llandybïe: Cyhoeddiadau Barddas, 1994), 3–16

KAA	*Kedymdeithyas Amlyn ac Amic*, ed. Patricia Williams (Caerdydd: Gwasg Prifysgol Cymru, 1982)
KLlB	William Salesbury, *Kynniver Llith a Ban* (orig. pub. 1567), ed. John Fisher (Cardiff: University of Wales Press, 1931)
LAG	Letters by Ann Griffiths
LDT	Letters by David Thomas (Dafydd Ddu Eryri)
LEE	Letters by Evan Evans (Ieuan Fardd)
LJJ	Letters by John Jones (Jac Glan-y-gors)
LlB	*Cyfreithiau Hywel Dda yn ôl Llyfr Blegywryd*, ed. Stephen J. Williams and J. Enoch Powell (Caerdydd: Gwasg Prifysgol Cymru, 1942)
LlTA	Morgan Llwyd, *Llyfr y Tri Aderyn* (orig. pub. 1653), ed. anon. (Caerdydd: Gwasg Prifysgol Cymru, 1974)
LTE	Letters by Thomas Edwards (Twm o'r Nant)
LUSS	Letters from Welsh settlers in the United States
MEW	Bishop Richard Watson, *Meddyliau yr Esgob Watson am y Cyfnewidiad Diweddar yn Llywodraeth Ffraingc* (Caerfyrddin: J. Ross, 1793)
MFf	'Mab y Fforestwr' (MS *c.*1600), in *RhG* i.122–30
MIG	'Llyma Vabinogi Iessu Grist', ed. Mary Williams, *Revue Celtique*, 33 (1912), 184–248
Misc.	Miscellaneous letters from Caernarfonshire
Owein	*Owein or Chwedyl Iarlles y Ffynnawn*, ed. R. L. Thomson (Dublin: Dublin Institute for Advanced Studies, 1968)
Ox.	'Glosau Rhydychen [The Oxford Glosses]: Mesurau a Phwysau', ed. Ifor Williams, *Bulletin of the Board of Celtic Studies*, 5 (1930), 226–48
PA	Huw Lewys, *Perl mewn Adfyd* (orig. pub. 1595), ed. W. J. Gruffydd (Caerdydd: Gwasg Prifysgol Cymru, 1929)
Peredur	*Historia Peredur vab Efrawc*, ed. Glenys Witchard Goetinck (Caerdydd: Gwasg Prifysgol Cymru, 1976)
PKM	*Pedeir Keinc y Mabinogi*, ed. Ifor Williams (Caerdydd: Gwasg Prifysgol Cymru, 1930)
PN	Hugh Jones (of Llangwm), *Enterlute Newydd; ar Ddull Ymddiddan rhwng Protestant a Neilltuwr: Gyd ag Ychydig o Hanes Ymrafael Opiniwnau a Fu er Amser Charles I Hyd yn Awr; A Byrr Grybwylliad am Ffalster, Cybydd-dod, a Chydwybod* (Mwythig: T. Wood, 1783)
Pwyll	*Pwyll Pendeuic Dyuet*, ed. R. L. Thomson (Dublin: Dublin Institute for Advanced Studies, 1957)
RhG	*Rhyddiaith Gymraeg*, i. *Detholion o Lawysgrifau 1488–1609*, ed. T. H. Parry-Williams (Caerdydd: Gwasg Prifysgol Cymru, 1954); ii. *1547–1618*, ed. Thomas Jones (Caerdydd: Gwasg Prifysgol Cymru, 1956)
Rhy.	Walter Davies (Gwallter Mechain), *Rhyddid: Traethawd a Ennillodd Ariandlws Cymdeithas y Gwyneddigion ar ei Thestun i Eisteddfod Llanelwy . . .* (Llundain: T. Rickaby, 1791)
SDR	*Chwedleu Seith Doethon Rufein*, ed. Henry Lewis (Caerdydd: Gwasg Prifysgol Cymru, 1958)
Slander cases	'An Analysis and Calendar of Early Modern Welsh Defamation Suits' (MSS 16th–19th c.), ed. Richard F. Suggett (SSRC Final Report (HR 6979), 1983)

SM   'The Surexit Memorandum', ed. John Morris-Jones, *Y Cymmrodor*, 28
          (1918), 268–79; 'The Welsh Marginalia in the Lichfield Gospels Part II:
          The "Surexit" Memorandum', ed. Dafydd Jenkins and Morfydd E. Owen,
          Cambridge Medieval Celtic Studies, 7 (1984), 91–120

StG   John Jones (Jac Glan-y-gors), *Seren tan Gwmmwl* (orig. pub. 1795); *Seren
          tan Gwmmwl a Toriad y Dydd*, ed. Thomas Jones (Liverpool: Hugh Evans
          a'i Feibion, 1923)

TChB   Thomas Edwards (Twm o'r Nant), *Tri Chryfion Byd, Sef Tylodi, Cariad, ac
          Angau. Yn y Canlyniad o Hyn, y Dangosir y Modd y mae r Tri yn Gryfion
          Byd* . . . (n.p. [?1789])

TD   John Jones (Jac Glan-y-gors), *Toriad y Dydd* (orig. pub. 1797); *Seren tan
          Gwmmwl a Toriad y Dydd*, ed. Thomas Jones (Liverpool: Hugh Evans a'i
          Feibion, 1923)

TN   *Testament Newydd ein Arglwydd Jesv Christ*, trans. William Salesbury (no
          imprint, [1567])

TWRP   *A Study of Three Welsh Religious Plays* (MSS 16th c.), ed. Gwenan Jones
          (Bala: R. Evans & Son, 1939)

W.   *Llyfr Gwyn Rhydderch*, ed. J. Gwenogvryn Evans with introduction by
          R. M. Jones (Caerdydd: Gwasg Prifysgol Cymru, 1973; new edn. of
          The White Book Mabinogion, ed. J. Gwenogvryn Evans (Pwllheli:
          J. Gwenogvryn Evans, 1907))

W. Ballads *A Bibliography of Welsh Ballads*, ed. J. H. Davies (London: Honourable
          Society of Cymmrodorion, 1911)

YAL   'Ystori Alexander a Lodwig' (MS *c.*1590, composed after 1515), ed.
          Thomas Jones and J. E. Caerwyn Williams, *Studia Celtica*, 10–11 (1975–6),
          261–304

YBH   *Ystorya Bown de Hamtwn*, ed. Morgan Watkins (Caerdydd: Gwasg Prifys-
          gol Cymru, 1958)

YCM   *Ystorya de Carolo Magno*, ed. Stephen J. Williams (Caerdydd: Gwasg
          Prifysgol Cymru, 1930)

YDG   Jonathan Hughes, 'Enterlute Histori y Dywysoges Genefetha' (National
          Library of Wales, MS Cwrtmawr 120A, 18th c. (composed 1744))

YLH   *Yny Lhyvyr Hwnn* (orig. pub. 1546), ed. John H. Davies (Bangor: Jarvis &
          Foster, London: J. M. Dent, 1902)

YRW   Richard Parry (?), *Ystori Richard Whittington, yr Hwn a Fu Dair Gwaith yn
          Arglwydd Maer Llundain. Wedi ei Gosod Allan mewn Interlute*
          (Caerfyrddin: J. Evans, 1812 (composed 1736))

YSG   *Ystoryaeu Seint Greal*, ed. Thomas Jones (Caerdydd: Gwasg Prifysgol
          Cymru, 1992)

YT   Elis Gruffydd, *Ystoria Taliesin: The Story of Taliesin* (composed 1540s), ed.
          Patrick K. Ford (Cardiff: University of Wales Press, 1991)

GRAMMATICAL GLOSSES

1P etc.	first-person plural
1S etc.	first-person singular
1S-GEN, etc.	first-person-singular genitive clitic
1S-ACC, etc.	first-person-singular object clitic
CL	clitic
COMP	complementizer
COND	conditional (imperfect subjunctive) verb form
CONJ	conjunctive pronoun
IMPER	imperative verb form
IMPERS	impersonal verb form
IMPF	imperfect-tense verb form
INF	infinitive
NEG	negative marker
PERF	perfect verb form/perfect aspect marker
PLUPERF	pluperfect
PP	past participle
PRD	predicative particle
PROG	progressive aspect marker
PRT	preverbal particle
REDUP	reduplicated pronoun
REL	relative marker
SUBJ	present-subjunctive verb form
VN	verbnoun
*	(in syntax) ungrammatical form; (in historical phonology) reconstructed form
**	(in historical syntax) hypothetical or predicted form, of uncertain grammaticality

Verbs unglossed for tense are present. Verbs unglossed for person are third person singular.

OTHER ABBREVIATIONS

AdvVSO	Adverb–Verb–Subject–Object
AgrSP	Subject Agreement Phrase
AP	Adverbial Phrase
AspP	Aspect Phrase
AuxSVO	Auxiliary–Subject–Verb–Object
CP	Complementizer Phrase (clause)
DP	Determiner Phrase (noun phrase)
DR	Diachronic Reanalysis
ECP	Empty Category Principle
GB	Government and Binding
Infl (I)	Inflection
IP	Inflection Phrase

LF	Logical Form
ModW	Modern Welsh
MW	Middle Welsh
NegP	Negation Phrase
NP	Noun Phrase
OV	Object–Verb
OVS	Object–Verb–Subject
OW	Old Welsh
PF	Phonetic Form
PP	Prepositional Phrase
SAuxVO	Subject–Auxiliary–Verb–Object
Spec	Specifier
SVO	Subject–Verb–Object
TP	Tense Phrase
t	trace
UG	Universal Grammar
VP	Verb Phrase
VSO	Verb–Subject–Object
V1	Verb-first
V2	Verb-second
XP	Any phrasal constituent

1. Introduction

The development of word order in Welsh is one of the greatest puzzles in the study of the historical syntax of the language. In its simplest terms, the puzzle is as follows. In Modern Welsh, the unmarked main clause word order is Verb–Subject–Object (VSO). In Middle Welsh, on the other hand, the verb-initial order is not common. The unmarked pattern is that known to traditional Welsh grammarians as the 'abnormal sentence' (*brawddeg annormal*), in which some element precedes the verb, resulting in orders such as Subject–Verb–Object (SVO), Object–Verb–Subject (OVS), Adverb–Verb–Subject–Object and so on. When we go back further, however, to Old Welsh, the Modern Welsh pattern apparently re-emerges: VSO is once again dominant. The question that arises is: can the language really have moved away from VSO and back again in the course of a thousand years? This is the puzzle that I consider in this book, in particular, the second part—whether (and if so how) Welsh word order moved back to VSO in the transition from Middle to Modern Welsh. In doing so, I shall use a Government and Binding (GB) (Principles and Parameters) framework to trace the development of Welsh word order from the fourteenth to the early nineteenth century. A number of related issues that have been overlooked in the substantial literature on the subject seem to have considerable relevance to this question, in particular the development of the subject pronoun system, the emergence of a system of affirmative main-clause complementizers in Modern Welsh (the 'pre-sentential particles'), and patterns of clausal coordination.

1.1. THE WELSH LANGUAGE

Before we turn to a detailed presentation of the problem, it is worth looking at the place of Welsh within the Celtic family of languages, since the testimony of a number of them bears substantially on the question of word order within Welsh itself.

Welsh is a member of the Brythonic sub-group of Celtic, the other main sub-group being Goidelic (Irish, Scots Gaelic, and Manx). Its sister languages within the Brythonic sub-group are Breton and Cornish. The parent language of all three is British, a language spoken across most of Britain during the first half of the first millennium AD and before. Languages closely related to British were spoken in Continental Europe at about the same time. Most important for the current discussion is Gaulish, a language spoken throughout France until its replacement by Vulgar Latin. It seems likely that the genetic relationship between Gaulish and British (and possibly some other Continental Celtic languages) is much closer than that between British and the Goidelic languages. In other words, the Goidelic languages and some varieties of Continental Celtic (Celtiberian) diverged from the other Celtic languages early. This view (the 'Gallo-Brittonic hypothesis'), adopted explicitly or implicitly in much of the literature on historical Celtic syntax, is justified in such works as Koch (1992) and Schmidt (1990, 1993), primarily on the basis of the evidence of the sound changes $*k^w > *p$ and syllabic $*n *m > *an *am$, common to British and Gaulish as distinct from Goidelic. For a dissenting view, see McCone (1992).

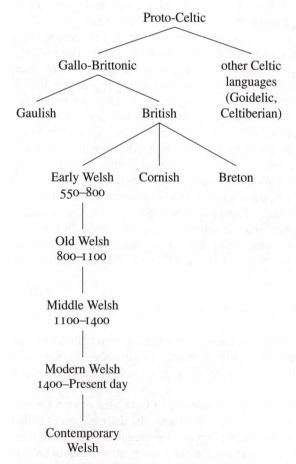

FIGURE 1.1. The periodization of Welsh and its position within the Celtic languages

Welsh is conventionally divided into four periods: Early Welsh, from the loss of final syllables to the earliest written records—that is, 550–800; Old Welsh 800–1100; Middle Welsh 1100–1400; and Modern Welsh 1400 to the present day (D. Simon Evans 1964: pp. xvi–xxi; Jackson 1953: 5–6; R. Brinley Jones 1979: 19–22; Lewis 1931: 96–108; Morris-Jones 1913: 6–8). Early Modern Welsh from 1400 to 1600 is sometimes used as a subdivision of Modern Welsh. The term Contemporary Welsh will be used where there are differences within the Modern period, in order to refer to the language spoken at the present day and used in the literature of the last hundred years. Where such differences are not an issue, however, the more neutral term Modern Welsh will be employed to cover even the contemporary language. The divisions between periods are approximate and based largely on extralinguistic criteria such as manuscript and literary tradition. While the periodization is not ideal for the current study, especially because of the lack of detail within the 'Modern' period, the periods will be used as arbitrary but convenient labels, to be supplemented by reference to specific dates as necessary.

The relationship between Welsh and the other Celtic languages and the periodization assumed within Welsh are summarized in Figure 1.1.

1.2.   NON-VSO ORDERS IN WELSH

In Modern Welsh, Verb–Subject–Object is the unmarked order in main clauses, as in (1). In neutral declarative main clauses, the verb may be preceded only by a closed set of 'presentential' particles (affirmative *fe* and *mi*, negative *ni(d)* and interrogative *a*) as in (2) or by certain adverbs as in (3).

(1)   *Gwelodd y   plentyn geffyl.*
        saw   the child   horse
        'The child saw a horse.'   (Stephen J. Williams 1980: 163)

(2)   *Fe   welsom y   tŷ   newydd.*
        PRT saw-1P the house new
        'We saw the new house.'   (Richards 1938: 99)

(3)   *Trannoeth   gwelais ef.*
        the-next-day saw-1S him
        'The next day I saw him.'   (Richards 1938: 99)

The affirmative particles cause soft mutation of the initial consonant of the following verb, hence *gwelsom* 'we saw' becomes *welsom* in (2) after *fe*.[1]

Despite the dominance of VSO today, until quite recently other orders were common in Literary Welsh. The central problem that will be addressed in this study is the status and development of non-VSO orders in the history of Welsh from the medieval period up to the nineteenth century.

There are two types of non-VSO order in Welsh, traditionally termed the *abnormal* and *mixed* orders, although the distinction between them is far from clear-cut. Traditional grammars such as Richards (1938) and Stephen J. Williams (1980) make virtually no reference to any historical change within the syntax of either type, except to say that the abnormal sentence is now archaic (hence the term 'abnormal'). I therefore cite examples from the rather incongruous mixture of texts and examples found in such grammars, leaving aside for the moment questions of historical development.

1.2.1.   *The abnormal sentence*

In the 'abnormal sentence' (*brawddeg annormal*) the verb is preceded by some phrasal constituent and a preverbal particle, which varies according to the nature of the preverbal constituent. Examples are given in (4) of a preverbal subject (4*a*), a preverbal object (4*b*), and a preverbal adverbial (4*c*).

(4) (*a*) A   'i ddisgyblion a   ddaethant ato . . .
　　　　 and his disciples   PRT came-3P to-him
　　　　 'And his disciples came to him . . .'
　　　　　　　　　　　　　　　　　(Matt. 8:25 (Stephen J. Williams 1980: 168))

　　 (*b*) *Eglwysi eraill a   ysbeiliais . . .*
　　　　 churches other PRT plundered-1S
　　　　 'I plundered other churches . . .'   (2 Cor. 11:8 (Richards 1938: 107))

　　 (*c*) *Am hynny y   digiais   wrth y   genhedlaeth honno*
　　　　 for that   PRT grew-angry-1S at   the people   that
　　　　 'For that reason, I grew angry at that people . . .'
　　　　　　　　　　　　　　　　　　　(Heb. 3:10 (Richards 1938: 109))

There has been a tendency amongst Welsh grammarians of the nineteenth and twentieth centuries to regard this word-order pattern as 'un-Welsh' and 'due to slavish imitation of the normal order of words in the English sentence, arising largely from translations' (Lewis 1942: 4, cf. also Dafydd Glyn Jones 1988: 131). Although largely erroneous (see especially Section 7.10) this view has coloured the discussion of the historical development of the pattern.

1.2.2.   *The mixed sentence*

A similar but distinct sentence type is that termed in traditional Welsh grammar the 'mixed sentence' (*brawddeg gymysg*). In this, some contrastively focused constituent is placed in preverbal position. The particle between this constituent and the verb is then determined in the same way as in the abnormal sentence.

(5) (*a*) *Y plentyn a   redodd adref.*
　　　　 the child   PRT ran   home
　　　　 '(It was) the child (that) ran home.'

(b) *Ceffyl a   brynodd y   dyn.*
   horse PRT bought   the man
   '(It was) a horse (that) the man bought.'

(c) *Ar y   pren y   canai   'r aderyn.*
   on the tree PRT sang-IMPF the bird
   '(It was) on the tree (that) the bird sang.'

(Stephen J. Williams 1980: 167)

Thus far, the mixed sentence appears to be formally identical to the abnormal sentence, with the only difference between them being a notional semantic or pragmatic one. However, a number of syntactic differences are said to exist between the two. The first is the different agreement patterns found with the two sentence types. In the abnormal sentence in (6), the verb agrees in person and number with the preverbal subject, whereas, in the mixed sentence in (7), the verb remains in its default third-person singular form, despite the presence of a plural preverbal subject.

(6)   *. . . a   'r publicanod hefyd a   ddaethant i'w   bedyddio . . .*
       and the publicans also PRT came-3P to+3P-GEN baptize-VN
       '. . . and the publicans too came to be baptized . . . '

(Luke 3:12 (Richards 1938: 107))

(7)   *Ei weledigaethau cyfrin ar natur a   dyn a   wnâi ei gyd-ddynion*
       his visions   secret on nature and man PRT made his fellow-men
       yn   oddefadwy iddo.
       PRD bearable   to-him
       '(It was) his secret visions on nature and man (that) made his fellow-men bearable to him.'   (Richards 1938: 100)

Unlike the abnormal order, the mixed order is found at all periods and in all registers of Welsh.

Agreement patterns in Welsh vary considerably over time (D. Simon Evans 1971), and to some extent this undermines the neat distinction between the two sentence types according to agreement.

A further difference is found in negative contexts. The negative marker appears after the preverbal constituent in the abnormal sentence in (8), but in front of it in the mixed sentence in (9). Note also a difference in the form of the negative marker—always *nid* in the mixed sentence, *ni* or *nid* before a word beginning in a vowel in the abnormal sentence.

(8)   *Ynfydion   ni   safant   yn dy   olwg.*
       foolish-people NEG stand-3P in your sight
       'The foolish shall not stand in your sight.' (Ps. 5:5 (Richards 1938: 107))

(9)   *Nid yn y   capel y   bydd ef.*
       NEG in the chapel PRT will-be he
       '(It is) not in the chapel (that) he'll be.' (Stephen J. Williams 1980: 167)

It is not at all clear that this is really a syntactic difference between the two types, since it reflects a difference in the sorts of meanings typically expressed using the abnormal order and the mixed order. In the focus mixed order, negation is typically negation of the focused element—that is, the sentence denies the fact that the predicate is true of the particular element focused. Negation, therefore, has scope only over the focused element. Not surprisingly, in this situation we find constituent negation, achieved in Welsh of all periods by placing a negative marker (invariably *nid*) immediately before the negated constituent. With the abnormal order, it is typically the entire proposition that is being negated, hence negation appears in its usually preverbal position. This supposed difference between the two sentence types thus seems to reflect indirectly an entirely unrelated distinction between constituent and clausal negation.

I shall make use of the traditional distinction between the abnormal and mixed sentences at various points in this study (see especially Sections 3.5 and 6.5). However, given the reservations expressed above, and the fact that agreement patterns are considerably more variable in the history of Welsh than this simple distinction suggests, I shall not give it the prominence that it has traditionally had. In any case, since the appearance of focused constituents in preverbal position is a constant feature of all periods of Welsh, there is relatively little to say about syntactic change in the mixed sentence. I concentrate instead on the historical development of the abnormal order.

1.2.3.   *'Abnormal' orders in the other Brythonic languages*

Before the historical evidence within Welsh is examined, it is worth noting parallels in the other Brythonic languages that need to be borne in mind when evaluating accounts of the developments within Welsh. Word order patterns in Breton and Cornish show striking similarities to the abnormal sentence in Welsh. In Breton and Cornish absolute sentence-initial verbs are virtually unknown. As in the Welsh abnormal sentence, the usual order has an arbitrary sentence-initial phrasal constituent, followed by a preverbal particle and then the verb and subject. Examples are given from Breton of SVO (10*a*), OVS (10*b*), and AdvVSO (10*c*).

(10) (*a*) *Me a   wel ar c'hazh.*
          I   PRT see the cat
          'I see the cat.'

     (*b*) *Ar c'hazh a   welan.*
          the cat   PRT see-IS
          'I see the cat.'

     (*c*) *Amañ e   welan ar c'hazh.*
          here PRT see-IS the cat
          'Here I see the cat.'   (George 1990: 238)

Aside from the striking parallelism between Breton and Cornish and Middle Welsh, there is one difference. In the Breton example in (10*a*) the preverbal subject in the 'abnormal' order does not trigger agreement on the verb. Instead the verb appears in its default third-person form. The same is true in Cornish. Contrast this with the agreement found in the abnormal but not the mixed sentence in Welsh.

Despite this difference, the general similarity between the three languages seems to suggest that some form of the abnormal order was available in the parent language. Any account of the development of Welsh word order should be consistent with the facts in these other languages.

1.3. THE RISE AND FALL OF THE ABNORMAL SENTENCE

A coherent view of the abnormal sentence in Middle Welsh must be compatible with an account of how it developed from the word-order patterns of Old Welsh, and how it developed into the patterns observed in Modern Welsh. The dominant view to date has been that Old and Modern Welsh present difficulties for an account that takes the evidence of Middle Welsh at face value. I consider first Old Welsh, then Modern Welsh.

1.3.1. *The Old Welsh evidence*

Dominant word-order patterns in Old Welsh are notoriously difficult to establish with any certainty. Contemporary prose sources are sparse, and consist largely of glosses on Latin texts or original Welsh texts based on Latin models. The volume of poetic texts is larger, but a number (*Canu Aneirin* and *Canu Taliesin*) are attested only in manuscripts dating from the Middle Welsh period. In all cases, the archaic and formalized nature of the poetic tradition makes it difficult to assess the significance of the poetry for the study of historical syntax. Nevertheless, Old Welsh has a significant contribution to make to the study of Welsh word order. Any claim that the abnormal sentence was a part of spoken Middle Welsh needs to be consistent with the word-order patterns attested for Old Welsh. Such consistency could be achieved either by claiming that the abnormal sentence developed out of some Old Welsh construction, or by claiming that some aspect of the Old Welsh literary language itself obscures developments in the spoken language.

Most accounts of the origin of the abnormal sentence have traced it back to the Old Welsh period. The two 'classic' accounts are the one set out in Lewis (1931) and Richards (1938); and that in Lewis (1942).

Lewis (1931: 117) and Richards (1938: 104–5) claim that in Old Welsh the subject could follow the verb, as in (11*a*), or precede it, as in (11*b*). The pattern in (11*b*) is not the same construction as the abnormal sentence, since no particle intervenes between subject and verb. Following Lewis and Richards, I give Old Welsh examples using Modern Welsh forms.

(11) (a) *Aeth gŵr i'r   frwydr.*
     went man to-the battle

(b) *Gŵr aeth i'r   frwydr.*
     man went to-the battle
     'A man went to battle.'   (Richards 1938: 105)

The language also had pseudocleft mixed sentences where a sentence-initial subject received contrastive focus and was followed by the particle *a*.[2]

(12)   *Gŵr a   aeth i'r   frwydr.*
       man PRT went to-the battle
       '(It was) a man (that) went to battle.'   (Richards 1938: 105)

The argument is that (12) influenced the form of (11*b*), resulting in the introduction of the particle *a* into it, and hence the innovation of the abnormal sentence. For Lewis, this development occurred in the literary language only, whilst verb-initial order came to prevail in speech. In his words, the abnormal order was 'a decorative literary form, and eloquent testimony to the importance of analogy in language and to the conservatism of the standard literary language' (Lewis 1931: 118; my translation).

The account raises two related difficulties. The SVO variant of the abnormal sentence is taken as the primary form to be accounted for. However, the orders Object + *a* + Verb . . . and Adverb + *y*(*d*) + Verb . . . are also possible manifestations of the abnormal order and their appearance must be accounted for too. Lewis ignores this problem, but Richards (1938: 105–6) suggests a solution: the same influence of the mixed sentence happened also with other types of preverbal constituent. Effectively this means that a hypothetical pseudocleft of the type in (14) influenced OVS sentences of the type in (13), resulting in the introduction of the particle *a* into them.

(13)   ***Y frwydr gwelodd y gŵr.*
       the battle saw   the man
       'The man saw the battle.'

(14)   *Y frwydr a   welodd y gŵr.*
       the battle PRT saw   the man
       'It was the battle that the man saw.'

However, this requires that the sentence in (13) was grammatical in Old Welsh, a fact not assumed at the outset of the account. A natural solution would be to widen the claim about the word-order possibilities at the outset. That is, one might claim that, rather than allowing both SVO and VSO, early Old Welsh had free (that is, pragmatically conditioned) word order. However, even this will not suffice, since given this claim the expectation would be that the SOV word order in (15) would be a freely available possibility. However, if that were the case, we would need to explain why this construction disappeared completely in the later language, where the abnormal sentence requires the verb to be (broadly speaking) in second position.

(15)   **Y gŵr y   frwdyr gwelodd.
       the man the battle   saw
       'The man saw the battle.'

A related concern is the fact that this account offers no evidence for the assumptions made about the starting point for the historical development of word order. It is not at all clear that the claim that Old Welsh allowed VSO or SVO (or, under the revised analysis, free word order) can be supported by textual evidence.

An alternative proposal is that of Lewis (1942), who partially addresses this last concern. Lewis argues that, since the evidence of Gaulish inscriptions suggests that it had 'free' word order, it can be assumed that its closely related sister language British also had free word order, which it retained as it developed into Old Welsh. The pivotal role in this account is played by object clitics. In Old Welsh, object pronouns were enclitic to the preverb of a compound verb as in (16).

(16)   *Deus dy-   -m- -gwares.*
       God PREVERB me deliver-SUBJ
       'May God deliver me.'   *(BT* 41. 2)

If the verb was not a compound verb, or if it was no longer perceived to be so, a particle *a* was inserted to which the object pronoun could cliticize, as in (17).

(17)   *Duw a-   -m difero.*
       God PRT me defend-SUBJ
       'May God defend me.'   *(H.* 33. 30)

This contrasted with the case of a full nominal object, as in (18), where straightforward SVO would be observed.

(18)   *Dewi differwys y   eglwysseu.*
       David defended his churches
       'David defended his churches.'   *(H.* 205. 1)

Comparison of (17) and (18) led to the introduction of the particle *a* into sentences like (18), and therefore the general introduction of the abnormal sentence into Welsh as well as Breton and Cornish. Again, however, this account neglects to account for the appearance of the object-initial and adverb-initial variants of the abnormal order.

More recently Mac Cana (1973) has proposed that the abnormal sentence develops from left-dislocation structures (*nominativus pendens*). This proposal has recently been revived in more radical form by Isaac (1996), who claims that the abnormal sentence and left-dislocation structures are in fact identical.[3] Such an account fails to explain the introduction of the preverbal particles into the construction at all.

Any of these proposals could in principle be reconciled with an account of the development of Welsh word order according to which the abnormal sentence was a spoken form in Middle Welsh or according to which it was limited to the literary variety. However, according to the account presented in Lewis (1931), the existence of verb-initial patterns in Old and Modern Welsh suggests that the literary and spoken languages diverged in Old Welsh, with the abnormal sentence developing in the literary language, while verb-initial word order remained the constant norm in speech. As will be seen below, this view has been taken up by a number of other scholars, and has become the dominant view in the field.

A feature of all of these accounts is the absence of any detailed textual analysis of Old Welsh word order. This deficiency has been remedied to some extent by Watkins (1987) and Isaac (1996). Watkins casts doubt on the starting hypothesis of the two standard accounts—namely, that earlier free Celtic word order survived in Old Welsh, either in a completely free form, as suggested by Lewis (1942), or in a reduced VSO/SVO form, as suggested by Richards (1938). Watkins shows that the evidence for free word order in Old Welsh is meagre, coming only from the highly formalized poetry. He shows that, on the contrary, verb-initial word order is characteristic of prose (Watkins 1987: 53–4). Watkins gives clear examples of VSO in Old Welsh texts, for instance (19), and argues that the predominance of such examples in these texts is evidence that VSO is the unmarked word order in Old Welsh.

(19)   . . . *prinit hinnoid .iiii. aues* . . .
            buys that   four birds
         'That buys four birds . . .'   (Ox. 234. 33)

The Old Welsh evidence nevertheless remains difficult to interpret. In Watkins's data, once examples of VSO in embedded contexts and examples in negative main clauses are removed,[4] we are left with relatively few examples of VSO. A few examples of the abnormal order are also found in Old Welsh, for instance (20), where the preverbal element is the subject.

(20)   *Gur dicones remedaut elbid a-n-guorit* . . .
            man created wonder   world PRT+1P-ACC+redeems
         'The man who created the wonder of the world redeems us . . .'

(Juv. 5a–b)

Watkins and a number of other scholars have drawn the conclusion that Old Welsh is essentially VSO with little evidence of the abnormal sentence (Fife and King 1991: 83–4; Mac Cana 1973: 113; 1991: 52). They contrast this with Middle Welsh where the abnormal sentence predominates. Given that they saw very little evidence of the abnormal sentence in Modern Welsh,[5] this has created an air of mystery surrounding appearance and disappearance of the abnormal sentence which has led to the development of the idea that it is a purely literary phenomenon, an issue to which we return shortly.

1.3.2. *The Modern Welsh evidence*

At first sight, the abnormal sentence appears to have disappeared mysteriously and completely in the Welsh language of today. The obvious, although perhaps hasty, conclusion is that, in the modern literary language from the sixteenth century onwards, and perhaps before, it was a purely literary construction, and that its downfall was due to a growing purist perception of it as being essentially an SVO word order borrowed from English. As Stephen J. Williams (1980: 168) points out: 'It is a construction very commonly found in literature as late as the beginning of the present century, when grammarians began to condemn it.' We find this attitude expressed even in nineteenth-century grammars. For instance, Hugh Hughes (Tegai) (1805–64) criticizes the 1588 Bible translation because it follows English with respect to word order rather than the original Hebrew (Hugh Hughes n.d.: 178). In John Mendus Jones's grammar of 1847 specific reference is made to the abnormal sentence in its SVO form as 'the English order' (*y drefn Seisonig*), albeit approvingly (John Mendus Jones 1847: 121–2). This certainly suggests that, in the nineteenth century, the abnormal order was recognized only in its SVO form, and that, even in this form, it was perceived at best to be a literary variant, at worst a foreign intrusion on the language.

Nevertheless, the abnormal order survives into Contemporary Welsh in popular usage in three contexts, highlighted by Lewis (1942: 20). Any account of the development of Welsh word order will need to be consistent with these remnants too.

The first context consists of fossilized expressions in the subjunctive, specifically *Duw cato pawb* 'God preserve (us) all' and *Duw cato ni* 'God preserve us'.

The second context is illustrated by an anecdote of Henry Lewis. He says: '. . . if we chanced in walking along a country road to meet straying cattle, and inquired the cause, we should as likely as not be told *y ffermwr adawodd y glwyd ar agor* "the farmer left the gate open"' (Lewis 1942: 20; see also Lewis 1931: 118–19). That is, in answer to a question of the type 'What happened?' we could expect an SVO abnormal sentence as the response. Richards (1938: 106) had made much the same point, saying that the abnormal sentence survives occasionally in spoken Contemporary Welsh especially in answer to a question. His example is *Sut torraist ti dy goes?* 'How did you break your leg?', answered with the SVO abnormal sentence *Fy nhroed lithrodd* 'My foot slipped'. Notice that the only form of the abnormal sentence referred to is the SVO form.

Finally, there is a small group of dialects in south-east Wales in which the abnormal sentence is said to be productive. In fact, its productivity even there is limited to one context—namely, SVO is found with pronominal subjects (Morgan

1952: 367; Morris-Jones 1913: 428; Ceinwen H. Thomas 1974: 119–21; Thomas and Thomas 1989: 76).[6] The construction is noted in particular for the dialects of the Ely Valley (Phillips 1955: 298–9) and Nantgarw (Ceinwen H. Thomas 1993: 307–8) in Glamorgan. The existence of a long-established dialect division between these and other dialects of Welsh is crucial in accounts where the abnormal sentence is claimed to be a literary phenomenon.

1.3.3.   *Accounts of the development of Welsh word order*

Given the supposed contrast of the linguistic testimony of Old and Modern Welsh on the one hand and Middle Welsh on the other, some scholars have rejected the idea that Welsh word order could have changed so markedly between Old and Middle Welsh, and then apparently returned to its old pattern in the transition to Modern Welsh. They have developed an account of the history of Welsh word order in which non-VSO patterns in Middle Welsh are an affectation of a literary language with little basis in speech. On this account, once the fashion abated in Modern Welsh, the written language returned to its 'natural' pattern. The evidence of Modern Welsh is taken strongly to support such a view in so far as there is little evidence for the abnormal sentence in contemporary Welsh dialects (Mac Cana 1979: 185–6, but see Section 1.3.2 above). The general feeling that in the nineteenth and twentieth centuries any continued use of the abnormal sentence has been due to literary or English influence has strengthened the instinct that the abnormal sentence could never have been a living form in Welsh. Of course, although tempting, this conclusion is by no means a necessary one.

1.3.3.1.   *The abnormal sentence as a literary phenomenon*

This view is developed in Mac Cana (1973), and Watkins (1977–8), and is given its fullest expression in Fife (1988) and Fife and King (1991). Fife argues generally that the abnormal order is a topicalization device, allowing topic-comment order to be realized. Its widespread use in Middle Welsh is, he claims, 'an exaggeration of a device already latent in the language' (Fife and King 1991: 144). It is developed into a literary syntax interrupting the otherwise continuous attestation of the 'normal' VSO pattern. It is thus claimed that non-VSO orders had originally a narrowly defined base in the spoken language but were spread artificially in the literary language by a variety of means, including literary fashion and translations. The conclusion is that in medieval Wales there was a sharp contrast between a VSO spoken language and a literary language in which the use of a topicalization device was virtually obligatory.

The loss of the abnormal sentence is then accounted for as the decline of this literary fashion. Fife claims that by the end of the Middle Welsh period

the effect of the overuse of the A[bnormal] S[entence] where it served no informative function may have been cloying to new generations of writers. Certainly in Morgan's Bible translation of 1588, the last bastion of the AS and which has served as sanction for would-be AS-users until today, the fronting of elements is prolific, often seemingly unrelated to any functional load it may carry. And the effect *is* cloying.   (Fife 1988: 129)

This view does not seem to be entirely coherent even without reference to empirical evidence. If the abnormal sentence was a topicalization device (and the evidence that Fife presents to this effect seems to be fairly conclusive), one wonders how writers for whom the abnormal sentence was a literary, consciously learned part of their language could have maintained thematic restrictions on its usage. How did they learn, for purposes of writing only, a quite complex rule which was entirely alien to their spoken language? Note that writers could not simply use SVO in literary texts—the rule required would be far more complex, requiring an awareness that constituents other than the subject could be fronted and a *conscious* awareness of the notion of 'topic'. It is hard to see how such a norm could be consciously learned, whereas topicalization as syntactic movement must clearly be universally available as a possibility for naturally acquired languages.

The view is also made inherently implausible by a curious and perilous reliance on 'intuitions' derived from knowledge of Contemporary Welsh. Fife says he finds the use of the abnormal sentence in the Welsh Bible 'cloying', and attributes his own intuitions to the 'new generation of writers' of Early Modern Welsh. It is important to stress here that such 'intuitions' are of no value in the study of historical syntax.

This view is very widespread in the literature on historical Welsh syntax. It goes back as far as Watkins's (1977–8) suggestion, based on and developing the views of Mac Cana (1973, see below) and Lewis (1931), that non-VSO orders spread in the literary language via translations from Latin and English, and that from narrative prose the abnormal order spread to the Welsh Bible, where its use is 'artificial' (Watkins 1977–8: 394):

the point is that this 'artificial' use is as 'abnormal' in terms of native Middle Welsh as it is in terms of Contemporary Welsh. It is quite certain that what caused the use of the Relative [=abnormal/mixed] Order to spread (and it was a literary spreading only) was the effect of translations from languages where the pattern Subject + Verb occurred either commonly (as in Latin) or natively (as in English).   (Watkins 1977–8: 395; my translation)

Again, this seems to reflect the modern intuition that non-VSO in Welsh is in some sense foreign to the language. This account ignores the frequent OVS pattern in Middle Welsh which has no obvious source of import; it is not clear what the justification is for the claim that Subject–Verb order is 'general' in (Medieval) Latin; and it is difficult to see why Early Middle English, rather than perhaps Anglo-Norman, should be cited as a prestige model for Welsh.

1.3.3.2. *The Southern British Dialect Hypothesis*
The view described above has often been linked to the idea of a syntactic division

between the southern dialects of British, the notional parent language of Welsh, Breton, and Cornish, and the other dialects of the language. The idea begins with Lewis (1942: 19), who suggests that the innovation of the abnormal sentence in late British flourished in the southern British dialects, becoming the normal order in Breton and Cornish.

This suggestion starts out from observations about similarities in word order between Middle Welsh and the two other Brythonic languages, Breton and Cornish. As we have seen (Section 1.2.3), sentences of the 'abnormal' type are the rule in these languages, and absolute sentence-initial verbs are virtually unknown (see George 1990 on Middle Breton; Timm 1989, 1991 on Modern Breton; and George 1991 on Middle Cornish). In Modern Breton, VSO appears to be somewhat more common but is still rare, and has been considered to be a recent purist innovation in imitation of Welsh (Timm 1989: 361). As in Middle Welsh, any element may precede a clause-second verb in a main clause in Middle Breton and Cornish.

The evidence from Breton and Cornish shows that non-VSO patterns must have some tradition as living forms in earlier stages of Brythonic. The evidence may point to their being possible in Late British, and there is thus apparently no reason to doubt the vitality of such patterns in spoken Middle Welsh.

Mac Cana (1973) picks up on these facts. Noting the Breton and Cornish evidence and the fact that an SVO order is found with pronominal subjects in the dialects of south-east Wales (cf. Section 1.3.2), he suggests tracing the syntax of all three varieties back to a common dialect within British, covering what is now southern England and south-east Wales. He suggests that there is evidence in Old Welsh for the order Subject Pronoun–Verb, but none for Nominal Subject–Verb (Mac Cana 1973: 117).[7] Mac Cana takes this to be the situation in British, with SVO for pronominal subjects having been borrowed from British Latin. In the south, the SVO order spread from pronominal subjects to all subjects, resulting in the innovation of the 'noun-initial' order (*sic*) in the southern British dialects, the forerunners of Breton and Cornish. The original situation, he claims, survives in the south-eastern dialects of Welsh, which allow the order Subject Pronoun–Verb but not Nominal Subject–Verb. In most of Wales, however, the preverbal subject pronoun 'tended to lose its nominal force and become a mere verbal particle' (Mac Cana 1973: 118). Hence in all Welsh dialects except those of the south-east, the only remnants of the 'noun-initial' orders in British are the presentential particles *mi* and *fe* (cf. example (2) above, and Section 1.3.3.4 below).

This leads him back to the claim that 'one can hardly avoid the conclusion that the "abnormal" sentence of MW is essentially a literary syntax which does not reflect the usage of spoken Welsh' (Mac Cana 1973: 115–16). The use of non-VSO orders in Middle Welsh is then accounted for as the influence of the dialects of the south-east on the literary language. Thus it is claimed that the abnormal sentence existed in speech in the Middle Welsh dialects of the south-east, and that, since Middle Welsh narrative prose is largely a product of the south, the abnormal order was used for it.[8] It had only ever been a spoken form in a small area of Wales.

Middle Welsh poetry was mainly a product of the northern Welsh principalities and so used VSO (Mac Cana 1973: 113). From the prose tales the construction is taken up into the Bible translation and from there into the standard language. More recently, this artificial word-order pattern was removed from the literary language, which was thereby brought much closer to speech and VSO order was restored.

I present in summary form what I understand to be the development postulated in Mac Cana (1973) in the 'family-tree' diagram in Figure 1.2.

1.3.3.3.   *Against the Mac Cana–Watkins–Fife account*

There are a number of ways in which this account could be tested. It could be rejected if it could be shown that British or Early Welsh did not show the required dialect division or patterns of word order; or if the abnormal sentence could be shown to be a spoken form in Middle Welsh; or if there is evidence that the abnormal sentence was used as a spoken form after the Middle Welsh period; or if it turned out that the presentential particles are of recent (post-twelfth century) origin.

In fact, the account has never really been put to the test. The first issue—the suggestion that a syntactic dialect split emerged in British—is simply unverifiable. However, there are plenty of sources available to come to some conclusion on the other questions. In fact, linguists working on historical Welsh syntax have generally been unnecessarily restrictive in their choice of sources of evidence. Studies are available of word order in Old Welsh (Watkins 1987); in a fairly narrow set of Middle Welsh texts, mainly the tales; some Early Modern Welsh literary texts (Fife 1991, and, in another tradition, D. Simon Evans 1968), and Modern Welsh fiction (Fife 1993). There is a large gap in coverage between the Early Modern Welsh texts (sixteenth and early seventeenth century) and the Modern Welsh fiction examined (mostly twentieth century). There also seems to be an almost complete lack of interest in the post-medieval non-literary sources.

It should immediately be apparent that a major empirical test for the account will come when texts, in particular non-literary ones, from the period from the sixteenth to the twentieth century are examined. Any evidence of the abnormal order or of developments which presuppose the abnormal order as their source is evidence to refute the account. Such an examination will be the subject of Chapter 5 and, in particular, Chapter 7 of this study. I aim to show that the evidence is fully consistent with step-by-step syntactic changes from a spoken language in which the abnormal sentence is fully productive, but not from a language in which the abnormal sentence is restricted to literary works. Work on developments in the dialects can also be of help in disproving the standard account. In particular, if it can be shown empirically that the syntactic dialect split between the south-east and the rest of Wales is of very recent origin, then the standard account is seriously undermined. The data presented in Chapter 7 do just this, suggesting that, in the eighteenth century, the main syntactic dialect division was between north and south Wales, rather than between the south-east and the remainder of the country.

It is also possible to argue, by demonstrating intricacies in the Middle Welsh system that are in accordance with Universal Grammar, but which would be very difficult to learn consciously as a prescriptive rule, that the observed syntactic data of Middle Welsh do indeed reflect the natural speech patterns of the writers. This is one of the main aims of the earlier parts of this study.

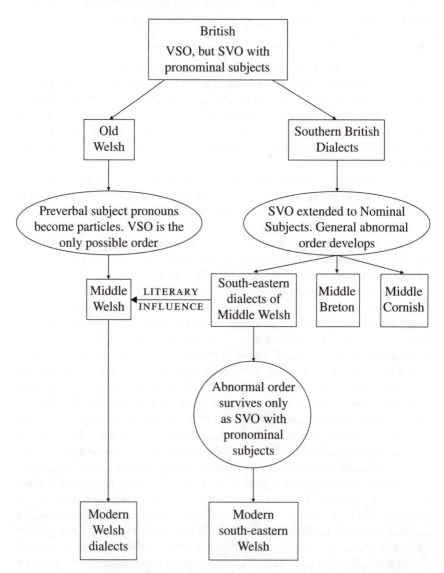

FIGURE 1.2. The Mac Cana–Watkins–Fife model of syntactic change in the Brythonic languages

Finally, the claim that southern prose texts use the abnormal order specifically because they are southern can be verified or refuted by paying attention to northern prose texts. If the abnormal order were native only to the south-east, then it would be expected that northern authors and scribes would either fail to use the southern pattern at all, reverting to their native verb-initial pattern, or that they would make mistakes in their use of the more refined aspects of the system. Consistent use of the abnormal pattern in texts with exclusively northern affinities would be difficult to reconcile with the standard account.

1.3.3.4. *The presentential particles*

Another issue which seems to be very closely connected to the history of word order in Welsh is the development of the presentential particles *mi* and *fe*. These particles appear optionally in affirmative main clauses in Modern Welsh (cf. example (2) above). Further examples are given in (21) and (22).

(21)   *Mi gei   boen bol   os bwyti di   ormod   o siwgr.*
MI get-2S ache stomach if eat-2S you too-much of sugar
'You'll get a stomach ache if you eat too much sugar.'

(Thorne 1993: 347)

(22)   *Fe fyddwn   ni gartre erbyn naw.*
FE be-1P-FUT we home by   nine
'We shall be home by nine.'   (King 1993: 138)

It seems clear that historically they have developed from homophonous first-person and masculine third-person pronouns (Koch 1991: 20–1; Lewis and Pedersen 1937: 245; Mac Cana 1973: 117–18; Morgan 1952: 367). In Modern Welsh they never co-occur with the negative particle or with subordinating complementizers, and it therefore seems clear that they are main-clause complementizers.

On Mac Cana's view the development of these particles proceeds in a very particular way. They are a survival of Old Welsh Subject Pronoun–Verb order, with 'secondary mutation' and a functional change of the pronoun to particle (Mac Cana 1973: 118–19). That is, they are not a development from the abnormal sentence. The Old Welsh Subject Pronoun–Verb order is well attested. An example is given in (23). It is clearly distinct from the abnormal order in that there is no particle *a*, and the verb (*lledin*, not *ledin*) does not undergo the soft mutation caused by this particle.

(23)   *Wy lledin.*
they killed-3P
'They killed.'   (*CA* 633)

This construction disappears completely in Middle Welsh. It is not entirely clear from Mac Cana (1973) what is claimed to happen next. The Subject Pronoun–Verb order is claimed to be the model for the development of the abnormal sentence. It must be lost very early in all dialects in which the abnormal order does not develop.

That is, in most dialects the functional change from pronoun to particle must happen earlier than the Middle Welsh period, otherwise there is nothing to prevent the pattern Subject Pronoun–Verb from acting as the model for the innovation of the abnormal sentence in these dialects.

Again, this account can be tested against detailed textual evidence for the post-medieval period. Evidence that *mi* and *fe* are of recent origin, or that they developed out of a fully-established system using the abnormal order, is evidence to refute this account. In the course of this study both types of evidence will be presented.

1.3.3.5.   *The Evans–Koch tradition*

There is an alternative approach, alluded to in D. Simon Evans (1968: 336–7) and Koch (1991), but not yet developed in any detail. In many ways this continues the earlier accounts of Melville Richards and Henry Lewis. According to Evans, the Old Welsh system was completely superseded in Middle Welsh by the abnormal sentence, presumably (although this is not explicitly stated) in speech just as much as in writing. Other orders, in particular main clause VSO and presentential particle + VSO, are then assumed to be much more recent innovations.

Koch elaborates a little for the early period, suggesting that the abnormal order is a pan-Brythonic innovation which was admitted only slowly into the literary language. This accounts for the meagre evidence for it in Old Welsh, even in prose: written Old Welsh reflects an older stage of the language before the adoption of the abnormal order (Koch 1991: 30).

This view is presented in Figure 1.3. It should be immediately clear that this view is considerably simpler and involves far less 'special pleading', such as references to unverifiable developments and resort to artificial literary languages to explain away contradictory evidence, than the standard account.

1.4.   THE AIMS AND METHODOLOGY OF THIS STUDY

It is an account along the lines of the Evans–Koch tradition that will be developed here. Detailed empirical evidence will be presented from Middle and Modern Welsh texts in support of the claims that the abnormal sentence pattern in Middle Welsh involved a system of rules that are rich and complex in their output but fully in conformity with Universal Grammar and phenomena found in other languages, including in particular the Germanic verb-second languages; and that a number of factors led to the loss of this rule from the language and its replacement by the Contemporary Welsh system with VSO and presentential particles.

For the Middle Welsh period I draw on exhaustive searching of Jarman's anthology of tales, *Chwedlau Cymraeg Canol* (*ChCC*), although other sources are also used extensively. For Early Modern Welsh, the anthologies of texts in the first two volumes of *Rhyddiaith Gymraeg* (*RhG*) have been most helpful, and have been supplemented by Suggett's (1983) calendar of slander-trial proceedings in Welsh courts and a number of other sources. For the eighteenth and nineteenth centuries a larger stylistically layered corpus is used, which will be discussed in more detail in Chapter 7. A full list of primary texts used is given in the References.

1.5.   WELSH SYNTAX IN A GENERATIVE FRAMEWORK

The analysis of word-order change in Welsh will be presented in a Government and Binding (Principles and Parameters) framework. The application of this framework to syntactic change is discussed fully in Chapter 2. Here, I give a brief outline of theoretical assumptions regarding the phrase structure of Modern Welsh. Discussion of the framework will be limited here to its application specifically to Welsh. For

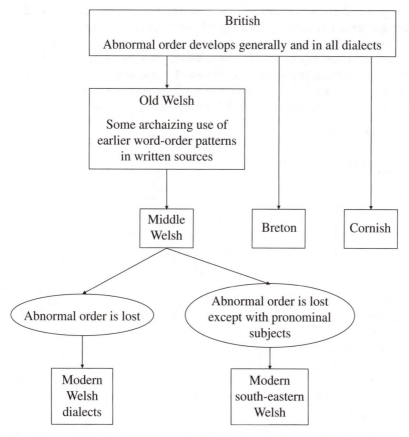

FIGURE 1.3. The Evans–Koch model of syntactic change in the Brythonic languages

a general intoduction to the theoretical framework adopted, see Haegeman (1994) and Ouhalla (1994). More detailed discussion of its application to the Celtic languages can be found in the introduction to Borsley and Roberts (1996).

The standard generative approach to the analysis of clause structure in Modern Welsh, going back in essence to Sproat (1985) and developed further in such works as Hendrick (1991), Koopman and Sportiche (1991), and Sadler (1988), argues that VSO is a derived word order, the result of verb movement. The major sentence constituents are generated in an SVO configuration. Auxiliaries and inflectional morphology are generated to the left of the subject in an inflectional node, I (Infl). Where there is no auxiliary, the lexical verb raises to Infl in order to give support to the inflectional morphology.[9] Updating to current theoretical assumptions, this assigns a structure like that in (25) to the simple VSO main clause in (24). The subject Noun Phrase (DP) is base-generated within the Verb Phrase (in SpecVP) and remains there, while the verb, generated in V, raises to Infl.

Before movement, theta-roles, abstract semantic labels indicating the function of each participant in an event, are assigned, for instance, agent to the element in SpecP, generally the subject, and patient to the sister of the verb. The patient will often be the object, but it may also be a subject in a passive or other raising construction. In this case the constituent to which the patient role is assigned will move for reasons of Case (see below). It is a requirement that each Noun Phrase should have exactly one theta-role (the Theta Criterion).

(24)   *Yfodd Dafydd gwrw.*
         drank Dafydd beer
         'Dafydd drank beer.'

(25)

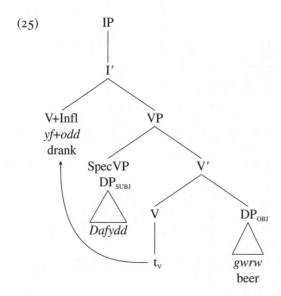

Evidence in support of this analysis comes from three constructions in which the verb fails to raise and in which the underlying SVO order can be seen. First, in periphrastic constructions in which tense and agreement inflection is carried by an auxiliary rather than the lexical verb, the word order in Modern Welsh is AuxSVO, as in the colloquial Welsh example in (26).

(26)   *Naiff Siôn ddarllen y   llyfr.*
        will Siôn read-VN the book
        'Siôn will read the book.'

This is as expected if the lexical verb raises only for morphological reasons. Raising of the nonfinite verb (verbnoun) is unnecessary because tense, person, and number inflection is already carried by the auxiliary *naiff*. This leaves the subject in a position where it precedes the nonfinite verb. The structure of (26), given in (27), is therefore taken broadly to represent the underlying order of constituents in Welsh.

(27)

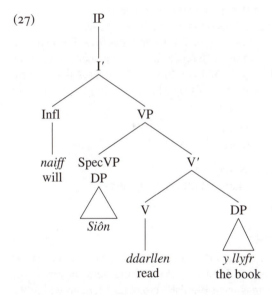

Secondly, the underlying SVO order surfaces in embedded nonfinite clauses as in (28). In the absence of tensed Infl in the form of tense and agreement morphology, the verb does not raise and remains in its nonfinite form. In Government and Binding theory there is a requirement that all Noun Phrases be assigned abstract Case (the Case Filter), independently of whether they manifest overt case morphology or not. Nominative Case is normally assigned by tensed Infl, that is, the morphology of the finite verb, in various configurations. However, since nonfinite clauses lack tensed Infl, a Case-assigning preposition *i* 'to' is also inserted (see Borsley 1986; Sadler 1988: 34–44; Tallerman 1993).

(28)   *Disgwyliodd Gwyn i Emrys weld   Megan.*
        expected   Gwyn to Emrys see-VN Megan
        'Gwyn expected Emrys to see Megan.'   (Borsley 1986: 68)

Finally, in 'absolute' constructions, nonfinite adjunct clauses, SVO is the only possible order. Again since these clauses are not tensed, we can assume that verb-raising induced by the presence of inflection is unnecessary and that consequently the subject appears in its underlying preverbal position.[10]

(29)   *Mynnodd fynd   i 'r gwaith, a   'r meddyg wedi dweud wrtho*
        insisted go-VN to the work,   and the doctor PERF say-VN to-him
        am orffwys.
        to rest-VN
        'He insisted on going to work, though the doctor had told him to rest.'
                                                (Stephen J. Williams 1980: 173)

This analysis requires that subjects be base-generated in the specifier of the Verbal Phrase (SpecVP) in Welsh (Koopman and Sportiche 1991: 218–21), or at least a position below the inflectional head to which the verb raises.

Verb-raising to Infl is a common feature of European languages. For instance, it is generally thought to account for the differences in adverb placement between English and French illustrated in (30) and (31). In French, adverbs like *souvent* 'often' must follow the finite verb, as in (30), whereas in English they must precede, as in (31).

(30) (*a*) **Jean souvent embrasse Marie.*
            John often   kisses   Mary

      (*b*) *Jean embrasse souvent Marie.*
            John kisses   often   Mary   (Pollock 1989: 367)

(31) (*a*) *John often kisses Mary.*

      (*b*) **John kisses often Mary.*

It is assumed that the position of the adverb *often/souvent* is constant, and marks the left edge of the Verb Phrase. In French (32*b*), a finite verb moves across this adverb, moving to Infl, whereas most English verbs (32*a*) remain within the Verb Phrase (Pollock 1989). The existence of verb movement in Welsh can be demonstrated by the position of negation relative to the verb (see below).

(32) (a)

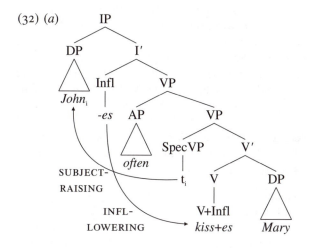

(b)

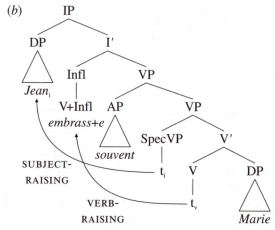

Variation in the position of the subject relative to auxiliary verbs shows that subjects move across auxiliaries in languages such as English and French, raising from SpecVP to SpecIP. This results in SAuxVO or SVO order. The appearance of verb-initial order in Welsh suggests that this movement does not take place, a more surprising fact. Koopman and Sportiche (1991) develop a Case-based account of why subjects in a language like Welsh should remain in the postverbal SpecVP position, rather than raising to SpecIP. This involves a Case-assignment parameter, according to which languages may vary according to whether abstract Nominative Case is assigned by Infl under agreement or government. They suggest that, in Welsh, Infl assigns Case only under government. Therefore SpecVP in Welsh is a Case-marked position, whereas SpecIP is not (Koopman and Sportiche 1991:

231). The subject in Welsh is therefore able to receive Nominative Case in its base-position in SpecVP, and does not need to raise to SpecIP to receive Case. The same configuration appears to be found in Irish (Chung and McCloskey 1987: 218–21; McCloskey 1991: 262) and Breton (Schafer 1995: 137).[11]

The analysis becomes somewhat more complicated once aspect and negation markers are included. There is evidence that the subject in Welsh undergoes 'short' movement from its base position, SpecVP, at least to a position within an intermediate projection dominating the aspect marker, SpecAspP.[12] Postulation of this movement is motivated by the fact that in Welsh the subject must precede aspectual particles in periphrastic constructions. For instance, in (33) the subject *Mair* precedes the progressive aspect marker *yn*.

(33)   *Mae Mair yn   canu.*
       is   Mair PROG sing-VN
       'Mair is singing.'

Similarly, the subject precedes the negative marker *ddim*, which can be assumed to be the specifier of a negative projection NegP (cf. Hendrick 1991: 194). Note that the inflected verb *aeth* also precedes negation, indicating that it has moved out of the Verb Phrase to Infl.

(34)   *Aeth hi ddim.*
       went she NEG
       'She didn't go.'   (Thorne 1993: 221)

Given these facts, we must suppose that the subject in Welsh undergoes 'short' movement to some functional projection lower than that in languages such as English and French (i.e. below the inflected verb in Infl), but higher than AspP and NegP. We are left with a structure for a main clause in Modern Welsh looking something like that in (35a) if the verb is synthetic, and (35b) if it is periphrastic, where XP stands for some as yet undefined maximal projection.

(35) (a) $[_{IP}$ V+I $[_{XP}$ Subj$_i$ t_V $[_{NegP}$ (*ddim*) t_V $[_{AspP}$ t_i t_V $[_{VP}$ t_i t_V]]]]]

    (b) $[_{IP}$ Aux $[_{XP}$ Subj$_i$ t_{Aux} $[_{NegP}$ (*ddim*) $[_{AspP}$ t_i $[_{Asp}$ *yn*] $[_{VP}$ t_i V]]]]]

If the negative marker *ddim* is a specifier of NegP, then the subject cannot raise to SpecNegP, and must raise to a functional projection above NegP.[13] Adopting an IP split into AgrSP and TP (Pollock 1989), we can achieve the required result by having the subject raise to SpecTP, assuming that this is the lower projection of the split IP (Chomsky 1995: 59–60), with the verb raising fully to AgrS. In a fully articulated phrase structure, the rule for Nominative Case-assignment in Welsh is therefore that Case is assigned by AgrS under government to the position SpecTP.[14] The general pattern for a Welsh main clause will be as in (36).[15]

(36) $[_{AgrSP}$ V+Infl $[_{TP}$ Subj$_i$ t_V $[_{NegP}$ (*ddim*) t_V $[_{AspP}$ t_i t_V $[_{VP}$ t_i t_V]]]]]

A full example with aspectual and negative markers is given in (37), with the structure in (38).

(37) *Dydy   Dafydd ddim wedi gweld y   ffilm.*
      NEG+is Dafydd NEG PERF see-VN the film
      'Dafydd has not seen the film.'

In (38) the auxiliary carries tense and agreement features (default features are required with a full lexical subject), raising from T to AgrS to do so. AgrS can assign Nominative Case to SpecTP under government, but to no other position. The subject *Dafydd* must therefore raise to SpecTP to receive Case. This produces the correct surface order.

(38)

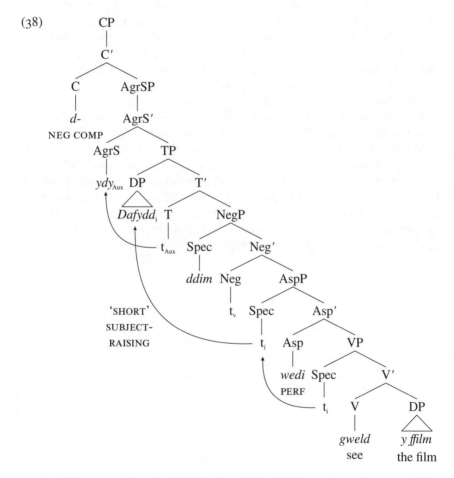

This is the phrase structure that I shall assume for Modern Welsh throughout the remainder of this study. It is the phrase structure towards which our account of the historical development of Welsh word order will lead us. In many cases, however, I shall for reasons of space and convenience amalgamate AgrSP and TP into IP, omit NegP where it is not relevant, and amalgamate AspP and VP into VP where the distinctions in question are not crucial to the point under discussion.

1.6.   THE STRUCTURE OF THIS STUDY

Before the historical data from Welsh are examined, Chapter 2 addresses a number of issues in the literature on generative approaches to syntactic change, in particular the notions of parametric and lexical change. I then move on in Chapter 3 to present an analysis of the abnormal sentence in Middle Welsh as a verb-second rule, specifically one involving A'-movement parallel to that found in relative clauses. In Chapter 4, apparent cases of verb-initial orders in Middle Welsh are examined. It is argued that they are merely a subtype of the verb-second rule, and that the language therefore has virtually no real instances of VSO. Chapter 5 discusses the status of subject pronouns of Middle Welsh, arguing that they gradually acquire clitic status. A major effect of this change is the spread of an expletive construction, which ultimately results in the innovation of the presentential particle *fe*. In Chapter 6, the instances of structural ambiguity and phonological weakening in Middle Welsh are drawn together. I argue that these allow a reanalysis of the verb-second rule as two constructions in Early Modern Welsh, one VSO and one SVO with A-movement parallel to English rather than A'-movement. Finally in Chapter 7, developments in the eighteenth century are considered, focusing on the change in order with pronominal subjects from SVO to VSO in most dialects, and the innovation of the second presentential particle *mi* and the spread of both particles (*mi* and *fe*) as unmarked affirmative complementizers.

2. Syntactic Change

One of the central concerns of any linguist looking at historical change must be the cause or causes of linguistic change. What aspect of the structure of a language or the environment in which it is spoken allowed a given change to take place? This is the Actuation Problem, formulated in Weinreich, Labov, and Herzog (1968: 102) as 'Why do changes in a structural feature take place in a particular language at a given time, but not in other languages with the same feature, or in the same language at other times?' Actuation is essentially an internal linguistic question. It is concerned with changes in the formal structures of language, specifically in linguistic competence. These changes may be influenced by performance during language acquisition. With syntactic change, the answer to why a change takes place typically involves such notions as structural ambiguity or external factors, such as phonological erosion.

There are other related questions in which social aspects may be more important. A new linguistic form need only appear in the speech of one speaker for there to have been an innovation, but change in the language as a whole requires the new form to spread. We may examine how social factors such as prestige and social and geographical mobility influence whether a linguistic innovation spreads and if so how it spreads.

Once this second question is faced, the important distinction between actuation and diffusion of change can be made. Actuation (or innovation) is the process by which a change is begun. It occurs at the moment when a new linguistic form or structure is created. Diffusion (or implementation), on the other hand, is the process by which new forms or structures are spread between different speakers or between different lexical items (Chen and Wang 1975; James Milroy 1992: 169–72; 1993: 219–26). A linguistic change is complete when it has diffused to all members of a language or dialect community. The difficulty for the historical linguist is that, whilst the evidence for diffusion, in the form of variation between texts, is often available, direct evidence for actuation and its causes is not.

Diffusion has generally been thought of in relation to the spread of new phonological variants. In application to syntax it is not nearly so clear that a purely social account of diffusion is appropriate. An intriguing question is why some changes spread rapidly through a community, whereas others spread only very slowly. For instance, English has pairs of related nouns and verbs which differ only in the position of the stress—for instance, *rébel* (noun) versus *rebél* (verb). The linguistic change that has brought these pairs about has taken 400 years, and is still far from completion. In 1934, there were 150 such items compared to only three in 1570 (Chen and Wang 1975). On the other hand, Middle English subordinate clauses changed their order from predominantly Subject–Object–Verb to predominantly Subject–Verb–Object in a short space of time in the twelfth century (Lightfoot 1991: 71). Why should such differences be found in the absence of any social explanations?

It seems reasonable to expect answers to this type of question to make reference to the type of linguistic change involved. That is, we can ask whether the method of actuation interacts with or affects the nature of diffusion (cf. Kroch 1989: 200). It may be that syntactic change is different from phonology in this respect. Syntax may be different inasmuch as the diffusing linguistic structures cannot be observed directly by those acquiring them. An underlying word order is not spread directly by observation as a sound change may be. Rather with syntactic change, learners must individually abstract a syntactic structure from what they hear. Under such circumstances, it is a reasonable possibility that diffusion is best thought of as multiple instances of the actuation of the same change.

These are the sorts of issues which an account of syntactic change and indeed linguistic change generally must face. Linguists have adopted a number of approaches to the actuation of syntactic change. One line of enquiry has developed out of the study of typology and universals. In this model, it is claimed that word-order change will be consistent with hierarchies of possible orderings ('Universal Consistency in History' (Hawkins 1983)). Other researchers have worked on the notion of recurrent paths of change (Aitchison 1989; Givón 1977). For instance, Givón suggests that VSO languages will typically develop into SVO languages via the extension of topicalization of the subject.[1] More recently, there has been a resurgence of interest in grammaticalization, in its weakest form, the change in status of full lexical items to grammatical markers (Hopper and Traugott 1993; Traugott and Heine 1991). An example would be the change in status of English *go* from a verb of motion to a marker of futurity. A number of the syntactic changes in Welsh are of this nature.

In this chapter, I do not discuss these approaches in any detail. Instead, the Principles and Parameters approach to the actuation problem and related issues is introduced and examined in some depth. This approach stems from the belief that a prerequisite for investigation of typological change is the explicit and detailed study of syntactic change in specific languages. Furthermore, the Principles and Parameters approach allows an explicit formulation of the role of children during the acquisition process in initiating change in the core grammar. The discussion will lead towards the presentation of some working assumptions with which to approach the data from the historical syntax of Welsh.

2.1.   ACQUISITION AS THE LOCUS OF CHANGE

The essence of the generative account of language change goes back to Andersen

(1973) and earlier. This account is based on the observation that 'any speaker's internalized grammar is determined by the verbal output from which it has been inferred' (Andersen 1973: 767). That is, the locus of change is the acquisition process. Children acquiring a language do not have direct access to its grammar but must recreate it. They make hypotheses on the basis of the data that they receive in the form of spoken utterances from parents, peers, and others around them (the **input** or **trigger experience**). They then test these hypotheses against more of that input, revising them where necessary. Some incorrect hypotheses may fail to be corrected or may be corrected only by what Andersen calls adaptive rules, rules used to 'patch up' the output of the grammar in order to make it conform to that of other speakers. Andersen suggests that speakers whose own output is produced using adaptive rules will be more sympathetic to children's failure to acquire them, and therefore will be less prone to correcting them. Children will thus be encouraged (indirectly) to acquire grammars from which even the adaptive rule has been dropped.

This view of change is, disregarding the role of parental correction, essentially that adopted in recent generative approaches. Children establish grammars on the basis of the output of those around them. Variation and unsystematic change in the nature of that evidence may lead children to construct grammars that differ in structure from that of adults. In particular, given insufficient exposure to less frequent pieces of evidence for the nature of the adult grammar, children may construct grammars that produce a surface output containing the commonest constructions, albeit possibly assigning them different structures, but which fail to produce less frequent constructions or which introduce new constructions not attested in the input.

2.2.   THE PRINCIPLES AND PARAMETERS MODEL OF CHANGE

Before outlining the Principles and Parameters approach to change, it is necessary to introduce the view of human language that underlies it. It has been suggested that adult grammars are radically underdetermined by the evidence available to children while they are acquiring them (Chomsky 1980; 1981: 3). As an example consider (1) and (2).

(1)   *I wonder who [the men$_i$ expected to see them$_i$].*

(2)   *The men$_i$ expected to see them$_{j \neq i}$.*

In (1), *them* has the same reference as *the men*, whereas in (2) it must have different reference, despite the fact that the two sentences superficially contain the same sequence of words. Children have no difficulty in acquiring these patterns, yet there is no direct evidence for them in the trigger experience (Chomsky 1986*b*: 7–9). Such properties of language must, therefore, be ascribed to innate, genetically preconditioned principles of the language faculty—that is, Universal Grammar.

Human languages are also observed to vary significantly, but not in unconstrained ways. A well-established tradition of typological studies shows, for
instance, that the position of syntactic heads with respect to their complements
tends to be fairly consistent within each language (Hawkins 1983, 1988). For
instance, languages like English, where the verb precedes the object, tend to have
prepositions (that is, the head precedes its complement), whereas languages like
Japanese, where the object precedes the verb, tend to have postpositions (that is, the
head follows its complement).

According to the Principles and Parameters model, the competence of a native
speaker can be reduced to innate universal principles of grammar, part of the
genetic endowment, with a limited set of parameters. The 'principles' are the
unchanging rules of each module of the grammar. An example would be the
Binding Conditions, which regulate the possible interpretations of pronouns and
anaphors. The 'parameters' are 'switches' which set the limits on possible variation
between languages, because children are free only to set each one either positively
or negatively on the basis of experience (Chomsky 1981: 3–9). Since the number
of parameters is highly constrained, the complexity of the task that children face
in learning their native language is greatly reduced. This provides an account of
how acquisition is possible with limited evidence. For a full exposition see
Chomsky and Lasnik (1993).

For instance, in the Principles and Parameters model, the typological observations made above about the relative position of heads and complements may be
reduced to a Head Ordering Parameter, a single 'switch' set either to head-first or
head-final order.

Under this account, it is anticipated that a number of surface cross-linguistic
differences can be reduced to the setting of a single parameter. Each parameter is
expected to be manifested in a number of exponent constructions. In the case of the
Head Ordering Parameter, one would hope to develop an account according to
which the presence of prepositions in a language follows automatically once the
head-first setting is established, say, on the basis of Verb–Object order in the
trigger experience.

Another example of a well-established parameter with multiple exponents is
the null subject parameter (Jaeggli and Safir 1989; Rizzi 1982). In the classical
formulation of this parameter, a positive setting determines three syntactic
properties of a language—namely, the presence of null subjects and of Free
Subject Inversion and the absence of *that*-trace effects. English, in (3), has none
of these properties. Null subjects in (3a) are ungrammatical. Free inversion of
the subject and verb in (3b) is also ill-formed. Finally, it is not possible to
A′-move a *wh*-element in subject position across an overt complementizer. That
is, in (3c), the presence of the complementizer *that* prevents movement of *who*.
Under standard analyses, *that* acts as a potential governor of the trace, but fails
to properly govern it. Therefore (3c) is a violation of the Empty Category
Principle (ECP), which requires that *wh*-trace and other empty categories be

properly governed by the closest potential governor (Chomsky 1986a: 47–8).

(3) (a) **Has spoken.*
(b) **Has telephoned John.*
(c) **Who$_i$ do you believe that* t$_i$ *will come?*

Italian, on the other hand, in (4), allows all three constructions:

(4) (a) *Verrà.*
will-come
'He/she will come.'

(b) *Verrà   Gianni.*
will-come Gianni
'Gianni will come.'

(c) *Chi$_i$ credi   che* t$_i$ *verrà?*
who believe-2s that   will-come
'Who do you believe (that) will come?'   (Rizzi 1982: 117)

All three are analysed as involving a null subject. Therefore, a language like Italian which allows null subjects will allow all three, whereas a language like English which does not will lack all three.

   Given a conception of the language faculty of this kind, a view of historical change emerges in which changes in these parameter settings are crucial. It is expected that changes in parameter settings will occur periodically, and that these parameter changes will affect all the constructions controlled by the parameter at approximately the same time. A central task of historical syntax is then to account for the mechanisms by which such parametric changes are possible. Accounts of syntactic change in a parametric framework have been attempted for various aspects of syntactic change in English (Kroch 1989; Lightfoot 1991; Roberts 1985, 1993b; Warner 1995), for the loss of verb-second and null subjects in French (Adams 1987; Clark and Roberts 1993; Roberts 1993b), the loss of null subjects in Swedish (Falk 1993; Platzack 1987: 396–8) and for the change from Object–Verb to Verb–Object order in Yiddish (Santorini 1992, 1995). See also the articles in Battye and Roberts (1995) and van Kemenade and Vincent (1997).

   The two most articulated accounts of how such a theory would operate are Lightfoot (1991) and Roberts (1993b). I shall examine these accounts in some detail, before moving on to discuss some of the difficulties that emerge, and establishing some working assumptions and hypotheses with which to approach the discussion of the history of Welsh phrase structure.

2.2.1. *Lightfoot (1991)*

In Lightfoot's (1991) model, parametric change begins with changes in the frequency with which certain constructions are chosen for use. Such changes do not of course involve a change in the grammar as such, since the set of grammatical sentences remains the same. However, frequency changes may reduce the availability of evidence for a particular parameter setting within the trigger experience, potentially to such an extent that at least some children adopt a different parameter setting from that of their parents. They then begin to produce performance with the 'incorrect' parameter setting, and therefore, through their own speech, provide additional *positive* evidence to others in support of the new parameter setting. Thus more and more children are led to set the parameter in the new way. Once a new parameter setting has been adopted, a number of other simultaneous changes in any other features linked to that parameter will follow naturally.

Lightfoot takes the example of the loss of underlying Object–Verb (OV) order in Old and Middle English. Because of a verb-second rule in Old English, the underlying OV order was generally obscured in surface data. Lightfoot asks how children could have acquired the correct underlying order, investigating first how children acquire it in a similar modern language, Dutch. Dutch children, he argues, can learn that the verb moves from its base position from the evidence of verb-second main clauses like (5), where the verb *vonden* and direct object *het idee* are not adjacent. Complements must universally be base-generated adjacent to their heads, therefore one of them must have moved.

(5)   *In Utrecht vonden   de mensen het idee gek.*
       in Utrecht found-3P the people the idea crazy.
       'In Utrecht people found the idea crazy.'   (Lightfoot 1991: 52)

Children are able to infer that the verb moves leftwards across the object in (5) from a position *following* the object from 'signposts' in Dutch which indicate the original position of the verb. These are elements such as separable verbal particles and negative markers which can be expected to be base-generated adjacent to the verb. After the verb has moved, these remain behind in post-object position, indicating that the verb itself moved from a position following the object. For instance, in (6) the separable particle *op* remains in post-object position, even though the verb *belt* has moved leftwards.

(6)   *Jan belt de hoogleraar op.*
       Jan calls the professor   up
       'Jan is calling the professor up.'   (Lightfoot 1991: 53)

Similar evidence for the position of the verb is available from modal constructions in (7) where the nonfinite lexical verb remains in its underlying clause-final position after the object.

(7)   *Jan moet de hoogleraar opbellen.*
       Jan must the professor   up-call
       'Jan must call the professor up.'   (Lightfoot 1991: 53)

According to Lightfoot, there was similar evidence in Old English. There are sentences like (8), parallel to (5), in which the verb is to the left of its object and non-adjacent to it.

(8)   *Þe   gegaderode Ælfred cyning his fierd.*
       then gathered   Alfred king his army
       'Then King Alfred gathered his army.'   (Lightfoot 1991: 60)

This allows the child to infer verb-raising. But how do children know the verb has moved from post-object position? The child learning Old English has access to a certain amount of evidence that may establish this. Separable verbal particles (for instance, stand *up*) appear in a number of positions in main clauses, but in some cases, as in (9), they occur in the clause-final position that would indicate the base-position of the verb.

(9)   *Þa   sticode him mon   þa eagon ut.*
       then stuck   him someone the eyes   out
       'Then someone poked his eyes out.'   (Lightfoot 1991: 61)

Further evidence would come from the existence of verb-final main clauses, as in (10). These would show the underlying OV order directly.[2]

(10)   *He hine an bigspell ahsode.*
       he him the parable asked
       'He asked him about the parable.'   (Lightfoot 1991: 63)

Gradually, the frequency of word-order patterns where the verb could not have been fronted, in particular verb-final main clauses like (10), declines. This change did not reflect a difference in the grammar, but rather an increasing propensity to choose certain options made available by the grammar rather than other possible options (Lightfoot 1991: 67). The verb-final word order in (10) had provided good evidence for underlying OV order, and thus its decline significantly reduced the evidence for that order.

Lightfoot argues that the decline in the frequency of this type of data led to the loss of OV order. Eventually there was simply insufficient evidence for a child acquiring English to set the appropriate parameter to the OV setting: 'Consequently, as matrix instances of object–verb diminished to a certain point, underlying object–verb order became unlearnable and the verb–order parameter came to be set differently' (Lightfoot 1991: 67).

The result was a parametric change from underlying Object–Verb to Verb–Object order in English. Under the parametric account of change, it is expected that a parametric change triggers changes in other exponents of the relevant parameter, resulting either in the rapid disappearance or appearance of particular constructions, or in assignment of a new structure to constructions which are not compatible with the old grammatical setting. In this case, Lightfoot links two other rapid changes to the parametric change in the relative order of the verb and its object. First, separable verbal particles like *ut* in (9), previously generated in a parallel way to objects, were reanalysed as (postverbal) adverbs everywhere, no longer prefixing to the verb in embedded contexts. Secondly, the change to Verb–Object word order spread rapidly to embedded clauses, where previously only OV had been possible.

Two points should be noted with respect to the model of parametric change. First, it is claimed that a parametric change results in the obsolescence of particular constructions rather than mere changes in frequency. Thus it is only when the parametric change takes place that OV order in subordinate clauses dies out. Up to this point, any changes have been changes in relative frequency only.

Related to this is the point that variation in the frequency of different word-order types is not in itself grammatical change, although it may be a significant factor in causing grammatical change. According to Lightfoot, 'this no more reflects a difference in grammars than if some speaker were shown to use a greater number of passive or imperative sentences. Rather, it reflects the kind of accidental variation that is familiar from studies in population genetics' (Lightfoot 1991: 67). Thus the drop in frequency of orders evidencing OV in early Middle English does not reflect a grammatical change.[3] On the other hand, the parametric change itself is characterized by the sudden obsolescence of syntactic patterns that were compatible only with the old parameter setting.

This then is a paradigm case of parametric change. A series of gradual changes takes place which have no grammatical significance. Grammatical competence remains the same, but the relative frequency of the output (performance) alters because of (unspecified) external factors. This unsystematic change in relative frequencies alters children's trigger experience in such a way that some children cease to have access to enough relevant data to be able to set the parameter correctly. Once some children set a parameter differently, they contribute to the trigger experience of the next generation simply by using the language, further impoverishing the data in favour of the old parameter setting, and perhaps introducing new constructions that provide positive evidence in favour of the new setting. Thus in the next generation, children are more likely to infer the new rather than the old parameter. The effect is a rapidly increasing propensity for children to set the parameter in the new rather than the old way.

2.2.2.   *Roberts (1993b)*

A similar account is offered in Roberts (1993*b*). In this model we begin with a **step**. This is a performance phenomenon, the appearance of a new construction or a change in frequency of an old one without any change in the grammar.[4] That is, the grammar and therefore the set of syntactic structures generated by the grammar remain the same. A change in frequency with which certain structures are selected in performance is perfectly possible for non-syntactic reasons, and thus no change in the grammar is necessary at this stage.[5] Essentially this part is the same as in Lightfoot's account.

Two mechanisms then operate to effect language change. Since performance is the input data for first-language acquisition, a change in the frequencies of constructions may alter the way in which a new generation of children analyse their language. For instance, in fifteenth-century French, children were exposed to an increased frequency of the pattern Adverb–XP–Verb and this had consequences for the acquisition of the verb-second rule (Roberts 1993*b*: 148) (see below).

Why should a step cause such a change? Children had previously had to reject some 'simpler' analysis of some construction because of counter-evidence in the triggering experience. However, as a consequence of the step, the aspect of the trigger experience which forced rejection of the simpler analysis becomes rarer, sufficiently so that it fails to lead the child to reject the simpler analysis. Alternatively, the evidence in favour of the new analysis becomes more frequent, and so more compelling to the child. Some children therefore adopt a new structure for a familiar construction. Roberts calls this a **Diachronic Reanalysis** (DR) (cf. Timberlake's (1977) 'Reanalysis').

The nature of the reanalysis is determined by another mechanism, the **Least Effort Strategy**, similar to Lightfoot's (1979) Transparency Principle. This states that:

(11)   Representations assigned to sentences of the input to acquisition should be such that they contain the set of the shortest possible chains (consistent with (*a*) principles of grammar, (*b*) other aspects of the trigger experience).   (Roberts 1993*a*: 228–9; 1993*b*: 156)

That is, all other things being equal, the child assigns to a given sentence of the input the syntactic structure involving least movement, regardless of the effect that this has on parameter settings. Essentially, this is a way of formalizing the intuitive notion of 'simplicity' of structure in terms of chain positions.

In order to allow the grammar to generate the new structure assigned to the particular construction, the child may have to infer a new parameter setting. 'DRs frequently create the conditions for parametric changes, by removing the structural evidence for a given parameter setting' (Roberts 1993*b*: 159).[6] This new setting causes unexpected and sudden changes to the set of grammatical sentences. Once a child adopts a new parameter setting, the structure of a number of constructions may have to be changed in order to accommodate the new setting. That is, the parameter change triggers other Diachronic Reanalyses (Roberts 1993*b*: 160). The changed parameter may also mean that old constructions simply cannot be generated by the grammar any more, and some new ones not generated by the previous grammar may suddenly appear: 'the elimination of structures is associated with parametric changes, but changes in frequency and status . . . of structures may be the consequence of lower-level factors, typically DRs' (Roberts 1993*b*: 198).[7] These steps may in turn feed back into the system perpetuating syntactic change.

The most important distinction between the two accounts is the postulation of

Diachronic Reanalyses as a separate phenomenon from steps and parameter changes in this model.

An example of parametric change in the Roberts model is the change in the setting of the Nominative Case Assignment Parameter in the history of French. Old French is a verb-second (V2) language, in which the verb is required to appear in second position in main clauses. Modern French is not. How can a parametric account explain the loss of verb-second?

According to Roberts, in a V2-language, C bears a feature [+Agr] which assigns Nominative Case. Nominative Case may be assigned either under government to a subject in SpecAgrP or by agreement to a subject in SpecCP, these options each being controlled by a parameter setting. The [+Agr] feature in C forces the verbal complex in Agr to raise to C to support it (Roberts 1993*b*: 52–5). Assuming further that the specifier position of [+Agr] must universally be filled, in such a language some element must move to SpecCP. The result is that the verb obligatorily occupies second position in main clauses.

During the Middle French period there is a rise in the frequency of orders where the verb appears later than in second position. This happens because in Old French, as in a number of V2-languages, a limited set of adverbs, such as *sans faille* 'without fail', do not trigger V2, and this set increases in size during Middle French. This is a step.[8] In Clark and Roberts (1993: 338) the introduction of these XSVO orders is related to a phonological factor, the cliticization of subject pronouns. Thus, by the fifteenth century, children acquiring French were being exposed to significantly more occurrences of the order Adverb–XP–Verb than their predecessors (Roberts 1993*b*: 148).

This invites a Diachronic Reanalysis of the CP with an adjoined adverb as an AgrP with the main verb in Agr and the subject in SpecAgrP (Roberts 1993*b*: 150–1). Such a structure is favoured because adjunction of adverbs and comple- ments to CP is cross-linguistically marked, but adjunction to AgrP is generally allowed. As a result of this Diachronic Reanalysis, main clauses in Middle French could be either CPs or AgrPs.[9] AgrPs resulted in (X)SVO order (since SpecAgrP could only be a subject position), whereas CPs allowed (Adv)–XP–V–(S)–O. The AgrP option was gradually preferred. This is reflected in the increasing statistical predominance of SVO word order in the fifteenth century. The Diachronic Reanal- ysis of CPs as AgrPs is dictated by the Least Effort Strategy, since it eliminates syntactic movement of the verb from Agr to C and of some other element to SpecCP.[10] For this system to operate, the [+Agr] feature on C must be optional, that is, the verb is no longer obliged to raise from Agr to C (Roberts 1993*b*: 154–7).[11]

In main clause AgrPs, Nominative Case is assigned under agreement by Agr to SpecAgrP, whereas in main clause CPs Nominative Case is assigned under government by [+Agr] in C to SpecAgrP. Reinterpreting many main clauses as AgrPs greatly increases the frequency with which Nominative Case is actually assigned by taking the agreement option rather than the government option (Roberts 1993*b*: 143).

Other Diachronic Reanalyses also weakened the trigger evidence for Nominative Case assignment under government. Consequently, during the sixteenth century, the evidence for Nominative Case under government became so weak that a parametric change excluded it from the grammar entirely. Verb-second depended crucially on this possibility, so the parametric change eliminated verb-second *entirely*, and also removed simple inversion and null subjects in French, both of which depended upon the possibility of Case-assignment under government (Roberts 1993*b*: 197).

A summary of the Roberts model of the development of the Nominative Case Assignment Parameter in French is given below.

STEP	Increase in frequency of Adverb–XP–Verb.
DIACHRONIC REANALYSIS	Some main clauses are reinterpreted as AgrPs rather than CPs. C is now only optionally [+Agr]. This option is chosen with increasing frequency reducing the evidence for Nominative Case assignment under government.
PARAMETRIC CHANGE	Nominative Case is assigned solely by agreement not under government.
OBSOLESCENCE	Of V2, simple inversion and null subjects.
DIACHRONIC REANALYSIS	Ambiguous examples are reanalysed in conformity with the new parameter setting—e.g. simple inversion is reanalysed as free inversion. C becomes unable to bear [+Agr].

2.3. SOME ISSUES IN SYNTACTIC CHANGE

These accounts raise a number of issues that need clarification. Here I shall concentrate on three such issues. First, I argue that there is a need to distinguish lexical change more clearly as a category of change distinct from parametric change. Then the distinction between Diachronic Reanalyses and parametric changes will be discussed. Finally, the question is raised as to how it is that children can initiate change despite evidence against the change in their linguistic environment.

2.3.1. *The nature of 'steps' and lexical change*

The first issue concerns the nature of the 'step' (or its equivalent in the Lightfoot model). One aspect of the concept of a step is relatively straightforward. Steps change the frequency of constructions that are already grammatical and thereby alter the conditions for acquisition without altering the grammar itself. They are thus located firmly in performance, and constitute the means by which current performance can influence future competence.

Another aspect of steps is more problematic. They are said to be able to introduce new constructions. It is not clear how this can happen without a change in the grammar. For instance, at some point in the history of French, AdvSVO orders are introduced as a step.

Clark and Roberts (1993) offer us the following explanation: children acquiring Middle French must have tried the hypothesis that subject pronouns in their language were clitics, and as such did not count for V2. Under this hypothesis, XSVO orders would have been possible if the subject was a pronoun. The introduction of AdvSVO is, therefore, due to the influence of the child's 'ultimately unsuccessful hypothesis that these pronouns were indeed syntactic clitics' which 'could . . . have given rise to XSV orders at the time when the subject-pronoun system was undergoing change' (Clark and Roberts 1993: 338 n. 19). However, the hypothesis that subject pronouns were syntactic clitics is one which is supposed eventually to be rejected by children, whereas the AdvSVO orders are produced by adults who should already have rejected the hypothesis during acquisition. The only way out for this explanation would seem to be to claim that children acquiring Middle French were unable to decide between clitic and full status for subject pronouns, in which case adults might treat them sometimes as clitics, sometimes as non-clitics. Yet Roberts's model of syntactic change does not allow for this kind of indeterminate parameter setting.

The only other solution seems to involve changes in the lexical entries of individual lexical items. For instance, in the case of adverbs found in AdvSVO orders, certain adverbs are licensed in their lexical entries to adjoin to CP (cf. notes 8 and 9). If this is so, then at least some steps must represent a type of true linguistic change, perhaps even of syntactic change, albeit distinct from parametric change. Other steps—for instance, 'drift' towards a favourite sentence type—may fall outside this, and are presumably amenable to description only in informal, perhaps pragmatic, terms.

This suggests that we should perhaps take the notion of lexical change in syntax more seriously. This is also the conclusion that emerges from a closer examination of Lightfoot's study of syntactic change in English.

Lightfoot (1991: 166–7) claims in his study of parametric change in English to have examined six new parameter settings. These are:

1. a move to an underlying verb–complement order, namely the move from OV to VO order discussed in Section 2.2.1 above);
2. the innovation of the ability of *to* to transmit Case and head-government properties of a governing verb;
3. the loss of D-structure oblique case;
4. the emergence of a reanalysis operation allowing V+P sequences to be treated as complex verbs for A'-movement as in *Who$_i$ did you* [$_V$ *speak to*] t$_i$?
5. the recategorization of 'premodal' verbs as modals;
6. the loss of V-to-I raising (see also Lightfoot 1993).

This gives the impression of a theory of syntactic change in which all syntactic change is parametric. However, as Hale (1994: 148) points out, these do not all seem to be parametric changes, at least in the sense in which that term has usually been defined. Changes 2, 4, and 5 are not obviously linked to any recognized parameter. If a theory of change involving parameters is to have any value, the set of possible parameters must be highly constrained (Lightfoot 1997: 254; cf. the role of parameters in explaining why children acquire language so easily, Section 2.2). We cannot accept highly language-specific features as being controlled by parameters. In particular, the properties of a single lexical item, as with *to* in Change 2, cannot possibly be controlled parametrically.[12] The recategorization of the premodals is described by Lightfoot himself as 'a change in lexical specifica-tions' which 'may have affected some items earlier than others' (Lightfoot 1991: 147; cf. the criticisms in Warner 1983 of Lightfoot's 1979 account of the modals). This can be understood as parametric only if there is some parameter allowing or disallowing modals in the lexicon, a move which seems to be completely unnecessary. It seems to violate the definition of parametric change both by being lexical and by proceeding gradually. In the case of the modals, it seems entirely reasonable to treat the isolation of the modals as a class as being the result of a series of changes in lexical specifications, largely the loss of exception features.

Finally it is hard to imagine that the reanalysis operation in Change 4 is anything other than a property specific to English, rather like *do*-insertion. In as much as it is a property of category sequences rather than individual lexical items, it may be a change in the peripheral (non-UG) grammar, but it can hardly be parametric.

Once again this brings us to the conclusion that we need to take more seriously the distinction between parametric and non-parametric change. A distinction that is implicit in the literature needs to be elaborated in an explicit manner. In the spirit of Lightfoot and Roberts, I assume that a fully articulated hypothesis of parametric change must begin by admitting three classes of syntactic changes—namely:

1. **performance changes** (≈steps)—e.g. increased frequency of a favoured word-order pattern;
2. **parametric changes**—e.g. a change in the configuration for Nominative Case-assignment;
3. non-parametric changes:
   (*a*) in the periphery (**peripheral changes**)—e.g. language-specific peripheral operations such as availability of *do*-insertion or V+P reanalysis;
   (*b*) in the lexicon (**lexical changes**)—e.g. feature changes in lexical and functional items listed in the lexicon.

These types should have distinct properties, both in terms of their effect on the grammar, and in terms of the patterns through which they are reflected in the speech community.

2.3.2.   *The status of Diachronic Reanalyses*

A further question is raised by the status of Diachronic Reanalyses in the Roberts model. It does not seem to be possible to maintain the distinction between a

Diachronic Reanalysis and, on the one hand, a parametric shift, and, on the other, a step.

Two scenarios spring to mind: either the reanalysed structure in a DR can be generated by the (old) grammar or it cannot. In the first scenario, we must ask why the DR did not happen much earlier—that is, why it was not simply triggered by an earlier parametric change. Presumably there was evidence in the earlier trigger experience to rule out the possibility that the new structure could be generated by the grammar of the language. In the second case, the DR must itself *immediately* trigger, in fact, be part of, a parametric change.

Let us consider these possibilities in relation to V2 in Old and Middle French. As a result of various steps, the child finds the verb increasingly in third position and reanalyses CPs as AgrPs to avoid the cross-linguistically dispreferred option of adjunction to CP (Roberts 1993*b*: 144–50):

(12) $[_{CP} \text{Adverb} [_{CP} \text{XP} [_{C} \text{Verb} [_{VP} t_V \text{NP}]]]]$

         $\Rightarrow$

(13) $[_{AgrP} \text{Adverb} [_{AgrP} \text{XP} [_{Agr} \text{Verb} [_{VP} t_V \text{NP}]]]]$

Previously the verb had been required to raise to V because of the presence of a feature [+Agr] on C (Roberts 1993*b*: 97). This feature had to be compulsory in order to ensure that V2 in main clauses was compulsory. The previous grammar could thus not generate (13). Roberts posits a DR whereby (12) is reanalysed as (13). In order to do this, [+Agr] must cease to be obligatory on C. Thus (13) *can* be generated by the later post-DR grammar. But this goes against the claim that this is a DR independent of parametric change involving no change in the grammar (Roberts 1993*b*: 158). The grammar *has* changed in that it no longer requires the [+Agr] feature on C, and this change has to be parametric (rather than lexical change or change in the peripheral grammar). There seems to have been a hidden parametric change (cf. note 11). This leaves us close to Lightfoot's conclusion that a Diachronic Reanalysis is really 'a particular type of parametric shift' (Lightfoot 1994: 577). In fact the change exhibits some of the other properties of parametric change. After the 'reanalysis' the XP is in SpecAgrP, a position reserved for the subject, and so the order Adverb–Object–Verb–Subject is rendered obsolete.[13]

It is conceivable that there might be DR-like developments independent of parametric shift. Suppose that, in the French example, the grammar is such that it is already capable of generating both (12) and (13), but earlier speakers in practice used only (12). That is [+Agr] is only optionally present on C. The Diachronic Reanalysis would therefore be the sudden use of the structure (13), where only (12) had been used before. Subsequently we get a gradual replacement of one of the available options (12) by the other (13), towards the end of which a parametric change is triggered.

In this case, it is hard to see how the DR differs in any way from a step—it is merely the first part of a step that applies to structures. The frequency with which an available structure is chosen rises from zero to above zero. Arguably under this scenario a DR takes place at the first point in time at which the new structure is actually chosen. That is, the fact that the grammar generates the new structure can be thought of as the pre-existing potential for a DR to take place, but it does not actually happen until the new structure is actually used in performance.

This scenario, of course, would be reflected by no surface changes, since it involves the replacement of one structure for a given string by another. It is, therefore, impossible to demonstrate, and a priori impossible to date the DR. It is also hard to see how the DR could be passed on from generation to generation unless it triggers some surface change in the form of a parametric change. Once again we are forced back to questions like: why is the new structure not used (at least to some extent) as soon as a grammar appears (historically) which allows it? To put it another way: how can a grammar exist which generates certain structures that are never used?

Given these difficulties with the second scenario, it seems that we must adopt the first as our view of parametric change. If so, DRs become subsumed under the notion of parametric change. We might think of a parametric change as consisting of two simultaneous phenomena: the DR (the child's failure to adopt the adult structure for leading construction(s)) and the parametric shift (the child's hypothesis about parameter settings based on the assignment of new structures in these cases).[14]

If so, the more relevant notion in the lead-up to the parametric shift is the potential inherent in a structure produced by the grammar for reanalysis and parameter shift, specifically some notion of **acquisitional ambiguity**. In this case, a construction has two possible structures only one of which is generated by the adult grammar. The other, however, is a tempting analysis for the child but one which should ultimately be rejected for independent reasons.

2.3.3. *Parametric change violates the input data*

Whether acquisitional ambiguity leads to syntactic (parametric) change or not depends upon the evidence available to children in favour of the conservative structure. If the quantity or quality of this evidence is insufficient to force the child to opt for the adult structure, then a DR will occur, triggering a parametric change. However, in any case, since the old parameter setting in the adult will result in instances of constructions compatible only with that parameter setting being produced in the trigger experience, Diachronic Reanalyses and parametric changes must occur despite evidence to refute them. As Lightfoot (1991: 14) puts it: 'It is well known that certain kinds of syntactic patterns become obsolete in certain speech communities at certain times. This means that sometimes children hear a form that does not trigger any grammatical device permitting it to be generated by the grammar and thus to occur in their mature speech.' For instance, in Roberts's French example, children must fail to establish that Nominative Case-assignment is possible under government despite the fact that they still have access to some

instances of verb-second structures with postverbal subjects that provide unambiguous evidence that this is indeed the case, such as *einsint aama la demoisele
Lancelot* 'thus loved the lady Lancelot' (Roberts 1993*b*: 85) (Lightfoot 1994: 573).

Thus, one possible criticism of the approach is that it is not clear how much
evidence is needed to fulfil the proviso that Diachronic Reanalyses must be
'consistent with . . . other aspects of the trigger experience'. This is a problem
familiar from Lightfoot's (1979) Transparency Principle, revived in contemporary
form as Roberts's Least Effort Strategy. Both are only *post hoc* ways of 'explaining' syntactic change. It is not made explicit precisely which aspects of the trigger
experience the representations must be consistent with. They do not define the
point at which a Diachronic Reanalysis and parametric change take place. The
problem of how much evidence is needed to set a parameter is, however, one that
needs to be faced in language acquisition too.

On the other hand, it is too much to expect any theory of language change to
have predictive power. If first-language acquisition is the locus of language change,
then change depends crucially on individual children responding to trigger
experiences which differ from one another randomly. There is considerable
extralinguistic input in the form of normative pressure against the use of certain
patterns, and thus against their appearance in the trigger experience, thus retarding
the appearance of parametric changes. But the extent of this and similar pressure
is determined by entirely non-linguistic factors. It can reasonably be argued that the
exact timing of parametric change is due to chance, but that, all other things being
equal, the probability increases as the trigger evidence declines.

It seems useful, however, to distinguish between sources of evidence that are
both structurally unambiguous and frequent enough to be of use in setting
parameters and those that are not. We can take the standard account of the null
subject parameter as an example (Rizzi 1982). Recall (from Section 2.2) that three
features are linked to the setting of this parameter—namely, the presence or
absence of null subjects, the possibility of Free Subject Inversion, and the presence
or absence of *that*-trace effects.

The Italian child will hear instances of null subjects fairly frequently, and this
will provide good ('robust') evidence that the null subject parameter should be set
positively. Contrast this with sentences involving the absence of *that*-trace effects.
These will be fairly rare, and it seems unlikely that the child could ever use them
as the basis for setting the parameter. Thus, whether the parameter continues to be
set positively in Italian depends crucially on sentences with null subjects remaining
frequent in performance. The frequency of the *that*-trace filter violations will
always be too low to be of any significance. The place of free subject inversion in
this is intermediate and would need to be the subject of empirical investigation.

If we make such distinctions, we can begin to consider what patterns of data
could be expected in texts during a period of parametric change. Logically, a theory
of parametric change predicts something like the following. Two types of
construction can be established with respect to each parameter.

First, we have those syntactic features that provide evidence for the setting of the parameter itself—for instance, the position of separable prefixes showed the base position of the verb in Old English, and so helped to set the OV/VO parameter (Lightfoot 1991: 61).[15] Potentially the direct output of the parameter is also the evidence for setting it. For instance, the null subject parameter can be set by the child hearing a sentence containing a null subject, and a positive setting for this parameter is the only way to generate null subjects. Changes in such features should be gradual. In a typical case, we expect gradual change (performance change) towards a reduction in evidence for the conservative parameter setting. Once the parameter setting itself changes, we expect sudden obsolescence of the option which provided evidence for the old parameter setting, or else its reanalysis. I shall call such a feature a **leading feature** with respect to a parametric change.

The second type of feature is directly sensitive to the setting of a parameter but does not directly provide (much) evidence for setting it. In Lightfoot's analysis of English word-order change, an example of this would be subordinate-clause word order in Old English. According to his degree-o learnability, embedded contexts are not used in parameter-setting, so subordinate-clause word order is not used to set the VO/OV parameter. However, once this parameter was reset at VO, word order in subordinate clauses changed suddenly to conform with the new parameter setting. I shall call such features **trailing features** with respect to a particular parametric change.[16] Such a feature need not show any signs of change until the parameter setting itself changes, since it can be fully current in performance without providing good evidence in favour of the conservative parameter setting. However, once the parameter change sets in, it should change suddenly. In this case reanalysis should not be an option, since the construction itself is not salient enough in the trigger experience to require that the child assign it a grammatical structure.

Another possible construction type is the construction which can be generated, albeit with a different structure, with both settings. Clearly such a construction provides no evidence for either setting. For instance, SVO word orders in a V2-language provide no evidence that the language is V2. The frequency of such a construction should not be affected by the parametric change. It may nevertheless be central to the parametric change in that the acquisitional ambiguity of the construction allows it to be reanalysed, thereby triggering a parametric change. Changes will, however, be observed in related constructions or in specific subtypes of the construction, which can be thought of as trailing changes themselves.

Given this view of change, we expect the observed data, inasmuch as they can be freed from sociolinguistic 'noise', to resemble the idealized situation presented in Figure 2.1.

A number of factors may be expected to prevent such patterns from appearing in actual data. Typically we may find corpora of texts showing mixed usage when parametric change predicts a sudden switch from old to new. Such non-categorical usage may have a number of simple explanations that are compatible with a

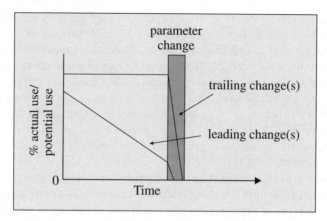

FIGURE 2.1. Idealized development of a parametric change

parametric single grammar model. Several sociolinguistic factors will complicate the picture.

Non-categorical usage at a community level may be the result of variation between individuals. Aggregate statistics for texts based on the performance of a number of individuals, or for multiple texts, may well show this type of pattern.

Non-categorical usage by an individual may be the result of style-shifting. Suppose individuals have a single acquired grammar at their disposal, which may contain either the new or the old parameter setting but not both. Does this mean that they must produce categorical usage pattern consistent only with one setting? In the Andersen tradition (cf. Section 2.1), the answer is clearly no. Such individuals may have learned, consciously or unconsciously, peripheral adaptive rules through which they produce the earlier pattern even though it is not native to them in the way that it was to earlier speakers. Writers will have access to a considerable body of earlier literature in their language, and to some extent will be 'quoting', consciously or unconsciously, from that body of literature, whether this be in the form of fossilized expressions or simply stylistic imitation. In literary contexts, areas of syntax covered by a (potentially implicit) norm may show high levels of usage of the conservative pattern. If the literary tradition is strong and continuous, there is no reason why the conservative pattern should not be maintained for many centuries. In speech and at lower stylistic levels, conservative usage is likely to be maintained less securely, to the extent that normative pressures are likely to be less pervasive there. Thus, in cases where there is a literary norm covering the syntactic pattern in question, non-categorical usage in literary texts cannot provide evidence against parametric shifts. However, where that norm is least pervasive, evidence should be available in their favour.

Social and stylistic variation is, therefore, not counter-evidence to the parametric model. The sort of counter-evidence required is the existence of variable usage and, in particular, gradual change with respect to a particular parameter by single individuals in a context not influenced by norms of usage.

It has been argued that, even allowing for such factors, the observed data are not always compatible with a parametric model that predicts that two parameter settings cannot coexist. Santorini (1992) claims that data from the history of Yiddish provide evidence that individuals may have access to both the old and the new settings for a given parameter. This is the **Double Base Hypothesis** that 'children have the ability to abduce more than one grammatical system from the primary data in the course of acquisition' (Santorini 1992: 619).

The argument runs as follows. Yiddish has moved from having head-final IPs (reflected in underlying Lexical Verb–Auxiliary order) to head-medial IPs (with the reverse underlying order). For instance, Early Yiddish had subordinate clauses like those in (14), where the Infl-element in bold is clause-final. In Modern Yiddish, as in (15), Infl precedes verbal adjuncts and complements.

(14)   . . . *ds   zi   droyf   givarnt **vern**.*
              that they thereon warned were
              '. . . that they might be warned about it.'

              (Santorini 1992: 606; 1995: 60)

(15)   . . . *oyb   dos yingl **vet** oyfn   veg zen a kats.*
              whether the boy   will on-the way see a cat
              '. . . whether the boy will see a cat on the way.'

              (Santorini 1992: 597; 1995: 54)

This is a change in a parameter controlling Head-Complement order in IP. Santorini extracts from her historical corpus those subordinate clauses consistent only with the old or only with the new parameter. We would expect, if each individual has only one parameter setting, that each text should contain only clauses requiring the old setting or only clauses requiring the new setting, but not both. In fact, the two coexist in a number of texts. The necessary adaptive rules to map from one parameter setting to the other would be complex and unnatural, she argues, hence the Double Base Hypothesis is used as a way out.[17]

Acceptance of the Double Base Hypothesis would have very serious consequences for the theory of syntactic change. It would mean that it would be impossible *in principle* to refute the parametric account of syntactic change on the basis of observed historical data. The observation that a change in a feature thought to be the subject of parametric variation is gradual could no longer be used against the parametric account—it could always be argued that a double base is involved. It also reduces the potential types of evidence available in favour of the parametric account, since the rate of progress of syntactic change through time becomes irrelevant. Indeed, variation in the speed of different syntactic changes becomes puzzling, since it makes one wonder why under some circumstances double bases seem to be available, whereas under other circumstances the language shifts suddenly from one parameter setting to another, without making use of the possibility of double bases, a possibility that should be freely available (cf. Traugott and Smith 1993: 437, 444). Thus, if such a possibility were available, it would be hard to see what the point of a parametric theory of change would be. Our starting assumption must, therefore, be to reject the Double Base Hypothesis unless strong evidence in its favour should emerge.

2.4.   THE FEATURES OF A PARAMETRIC CHANGE

Certain of the anticipated features of a parametric change have already been mentioned, specifically abruptness and obsolescence. Let us now turn to examine the full range of features that has been suggested.

Lightfoot (1991: 167–9) gives the following six characteristics of parametric change:

1. Each parameter change is manifested by a cluster of simultaneous surface changes.
2. Parameter changes sometimes set off 'chain reactions' in the form of other parameter changes.
3. changes involving new parameter settings take place more rapidly than non-parametric changes.
4. new parameter settings cause the total disappearance of old constructions.
5. any significant change in meaning is generally a by-product of a new parameter setting.
6. new parameter settings occur in response to shifts in unembedded data only.

As noted by Hale (1994: 149), this set of properties is unsatisfying. The difference between Feature 1 'a cluster of simultaneous surface changes' and Feature 2 'chain reactions' is hard to maintain purely in terms of data. In fact the distinction is entirely theory-internal and should be defined as such. With Feature 5, it is unclear what would constitute a 'significant change in meaning'. Feature 6 is a hypothesis open to empirical investigation (in acquisition studies rather than historical syntax), but a priori seems rather unlikely. In any case, it can hardly be taken as a defining property of parametric change.

This leaves us with a reduced set of core features that a theory of parametric change must hypothesize. The distinction that Lightfoot makes between simultaneous surface changes and chain reactions reflects a distinction inherent in the definition of parameter. Since a parameter by definition has exponents in a number of areas of (surface) grammar, a change in parameter setting will have immediate changes in a number of areas. Other changes are possible, perhaps changes in other parameters, but these are not directly attributable to the parameter change itself. In particular, the changes brought about by the parameter change in the first place will alter the input data for the next generation of children, perhaps considerably reducing the evidence for the 'correct' setting of some other parameter. On the other hand, they may not, and in any case parametric shifts could be brought about by means other than by such chain reactions. There therefore seems to be little point in concentrating on Feature 2 of parameter changes, especially since it confuses the situation with respect to Feature 1. Feature 1, however, lies at the heart of the notion of parameter as an abstract switch with a number of surface exponents. If the switch changes, we must expect wide-ranging effects on the surface.

The binary nature of parameters means that Feature 3 is also a logical necessity in such a theory. Parametric change must be swift because, assuming there are no parameter settings like 'Either' or 'Mostly' (cf. the objections to the Double Base Hypothesis above), there can be no intermediate grammars between one parameter setting and another. Contrast the situation in historical lexical semantics, where old and new meanings of a word may coexist for centuries, or in morphology, where erosion of inflectional endings may proceed via many intermediate stages.

In fact, given that single parameters have multiple exponents, we can make a stronger claim. The new parameter setting as a whole 'diffuses'. It is therefore not possible, at least to the extent that usage reflects naturally acquired rather than consciously learned norms, for part of a parametric shift to be taken over—we do not expect to find a new syntactic pattern that a parameter shift introduces to spread without the other syntactic effects of the parameter shift spreading with it. Kroch (1989) argues that a given syntactic change appears simultaneously in the environments to which it will apply, but at varying initial levels of dominance. He further claims that thereafter change proceeds at a constant rate in each environment. It may be that this is the way in which we should envisage the diffusion of an entire parameter setting. I shall refer to this property of parametric change as **uniform diffusion**.

Finally, obsolescence should be a feature of parametric change, rather than smooth changes in frequency of use. If the core grammar changes, then the set of sentences that it generates must change also. One consequence will typically be the elimination of constructions. These constructions will have been relatively infrequent in performance, since they failed to prevent the parameter shift. Note that this does not suffice to define a parametric change: obsolescence may well be a feature of lexical change also.

A theory of parametric change also requires a modification of the notion of 'diffusion', and of the distinction between actuation and diffusion. It is clear that parameter settings themselves cannot diffuse, since children do not have direct access to them in the way that they have direct access to, say, sound changes. Diffusion of syntactic change, under the parametric model, is, therefore, of a very different nature from diffusion of, say, phonological change (contra Hale 1994: 150–1; Traugott and Smith 1993: 436). Each time a new individual adopts the new parameter, it is via the same procedure as the first individual. Each speaker discovers the parameter change anew. A parametric shift spreads in so far as the change of parameter setting in one speaker or group of speakers tilts the trigger experience of children towards the new setting. That is, once one speaker shifts to the new setting, the amount of data in favour of the old parameter setting falls, whilst the amount of data in favour of the new parameter setting rises. Children exposed to speakers with the new setting are more likely to acquire that setting. The directionality of the change is thus maintained. In that sense, the spread of a syntactic change involves multiple actualization of a change rather than diffusion. Of course, the extent to which this multiple actualization occurs is likely to be influenced by sociolinguistic factors—the shape of social networks, the extent to which data come from speakers with social prestige, and so on.[18]

2.5. WORKING ASSUMPTIONS

The above discussion leads us to reject some of Lightfoot's features of a parametric change. Instead, we can concentrate on a smaller number of expected core features. If the hypothesis of parametric change is correct, it should be possible to identify parametric changes in the following setting.

First, the evidence for the conservative parameter setting declines as the result of a performance change in a leading construction, owing to non-syntactic (most likely phonological or pragmatic) factors or lexical change. Other constructions which use the old parameter setting are acquisitionally ambiguous—that is, amenable to an alternative preferred (by the Least Effort Strategy) structural analysis. The decline in evidence for the old parameter setting from the leading feature allows the ambiguous construction to be reanalysed in a way consistent only with the new parameter setting (a Diachronic Reanalysis). The parameter is then set to the new setting. The notion of reanalysis can be retained as a means of showing this, but the reanalysis is inevitably part of a parametric change. Unless the leading construction is amenable to reanalysis, it will become obsolete. Changes in trailing constructions are triggered simultaneously and are completed quickly.[19] Either such constructions become obsolete or they are innovated as appropriate. The surface changes should, in so far as the effects of sociolinguistic and dialectal variation allow us to tell, take effect rapidly. Diffusion of the parametric shift is indirect, via multiple (re)actualization. Inasmuch as the new setting in one speaker's grammar reduces the frequency of leading constructions still further, the new parameter setting quickly diffuses through the community. All surface exponents of the shift will be affected to the same extent in any given dialect or sociolect.

Alongside parametric change, some grammatical change may be lexical. This may show variability between different items of the same syntactic category. On the other hand, suddenness may also be a property of this type of change, in so far as it involves features that may be set only positively or negatively in the lexicon.

The exact properties of such changes will need to be the subject of further empirical investigation.

We have now established a framework in which to discuss syntactic change. In the next two chapters I shall move away from the question of historical change to present a synchronic account of the verb-second system of Middle Welsh. However, I shall return to the question of syntactic change in the following chapters, examining how the framework developed here can be applied to word-order changes and related changes in Early Modern Welsh.

3. Verb-Second in Middle Welsh

This chapter deals with the central word-order patterns of Middle Welsh. It develops a synchronic analysis of the abnormal sentence as a verb-second (V2) phenomenon parallel to similar phenomena in the Germanic languages and in Breton. The discussion shows that, with minor modifications to deal with adverb-placement rules, the standard analysis of verb-second is applicable to Middle Welsh. Restrictions on movement, parallel to those affecting relative clauses, justify the conclusion that in most cases moved preverbal constituents undergo A′-movement. A number of other aspects of the abnormal sentence will also be explored, specifically how it interacts with negation and how the observed agreement patterns can be accounted for. As well as providing an analysis of the construction, the chapter aims to show that the abnormal sentence manifests such intricate rules and cross-linguistic parallels that it is inconceivable that it could be an artificial literary construction.

The discussion in this and the next two chapters is based on data drawn from a number of Middle Welsh texts. Principally these are *Y Bibyl Ynghymraec* (*BY*), *Brut y Brenhinedd* (Cotton Cleopatra B. v. (*BB₁*) and Llanstephan 1 (*BB₂*)), *Brut y Tywysogyon* (Peniarth 20 (*BTy₁*) and the Red Book Version (*BTy₂*)), *Chwedlau Cymraeg Canol* (*ChCC*), *Historia Gruffud vab Kenan* (*HGK*), *Kedymdeithyas Amlyn ac Amic* (*KAA*), *Mabinogi Iessu Grist* (*MIG*), *Owein*, *Pedeir Keinc y Mabinogi* (*PKM*), *Peredur*, *Ystorya de Carolo Magno* (*YCM*), and *Ystoryaeu Seint Greal* (*YSG*). Additional material is also taken from D. Simon Evans (1964).

Recent research (Peter Wynn Thomas 1992, 1993) has raised the possibility of recognizing dialect variation within Middle Welsh at a phonological and morphological level, and it is hoped that the use of these texts will allow us to test for dialect variation at the syntactic level also. Although Middle Welsh prose has traditionally been traced to south Wales (Peter Wynn Thomas 1992: 287, 1993: 18; G. J. Williams 1969: 4, 37, 75–7), a number of texts can be linked to north Wales on the basis of both linguistic and nonlinguistic evidence. This is true of several of the texts used here. The versions of *Brut y Brenhinedd* in Cotton Cleopatra B. v. and Llanstephan 1, the Peniarth 20 version of *Brut y Tywysogyon*, *Historia Gruffud vab Kenan* (Peniarth 17), *Y Bibyl Ynghymraec* (Peniarth 20), and *Kedymdeithyas Amlyn ac Amic* (Red Book of Hergest) all have northern links. D. Simon Evans (*HGK*, pp. ccxcviii) suggests that a number of linguistic (phonological and morphological) features may link the *Historia* with the north; Peter Wynn Thomas's studies offer quantitative linguistic evidence in support of locating this text, the Llanstephan I version of *Brut y Brenhinedd*, *Brut y Tywysogyon* (Peniarth 20), *Y Bibyl Ynghymraec* (Peniarth 20), and *Kedymdeithyas Amlyn ac Amic* in the north.[1] Daniel Huws has suggested that the Peniarth 20 manuscript may have been compiled in the scriptorium at Valle Crucis in north-east Wales (Huws 1991: 11). The same hand is used in *Y Bibyl Ynghymraec* (Peniarth 20) and in *Dares Phrygius* (Cotton Cleopatra B. v.) (*BY*, pp. lxxxvii–lxxxix) and in other parts of these two manuscripts (*BTy₁*, p. xx), a fact which may allow us to trace the Cotton Cleopatra B. v. version of *Brut y Brenhinedd* to the same scriptorium, almost certainly in the north-east.

Inclusion of these texts allows us to test for syntactic dialect variation in the constructions examined in this chapter. Since variation is known to exist in phonology and morphology between these and the majority southern texts, the absence of variation on a syntactic level would be evidence that the abnormal pattern was native to the whole of Wales, and would therefore be evidence against the Southern British Dialect Hypothesis (Section 1.3.3.2). Throughout this chapter I have therefore tried to include examples of each construction under discussion from texts with both northern and southern associations, even where such variation is not explicitly referred to.

3.1. THE ABNORMAL SENTENCE IN MIDDLE WELSH

Let us first consider the basic properties of word order in Middle Welsh. Recall that in Middle Welsh the verb generally appears in non-initial position in main clauses. It is preceded by a wide range of constituents in so-called abnormal sentence. It is (virtually) obligatory for there to be at least one preverbal constituent in affirmative main clauses, and quite frequently there is more than one preverbal constituent. Some of the various possibilities are exemplified in (1). In (1*a*) the subject is preverbal, in (1*b*) the direct object, in (1*c*) an adverbial adjunct, in (1*d*) an adverbial complement, and in (1*e*) the Verb Phrase complement of an auxiliary. In (1*f*) a nonfinite verb (verbnoun) is fronted from within the VP complement of an auxiliary. These patterns appear regularly in both southern and northern Middle Welsh texts.[2]

(1) (*a*) A' r *ederyn a* *doeth y* 'r *ynys honn.*
And the bird   PRT came to the island this
'And the bird came to this island.'   (*PKM* 38. 12–13)

(*b*) *Ac ystryw a* *wnaeth y* *Gwydyl.*
And trick PRT made the Irish
'And the Irish played a trick.'   (*PKM* 44. 11)

(*c*) *Yn Hardlech y* *bydwch* *seith mlyned ar ginyaw . . .*
In Harlech PRT be-FUT-2P seven years at dinner
'In Harlech you will be at dinner for seven years . . .'   (*PKM* 45. 2–3)

(d) *Atref   y   doeth Arthur . . .*
homeward PRT came Arthur
'Arthur came home . . .'   (*CO* 927)

(e) *A   chymryt y   golwython a   wnaethant . . .*
And take-VN the steaks   PRT did-3P
'And they took the steaks . . .'   (*Owein*, 24)

(f) *Gwyssyaw   a   oruc Arthur milwyr yr ynys   honn . . .*
summon-VN PRT did Arthur soldiers the island this
'Arthur summoned the soldiers of this island . . .'   (*CO* 922–3)

A preverbal particle appears between the clause-initial constituent and the verb. This particle is *a* if the constituent is the subject or direct object of the verb as in (1a) or (1b), or the nonfinite complement of an auxiliary as in (1e) or (1f). After a fronted adjectival or nominal predicate complement of verbs like *bot* 'to be' the rule is that the verb undergoes soft mutation without any preceding particle, as in (2).

(2) (a) *A   llawen vu   Arthur wrth y   kennadeu . . .*
and happy was-PERF Arthur at   the messengers
'And Arthur was happy at the messengers . . .'   (*YSG* 168)

(b) *. . . a   drwc vv   gan y   tywysogion ereyll hynny.*
and bad   was with the princes   other that
'. . . and the other princes were displeased at that.'   (*BTy*₁ 295a. 18–20)

Otherwise—that is, mostly with adverbial elements in preverbal position—the particle is *y(d)*, as in the remaining examples. The particle *a* triggers soft mutation of the initial consonant of the following verb, whilst *y(d)* does not trigger any mutation at all. The rules determining the choice of particle are enforced rigidly and show no regional variation.

In the absence of any other element as topic, and indeed sometimes even with a preverbal adverb, an expletive ('dummy') third-person singular masculine pronoun *ef* may be inserted in topic position, as in (3).

(3) (a) *Ef a   doeth makwyueit a   gueisson ieueinc y*
it PRT came squires   and lads   young to+3SM-GEN
diarchenu . . .
disrobe-VN
'There came squires and young lads to disrobe him . . .'   (*PKM* 4. 8–9)

(b) *Ef a   daw   glaw gwaet . . .*
it PRT will-come rain blood
'There will come rain of blood . . .'   (*BB*₁ 125. 5)

This construction is constrained in certain important respects that will be dealt with more fully in Chapter 5.

In negative main clauses the verb is in general in initial position, preceded only by the negative marker itself. An example is given in (4). However, exceptions to this pattern do occur, and will be discussed fully in Section 3.6.

(4)   *Ny   welei   ef y   twrwf   rac tywyllet y   nos.*
       NEG saw-IMPF he the commotion for so-dark the night
       'He could not see the commotion because the night was so dark.'

                                                       (*PKM* 22. 23)

In most embedded clauses, the verb obligatorily appears immediately after the complementizer, as in (5), resulting in VSO order.[3]

(5) (*a*) *A   chyt   archo   ef yti   rodi   yr eil,   na*
          and though implore-SUBJ he to-you give-VN the second NEG
          dyro . . .
          give-IMPER
          'And though he implore you to give him the second, do not give (it) . . .'

                                                       (*PKM* 3. 19–20)

    (*b*) *A   phan welas y   brenhin hynny a   barwnyeit y   llys, ny   bu*
          and when saw   the king   that   and barons   the court NEG was
          hoff ganthunt.
          glad with-them
          'And when the king and the barons of the court saw that, they were not pleased.'   (*YSG* 17–18)

The relative frequency of main-clause word-order patterns in Middle Welsh has been the subject of much investigation. A summary of the findings of recent quantitative studies is given in Table 3.1. The statistics are based, with minor variations between studies, on a count of all main affirmative declarative clauses in the texts, excluding copular structures (see e.g. Poppe 1989: 43; 1990: 445; 1991*a*: 168). That is, the data exclude negative, interrogative, and imperative clauses, and replies, for which separate word-order rules apply. The table is intended to convey the general impression of how great the difference is between Middle Welsh word order and the regular VSO order of Modern Welsh according to recent text-based studies. It can be seen that abnormal sentences form the overwhelming majority of main affirmative clauses. Absolute verb-initial (V1) clauses, although attested in these texts, form only a small fraction of the proportion that we would expect in Modern Welsh.[4]

The most important fact to emerge from Table 3.1 is that in Middle Welsh texts a wide range of preverbal elements is found. Preverbal adverbial phrases and clauses, nominal and pronominal subjects, nominal objects, and verbnouns and nonfinite Verb Phrases are all well represented in Middle Welsh texts.

On the basis of this and other evidence, Poppe has formulated the syntactic rule for the order of constituents in Middle Welsh main clauses as:

(6) $(C_2), C_1 V (S) (O)$

where

C_1 = a fronted constituent which governs the [choice of] particle
C_2 = a second fronted constituent
V = inflected verb
S = (non-fronted) subject
O = (non-fronted) object   (Poppe 1989: 51; 1990: 447; 1991a: 200; 1991b: 18)

That is, in Middle Welsh one constituent precedes the verb in an affirmative declarative main clause. The C_2 position is required for cases of 'multiple fronting' where two constituents precede the verb (see Section 3.3).

Fife has convincingly proposed that preverbal constituents in Middle Welsh exhibit the thematic properties of topics (Fife 1988; Fife and King 1991).[5] Poppe, whilst maintaining that all preverbal constituents are instances of fronting (topicalization), has also suggested that the set of elements which may occupy the C_2 position is different from that which may occupy the C_1 position. He states that 'the C_1 position is occupied by a constituent acting as topic or focus for the sentence, the C_2 position is (normally) reserved for a scene-setting adverbial or a left-dislocated constituent' (Poppe 1989: 61).

The schema in (6) and Poppe's commentary upon it will be taken as a basis for

TABLE 3.1. *Word-order patterns in Middle Welsh affirmative main clauses*

Text	Abnormal sentences by clause-initial constituent (%)					V_1 (%)	Sample Size
	Adv	S^{NOM}	S^{PRO}	O^{NOM}	V/VP		
Branwen	41	17	16	8	14	4	181
Breuddwyd Maxen	43	5	16	20	8	9	154
Breudwyt Ronabwy	45	12	6	9	26	2	139
Culhwch ac Olwen	25	16	12	12	26	9	253
Ked. Amlyn ac Amic	47	5	7	6	32	3	293
Cyf. Lludd a Llefelys	39	24	22	4	10	0	67
Manawydan	24	6	31	12	27	0	154
Pwyll	38	11	22	10	17	3	376

Notes:
Adv   Adverbial phrase/clause (incl. adverbial complement)
S^{NOM} Nominal subject
S^{PRO} Pronominal subject
O^{NOM} Nominal object
V/VP   Verbnoun/Nonfinite Verb Phrase
V_1 Finite verb in initial position

Sources: Poppe (1989, 1990, 1991a, 1991b, 1993), Watkins (1977–8, 1983–4, 1988, 1993).

further development. It will be shown that the C_1 and C_2 positions are fundamentally different in nature, corresponding in a GB framework to the Specifier position of CP and a CP-adjoined position respectively. In the spirit of recent work on verb-second phenomena in the Germanic languages, I shall argue that C_1 constitutes a landing site for syntactic movement, whereas C_2 is unconnected with movement. Thus it is proper to speak of 'topicalization' and 'fronting' with respect to position C_1 only. Adverb placement and left-dislocation structures in Middle Welsh will also be investigated. It will be argued that certain types of adverb placement are independent of topicalization, necessitating the postulation of an additional immediately preverbal syntactic position.

3.2. VERB-SECOND RULES

The data presented above suggest that the abnormal sentence in Middle Welsh is a verb-second phenomenon like that found in most modern Germanic languages. The examples in (7) show the equivalent phenomenon in German. The verb in a main clause must occupy second position. In (7*a*) it is preceded by the subject, in (7*b*) by the direct object, and in (7*c*) by an adverb. German, like most V2-languages, shows word-order asymmetries between main and subordinate clauses. In subordinate clauses with an overt complementizer the verb must appear in final position, as in (8).

(7) (*a*) *Peter hat gestern   ein Auto gekauft.*
       Peter has yesterday a   car   bought

    (*b*) *Ein Auto hat Peter gestern   gekauft.*
       a   car   has Peter yesterday bought

    (*c*) *Gestern   hat Peter ein Auto gekauft.*
       yesterday has Peter a   car   bought
       'Peter bought a car yesterday.'

(8)   *Ich weiß, daß Peter gestern   ein Auto gekauft hat.*
       I   know that Peter yesterday a   car   bought has
       'I know that Peter bought a car yesterday.'

    The verb-second phenomenon in Germanic has received much scholarly attention in recent years. It is now widely accepted that the embedded position of the verb is basic, with main clauses being derived by raising of the verb to C, and obligatory movement (topicalization) of some phrasal constituent to SpecCP.[6] In German, this means underlying SOV, with obligatory XVSO in main clauses. Accordingly, the structure of (7*b*) would be that given in (9). The auxiliary *hat* raises from I to C, licensing movement ('topicalization') of the object *ein Auto* to

SpecCP in sentence-initial position.[7] The account is developed for German in den Besten (1983) and Haider (1986), for Danish and Faroese in Vikner (1994), for Norwegian in Taraldsen (1986), and for Swedish in Platzack (1986) and Holmberg and Platzack (1991). See also Schafer (1994, 1995) for Breton.

(9)

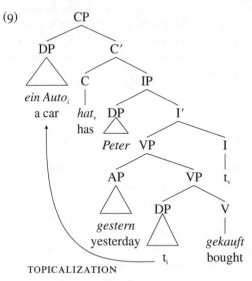

TOPICALIZATION

The main motivation for this analysis is the asymmetry between main and embedded clauses witnessed in German, Dutch, and the Scandinavian languages.[8] In German, verb-second does not apply in embedded clauses introduced by an overt complementizer, and the finite verb obligatorily appears in its underlying clause-final position. The analysis of V2 accounts for this fact naturally. The presence of a complementizer in C prevents movement of the verb from I to C, and, assuming that movement of the preverbal constituent is dependent upon this movement—that is, a tensed verb in C licenses the filling of SpecCP—it also blocks V2.

Once allowance is made for the fact that Middle Welsh, unlike German, is head-initial, this account can be transferred straightforwardly to the data given for Middle Welsh above. The structure of the main constituents in (1*b*) would then, assuming an articulated IP, be that given in (10). The verb raises in steps to C, and the direct object (A′-)moves to the topic position SpecCP. Assuming that verb movement to C is compulsory, the verb must appear in second position. Since the position preceding the verb is not an argument position, it may freely be occupied by a constituent of any type, thus allowing for the other possibilities in (1). I assume that AgrS assigns Nominative Case under government to SpecTP, and that it continues to do so even after it raises along with the verb to C. The subject therefore raises only as far as SpecTP, as in Modern Welsh. For motivation, see the analysis of agreement (Section 3.5) and expletive subjects (Section 5.2.1).

(10)

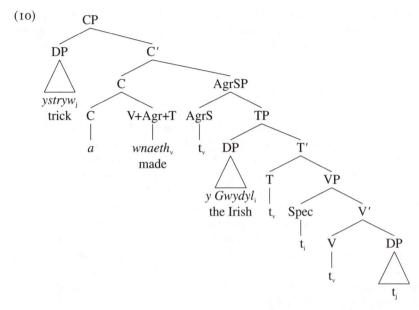

There remain questions regarding the status of the preverbal particle *a* and the movement of the verb from AgrS to C. I shall return to these in Section 3.3.3.[9]

A number of suggestions have been made suggesting how the verb-second parameter should be formulated. Most have attempted to reduce it to some more basic property of the grammar.

Rizzi (1990) suggests that in V2-languages the head of CP bears the features [+C, +I]—that is, it is a hybrid category between C and I. He further assumes, following Laka (1990), that Tense must raise to c-command all [+I] categories. This forces raising of the verb to C. The hybrid category also licenses a topic constituent in its specifier position.

Platzack (1986: 31, 39) adopts a Case-based approach, according to which Nominative Case in V2-languages is assigned by a [+Tense] feature in C. Assuming that Case assigners must be lexically realized, either C must contain an overt complementizer or the finite verb must raise to it.

In the minimalist program, it could be assumed that V2 is triggered by the presence of a strong D-feature on C which must be checked by raising of an element to SpecCP (cf. Schafer 1994: 33, and the case of *wh*-raising, Chomsky 1995: 232).

For present purposes it matters little which, if any, of these is correct. For fuller discussion of these and other suggestions see Vikner (1995: 51–64). We can assume the existence of a V2-parameter, which forces movement of the verb to C and movement of some phrasal constituent to SpecCP. The question of whether this parameter itself is derived from some other property of the grammar can be left open. The parameter is set positively in Middle Welsh and German, but negatively in Modern Welsh and English. Discussion of how these settings could be acquired by children is deferred until Chapter 6.

3.3.   VERB-SECOND AND ADVERB PLACEMENT

This account of V2 is complicated by the adverb-placement rules of Middle Welsh. In the Germanic languages, with a few language-specific exceptions, an adverb is not permitted to precede the verb in a V2-structure. On the other hand, quite frequently in the Middle Welsh tales, a number of constituents precede the finite verb in a main clause. On the basis of this, Poppe (1991*b*: 18–20) speaks of 'multiple frontings', and, at first glance, these make it appear that Middle Welsh is perhaps not verb-second at all. Poppe allows for these extra preverbal constituents to occupy the position C_2 in the schema in (6) in the case of double frontings, and he is in principle willing to allow for triple frontings if three or more constituents precede the verb by the addition of an extra C_3-position, and so on, in front of C_2 (Poppe 1989: 51 n. 5). The logical conclusion is to expand the word-order formula for Middle Welsh to that given in (11).

(11) $(C_n \ldots C_3\, C_2)\, C_1\, V\, (S)\, (O)$

This seems to require a radical revision of the basic analysis presented above. In particular it implies that topicalization is recursive, and should therefore be treated in GB terms as adjunction, rather than as movement to a unique specifier position. An analysis of the abnormal sentence in this spirit, involving multiple adjunction to CP, is presented in Tallerman (1996).

However, there is evidence that topicalization is not recursive, and that there are several qualitatively different syntactic positions that precede the verb in Middle Welsh. It appears that the standard V2-analysis can be defended with relatively minor refinements.

The 'multiple frontings' can be divided into three separate categories: pre-topic adverbials, interposed adverbials, and left dislocations. These will be described briefly below, and an integrated analysis of them will be attempted.

3.3.1.   *Pre-topic adverbs*

The standard examples of 'multiple frontings' cited by Poppe involve one or more adverbials preceding a subject, object, or nonfinite-verb complement of an auxiliary. Typically, it is this last constituent that determines the choice of preverbal particle. The belief that it is this last element which is the real topic is implicit in the way the data in the studies cited in Table 3.1 are prepared. Typically in such studies constituents preceding the one determining the preverbal particle are ignored for the purposes of determining the word-order type.

Some of the attested sequences of 'multiple frontings' are illustrated in (12). In (12*a*) the sequence adverb + subject precedes the verb; in (12*b*) adverb + direct object; in (12*c*) adverb + VP; and in (12*d*) adverb + adverb.

(12) (*a*) *Hir   bylgeint Guydyon a   gyuodes.*
      Early-morning Gwydion PRT got-up
      'Early next morning, Gwydion got up.'   (*PKM* 82. 5–6)

   (*b*) *Yr   hynny pymhet ran y Iwerdon a   wnaeth yn   diffeith.*
      Since that   fifth   part to Ireland PRT made   PRD desolate
      'Because of that he laid waste to a fifth of Ireland.'   (*CO* 1069–70)

   (*c*) *Ac uelly agori   y   drws a   oruc y   gwr llwyt.*
      and so   open-VN the door PRT did   the man grey
      'And so the grey man opened the door.'   (*YSG* 188)

   (*d*) *A   hep   ohir, o   gyt gyghor y   wyrda   y   rodes ef y   dvy*
      and without delay from counsel   his noblemen PRT gave   he his two
      uerched hynhaf ydav   y   tywyssogyon yr Alban   a   Chernyv . . .
      girls   eldest   to-him to princes   the Scotland and Cornwall
      'And without delay, following his noblemen's counsel, he gave his two
      eldest daughters to the princes of Scotland and Cornwall . . .'

                                           (*BD* 27. 14–16)

Examples of more than two elements preceding the verb are given in (13). In (13*a*) two adverbs precede a subject; and in (13*b*) two adverbs precede a fronted verb-noun. This pattern is particularly characteristic of chronicles.

(13) (*a*) *Ac vrth hynny, hyt tra   vu   veu   uyg kyuoeth a   gallu   rodi*
      and at   this   as-long-as was mine my riches   and power give-VN
      da   ohonaf, pavb   a   'm   carei.
      wealth of-me   everyone PRT IS-ACC loved
      'And because of this, as long as my riches and power to give were mine,
      everyone loved me.'   (*BD* 29. 15–16)

   (*b*) *Ac yn y   lle   eissyoes ymgynnullav a   wnaethant ar Vedravt*
      and in the place however gather-VN   PRT did-3P   to Medrod
      y   wasgaredicyon o   bob   man . . .
      the scattered-ones   from every place
      'And there, however, the scattered ones gathered with Medrod from all
      sides . . .'   (*BD* 183. 22–4)

The number of constituents that may precede the verb in this pattern appears to have no upper limit. Poppe (1991*a*: 178; 1991*b*: 19) cites examples of up to four preverbal adverbials plus an argument from *Brut y Brenhinedd* (cf. also Fife and King 1991: 90). Indeed, the observation of this pattern has served quite unjustifiably to strengthen the belief that the abnormal sentence is a literary fashion (Fife and King 1991: 89–90).

Typical adverbs in this position are *yna* 'then', *am hynny* 'because of this', *wrth hynny* 'upon this', *yuelly* 'thus', and clauses headed by *gwedy* 'after'. There are two important features of this pattern. First, all the preverbal constituents except the last are required to be adverbial. Secondly, the choice of preverbal particle is determined by this last preverbal constituent. Accordingly, the particle is *a* in (12a–c) after a subject, object, or nonfinite VP, but *y(d)* in (12d) after an adverbial.

3.3.2. *Interposed adverbs*

Although the most frequently attested pattern of 'multiple fronting' is that discussed above, another exists in which an adverb occurs immediately before the preverbal particle. It is thus possible for there to be a sequence of preverbal constituents in which one of the earlier constituents may be non-adverbial. It can be argued that the adverb in this structure is in a syntactic position distinct from that occupied by pre-topic adverbials. Some of the possible sequences in this category are exemplified in (14)–(16). In the examples in (14), an adverb intervenes between the preverbal subject and the verb.[10] In (15) the adverb intervenes between a preverbal object and the verb (see also *BD* 27. 12, 29. 16; *BTy₂* 40. 13; *BY* 27. 22; *HGK* 11. 14); and in (16) between a fronted verbnoun or VP and the finite verb (cf. also *BD* 184. 28; *BTy₁* 247b. 1; *KAA* 578).

(14) (*a*) *A   Lawnslot yna a   dywawt . . .*
and Lancelot then PRT said
'And Lancelot then said . . .'   (*YSG* 121)

  (*b*) *Gwalchmei yn ieuenctit y   dyd a   deuth y dyffryn . . .*
Gwalchmai in youth   the day PRT came to valley
'Early in the day Gwalchmai came to a valley . . .'   (*Peredur*, 59. 9–10)

(15) (*a*) *Hwnnw hagen   a   darogannwys y   corr   a   'r gorres   it . . .*
That   however PRT foretold   the dwarf and the dwarfess to-you
'That, however, the dwarf and dwarfess foretold for you . . .'

                                           (*Peredur*, 35. 15–16)

  (*b*) *Dychymic Rolant yna a   ganmolawd pawb . . .*
idea   Rolant then PRT praised   everyone
'Then everyone praised Roland's idea . . .'   (*YCM* 118. 12)

(16) (*a*) *Ac   atteb   yna a   oruc Aigolant . . .*
And answer-VN then PRT did   Aigolant
'And then Aigolant answered . . .'   (*YCM* 21. 17)

  (*b*) *Medylyaw heuyt a   dylyaf   i . . .*
think-VN   also PRT should-1s I
'I should also think . . .'   (*KAA* 576)

Once more, a number of adverbs may intervene between the topic and the verb, as can be seen from the examples in (17). The number of interposed adverbs again appears to have no upper limit.

(17) (*a*) *Minneu Turpin Archesgob, o   awdurdawt yr Arglwyd, ac o*
          I-CONJ Turpin Archbishop, from authority   the Lord   and from
          'm bendith inheu   a   'm ellygedigaeth, a'e
          my blessing I-CONJ and my absolution   PRT+3S-ACC
          rydhawn   o   bechodeu.
          release-COND-1S from sins
          'I, Archbishop Turpin, from the authority of the Lord and from my own
          blessing and absolution would release him from (his) sins.'

(YCM 14. 18–20)

     (*b*) *An heneiteu ni, drwy   y   fyd   a   gynhalywn, wedy an hageu*
          Our souls   we through the faith REL uphold-1P, after our death
          a   ant   y baratwys . . .
          PRT go-3P to Paradise
          'Our souls, through the faith that we uphold, after our death will go to
          Paradise . . .'   (*YCM* 18. 23–4)

The most common interposed adverbs are (*yr*) *eilweith* 'for the second time', *eiss(y)oes* 'nevertheless', *heuyt* 'also', *hagen* 'however', and *yna* 'then'. However, the construction is not restricted to these adverbs and the set of potential interposed adverbials appears to be fairly indefinite. The wide range of potential adverbs in this construction can be seen in example (17*b*) above, where two heavy adverbial phrases intervene between the subject and the verb.

Interposed adverbs can be distinguished from pre-topic adverbials as discussed in Section 3.3.1 provided that the topic is defined as the element which conditions the choice between *a* and *y(d)* as preverbal particle. In that case, the topic in multiple-fronting constructions is the preverbal element closest to the verb. In the interposed-adverb construction in (14)–(17), however, the adverb next to the verb does not result in *y(d)* being selected. Instead, the preverbal particle is determined by some element preceding that adverb, as the examples above demonstrate.

We can analyse preposed adverbs as adverbs preceding the topic, and interposed adverbs as adverbs following the topic. This is the conclusion to which we are inevitably drawn if we want to maintain the economical assumption that the choice of preverbal particle is determined solely by the element in SpecCP. Under this approach, we must claim that this position is constant, and that there are two syntactic positions for the adverbs in question. Pre-topic adverbs must occupy a recursive position preceding SpecCP. Clearly, adjunction to CP is the only possibility.

The position of the 'interposed' adverbs is less clear. Several possibilities exist, and these will be discussed below. For the moment, I shall simply refer to this immediately preverbal position as C_0 since it follows C_2 and C_1 in Poppe's schema.

We can thus think of the particles *a* and *y(d)* as topic-agreement marking on the verb. This is to be preferred to Poppe's schema as it stands, since otherwise there will be no way to account for the fact that, in some instances, the preverbal particle is determined by the immediately preverbal constituent (C_1), but in others by an earlier constituent $(C_2$ and beyond). A first approximation to the schematic structure of a main clause in Middle Welsh is then that given in (18). The preverbal particle is the head of CP. It stands in a Spec-head configuration with a phrasal constituent in SpecCP, with which it checks for agreement (cf. the Aff-Criterion of Schafer 1995: 152–3). 'Preposed' adverbs then appear to the left of the topic, adjoining to CP.

(18)

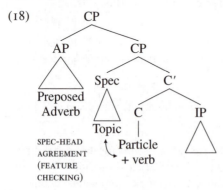

3.3.3. *Adverb classes*

It is possible to go further in describing the possible exceptions to the rule of single compulsory topicalization (V2-requirement). The ability of particular adverbs to participate in pre-topic and interposed adverbial constructions is in fact conditioned by the nature of the elements involved. Many adverbs have a fairly unconstrained distribution, and may appear freely in the pre-topic position, the topic position, and the interposed position. The prime example of such an adverb is *yna* 'then'. Other adverbs, however, obey conditions on their position that shed light on the nature of the positions themselves. The adverbials that will be considered here are *hagen* 'however', *heuyt* 'also', *eiss(y)oes* 'nevertheless', *(yr) eilweith* 'for the second time', and adverbs of the form preposition plus demonstrative pronoun, for instance, *am hynny* 'for that (reason)'. Discussion of manner adverbs will be postponed until a general framework to account for adverb placement has been established.

Let us begin with the last group, demonstrative PP adverbs. These adverbs are common discourse connectives, referring back directly to an element in the immediate context, and for this reason will be referred to as topic adverbs. The commonest examples are *am hynny* 'as a result of that', *ar hynny* 'thereupon, next', *gan hynny* 'since this is/was so', *gwedy hynny* 'after this', *wrth hynny* 'thereupon, next', and *yr hynny* 'since then; despite that'. These adverbs occur only marginally in the interposed post-topic position. However, they may act as topics in their own right, alone fulfilling the V2-requirement as in (19), or they may precede another constituent which itself functions as topic as in (20).[11]

(19) (*a*) . . . *ac am hynny y   cant   y   corn.*
          and for that   PRT sounded the horn
          '. . . and for that reason he sounded the horn.'   (*YCM* 158. 15–16)

    (*b*) *Gwedy henne ybu   pedeir blyned en hedwch . . .*
           after   that   PRT+was-PERF four   years   in peace
           'After that there was four years of peace . . .'   (*BTy*₁ 293a. 12–13)

(20) (*a*) *Ac ar hynny, Oliuer a   giglev twryf   y   pagannyeit . . .*
          and on that   Oliver PRT heard commotion the Pagans
          'And then, Oliver heard the commotion from the Pagans . . .'
                                        (*YCM* 139. 28)

    (*b*) *Ac am hynny ev   nackau   ar gwbyl   aorugant.*
           and for that   3P-GEN refuse-VN completely PRT+did-3P
           'And for that reason they refused them completely.'   (*BB*₁ 86. 6–7)

Conversely, sentences like the hypothetical (21), which parallels (20*a*) but where the adverb intervenes between topic and verb, are barely attested. The few exceptions (*BB*₁ 85. 5; *BTy*₁ 227b. 15; *KAA* 300; *Peredur*, 22. 11, 30. 13; *PKM* 21. 9; *YSG* 1428) are numerically insignificant in comparison with the vast number of examples conforming to the general pattern above.

(21)   **Ac Oliuer ar hynny a   giglev twryf   y   pagannyeit . . .*
          and Oliver on that   PRT heard commotion the Pagans
          'And Oliver then heard the commotion from the Pagans . . .'

Since these adverbs consist of a Prepositional Phrase, they have an alternative interpretation as complements selected by a particular verb. For instance, *ar hynny* may be the indirect object of a verb such as *trigaw (ar)* 'to decide (on)'. When they are argument PPs, these phrases *must* occupy the topic position and cannot precede another topic. That is, we find in Middle Welsh sentences such as those in (22) (cf. also *LlB* 60. 18; *Peredur*, 47. 1; *PKM* 26. 19; *YCM* 66. 1; *YSG* 4830).

(22) (*a*) *Ac ar hynny y   diskynyssant.*
          and on that   PRT decided-3P
          'And on that they decided.'   (*PKM* 38. 5–6)

    (*b*) *Ac ar hynny y   trigyassant y   nos   honno.*
           and on that   PRT agreed-3P   the night that
           'And on that they agreed that evening.'   (*Peredur*, 44. 14)

Here the verbs in question are *diskyn ar* 'to decide on' and *arfer o* 'to use, make use of', both of which select specific prepositions. In fact it is a property of Middle Welsh argument PPs in general that if they appear preverbally they must occupy the topic position. Traditionally these have been included in the 'adverb' category, and their distinctive pattern of distribution has consequently been underemphasized.[12] The two major groups of PPs of this type are the complements of verbs that selected a particular preposition and the complements of verbs of motion. The former is illustrated in (23) using the verb *aruer o* 'to use, make use of', the latter in (24).[13]

(23)   . . . *ac o dwill   abrat   yd aruer y   rei   marwawl wedy*
              and of deception and-treachery PRT use   the ones mortal   after
         na   allwynt   amgen.
         NEG can-SUBJ-3P otherwise
         '. . . and mortals use deception and treachery once they can do nothing else.' (*BB₁* 77. 3–4)

(24)   . . . *ac yny erbynn ynteu y   doeth ywein achadwaladyr* . . .
              and against-him   PRT came Owain and-Cadwaladr
         '. . . and against him came Owain and Cadwaladr . . .'

                                                            (*BTy₁* 175a. 9–12)

In both these cases the argument PP occupies the topic position. Sentences such as those in (25), with these constituents in pre-topic or post-topic position, are not attested.[14]

(25) (*a*) **Ac ar hynny y dynyon a   drigassant* . . .
              And on this   the men   PRT decided-3P
         'And on this the men decided . . .'

     (*b*) **Y   dynyon ar hynny a   drigassant* . . .
              the men   on this PRT decided-3P
         'The men decided on this . . .'

   The remaining adverbs under consideration are not pragmatically topics in the way that the demonstrative adverbs are. In terms of their distribution they fall into two groups. *Hagen* 'however' and *heuyt* 'also' are found in the interposed position as in (26) (cf. also (15*a*) and (16*b*) above), but never in the topic position itself or in the pre-topic position.[15]

(26) (*a*) *Amlyn iarll hagen   a   oed yn   clybot   yr ymadrodyon megys*
              Amlyn earl however PRT was PROG hear-VN the phrases   as-if
         trwy   y   hun . . .
         through his sleep
         'Earl Amlyn, however, was hearing the phrases as if through his sleep.'

                                                            (*KAA* 533–4)

     (*b*) *Y nos heuyt yssyd yn   dyuot   arnam.*
              the night also is   PROG come-VN on-us
         'Night is also coming upon us.' (*YSG* 1253–4)

It is reasonable to suppose that these adverbs right-adjoin to the Noun Phrase (DP) or other phrase in topic position. This is suggested by three considerations. First, German, an otherwise very strict V2-language, allows apparent violations of V2 just in this sort of situation—namely, with *aber* 'but, however' in second position as in (27). Positing that *aber* right-adjoins to some constituent provides us with a restrictive account of German word order. It allows us to distinguish between the small group of adverbs that may adjoin to the topic in both German and Middle Welsh from the much larger group that may adjoin to the interposed position in those languages like Welsh that make such a position available.

(27)   *Johann aber wird spät kommen.*
        Johann but   will late come-INF
        'Johann, however, will arrive late.'

Secondly, adverbs such as German *aber* and Middle Welsh *hagen* and *heuyt* exhibit scopal distinctions. In (27) *aber* has scope over *Johann*—Johann rather than, say, Peter will arrive late. Contrast this with (28), where it has scope over the Verb Phrase—Johann will arrive late, rather than arriving early.

(28)   *Johann wird aber spät kommen.*
        Johann will but late come-INF
        'Johann will come late, however.'

It is natural to expect an account of this phenomenon that derives scope from the syntactic position of the adverb. Specifically, it would be anticipated that the adverb c-commands the element over which it has scope. This will be the case in (27) only if *aber* adjoins to the subject DP. The argument carries over naturally to Middle Welsh.

Finally, unlike other interposed adverbs, Middle Welsh *hagen* and *heuyt* may precede a Noun Phrase standing in apposition to a topicalized subject as in (29) (cf. *KAA* 239 with *hagen*). On the reasonable assumption that Noun Phrases in apposition occupy an adjoined position, it must be concluded that the adverbs too right-adjoin to the topic.

(29)   *Arthur heuyt, brenhin brenhined enys   Brydein a   rysswr honneit*
        Arthur also   king   kings   island Britain and hero   celebrated
        clotvaur,   a   wnaeth deudec prif emlad en erbyn y   Saesson . . .
        praiseworthy PRT made   twelve main attack against the Saxons
        'Arthur too, king of the kings of the island of Britain and praiseworthy celebrated hero, made twelve main attacks against the Saxons . . .'
                                                                        (*HGK* 11. 25–7)

Finally, consider the distribution of two other non-topic adverbs *eiss(y)oes* 'nevertheless' and (*yr*) *eilweith* 'for a second time'. *Eiss(y)oes* may appear in the interposed position, as in (30) (cf. also *BD* 26. 18; *FfBO* 35. 32, 36. 19; *HGK* 3. 20; *YCM* 27. 14) or in the pre-topic position, as in (31) (see also *BD* 147. 33, 148. 3,

149. 6, 183. 17 etc.; *Owein*, 115, 141; *Peredur*, 33. 17, 53. 23; *PKM* 20. 8, 61. 3; *YSG* 139, 5625, 5640). (*Yr*) *eilweith* appears only in the interposed position, as in (32) (cf. also *FfBO* 37. 2; *YCM* 140. 23, 141. 4, 142. 3). Both, of course, may also appear postverbally. Neither is attested in the topic position itself.

(30)   *Haralld eissyoes   a   wledychus tros wynep Ywerdon . . .*
       Harald nevertheless PRT ruled   over face   Ireland
       'Harald nevertheless ruled over the face of Ireland . . .'

                                                              (*HGK* 3. 28–4. 1)

(31)   *Ac eissyoes   nessau   a   orugant attaw . . .*
       and nevertheless approach-VN PRT did-3P   to-3SM
       'And nevertheless they approached him . . .'   (*Owein*, 585–6)

(32)   *. . . agwilim   vrenhin lloegyr yr eilweith   a   gyffroes llu*
       and-William king   England the second-time PRT raised   force
       mawr . . .
       big
       '. . . and William king of England for the second time collected a great force . . .'   (*BTy₁* 91b. 26–8)

These distributional patterns are summarized in Table 3.2.

It was argued above that adverbs like *hagen* 'however' and *heuyt* 'also' right-adjoin to the topic. There is, therefore, no need to accommodate them into the V2-system, and they will not be considered further here. This leaves us with two other groups of adverbial in Middle Welsh, which will be referred to as topic adverbials and non-topic adverbials, plus a group of argument PPs, which may be identical in form to topic adverbials. Topic adverbials may occupy the topic position or precede the topic. Non-topic adverbials follow the topic, and in some cases may precede it. Some adverbials, like *yna* 'then', may of course be both topic and non-topic adverbials, and are thereby free to occupy either position. Finally, argument PPs must occupy the topic position.

To accommodate these facts, we need two recursive syntactic positions for topic and non-topic adverbials in addition to SpecCP. I suggest that these positions and the restrictions on adverb placement can be incorporated into a V2-analysis of Middle Welsh word order using fairly standard assumptions.

TABLE 3.2. *Distribution of preverbal adverbs and argument PPs in Middle Welsh*

Adverbial type	Example	Possible positions		
Topic adverbial	*guedy hynny* 'after that'	C_2	C_1	
Argument PP	(*trigaw*) *ar hynny* '(decide) on that'		C_1	
Constituent adverbial	*hagen* 'however', *heuyt* 'also'			C_0
Non-topic adverbial	*eiss(y)oes* 'nevertheless'	(C_2)		C_0

Notes: C_0 = interposed position
       C_1 = topic position
       C_2 = pre-topic position

Argument PPs are selected and theta-marked by a verb, and must therefore, under standard assumptions (cf. the Uniformity of Theta Assignment Hypothesis (Baker 1988: 46)), originate in their canonical position as complements of the verb and move to preverbal position by topicalization. On the other hand, it is reasonable to assume that elements that are not selected by the verb can originate in a preverbal adjoined position.

The distribution of adverbials follows if we assume that SpecCP (C_1) is the unique landing-site for movement to preverbal position—that is, that movement of arguments to adjoin to CP is impossible. The element that moves to SpecCP is the one that determines the preverbal particle. Since this position can be filled *once only* by movement, it is impossible for two elements selected by the verb to precede that verb in Middle Welsh. The result of these assumptions is that argument PPs, along with subjects, and direct and indirect objects, all of which must originate in a postverbal position because they are selected by the verb, can reach the preverbal position in Middle Welsh only as the result of movement. They are generated in postverbal positions and move to occupy, and thereby saturate, the topicalization position SpecCP (C_1). The result is that, as we have found, such elements may, in fact must, satisfy the V2-requirement alone, and may not co-occur with one another in preverbal position.

Non-arguments are free to originate in preverbal position and are able to circumvent the ban on multiple topicalization by occupying an adjoined position other than SpecCP. Elements adjoined to CP (C_2) can receive a similar topic interpretation. This position appears to have a discourse function related to that of the topic position itself. There seem to be two differences between it and the topic position proper. First movement *to* the pre-topic position is not possible. Secondly, whereas the topic position must be filled by an element whose referent is already present in the discourse, the pre-topic position may also be occupied by elements like *eiss(y)oes* 'nevertheless' that are not present in that discourse but which nevertheless indicate the pragmatic relation of one sentence to another. The result is that non-argument demonstrative PPs may appear there, as well as some other adverbs: *eiss(y)oes* 'nevertheless', which has a discourse function, but not *(yr) eilweith* 'for a second time', which does not.

In this way, topic adverbials not selected by the verb are free to originate in preverbal or postverbal position. If they originate in preverbal position, they will be adjoined to CP throughout, and will be able to co-occur with an element topicalized by movement to SpecCP. If they originate postverbally, they may optionally move to SpecCP, thereby alone satisfying the obligatory topicalization requirement.

Finally, a third, non-topic position, must be posited (C_0). This position is neither the landing site for movement, nor associated with a topic interpretation. Once again, this position may not contain any element selected by the verb. It is, there-fore, necessary that the element which occupies it be neither highly topical nor an argument of the verb. Thus, it may be filled only by non-topic adverbials.

We conclude that in Middle Welsh only one element selected by a verb may precede that verb, and that, in these terms, there is no such thing as 'multiple fronting' or 'multiple topicalization' in Middle Welsh.[16] Topicalization in Middle Welsh is not recursive.

There remains the question of precisely where in the structure post-topic adverbs (C_o) are to be put. If the standard analysis of V2 is to be maintained, this position must precede the verb in C, but follow the topic in SpecCP. Adjunction to C′ seems the obvious possibility (the C′-analysis). Bowers (1993: 605–16) develops an analysis of adverb placement in English and French in which adverbs are licensed by specific projections to adjoin at the X′ level. The C′-analysis would be in the spirit of this approach—Middle Welsh would have a class of adverbs licensed by C to adjoin to C′. However, it has widely been assumed that adjunction of phrasal categories is possible only to other phrasal categories (Chomsky 1986a: 4; cf. Kayne 1991: 652; Rizzi and Roberts 1989: 12; Vikner 1994: 140). If we maintain this assumption, then such an adjunction structure must be ruled out.

The alternative is to adjoin the adverbs to the functional projection immediately below CP, say AgrSP, in which case the verb must fail to raise to C. This leaves two possibilities for the preverbal particle. It could be a complementizer lowering from C to I, as McCloskey (1996) has suggested for Irish complementizers. However, this would violate general constraints against lowering rules. Alternatively it could be introduced as a verbal affix in a position below C in the clause— for instance, as the head of a polarity projection in place of NegP (Schafer 1995). In this case, the preverbal particles would have to raise covertly in order to check agreement features in CP, thereby ensuring the correct preverbal particle is chosen in accordance with the category of topic in SpecCP.

McCloskey (1996) discusses the evidence in favour of complementizer-lowering. In Modern Irish, adverbs modifying an embedded clause may precede the complementizer, as in (33), but may not follow it. McCloskey assumes these adverbs to be adjoined to IP, and therefore to mark its left periphery. This means that the complementizer must end up in IP, in a position lower in the clause than the adverb.

(33)   *Deiridís an chéad Nollaig   eile   go   dtiocfadh   sé aníos.*
        said-3P the first   Christmas other COMP would-come he up
        'They used to say that next Christmas he would come up.'

(McCloskey 1996: 55)

Similar facts are found in Middle Welsh. The example in (34) demonstrates that adverbs may precede the complementizer in an affirmative embedded clause. An equivalent example in a negative embedded clauses is given in (35) (see also preceding affirmative embedded clauses *BB₁* 83. 2; *BD* 26. 24 = *BB₂* 16, *BD* 27. 7; *BTy₂* 104. 32; *FfBO* 38. 13; *KAA* 372; *PKM* 10. 29; *SDR* 1061; *YSG* 1580, 3399,

4447, 4494; preceding negative embedded clauses *KAA* 474; *PKM* 15. 5; *YSG* 504, 555).

(34)   *Ac ef a   debygei, ar yr eil   neit, neu ar y   trydyd,*
      and he PRT supposed on the second leap or   on the third
      y   gordiwedei.
      COMP+3S-ACC catch-up-IMPF
      'And he supposed that on the second leap or on the third he would catch up with her.'   (*PKM* 12. 3–4)

(35)   *Ac yn y   drych y   gwelas senedwyr Ruuein, pa   deyrnas*
      and in the mirror PRT saw   senators Rome   which kingdom
      bynnac a   geisynt,   na   wrthwynepei neb   udunt.
      ever   PRT seek-COND-3P NEG oppose-COND anyone to-them.
      'And in the mirror the senators of Rome saw that whichever kingdom they sought no one would oppose them.'   (*SDR* 483–5)

It seems reasonable to link this property of Middle Welsh to the fact that the language allows adverbs to intervene between the topic and the verb. There is every reason to suppose that a single syntactic position is made available in both cases. However, this brings us no closer to a decision as to the precise nature of that position. In the case of both Irish and Middle Welsh, the correct word order would result regardless of whether the adverbs in question adjoined to C' or to AgrSP (IP).

Superficially, it would appear that cross-linguistic variation in V2-phenomena is better accounted for by the AgrSP-analysis than by the CP-analysis. It is unusual for adverbs to have the ability to intervene between the topic and the verb in V2-languages. For instance, main clauses parallel to the Middle Welsh cases discussed above are ungrammatical in German (36a) and Breton (36b).

(36) (a) **Johann wahrscheinlich wird spät kommen.*
      Johann probably   will late come-INF
      'Johann will probably arrive late.'   (Travis 1991: 360)

    (b) **Maia er   gegin   he deus graet bara.*
      Maia in-the kitchen has-3SF made bread
      'Maia made bread in the kitchen.'   (Schafer 1995: 141)

A natural way to account for this difference would be to suggest that the verb in Middle Welsh does not raise to C, but instead remains in AgrS, whereas, in the other V2-languages, the verb always raises to C. If it is then assumed that post-topic adverbs are a group of adverbs that always adjoin to AgrSP, then they will precede the verb in Middle Welsh, but not in the other V2-languages. If, on the other hand, the verb raises to C in all V2-languages, it is not clear why Middle Welsh should allow preverbal adverbs. The standard analysis of V2 depends crucially on adjunction to C′ being banned (cf. Thráinsson 1994: 161 n. 9) in order to rule out verb-third structures in languages like German.

There is nevertheless evidence that the availability of C′-adjunction must itself be subject to cross-linguistic variation. Instances of apparent C′-adjunction do in fact occur in some V2-languages other than Middle Welsh. For instance, the verb may appear in third position in Swedish and Icelandic with the adverb *bara* 'just', as in (37) (see also Thráinsson 1986: 174–5).[17]

(37)   *Hann bara hló   að mér.*   (Icelandic)
        Han   bara skrattade åt mig.   (Swedish)
        he   just laughed at me
        'He just laughed at me.'   (Sigurðsson 1990: 63 n. 6)

Since the verb in these languages unquestionably raises to C, it could not be hoped to extend the AgrSP-adjunction account of Middle Welsh adverb placement to these languages.

Indeed, the problem of adverb placement within CP extends beyond V2-languages. Consider the English example in (38).

(38)   *What in the end did Mary decide on?*

Given the standard analysis of inversion in *wh*-questions in English as involving movement of the finite verb to C, the example in (38) presents us with precisely the same problem as the interposed adverbs in Middle Welsh. If the analysis of inversion is to be maintained, then adjunction of the adverbial *in the end* to C′ must be permitted.

Given such data, the only possible account of the contrast between German and Breton, on the one hand, and Middle Welsh and English, on the other, must be to allow cross-linguistic (lexical) variation in the possible positioning of adverbials. Certain adverbials are licensed lexically to adjoin to C′ in English, Swedish, Icelandic, and Middle Welsh, but not in German and Breton.

I shall therefore assume the C′-analysis on the grounds that adjunction to C′ must be made available in other languages, and in particular that it must be an axis of variation between V2-languages. There is conversely no such widespread variation attested in the possibilities for complementizer-lowering or for covert movement to C. The issue remains, however, an open one.

This also leaves us with the question of whether the verb itself raises to adjoin to the preverbal particle in C or not. Middle Welsh shows VSO word order even in subordinate clauses where the verb cannot raise to the filled C-position and so must be in AgrS. It must be concluded that the subject follows AgrS, most plausibly occupying SpecTP. Movement of the verb from AgrS to C in main clauses will therefore be entirely string-vacuous. I shall nevertheless assume that this movement does take place, partly on the grounds that there is solid word-order evidence in favour of it in all other V2-languages, and partly because the preverbal particles must always *immediately* precede the verb, a fact which suggests that there is no adjunction position between them.

3.3.4. *Manner adverbs*

Manner adverbs provide another case of a clearly differentiated pattern of distribution that bears upon an account of Middle Welsh word order, and their distribution seems to be consistent with the sort of account developed so far. As an example let us now investigate the behaviour of a typical manner adverb of the form predicative particle *yn* + adjective, *yn gyflym* 'quickly'.

Manner adverbs occur in three syntactic positions in Middle Welsh: in a far-right postverbal position, in the topic position, or preceding the topic. Examples of these three patterns are given with the adverb *yn gyflym* in (39)–(41). The postverbal (VP- or V′-adjoined) use, shown in (39), is irrelevant to an account of topicalization. In (40), *yna* 'then' is in pre-topic position adjoined to CP, with *yn gyflym* acting as the topic in SpecCP. In (41) the adverb co-occurs with a nonfinite verb in the topic position, and presumably is itself adjoined to CP (cf. also *BB₁* 180. 12; *ChCC* 68. 8; *KAA* 538).

(39)   . . . *nessau*   *a*   *oruc attaw yn gyflym* . . .
            approach-VN PRT   did   to-him quickly
            '. . . he approached him quickly . . .'   (*ChCC* 68. 18–19)

(40)   *Ac   yna   yn gyflym yd   eynt*   *am benn yr   honn a*
            and then quickly   PRT went-IMPF-3P against   the one REL
            vynnynt . . .
            wanted-IMPF-3P
            'And then quickly they attacked the one that they wanted . . .'
                                                                                            (*SDR* 485–7)

(41)   *Ac   yn gyulym kyuodi   a   wnaeth Frollo* . . .
            and quickly   arise-VN PRT did   Frollo
            'And quickly Frollo arose . . .'   (*BD* 156. 2–3)

In terms of the account presented above, manner adverbs have a distribution identical to that of demonstrative PPs, occupying SpecCP or adjoining to CP. Crucially, we do not find *yn gyflym* adjoining to C′.

Manner adverbs modify the Verb Phrase rather than the sentence, so, if the spirit of the account above is carried through, they should be required to move from a postverbal position (say adjoined to V′) to a preverbal position. The only admissible preverbal landing site for topicalization is SpecCP, given that we have ruled out movement *to* either of the preverbal adjunction sites. The analysis thus implies that manner adverbs should act like argument adverbials and be restricted to SpecCP.

At first sight, there seem to be some apparent counter-examples with phrases resembling manner adverbs occupying the post-topic position, suggesting that they should be permitted to adjoin to C′ (cf. also *BTy*₂ 20. 30, 20. 32, 22. 3, 36. 19):

(42) (*a*) *Gruffud enteu,   o 'e gnotaedic deuaut, en vudugaul*
       Gruffydd he-CONJ of his usual   custom PRD victorious
       a'e   hemlynvs wynteu . . .
       PRT+3P-ACC pursued   them-CONJ
       'Gruffydd too, after his usual custom pursued them victoriously . . .'
(HGK 16. 2–3)

(*b*) *Ac wynteu   yn vuyd   a   gyfarchassant well idaw   ynteu.*
    and they-CONJ PRD obedient PRT greeted-3P   to-3SM him-CONJ
    'And they too obediently greeted him.'   (*YSG* 3021–2)

On closer inspection, however, it seems that these are not really manner adverbs at all. For instance, in (42*a*), it is Gruffydd and not the event of pursuing that is victorious, and, in (42*b*), it is they and not the event of greeting that are obedient. Contrast this with, say, (41), where it is not Frollo but the event of arising that is quick. The ambiguity is parallel to that found in Modern Welsh with 'adverbs' of the form predicative particle *yn* + adjective. These can be ambiguous between a predicate reading and an adverbial reading. In a sentence like (43), the 'adverb' *yn falch* 'proud' may be interpreted as describing either Rhodri or the event of going away.

(43)   *Aeth Rhodri i ffwrdd yn   falch.*
       went Rhodri away   PRD proud
       'Rhodri went away proudly/Rhodri went away satisfied.'

Other possible exceptions (*BTy*₁ 79a. 24, 79b. 6, 82b. 25, 166b. 17; *YSG* 3628, 3875, 4034) seem to involve adverbs modifying the subject rather than the verb.

The appearance of manner adverbs adjoined to CP can be left aside for the moment, until full discussion of left dislocation in Middle Welsh. It is sufficient to note at present that the absence of manner adverbs in the position adjoined to C′ is expected given the claims that adjunction to C′ is base-adjunction only, and that manner adverbs originate within VP.

3.3.5. *Left dislocation*

The conception of topicalization outlined above rules out sequences containing multiple topicalization of arguments, since these would involve a doubly filled SpecCP. Some of the sequences in question are given in (44).

(44) (*a*) Direct object–Subject
       *Eur Myrdin a   rodes i Arthur.
       gold Merlin PRT gave to Arthur

(*b*) Argument PP (indirect object)–Subject
       *I Arthur Myrdin a   rodes eur.
       to Arthur Merlin PRT gave gold

(*c*) Argument PP (indirect object)–Direct object
*I Arthur eur a   rodes Myrdin.
to Arthur gold PRT gave Merlin

(*d*) Direct object–Argument PP (Indirect object)
*Eur i Arthur y   rodes Myrdin.
gold to Arthur PRT gave Merlin
'Merlin gave gold to Arthur.'

Such sequences appear to be unattested in Middle Welsh.[18]

In sentences such as those in (44), both topics are verbal arguments and would therefore have to be generated in their canonical postverbal position. One would be able to move to SpecCP, but the other could not adjoin to CP or C′, and so the second 'topic' could not appear preverbally.

The ban on multiple topicalization proposed above appears to rule out sequences where a direct or indirect object is topicalized along with the subject—that is, sentences of the type in (45).

(45) (*a*) Direct object–Subject
*Eur Myrdin a   rodes i Arthur.
gold Merlin PRT gave to Arthur

(*b*) Argument PP (indirect object)–Subject
*I Arthur Myrdin a   rodes eur.
to Arthur Merlin PRT gave gold

(*c*) Subject–Direct object
Myrdin eur a   rodes i Arthur.
Merlin gold PRT gave to Arthur

(*d*) Subject–Argument PP (indirect object)
Myrdin i Arthur y   rodes eur.
Merlin to Arthur PRT gave gold
'Merlin gave gold to Arthur.'

While this appears to be the correct prediction for the first two sequences given here, it fails on the second two. We do, in fact, find subjects preceding topicalized direct or indirect objects, or other elements selected by the verb, as can be seen from (46) (cf. also *BD* 160. 26, 160. 27; *BTy*₂ 74. 5; *FfBO* 41. 5; *Owein*, 62; *PKM* 2. 16, 4. 9, 26. 3).

(46) (*a*) *A   minneu ederyn ieuanc oedwn.*
and I-CONJ bird   young was-1S
'And I (too) was a young bird.'   (*CO* 851–2)

(b) *Y   llu   a   welvch chui raccw yn avch erbyn, o   amrauael*
the force REL see-2P you yonder against-you   from various
enyssed yd   henynt . . .
islands PRT come-3P
'The forces that you see yonder (coming) against you come from various
islands.'   (*BD* 184. 29–30)

There are also examples in Middle Welsh texts of objects preceding topicalized
elements selected by the verb, as in (47) (cf. also *BB*₁ 139. 6, 187. 19; *BM* 8. 24,
12. 7; *BR* 5. 30; *ChCC* 64. 18; *CLlLl* 164; *Peredur*, 7. 6, 66. 12; *PKM* 6. 21, 8. 15,
15. 19; *YCM* 14. 7, 23. 26; *YSG* 590).

(47) (a) *Ac a   geueis, mi a'e   crogaf.*
and REL found-IS I PRT+3S-ACC hang-IS
'And what I have found, I shall hang (it).'   (*PKM* 61. 7)

(b) *Y   gymeint a   wypwyf   i, mi a'e   dywedaf.*
PRD as-much REL know-SUBJ-IS I I PRT+3S-ACC tell-IS
'As much as I know, I shall tell (it).'   (*CO* 904–5)

In such examples, however, a resumptive clitic or agreement element always
appears alongside the verb, indicating that in these cases the position of the object
is left dislocation, accompanied by contrastive intonation and so on, rather than
topicalization.[19] Parallel examples with preposed subject and resumptive subject
pronouns are attested, but are much rarer:

(48) (a) *A   'r lladron, . . . wynt a   deuthant drachefyn tu a   'r twr.*
and the thieves   they PRT came-3P back   towards the tower
'And the thieves, . . . they came back towards the tower.'   (*SDR* 280–3)

(b) *Pwy bynnac . . . a   dwyllo   vnweith, ef a   dwyll*
who ever   REL deceive-SUBJ once   he PRT deceive
eilweith   os dichawn.
a-second-time if is-able
'Anyone . . . who deceives once, he will deceive a second time if he can.'
(*YCM* 115. 19–20)

There is no reason to expect an uneven distribution of sentence types, and it seems
clear that the examples of preposed subjects followed by another element selected
by the verb are in fact examples of subject left dislocations parallel to the examples
of left dislocations of direct objects given above. Because Middle Welsh allows
null subjects freely, the resumptive pronoun required in the canonical subject
position can itself be null, when a subject is left dislocated. This option is not
available with left-dislocated objects, since Middle Welsh does not permit null
objects without an object clitic. We can assume that such left-dislocated elements
adjoin to CP. The resumptive element is required either because only base-

adjunction to CP is permitted or because movement across CP is a subjacency violation. Either way, adjunction of an argument to CP must result in left dislocation with a resumptive element. The fact that manner adverbs can move to adjoin to CP suggests that the latter option should be taken.

Given that we have already analysed pre-topic adverbs as adjoining to CP, and given that this is the position standardly assumed for left-dislocated elements, we might expect problems to arise in keeping the two elements apart. However, it seems that these two positions can be treated as variant manifestations of the same position.

The most important evidence comes from some a priori very surprising evidence about ordering. If pre-topic adverbs and left dislocations were separate, we would expect all left dislocations to precede pre-topic adverbs. However, in fact, a left-dislocated constituent may follow a pre-topic adverbial, suggesting that they are the same type of element for positioning purposes (cf. also *BB*₁ 198. 17; *CO* 875; *FfBO* 41. 5; *Owein*, 20; *YSG* 735, 1054, 2606):

(49) (a) *"Arglwyd," heb ynteu, "rac guelet gwr kyuurd a*
     lord   said he-CONJ lest see-VN man of-such-rank as
     thidi   yn y   gueith hwnnw, punt a   geueis   i o
     you-REDUP in the act   that   pound REL received-1S I from
     gardotta, mi a'e   rodaf   it . . ."
     beg-VN I PRT+3S-ACC give-1S to-you
     '"Lord," he said, "lest I should see a man of such rank as you in that act, a pound that I received from begging, I shall give (it) to you . . ."'
                                   (*PKM* 62. 9–11)

   (b) *Tra vych   vyw, kymeint ac a   edeweis   i yti,   mi*
      while be-SUBJ-2S alive as-much as REL promised-1S I to-you I
      a'e   kywiraf.
      PRT+3S-ACC fulfil-1S
      'As long as you are alive, everything that I have promised you, I shall fulfil (it).' (*KAA* 565–6)

In the absence of any difference in syntactic position, we may seek a basis for the distinction between left dislocation and pre-topic adverb placement in their different behaviours with respect to resumptive elements. Left dislocations must be matched by a later resumptive element, whereas there is no such resumptive element in the case of pre-topic adverbs. Topic adverbials (like *ar hynny* 'thereupon') may simply be base-generated in the CP-adjoined position, since they are not interpreted as binding a lower position in the clause. Manner adverbs, however, must clearly move from a position modifying the verb. The fact that they do not require an overt resumptive element may simply relate to their status as adverbs. That is, the position adjoined to CP may be occupied by either nominal or adverbial constituents, with only the former requiring overt resumptive elements. The intonational break that is generally found between left-dislocated elements and the clause, and which is assumed for Middle Welsh also, might appear to weigh against this view. However, it could easily be the case that there is also a comparable intonational break between pre-topic adverbial elements and the main part of the clause.

3.3.6. *Further evidence from imperatives*

The syntactic behaviour of imperative forms of the verb in Middle Welsh provides further data supporting the distinction between the pre-topic CP-adjoined position and the SpecCP topic position. Imperatives do not co-occur with either of the preverbal particles *a* and *y(d)*. The question is whether they permit topicalization to take place over them. If the topic position SpecCP is licensed by the preverbal particles as has been claimed, it would be expected that SpecCP should be obligatorily empty with imperatives.

We find examples of subjects preceding imperatives, as in (50).

(50)   *Ar   ny   dylyo   eisted ar vwrd Iessu Grist   aet*
        REL NEG has-right-SUBJ sit-VN at table Jesus Christ go-IMPER-3S
        allan . . .
        out
        'Anyone who does not have the right to sit at the table of Jesus Christ, let
        him go out . . .'   (*YSG* 5419)

It seems reasonable, however, to treat these as containing a 'vocative' left-dislocated DP, followed by an imperative third-person-singular verb with a null subject. This interpretation is supported by an example such as (51), where, in a seventeenth-century punctuated text, a comma is inserted between the 'subject' and the imperative verb.

(51)   *Y   sawl sydd   gantho   glûst i   wrando, gwrandawed.*
        the one is-REL with-him ear   to listen-VN listen-IMPER-3S
        'He who has an ear to listen, let him listen.'   (*LITA* 77. 18–19)

Thus, although this type is quite common in Middle Welsh texts, it does not supply any clear evidence for the topicalization of subjects over imperatives. There are also no cases of topicalization of objects over imperatives.

Such a finding begins to suggest that topicalization across an imperative is simply impossible in Middle Welsh. If so, the behaviour of adverbials with respect to imperatives is significant. Certain types of adverbial may indeed precede an imperative, but the choice is not as free as it is with other forms of the verb. Typical examples of adverbs preceding an imperative are given in (52).

(52) (*a*) *Ac vrth hynny ymledvch   dros avch gulat . . .*
          and for that   fight-IMPER-2P for your country
          'And for that reason fight for your country . . .'   (*BD* 148. 15)

(b) . . . *ac   o cheissiant deffroi   neb   or   llu,   dywet*
          and if try-3P   wake-VN anyone of-the army say-IMPER-2S
     nat   reit   vdunt   namyn dyuot   wynt eu huneyn.
     NEG+COMP necessary to-them except come-VN they themselves
     '. . . and if they try to wake any of the army, say that they only need to
     come themselves.'   (*BB*₁ 13. 16–14. 1)

Example (52*a*) contains the connective *wrth hynny*, which unambiguously refers back to an element already mentioned, and thus has a clear claim to status as topic. Other pragmatically similar adverbs found in this position include other PPs with *hynny* 'that' as their object, as well as other topic adverbs such as *yna* 'then' and *yno* 'there'. Example (52*b*) shows that adverbial clauses may precede an imperative.[20]

   These adverbials are of the type that, as was seen earlier, can accompany an argument topic, leading to apparent instances of 'multiple topicalization'. It was concluded that these adverbials were not required to occupy the topic position SpecCP. In other words, the adverbials that precede imperatives are always non-argument topics, elements which may adjoin to CP in the analysis above. It therefore seems reasonable to suggest that the presence of an imperative verb inhibits a true topicalization position and a position for non-topic adverbs. Consequently only elements that are permitted to adjoin to CP may precede an imperative verb. This provides further justification for the analysis of topicalization presented above.

3.3.7. *Conclusions about adverb placement*

The discussion of adverb-placement rules has allowed us to maintain the hypothesis that Middle Welsh is a V2-language in which the verb obligatorily raises to C in main clauses, and some other constituent moves to SpecCP. In contrast to many other V2-languages, notably German, Middle Welsh makes two other recursive preverbal positions available. One (adjunction to CP) is reserved for adverbials with a topic or discourse-connective interpretation, and left dislocated elements. I have argued that such adverbials are in fact left dislocated, but because of their status (as adjuncts or as adverbs) they may be base-generated in this position or, if moved (in the case of manner adverbs), they do not require overt resumptive elements. The other recursive preverbal position involves adjunction to C′, and is reserved for adverbs lacking a topic interpretation. This latter position is invisible to movement rules, and may not therefore be occupied by arguments or any other elements (manner adverbs) that must be generated in a lower position.

   The hypothesis that this V2-pattern is a natural part of spoken Middle Welsh rather than an artificial literary invention has been supported inasmuch as the system, including the intricacies of adverb placement, is maintained consistently and in texts from all parts of Wales.

As a summary of the analysis, (54) shows the structure of the sentence in (53), where all three preverbal positions are filled. The subject undergoes topicalization to SpecCP, and the verb raises in steps to C. The adverb *yna* 'then' is base-generated adjoined to CP where it receives a topic interpretation. The adverb *drwy ei hun* 'through his sleep' is base-generated adjoined to C′, and thus does not receive such an interpretation.

(53)   *Yna Arthur drwy   ei hun   a   weles gaer.*
        then Arthur through his sleep PRT saw   castle
        Then Arthur through his sleep saw a castle.'

(54)

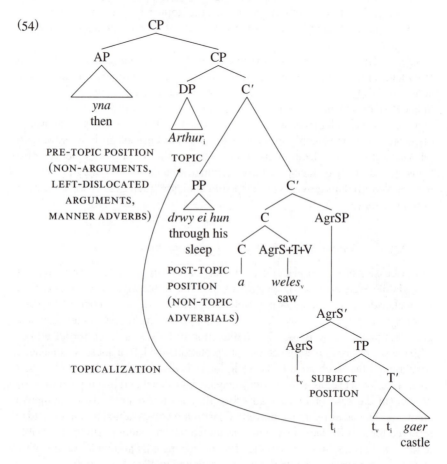

3.4.   TOPICALIZATION AS A′-MOVEMENT

Thus far, it has been tacitly assumed that, in parallel with verb-second topicalization in Germanic languages, topicalization movement to SpecCP in the Middle

Welsh abnormal sentence is A'-movement—that is, movement out of a Case-marked position—rather than A-movement—movement from a position where Case fails to be assigned to one where it does (such as object-to-subject raising in passives). This claim can be motivated explicitly by a comparison of the properties of topicalization constructions with other instances of A'-movement, such as relative clauses and *wh*-questions.

Traditional grammars of Welsh have long noticed the formal similarities between the abnormal sentence and relative clauses, specifically in the identical choice of particles used (Armstrong 1987–8; Stephen J. Williams 1980: 168). It turns out that the parallelisms are even more striking, and that the conditions on the two constructions are exactly parallel, a fact which confirms the hypothesis that both are instances of A'-movement.

I shall first examine the properties of A'- and A-constructions in standard environments, relative clauses and passive constructions respectively, before looking specifically at the constraints on topicalization. Armstrong (1987–8) has been invaluable as a source of data on complex relatives.

3.4.1. *Properties of A'-movement in relative clauses*

Consider first Middle Welsh relative clauses as a paradigm example of an A'-construction. A'-movement can be seen most clearly in those relative clauses, particularly non-restrictive ones, where Middle Welsh has an overt *wh*-element in the form of one of the demonstrative pronouns *yr hwnn* 'the one (m.)', *yr honn* (f.), *yr hynn* (n.), *y rei* (pl.) acting as a relative pronoun. Examples are given in (55) and (56). Henceforth the gap on which the relative clause has been formed is marked as ____. A relative formed on subject position is shown in (55). Example (56) illustrates pied-piping, where a preposition is extracted along with its *wh*-phrase.

(55)   *Ac oddyna . . . y   kerddws y lys   Henri, vrenhin Lloegyr, yr hwnn*
       and thence   PRT walked to court Henry king   England the one
       a   vu   ____ vrenhin yn   nessaf y 'w vrawt.
       PRT was-PERF ____ king   PRD next   to his brother
       'And from there he went to the court of Henry, king of England, who became king after his brother.'   (*HGK* 28. 1–2)

(56)   *. . . a   chynysgaedu yr eglwysseu, yn y   rei   y   daroed*
           and endow-VN   the churches   in the ones PRT happened-IMPF
       cladu   y   merthyri hynny ____, o deilyngdawt a   breint   a
       bury-VN the martyrs these   ____ of worth   and privilege and
       thir a   daear.
       land and earth
       '. . . and endow the churches in which these martyrs had been buried with worth and privilege and land and property.'   (*KAA* 802–4)

This pattern confirms the existence of two positions at the head of the relative clause, one for the relative pronoun and one for the particle. The natural assumption is that the pronoun occupies SpecCP, moving there from the gap left later in the clause, while the particle itself is a complementizer in C, as was claimed above for topicalization structures.

It is generally believed that relative pronouns were introduced into the literary language in imitation of Latin, French, and English (D. Simon Evans 1964: 66). More commonly, Middle Welsh relative clauses involve no overt *wh*-element. However, the presence of a phonetically null equivalent to the relative pronoun (null operator) can be inferred from the fact that the complementizer in a relative clause alternates between *a* and *y(d)* in agreement with the gap in the relative clause. Examples are given in (57)–(59).

(57)   *y   megineu a   oed   ____ wedy eu   gossot yg kylch y*
        the bellows REL was-3S ____ PERF 3P-GEN set-VN around the
        ty
        house
        'the bellows that were set up around the house'   (*PKM* 36. 15)

(58)   *a   'r arglwydiaeth a   gaussam   ninheu ____*
        and the government   REL received-1P we   ____
        '. . . and the government that we had . . .'   (*PKM* 8. 15–16)

(59)   *y   noss y   keueist y   mab ____*
        the night REL got-2S the boy ____
        'the night that you had the boy'   (*PKM* 23. 25)

The situation is analogous to an English relative clause like (60), where the overt *wh*-element is optional. Unlike in English, however, there is a strong preference in Middle Welsh for the variant in which the *wh*-element is non-overt.

(60)   *the teacher (who(m)) I saw ____ on the street*

It should be clear from the examples in (57)–(59) that the pattern of alternation in the complementizer in standard cases of relative clauses is identical to that in the abnormal sentence. If the gap is in subject or object position, the particle used is *a*, and if the gap is in an adjunct position *y(d)* is used.

Traditionally Welsh grammarians distinguish two relative-clause formation strategies, termed direct (*rhywiog*) and indirect (*afrywiog*) (D. Simon Evans 1964: 60–7; Richards 1938: 66). The distinction is based on twentieth-century Literary Welsh. Direct relatives are those formed on the subject position or on the direct object position of a synthetic verb using the particle *a*. In these cases default agreement is found—that is, third-person-singular subject–verb agreement in subject extractions, and absence of object clitics in object extractions. Examples (57) and (58) above are direct relatives. Notice that, in (57), the verb appears in its default third-person-singular form even though the antecedent is plural.

All other relative clauses are indirect. Indirect relatives in twentieth-century Literary Welsh use exclusively the particle *y(r)* (MW *y(d)*, *yr*) and are found with 'full' agreement where this is possible. So, for instance, in (61), a Contemporary Literary Welsh example of an indirect relative formed on the object position of a preposition, the preposition appears in a third-person-singular-feminine form in agreement with the feminine antecedent.

(61)   *yr ysgol yr   awn   iddi   ____*
         the school REL go-1P to-3SF ____
         'the school that we'll go to'   (Stephen J. Williams 1980: 53)

A number of generative analyses of Welsh relative clauses have retained the distinction between direct and indirect relatives, assimilating it to a distinction between movement (direct) and resumptive (indirect) strategies (Awbery 1977; Sadler 1988). According to these analyses, direct relatives involve movement of a null operator, which, like lexical (non-pronominal) Noun Phrases generally in Welsh, does not trigger full agreement.[21] Indirect relatives, on the other hand, involve no such movement. Instead, full agreement licenses a null resumptive element. Essentially, the intuition behind these analyses is that indirect relatives actually contain a resumptive pronoun despite first appearances. The relative clause in (61) is, therefore, to be understood as 'the school that we'll go to it', rather than as a 'true' relative clause.

There are a number of difficulties with such an account (see de Freitas and Noonan 1993, and especially Rouveret 1994). Discussion here is limited to two that are particularly relevant to Middle Welsh. For other approaches to Modern Welsh relative clauses, see also Harlow (1981, 1983), Sells (1983, 1987), and Tallerman (1983, 1990).

First, not all relative clauses involving *y(d)/y(r)* contain a resumptive element. As Rouveret (1994: 380) has pointed out, relatives formed on adjunct positions require *y(r)* in Contemporary Welsh, as in (62), yet they do not contain any resumptive element to license the non-movement strategy. The same is true of Middle Welsh. This suggests that the movement/resumptive distinction is not coterminous with the distinction between *a* and *y(r)*, and that a movement strategy must be made available even for indirect relatives, at the very least when they are formed on adjunct positions.

(62)   *Dyna 'r unig dro y   gwelais ef.*
         that's the only time REL saw-1S him
         'That's the only time I saw him.'   (Stephen J. Williams 1980: 167)

This is also true in the case of pied-piping in (56) above. There, the whole Prepositional Phrase *yn y rei* 'in which' is in clause-initial position and there is no resumptive element at the relativization site. This rules out an analysis involving a resumptive strategy. We can conclude that in that case too the particle $y(d)$ co-occurs with movement.

Secondly, in Middle Welsh, the correlation between the particles and full or default agreement does not hold. Examples of relative clauses formed on the object of a preposition are given in (63) and (64). In (63) the particle $y(d)$ is used, as in twentieth-century Literary Welsh; in (64) the particle is *a*. The use of *a* in these structures is paralleled in Modern Breton relative clauses (Trépos n.d.: 189).

(63)   *ty   y   ganhei   yndaw* ____ . . .
       house REL fit-COND in-3SM ____
       'a house that he would fit into'   (*PKM* 42. 4)

(64)   *ffiol eur a   anho   llawn diawt y   brenhin yndi*   ____
       vial gold REL fit-SUBJ full   drink the king   in-3SF ____
       'a golden vial that the king's fill of drink would fit into'   (*LlB* 3. 22)

The same variation is found in relatives formed on possessive Noun Phrases (65) and (66) (see D. Simon Evans 1964: 65). Relative clauses formed on the objects of nonfinite verbs are considered in more detail below.

(65)   *Cledyf a   uo   eur neu aryant ar y   aual*   ____ . . .
       sword REL be-SUBJ gold or   silver on 3SM-GEN pommel ____
       'A sword on whose pommel there is gold or silver . . .'   (*LlB* 98. 15–16)

(66)   *y   gwr y   lladawd ywein y   vrodyr*   ____
       the man REL killed   Owain 3SM-GEN brothers ____
       'the man whose brothers Owain killed'   (*BTy*₁ 108a. 3–5)

On the standard account the inflected preposition *yndaw* in (63) licenses a resumptive null pronominal object parallel to that in (61). However, if *a*-relatives involve movement, this cannot be claimed for (64). Instead, we must posit a mechanism whereby movement of the object of a preposition triggers full agreement on that preposition. Formally, this can be implemented by forcing movement to proceed via a Prepositional Agreement projection (AgrPP; cf. Kayne 1989*a*). Parallel reasoning applies the possessive relatives in (65) and (66).

Considerations such as these lead us to conclude that some cases where $y(d)$ is used must involve movement, and that some cases where agreement is found must also involve movement. The analysis must include mechanisms that allow for these two possibilities. I suggest that the choice of particle in A′-constructions is linked both to the category membership of the item in SpecCP (Noun Phrase, Adverbial Phrase, etc.) and to whether movement has taken place. If no movement has occurred, the particle is $y(d)$. This option is available for all oblique positions. If movement has occurred, then the form of the particle is determined by the category of the phrase moved to SpecCP, *a* if this is nominal, otherwise mostly $y(d)$.

Formally this may be implemented by assuming that operators that undergo movement are marked with categorial features of the position from which they moved. That is, an operator may be a DP or an AP before movement to SpecCP, and the correct form of the complementizer is ensured by checking in a Spec-head configuration within CP. Conversely operators that originate in SpecCP and bind a resumptive pronoun are unmarked for categorial features. Unmarked operators trigger $y(d)$ as the complementizer.

As an example, the analysis suggested for the three possibilities for relative clauses formed on the PP-position is given in (67). The case of preposition stranding with *a* as the relative particle (in (64)) is shown in (67*a*). Here, a nominal (DP) operator originates as the object of the preposition. This operator is forced to move to SpecCP via an intermediate specifier position (shown here as SpecPP for the sake of simplicity), where Spec-head agreement with the preposition ensures full agreement. The case with preposition stranding and $y(d)$ is shown in (67*b*) (representing (63)). Here there is no movement. An operator with unspecified features originates in SpecCP and binds a resumptive null pronoun, which is the object of the preposition. Full agreement is required on the preposition in order to license this null pronoun. Finally, the (literary) pied-piping case in (56) is shown in (67*c*). Here an overt *wh*-phrase PP moves directly to SpecCP. It is marked as a PP, hence determines the form of the particle as $y(d)$.

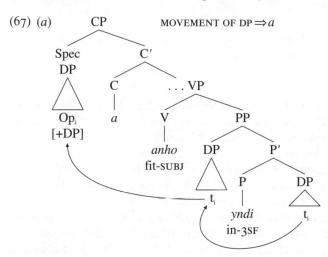

(67) (*a*)   CP   MOVEMENT OF DP ⇒ *a*

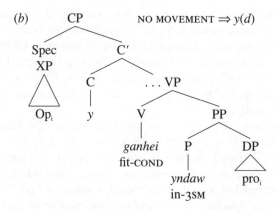

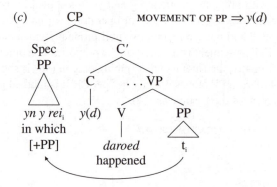

It is an analysis of this sort that will be assumed for relative clauses and A'-constructions generally. The central question for consideration is whether such an analysis can be extended to Middle Welsh V2-structures.

Also relevant to this question are a number of other special cases of relative clauses. If the same features are found in V2-structures, then we have evidence that a common analysis is justified. Consider first the pattern of data found for relative clauses formed on embedded positions. Relative A'-movement is possible from nonfinite clausal complements of a wide range of verbs. This includes movement of arguments from the complement clauses of both bridge verbs (68) (see also *BB*₁ 121. 8; *BD* 198. 15; *HGK* 21. 24; *KAA* 47, 180; *MIG* 191. 7; *W.* 184. 20, 408. 6); adverbial adjuncts from the same clauses (69) (see also *BB*₁ 99. 9; *FfBO* 44. 25; *PKM* 57. 1, 78. 9); and movement out of the complement clauses of control verbs (70) (see also *KAA* 56).

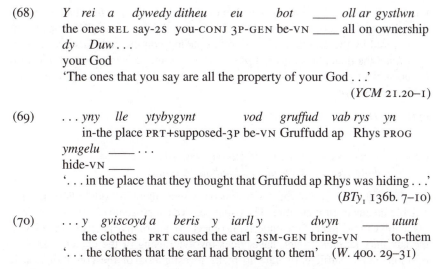

(68)   *Y   rei   a   dywedy ditheu   eu   bot   ____ oll ar gystlwn*
       the ones REL say-2S you-CONJ 3P-GEN be-VN ____ all on ownership
       dy   Duw . . .
       your God
       'The ones that you say are all the property of your God . . .'

                                                    (*YCM* 21.20–1)

(69)   *. . . yny   lle   ytybygynt   vod   gruffud vab rys   yn*
          in-the place PRT+supposed-3P be-VN Gruffudd ap   Rhys PROG
       ymgelu   ____ . . .
       hide-VN ____
       '. . . in the place that they thought that Gruffudd ap Rhys was hiding . . .'

                                                    (*BTy*₁ 136b. 7–10)

(70)   *. . . y   gviscoyd a   beris   y   iarll y   dwyn   ____ utunt*
         the clothes PRT caused the earl 3SM-GEN bring-VN ____ to-them
       '. . . the clothes that the earl had brought to them'   (*W.* 400. 29–31)

As far as it is possible to establish, the choice of particle is identical to that found in unembedded contexts. Such data confirm that A'-movement is permitted from embedded positions in Middle Welsh.

The second feature worth noting is the fact that overt resumptive pronouns are possible in direct-object position in relative clauses that would otherwise be ambiguous. This can be seen in (71). In the absence of the resumptive pronoun *ef*, this example would have the additional reading 'the boy who made Lancelot a knight' (cf. also *YSG* 2185, 3066, 5440). The same strategy is used in Breton to disambiguate V2-structures there (Timm 1988: 80).

(71)   *. . . am   y   mab a   ry   wnathoed   Lawnslot ef   yn*
          about the boy REL PERF made-PLUPERF Lancelot him PRD
       varchawc urdawl.
       knight
       '. . . about the boy whom Lancelot had made a knight.'   (*YSG* 60–1)

This construction is rare and has the flavour of a 'last-resort' strategy. There is, therefore, no need to incorporate it into our core analysis. However, if V2-structures and relative clauses share their essential features, it is expected that they will pattern alike with respect to this construction too.

3.4.2. *A-movement in passives*

The other candidate for the type of movement involved in Middle Welsh V2–structures is A-movement, standardly found across languages in passives and with raising predicates like *seem*. Broadly speaking, A-movement relates the position of *Jane* in (72) and (73), and in (74) and (75). In (73) *Jane* has A-moved from the object position of *arrest* (cf. (72)) to the subject position. This movement is triggered by the presence of passive morphology on the verb *was arrested*. In (75) *Jane*, the thematic subject of *play football*, A-moves across a nonfinite verb to the subject position of the verb *seem*, a raising predicate lacking a thematic subject of its own.

(72)   *The police arrested Jane.*

(73)   *Jane was arrested by the police.*

(74)   *It seems that Jane played football yesterday.*

(75)   *Jane seems to have played football yesterday.*

It is difficult to be sure of the conditions on A-movement in Middle Welsh, since reliable instances of it are rare. The usual passive (impersonal) construction does not involve movement of the underlying object. An alternative passive formed with the auxiliary *kaffael* 'to get, have' does involve raising of the object to subject position, but is sufficiently rare to make investigation of the conditions on it impractical. Middle Welsh also appears to have few raising verbs and adjectives. However, a comparison with Modern Welsh reveals differences between A′-movement and A-movement there that seem to be useful diagnostics even in Middle Welsh.

As has already been noted, Modern Welsh allows A′-dependencies to be formed on the object of a preposition. However, A-movement from within a Prepositional Phrase is not possible. The examples in (76) show this using passives with the auxiliary *cael* 'to get, have'.

(76) (*a*)   *Cafodd y gwallau eu   cywiro   _____.*
              got   the mistakes 3P-GEN correct-VN _____
              'The mistakes were corrected.'

     (*b*)   **Cafodd y gwallau (eu)   sylwi   arnynt _____.*
              got   the mistakes (3P-GEN) notice-VN on-3P _____
              'The mistakes were noticed.'

In (76*a*) passivization raises the direct object of a transitive verb to subject position. This is attempted with the object of a preposition in (76*b*), but fails. This salient difference between the two types can be used to determined the nature of movement in the Middle Welsh abnormal sentence. The same difference can be noted with movement from embedded positions.

3.4.3.   *Conditions on topicalization*

Examination of the properties of movement in the abnormal sentence shows that they parallel those in relative clauses very closely. Topicalization from within an embedded clause is well attested in Middle Welsh, although it often meets with the disapproval of editors of Middle Welsh texts (cf. *FfBO*: 69). A selection of examples is given below. In (77) we find topicalization from the subject position of the nonfinite clausal complement of the bridge verbs *tebygu* 'to suppose' (see also *BM* 3. 3, 3. 5; *BR* 3. 27; *W.* 42. 4), *dywedut* 'to say' (see also *BY* 10. 3, 10. 10; *EWGT* 44. 18; *FfBO* 32. 15; *YCM* 1. 3), *gwybot* 'to know' and *credu* 'to believe' (*FfBO* 43. 24). In all these cases agreement marking shows up on the embedded nonfinite verb, which in all cases is *bot* 'to be', and the direct preverbal particle *a* is used.

(77) (*a*) *Toat   y   neuad a   tebygei   y   vot   ____ yn   eur oll.*
        ceiling the hall   PRT supposed-IMPF 3SM be-VN ____ PRD gold all
        'The ceiling of the hall he supposed to be all gold.'   (BM 3. 3)

   (*b*) *A   'r llef hwnnw a   debygem   ni y   uot   ____*
        and the cry that   PRT supposed-IMPF-1P we 3SM be-VN ____
        oblegyt meistyr uffern.
        because master hell
        'And that cry we supposed was because of the master of hell.'
                                                            (*YSG* 749–50)

   (*c*) *Wyth oes byt   a   dywedir   eu bot   ____.*
        eight age world PRT say-IMPERS 3P be-VN ____
        'There are said to be eight ages of the world.'   (*BY* 10. 3)

   (*d*) *Plant   a   wnn   i y   uot   ____ idi   hi.*
        children PRT know-1S I 3SM be-VN ____ to-3SF her
        'I know that she has had children.'   (*PKM* 21. 16–17)

Topicalization is also found from the adjunct (78*a*) and complement (78*b*) (see also *FfBO* 40. 31) positions of such clauses. In these cases, the particle is *y(d)*.

(78) (*a*) *. . . ac ar hyt y bont y   tebygei   y   vot   yn*
              and along the bridge PRT supposed-IMPF 3SM be-VN PROG
        dyuot   ____ y 'r llong.
        come-VN ____ to the ship
        '. . . and he thought he was coming along the bridge to the ship.'
                                                            (*BM* 2. 14–15)

   (*b*) *Mawr y   dywawt y gwr y mi y   vot   ef ____.*
        big   PRT said   the man to me 3SM be-VN he ____
        'The man said to me that he was big.'   (*Owein*, 123)

Finally, movement is possible from the subject, object, and adjunct positions of the complement of a number of control verbs—for instance, *mynnu* 'to want' in (79) (see also *CO* 575), *peri* 'to cause' in (80) (see also BF ix. 327. 28; *BTy₁* 216b. 9), *keyssyaw* 'to try' in (81), and *darparu* 'to try' in (82).

(79) (*a*) *Ac Arthur a   Gwenhwyuar a   uynhaf eu   bot   ____ yn*
and Arthur and Guinevere   PRT want-1S 3P-GEN be-VN ____ PRD
rodyeit   ar y   uorwyn.
givers-away on the maiden
'And Arthur and Guinevere I want to give the maiden away (in mar-
riage).'   (*ChCC* 71. 14–15)

   (*b*) *Ker bron   y   brenhin yssyd arnaf i   y   mynhaf bot   y*
in-front-of the king   is-REL on-1S me PRT want-1S be-VN the
gyfranc y rof   i   a   thi ____.
combat between me and you ____
'I want the combat between me and you to be in front of the king who
rules over me.'   (*Peredur*, 58. 28–9)

(80) (*a*) *Y   ty   hwnnw a   peris   ef y   adeilat   ____ o   wyal*
the house that   PRT caused he 3SM-GEN build-VN ____ from sticks
gwynnyon . . .
white
'That house he had built from white sticks . . .'   (*LlB* 1. 9–10)

   (*b*) . . . *ar   llall a   beris   ef y   bot   ____ oe vlaen   ef*
and-the other PRT caused he 3SF-GEN be-VN ____ in-front-of him
e hvnn.
himself
'. . . and the other he ordered to be in front of him himself.'

                                                 (*BB*₁ 149. 17)

(81)   *A   'r rei   hynny yd   oet   wyr Groec yn   keyssyav eu*
and the ones these   PRT was men Greek PROG try-VN   3P-GEN
dwyn   ____ y arnav . . .
take-VN ____ from-on-him
'And these ones the Greeks were trying to take from him . . .'

                                                (*BD* 5. 6–7)

(82)   . . . *canys holl genedyl Saesson a   derpereist   ti   eu   dihol*
for   all   nation   Saxons PRT prepared-2S you 3P-GEN expel-VN
____ yn llvyr   o   'r enys   hon . . .
____ completely from the island this
'. . . for you prepared to expel the whole Saxon nation from this island.'
                                                (*BD* 203. 7–8)

In all cases the particle is the same as the one in the equivalent unembedded
topicalization. Topicalization does not appear to be found from within an embedded
finite clause.

Abnormal sentences and relative clauses also pattern alike with respect to the
possibilities for extraction from Prepositional Phrases. Topicalization is found

freely from within a PP in Middle Welsh, as the examples in (83) demonstrate. The particle is generally *a* (see also *BSM* 12. 10; *HGK* 17. 13; *PKM* 46. 5, 48. 2; *YSG* 2282, 4719).

(83) (*a*) *A   meir a   Iosep a   oed arnadunt* ____ *ouyn y   bobyl.*
      and Mary and Joseph PRT was on-3P   ____ fear the people
      'And Mary and Joseph were afraid of the people.'   (*MIG* 195. 25–6)

    (*b*) *Madawc uab Maredud a   oed idaw   ____ Powys yn y   theruyneu.*
        Madog ap Maredudd PRT was to-3SM ____ Powys in its extremes
        'Madog ap Maredudd ruled Powys in its entirety.'   (*BR* 1. 1–2)[22]

    (*c*) *Y Tobias vry   a   dywetpwyt   y   gethiwaw y rwng y*
        the Tobias above REL said-IMPERS 3SM-GEN enslave-VN between the
        dec llin, a   vv vab ydaw   ____ o   Anna . . .
        ten tribes PRT was son to-3SM ____ from Anna
        'The Tobias of whom it was said above that he was enslaved among
        the ten tribes had a son by Anna . . .'   (*BY* 40. 15–16)

    (*d*) *Y prenneu ereill a   deuei   ffrwyth arnunt* ____ . . .
        the trees   other PRT grew-IMPF fruit   on-3P ____
        'Fruit grew on the other trees . . .'   (*YSG* 4387–8)

However, the particle *y(d)* is also found, albeit rarely. The examples in (84) and (85) from similar contexts in the same text demonstrate the unconditioned nature of the variation between the two (for other instances of *y(d)*, see *BY* 45. 27; *PKM* 14. 10, 57. 17).

(84)   *Brenhin y   wlat honno . . . a   oed idaw   ____ o   wraged kymeint*
      king   the land that   PRT was to-3SM ____ of wives   so-many
      ac yd oed ydaw   trychant   o veibyon a   merchet.
      as PRT was to-3SM three-hundred of sons   and daughters
      'The king of that land had so many wives as to have three hundred sons
      and daughters.'   (*FfBO* 43. 11–13)

(85)   *Y brenhin hwnnw yd   oed ydaw   ____ na[w] mil   o*
      the king   that   PRT was to-3SM ____ nine   thousand of
      eliphanyeit dof . . .
      elephants   tame
      'That king had nine thousand tame elephants . . .'   (*FfBO* 43. 14–15)

Again, this is the same pattern as that found with relative clauses, but differs fundamentally from that found in passive A-movement.

If the parallelism between relative clauses and topicalization in the abnormal sentence is to be maintained, then it is expected also that topicalization of a possessive Noun Phrase will be possible on the same conditions as the formation of relative clauses on possessive Noun Phrases. Examples appear to be lacking from the Middle Welsh tales and romances. Given that relative clauses formed on this position are also exceedingly rare, this is perhaps not surprising. The following sixteenth-century example suggests that the relevant construction was probably grammatical at the earlier period also:

(86)   *Ac er   hynny Pompeius a   dorred   i   benn . . .*
        and despite that   Pompeius PRT cut-IMPERS 3SM-GEN head
        'And despite that Pompeius had his head chopped off . . .'

                                                              (*RhG* i. 14. 9 (MS 1508–10))

Examples are attested up to the early seventeenth century (see D. Simon Evans 1968: 324).

Finally, the last-resort use of overt resumptive pronouns for disambiguation is also common both to relative clauses and to the abnormal sentence. Example (87) would have the additional reading 'And he made Demetrius a priest' if it were not for the overt resumptive object pronoun *ef* (see also *BY* 18. 25, 27. 23, 36. 19, 37. 12, 54. 1, 60. 22; *YSG* 2591). Once again these data are confirmed by the existence of a parallel disambiguation strategy in Modern Breton (Timm 1988: 80).

(87)   *A   hwnnw a   wnaeth Demetrius ef   yn   effeiryat.*
        and that-one PRT made   Demetrius him PRD priest
        'And Demetrius made him priest.'   (*BY* 53. 11)

These similarities in points of detail between relative clauses and the abnormal sentence in Middle Welsh are so strong that we are forced to conclude that the linguistic mechanisms involved in them are identical. Extension of the analysis of relative clauses to the abnormal sentence also accounts for an obvious puzzle in the formation of the abnormal sentence: why do abnormal sentences that begin with a Noun Phrase corresponding to a gap in an oblique (object of preposition or possessive) position fluctuate between (preferred) use of *a*, and use of *y(d)*? This analysis provides the answer that the two are structurally different. The former involves actual A′-movement of an operator, whereas the later involves a null resumptive pronoun.

Our conclusion that the abnormal sentence in Middle Welsh involves A′-movement is not particularly unexpected given that topicalization in other V2-languages is also generally A′-movement. However, we shall see in Chapter 6 that the similarities between topicalization and relative-clause formation are in fact not a feature of all periods of Welsh. Significant differences emerge which call for an explanation.

3.5.   TOPICALIZATION AND SUBJECT–VERB AGREEMENT

There is one important area where the syntax of the abnormal sentence in Middle Welsh differs from that of relative clauses—namely, subject–verb agreement. The data, although difficult to assess, seem to suggest that some cases of the abnormal sentence in Middle Welsh should be analysed as involving A-movement. The suggestion is that the possibility of SpecCP acting as an A-position in Middle Welsh provided one starting point for the loss of V2-topicalization more generally.

As is well known, verbs in Modern Welsh show morphological agreement with a postverbal subject only if it is pronominal (Sadler 1988: 50–1; cf. also the similar Complementarity Principle devised for Breton in Stump 1984, 1989). The same is true in the main for Middle Welsh. However, if the subject is preverbal, it shows agreement in non-contrastive (abnormal) main clauses in Middle Welsh whether it is pronominal or not. Since the default agreement form is identical with the third-person singular, this agreement shows up only in the third person plural and with conjoined subjects in other persons.

As was mentioned in the Introduction (Sections 1.2.1–2), Welsh grammarians have traditionally made a distinction between the abnormal and mixed sentences. These are superficially very similar V2-structures. When a subject is fronted in the mixed sentence, as in (88), there is no subject agreement on the verb, whereas with a fronted subject in the abnormal sentence in (89) there is. The difference in agreement correlates with the difference in contrastive focus on the subject (cf. the Modern Welsh examples (6) and (7) in the Introduction).

(88)   *Mi ae   heirch.*
       I   PRT+3S-ACC seek
       '(It is) I (who) seek him.'   (*W.* 479. 24)

(89)   *A   'r guyrda   a   doethant y gyt . . .*
       and the noblemen PRT came-3P together
       'And the noblemen came together . . .'   (*PKM* 21. 12)

Relative clauses formed on the subject position do not show subject–verb agreement (D. Simon Evans 1964: 61). In this respect, the mixed sentence behaves like a relative clause, whereas the abnormal sentence does not. The question that arises is, therefore, how these different agreement patterns can be accounted for.

There seem to be a number of reasons for believing that, in V2-languages, the landing site for topicalization SpecCP may under some circumstances be an A-position (Cardinaletti 1990*b*: 82–3; Diesing 1990: 47–9; Taraldsen 1986: 17–18). The principal motivation comes from the evidence of Yiddish stressed pronouns. In Yiddish, non-subject pronouns may precede the verb in main clauses only if they bear contrastive stress. Much the same applies to German (Travis 1991: 359; cf. also Cardinaletti's account of German expletives discussed below). Diesing argues that, when it hosts subjects, the topic position (SpecIP in her analysis) may be an A-position, but that, when it hosts non-subjects, it must act as an A'-position. The topic/focus interpretation of preverbal elements is then due to their being operators in an A′-position. Subjects may occupy an A or A′-position, so may or may not receive a topic/focus interpretation. This allows the behaviour of the pronouns to be stated as follows: a pronoun topicalized by A′-movement must be contrastively stressed.

This suggests an approach to agreement differences between the abnormal sentence, on the one hand, and the mixed sentence and relative clauses, on the other, in terms of the A/A′-distinction. If SpecCP is an A-position, (A-)movement of the subject must proceed stepwise through SpecAgrSP (due to Relativized Minimality). If movement to SpecCP were direct, the trace of the moved subject would fail to be A-bound within its governing category by its antecedent in SpecCP. Movement via the functional projection immediately below SpecCP is required—that is, AgrSP. So, if SpecCP is an A-position, the subject must pass through SpecAgrSP. On the assumption that subject agreement is the morphological realization of Spec-head agreement in AgrSP, the result is obligatory subject–verb agreement. An 'abnormal' sentence results.

On the other hand, if SpecCP is an A′-position, Binding Condition A is irrelevant, and the subject may move directly from SpecTP (where it receives Nominative Case) to SpecCP. This movement does not pass through SpecAgrSP, so there is no agreement on the verb. The result is the mixed sentence. The structures of the mixed sentence (88) and the abnormal sentence (89) under this analysis are given in (90) and (91) respectively.

(90)

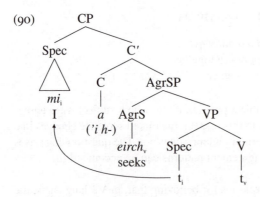

(91)

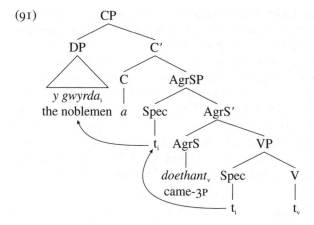

How do these structures relate to thematic interpretations? In the case of preverbal subjects it is straightforward to make a distinction between subjects in SpecCP as an A-position and those in SpecCP as an A′-position. We can argue that, when SpecCP is an A-position, it is interpreted as involving no contrastive stress (the abnormal sentence), but that, when it is an A′-position, there is contrastive stress (the mixed sentence).

For other possible topicalized constituents the situation is more complex. A-movement of other constituents to SpecCP seems to be ruled out by Relativized Minimality. If so, SpecCP is always an A′-position for non-subjects. Yet clearly non-subjects may appear preverbally in non-contrastive readings in Middle Welsh. We thus have to allow for SpecCP as an A′-position to be associated with a non-contrastive reading.[23] In fact, this seems to be a general property of V2-languages as opposed to non-V2-languages. If a language requires movement to SpecCP, then A′-movement to that position does not give a contrastive reading, whereas, in a language like English where such movement is not required, constituent fronting always entails contrastive focus.

Curiously, on the point of agreement, Middle Welsh and Breton diverge. In Breton, the verb fails to agree with any non-pronominal subject, whether it is preverbal or postverbal, as can be seen in (92). How can our account be extended to account for this?

(92) (a) *Ar vugale   a   lenn/*lennont levrioù.*
     the children PRT read/ read-3P books

  (b) *Levrioù a   lenn/*lennont ar vugale.*
     books   PRT read/ read-3P the children
     'The children are reading books.'   (Stump 1984: 292)

I suggest that, whereas Welsh allows subjects to A-move (in the abnormal sentence) or A′-move (in the mixed sentence), giving two different agreement patterns, topicalization of subjects in Breton is restricted to A′-movement.

This view is supported by another difference between the two languages. It is well known that expletive subjects cannot undergo A′-movement (Cardinaletti 1990*b*: 82). This is clearly the case in German V2-structures. Assume that German A′-movement may cross clause boundaries whereas A-movement cannot. The appearance of an expletive subject in initial position in (93) is consistent with it having A-moved there. For it to appear in initial position in (94), however, it must have undergone A′-movement, since it has moved out of the lower clause. The ungrammaticality of (94) suggests, therefore, that A′-movement of expletives is impossible.

(93)   *Es$_i$ wurde* t$_i$ *viel   getanzt.*
        it   was   much danced
        'There was much dancing.'

(94)   **Es$_i$ glaube ich,* t$_i$ *wurde* t$_i$ *viel   getanzt.*
        it   believe I   was   much danced
        'I believe that there was much dancing.'

It is hard to see how a V2-language in which SpecCP is solely an A′-position can allow expletive subjects there at all. The fact that both Middle and Modern Breton lack any equivalent to the Middle Welsh expletive subject *ef* supports this analysis of the difference between the two languages with respect to agreement.

3.6. TOPICALIZATION AND NEGATION

The interaction of topicalization and negation provides clues as to structure during the later development of verb-second. For this reason, the Middle Welsh facts will be mentioned here (see also D. Simon Evans 1964: 173–4).

In general, the negative marker *ny*(*t*) blocks topicalization in Middle Welsh. The result is that most negative main clauses have the order Negative Marker–Verb–Subject–Object, as in (4) repeated here as (95).

(95)   *Ny welei   ef y twrwf   rac tywyllet y nos.*
        NEG saw-IMPF he the commotion for so-dark the night
        'He could not see the commotion because the night was so dark.'
                                                                    (*PKM* 22. 23)

In a small proportion of cases, however, topicalization is found across a negative. In the examples in (96), a subject is topicalized across the negative.

(96)   (*a*) *A   hynny ny   thygywys idaw.*
              and that NEG availed   to-him
              'And that didn't work for him.'   (*PKM* 11. 2)

(b) *Y rei emelldigedic ny chaffant vy nhyrnas i.*
the ones damned NEG receive-3P my kingdom me
'The damned ones shall not receive my kingdom.' (CDd 27. 23)

Direct objects may also be topicalized over a negative. If they are, the negative marker may, but need not, appear with an object clitic *-s*. Examples where this has not occurred are given in (97). In (98) this option is chosen.[24]

(97) (a) *. . . ac attep ny chauas ef genthi hi yn hynny.*
and answer NEG received he with-3SF her in that.
'. . . and he received no answer from her in that (respect).'

(PKM 7. 12–13)

(b) *. . . ac amgen ledyr no hwnnw ny phrynei ef . . .*
and other leather than that NEG bought-IMPF he
'. . . and he would buy no other leather than that . . .'

(PKM 54. 13–14)

(98) (a) *. . . a 'r arglwydiaeth a gaussam ninheu y ulwydyn honno,*
and the government REL had-1P we-CONJ the year that
nys attygy y gennym, ot gwnn.
NEG+3S-ACC take-back-2S from with-us surely
'. . . and surely you will not take back from us the (good) government that we have had this year.' *(PKM 8. 15–16)*

(b) *. . . a hynny nys gallei.*
and that NEG+3S-ACC could
'. . . and that he could not do.' *(YSG 1780–1)*

Finally, (99) shows topicalization of a VP, again with an optional *-s* clitic on the negative marker.

(99) (a) *Eissyoes y odiwes ef nys gallassant.*
however 3SM-GEN catch-up-with-VN him NEG+3S-ACC could-3P
'However, they could not catch up with him.' *(YSG 1248)*

(b) *. . . na chlybot na gwelet nys gallei . . .*
neither hear-VN nor see-VN NEG+3S-ACC could
'. . . he could neither hear nor see . . .' *(YSG 5200–1)*

I assume that negative marker *ny(t)* is base-generated in C.[25] This assumption is motivated by the complementary distribution between it and the preverbal particles. There is also the fact that Middle Welsh has negative complementizers *cany(t)* 'because . . . not', *kyny(t)* 'although . . . not', and *ony(t)* 'if . . . not'.

The simplest hypothesis would be to transfer the analysis of affirmative main clauses to negative ones, allowing merely for the optionality of movement in the latter. If V2 in affirmative clauses is triggered by a feature on the preverbal particles, it could be that this feature is simply optional on the negative particle.

There remains, however, the difficulty of the two patterns attested with movement of direct objects across the negative. If negative clauses were exactly parallel to affirmative clauses, we would expect an equivalent object clitic *'i* to appear in affirmative V2-structures with fronted objects, yet this does not happen.[26]

One possibility would be to analyse the variant in (98) with the object clitic as involving left dislocation, with the object clitic licensing a null object *pro* (cf. Isaac 1996: 58–9). This is indeed what the editor of (98*a*) has done by inserting a comma between the fronted object and the negative marker. In this case, (98*b*), for instance, would be interpreted as 'That, he couldn't do it'.

However, there is good reason to reject this suggestion. The set of possible sentence-initial elements includes non-referential quantifiers like *dim* 'anything, nothing', as can be seen from the examples in (100).

(100) (*a*) . . . *eissyoes dim o Seint Grail nys   gweles ef.*
           however none of Holy Grail NEG+3S-ACC saw   he
           '. . . however, he did not see the Holy Grail at all.' (*YSG* 1335)

    (*b*) *"Dim o 'r gennyat," heb hi, "nys   keffy   di."*
           none of the permission said she NEG+3S-ACC have-2S you
           ' "You shall not have any permission," she said.' (*YSG* 1735–6)

Non-referential quantifiers are cross-linguistically resistant to left dislocation. For instance, the example in (101) shows that in Italian *nessuno* 'no one' may not be left dislocated. Parallel facts are found in French (Brandi and Cordin 1989: 118–19; Rizzi 1986: 394–7; Roberts 1993*b*: 64).

(101) **Nessuno, lo   conosco in questa cittá.*
        no one   him-CL know-1S in this   city
        'No one, I know him in this city.'
        (Intended reading: 'I know no one in this city.') (Rizzi 1986: 395)

If sentences like (100) involved left dislocation, they would be parallel to (101), an undesirable consequence from a comparative perspective.

Another possibility is that the object topic, although in SpecCP rather than in a left-dislocation position, does not undergo movement. We could claim that the negative particle in fact blocks all movement. Instead resumptive *pro* is inserted in object position, acting as a pronominal variable bound by a topic base-generated in SpecCP. This is a standard approach to negation in relative clauses in Modern Welsh (see Awbery 1977; de Freitas and Noonan 1993). In SNegVO sentences this would be indistinguishable from a movement analysis—*pro* would be licensed by the verbal inflection, but the verb would have shown inflection even if movement had been possible. In ONegVS order, object *pro* would have to be licensed. The object clitic -*s* would suffice to do this. However, the type of sentence without the object clitic would be difficult to account for, since it is hard to see how object *pro* could possibly be licensed in this case. We must, therefore, reject this possibility.

This suggests that, in fact, a movement analysis of negative V2 is required. We must assume that the negative marker does allow movement of a subject or object, across it. In the case of the object, the possibility of agreement suggests that movement is via some agreement projection, say AgrOP (cf. Kayne 1989*a*, and the analysis of Middle Welsh A'-movement above). Such cyclic movement is perhaps forced because direct A'-movement skipping the A'-specifier position SpecNegP will violate Relativized Minimality.

If movement via SpecAgrOP is required, why is the object-agreement clitic only optional? This seems to be a more general property of the clitic in question. Other agreement elements in Middle Welsh appear whenever the agreement trigger is pronominal. However, -*s* does not appear consistently in this environment. Compare the parallel sentences in (102) with -*s* and (103) without.

(102) . . . *nys   aroaf   i euo.*
       NEG+3S-ACC wait-1S I him
       '. . . I shall not wait for him.' (*Peredur*, 14. 13–14)

(103) *Ac yr   hynny hyt hediw ny   thorreis i ef.*
       and since then   until today NEG broke-1S I it
       'And since then until today I have not broken it.' (*ChCC* 67. 25–6)

We conclude that V2 in negative contexts differs in two ways from the standard analysis of V2 presented above. First, movement to SpecCP is optional, perhaps owing to lexical differences between the negative and affirmative preverbal particles. Secondly, the presence of negation forces movement of objects to be via an object-agreement projection, the result of which is the optional appearance of -*s* on the negative marker.

3.7. THE RISE OF VERB-SECOND

The detailed ways in which the verb-second rule of Middle Welsh conforms to verb-second rules in other languages, and the fact that it shows complex interactions with adverb-placement rules, negation, and embedded clauses all suggest that it was indeed a living part of spoken Middle Welsh rather than a literary invention. Such a view of Middle Welsh word order naturally raises the question of how such a system arose. More specifically, it is incumbent upon a proponent of such an account to demonstrate that it is possible to formulate an account of Old Welsh word order consistent with the word-order facts hypothesized for Middle Welsh. Let us now turn to this question. Discussion is limited to affirmative main clauses. Embedded clauses and, with some exceptions in poetry, negative main clauses are verb-initial in Old Welsh as in Middle and Modern Welsh.

First, consider Old Welsh poetry. A wide variety of word orders is attested in Old Welsh poetry. The examples below are taken primarily from *Canu Aneirin*

(*CA*) (see Lewis 1950), although it appears that much the same evidence could be found in any of the Old Welsh poetic texts. These word orders can broadly be divided into two groups. The first group is unrelated to the verb-second structure in that it lacks the preverbal particles that characterize verb-second. The major sentence constituents may be found in virtually any order. At the very least the following are attested: VSO in (104), SVO in (105), OV(S) in (106), VOS in (107), and SOV in (108).

(104)   *Eveis   y win   a   med   e   mordei.*
          drank-1s I wine and mead in great-halls
          'I drank wine and mead in great halls.'   (*CA* 221)

(105)   *Gwr Gwned   divudyawc dimyngyei   y   gat.*
          Men Gwynedd ferociously prepared-3s the battle
          'The men of Gwynedd ferociously prepared the battle.'   (*CA* 794–5)

(106)   *Teithi etmygant, tri   llwry   nouant . . .*
          right   honour-3P three javelin stain-3P
          'They honour right, they stain three javelins . . .'   (*CA* 178–80)

(107)   *Trauodynt   eu   hed   eu   hovnawr.*
          departed-3P their dwelling-place their fears
          'Their fears departed their dwelling place.'   (*CA* 85)

(108)   *Meiryon eu   tretheu dychynnullyn.*
          stewards their taxes   collected-3P
          'Stewards collected their taxes.'   (*AP* 21)

This evidence is open to two interpretations. Lewis (1942) saw the freedom of word order in the early poetry as evidence of archaism, and suggested that word order was highly flexible at an early period. Others have been less believing: for instance, Greene (1971: 9) dismisses it as 'simply an example of poetic licence'. The evidence of Old Welsh prose is crucial in deciding between these two views.

    Verb-second structures are also attested. Syntactically they are already fully developed in Old Welsh poetry. That is, the same options for the preverbal particle are available (and required) as in Middle Welsh. With a preverbal subject or object, the particle *a* is required, as in (109) and (110); with a preverbal adverbial, *y(d)* (OW *e(d)*) is required, as in (111); and with a preverbal nominal or adjectival predicate, a soft mutation on the initial consonant of the verb is found in place of any preverbal particle, as in (112).

(109)   *Mab Syvno . . . a   werthws e   eneit er   wyneb grybwyllyeit.*
          son Sywno   PRT sold   his soul for honour mention
          'The son of Sywno . . . sold his soul for the mention of honour.'
                                                                              (*CA* 212–14)
(110)   *Med a   dalhei.*
          mead PRT earned-IMPF
          'He earned his mead.'   (*CA* 22)

(111)   *E am   lavnawr coch gorvawr gwrmwn   dwys dengyn ed*
         along-with blades   red   great   dark-sockets close steadfast PRT
         emledyn   aergwn.
         fought-3P heroes
         'Along with red blades, in great dark sockets, in close ranks, steadfastly
         heroes fought.'   (*CA* 76–7)

(112)   *. . . a   gwenwyn vu.*
              and poison   was-PERF
         '. . . but it was poison.'   (*CA* 69)

The syntactic patterns in (109)–(112) cannot be due to poetic licence, since poetic licence cannot use a rule that has not yet entered the language.[27] The rule for agreement between the preverbal particle and topic cannot simply have been invented by the Old Welsh poets, since it is identical to later Middle Welsh. The rule must, therefore, have been continuously present in the grammar from the Old Welsh period onwards. The essential difference between Old Welsh poetry and Middle Welsh is therefore that, while in Middle Welsh verb-second structures are essentially obligatory in affirmative main clauses, Old Welsh poetry allows a choice between the verb-second 'abnormal' structure and a variety of other word orders.

A comparison with Old Welsh prose sheds further light on the question of whether these other word orders are reflections of spoken Old Welsh, or whether they are merely poetic devices. Old Welsh prose texts show more consistency in their word order than poetry does. As Watkins (1987) has shown, by far the commonest pattern is the verb-initial one illustrated in (113). However, a number of cases of the 'abnormal' pattern, in (114), are attested.

(113) (*a*) *Amgucant   pel   amtanndi . . .*
              disputed-3P long about-3SF
              'They disputed long about it . . .'   (SM)

      (*b*) *Rodesit Elcu guetig   equs . . .*
            gave   Elgu afterwards horse
            'Elgu gave afterwards a horse . . .'   (SM)

      (*c*) *. . . ha   chepi   hinn inguir*
                and find-2s this in-true
            '. . . and you will find this to be true.'   (CF 21)

(114)   *mormarh tutnred harodes   alt guhebric deo $_7$ sancti elivdo.*
         Morfarch Tudnred PRT+gave Allt Gwefrig God and St.   Eliudd
         'Morfarch Tudnred gave Allt Gwefrig to God and St. Eliudd.'

                                                             (Chad 7)

On the natural assumption that Old Welsh prose is a better reflection of spoken Old Welsh than poetry is, it seems likely that, of the many attested orders of Old

Welsh poetry, only the verb-initial pattern and the verb-second pattern were found in speech. This suggestion is entirely consistent with the view of Middle Welsh word order presented above. In spoken Old Welsh, both absolute verb-initial main clauses and main clauses of the verb-second type were possible. A plausible characterization of the difference between the two is that the verb-initial order was the neutral order and the verb-second order was simply a reduced form of the cleft construction. It appears that this construction increased in frequency, shifting as it did so from a cleft interpretation to an interpretation as a topicalization construction. Eventually the verb-second structure, now completely bleached of any cleft interpretation, ousted the verb-initial construction. The spread of the cleft construction must already have been well advanced by the Old Welsh period, since the verb-second structures that result from it are obligatory in all the medieval Brythonic languages.

This hypothesis also helps to account for another curious fact about Middle Welsh word order—namely, the surprisingly high frequency with which verb-initial affirmative main clauses are found in one Middle Welsh text—namely, *Culhwch ac Olwen (CO)*. Particularly significant is the fact that in *Culhwch ac Olwen* verb-initial main clauses frequently lack a preverbal particle. These clauses are therefore structurally identical to Old Welsh examples of the verb-initial order, but are sharply differentiated from later Middle Welsh, where verb-initial main clauses are nearly always found after a preverbal particle and generally in coordination structures (see Section 4.2 below). Examples are given in (115) (see also *CO* 50, 107, 173, 535, 555, 1043, and numerous other examples with the verbs *dywedut* and *amkawdd/amkeuddant* 'to say').

(115) (a) *Gorucpwyt   hyn[n]y.*
            do-PAST-IMPERS that
            'That was done.'   (*CO* 519)

       (b) *Gouynnwys y   gwyr y Arthur peth oed ystyr   yr hwch hwnnw.*
            asked   the men to Arthur what was meaning the pig   that
            'The men asked Arthur what the meaning of that pig was.'

                                                                (*CO* 1074–5)

Culhwch ac Olwen is generally believed to be the earliest of the Middle Welsh prose tales. Bromwich and Evans date the composition of the surviving redaction to the late eleventh century (*CO*, pp. lxxxi–ii), and stress the linguistically archaic nature of the text (*CO*, pp. xv–xviii). In their study of the syntax of copular constructions, Watkins and Mac Cana (1958: 17) consider *Culhwch ac Olwen* to be a conservative text, occupying an intermediate position between Old and Middle Welsh usage. In the field of word order, it is natural, therefore, to interpret the instances of verb-initial word order that it contains as providing evidence for a stage of the language at which the Old Welsh verb-initial order was obsolescent but had left traces in the literary tradition. Note also that (115*a*) is found only in the earlier (White Book) manuscript, being replaced with a verb-second order in the later (Red Book) manuscript. The Red Book version indulges in modernization of other linguistic features (*CO*, pp. xii–xiii). These facts confirm the suspicion that the verb-initial construction was perceived as archaic by the fourteenth century (cf. also *CO* 50).

According to this account, there was at an early stage no difference between the mixed (cleft) sentence and the abnormal (verb-second) sentence. This claim is borne out by the fact that in Old Welsh poetry abnormal sentences with plural pre-verbal subjects show both agreement between subject and verb and lack of agreement indifferently. Compare agreement in (116) with lack of agreement in (117).

(116)   *Gwyr a   gryssyassant buant   gytneit.*
         men PRT attacked-3P were-3P together-leaping
         'Men attacked, they leaped forward together.'   (*CA* 353)

(117)   *Gwyr a   aeth   Gatraeth buant   enwawc.*
         men PRT went-3S Catraeth were-3P famous
         'Men went to Catraeth, they were famous.'   (*CA* 235)

Lack of agreement is the norm in all attested stages of Breton (cf. (92*a*) above) and in Cornish, suggesting that this was the rule in the parent language, and there-fore that (117) represents the conservative pattern in Welsh. It has already been demonstrated that this pattern of agreement is the one typical for relative (A'-)constructions in Welsh. If the verb-second construction developed from the generalization and grammaticalization of the cleft construction, this is precisely what would be expected. Agreement typical of (relative) A'-constructions would be found at the early stages of that process. One consequence of the shift from a relative-like A'-construction to an unmarked main-clause word-order pattern could be a move away from agreement typical of A'-constructions to agreement typical of A-constructions.

3.8. CONCLUSION

In this chapter we have seen that Middle Welsh has a verb-second rule. The standard analysis of verb-second as (predominantly) A'-movement to SpecCP can be justified for the language on the basis of evidence from movement restrictions. Apparent complications with adverb placement make Middle Welsh a somewhat unusual verb-second language, but require relatively superficial changes to the standard analysis, involving only lexical rules on possible adverb positions. Other facets of the V2-system, involving movement restrictions, negation, and agreement have been examined and integrated into such an analysis.

4. Verb-First in Middle Welsh

Absolute verb-initial (V1, verb-first) clauses, where at most only the preverbal particle *y(d)* precedes the verb, are not common in Middle Welsh. On average the frequency of absolute V1, excluding negative clauses and other contexts where it is compulsory, is close to nil in Middle Welsh texts, and in no text which has ever been investigated does it exceed 10 per cent (see Table 3.1).

Despite this, Fife and King (1991: 89) claim that V1 is one of two non-emphatic word orders in Middle Welsh. Poppe similarly emphasizes that it is a grammatical word-order type in Middle Welsh (1990: 454; 1993: 104). In this chapter I claim that, far from being a basic word-order type in Middle Welsh, V1 with synthetic verbs is in a certain sense almost non-existent. The examples that we do have can be viewed as special cases of verb-second found in coordinate structures and in similar narrative continuity contexts. We must therefore look to the later period discussed in Chapter 6 for the development of a true V1-pattern in Welsh.

4.1. THE GRADUALIST ACCOUNT OF THE RISE OF V1

Fife (1991) has suggested that there was a gradual rise in the use of verb-initial main declarative clauses in Welsh, with the sixteenth century occupying a transitional position between Middle and Modern Welsh. His study of literary texts of the sixteenth century purports to show that at this time the frequency of absolute verb-initial word order in main clauses ranged from 15 to 20 per cent. This contrasts with his study of Contemporary Welsh word order, which suggests that the equivalent figure for verb-initial clauses is now between 50 and 66 per cent (Fife 1993).[1] Comparing these figures with Middle Welsh, he suggests that there has been a gradual and steady increase in the use of this order in the history of Welsh.

If such a gradualist position could be maintained, the evidence in support of it would present some difficulties for a parametric approach to syntactic change. We have posited the V2-requirement to be a parameter of Universal Grammar. A language with a positive setting of this parameter will not allow core verb-initial structures.[2] The introduction of verb-initial structures therefore requires a change in parameter setting, which in turn entails a shift in the grammaticality of verb-initial orders as unmarked structures.

In fact, however, the evidence on which the gradualist account is based is flawed, and closer documentation of the spread of the V1-order in the history of Welsh shows that it needs to be amended substantially. In Section 4.4 it will be shown that the statistics given in Fife (1991) suggesting a gradual rise in V1-orders are misleading. First, however, I examine V1-structures in Middle Welsh, arguing that they can be dealt with naturally within a V2-account of that language.

4.2. SENTENTIAL COORDINATION AND V1 IN MIDDLE WELSH

The rules for word order in Middle Welsh interact closely with those for coordination. The patterns of word order observed in the second conjuncts of pairs of conjoined clauses differ significantly from those found elsewhere. In particular, virtually all of the instances of verb-initial word order are found in the second conjunct of conjoined clauses.

In a number of studies of Middle Welsh word order, difficulties have been noted with conjoined clauses—in particular, difficulties in assimilating them to the usual pattern of Topic–Verb–X. For instance, in (1), discussed by Poppe (1989: 45), there appears *syntactically* to be an adverbial topic deleted under identity ('understood') in the second and subsequent clauses. This would be sufficient to account for the appearance of the particle *y(d)*, implying agreement with an adverbial topic, in the second and subsequent conjuncts.

(1) *Parth ac ynys Prydein y   doethant dros vor a   gweilgi. Ac y*
    towards island Britain PRT came-3P over sea and ocean   and PRT
    goresgynnwys yr ynys ar Veli mab   Manogan, a   'e ueibon, ac
    conquered   the island on Beli son-of Manogan, and his sons,   and
    y   gyrrwys ar uor wynt, ac y   deuth racdaw hyt yn   Aruon,
    PRT+3P-ACC drove   on sea them, and PRT came onward as-far-as Arfon
    ac yd adnabu   yr amherawdyr y wlat mal   y
    and PRT recognized the emperor   the land as-soon-as PRT+3S-ACC
    gwelas.
    saw.
    'Towards Britain they came over sea and ocean. And he [Emperor Macsen] conquered the island from Beli son of Manogan and his sons, and drove them into the sea, and advanced to Arfon, and the emperor recognized the land as soon as he saw it.' (*BM* 8. 12–17)

However, semantically the topic of these clauses cannot be reconstructed as identical with the topic of the first clause—namely, *parth ac ynys Prydein* 'towards Britain'—even though, since it is an adverb, this would be a syntactically acceptable reconstruction. The required interpretation of the second clause as 'Towards Britain he conquered the island . . .' would simply be incoherent. This leads Poppe to reject (1) as an instance of topic deletion under identity. The problem of why the particle *y(d)* appears in the second and subsequent conjuncts of course remains. A similar example from *Breudwyt Ronabwy* is given in Poppe (1990: 448).

4.2.1. *Conjoined structures in Middle Welsh*

It seems that the difficulties with such clauses are part of a wider problem involving the rules of coordination and the possibilities for non-overt topics in Middle Welsh. In Middle Welsh, if a series of conjoined clauses have the same topic, the topic may be omitted in all the clauses after the first. Thus, many instances of clause-initial verbs in Middle Welsh can be construed as syntactically dependent on an adverb or some other topic in the preceding clause (Poppe 1989: 45).

Consider, for instance, the examples in (2)–(5). The examples in (2) show a subject topic in the first clause followed by a second clause with a subject gap (henceforth marked as ____) in the clause-initial topic position. The topic in the second clause must be a subject because the preverbal particle is *a*, the form required in agreement with a subject or object.[3]

(2) Subject topic

    (*a*) *A*   *chanys bu, a*   *'y*   *dala*   *hi, mi a*   *rodaf Pryderi*
       and since   was and 3SF-GEN catch-VN her, I   PRT give-1S Pryderi
      a   *Riannon it*   *ac* ____ *a*   *waredaf*   *yr hut*   *a*   *'r lletrith*
      and Rhiannon to-you and ____ PRT remove-1S the spell and the magic
      y   *ar Dyuet.*
      from on Dyfed.
      'And since it was and she was caught, I shall give Pryderi and Rhiannon to you and remove the spell and magic from Dyfed.'   (*PKM* 64. 18–20)

    (*b*) . . . *ac ef a*   *ryuelawd a*   *hwnnw ac* ____ *ay*   *delhiis*
       and he PRT warred   with that-one and ____ PRT+3S-ACC caught
      ac ____ *ay*   *rodes yngkarchar. ac* ____ *a*   *ladawt y*
      and ____ PRT+3S-ACC put   in-prison   and ____ PRT killed   his
      deu vab. ac ____ *a*   *gymyrth y*   *dyrnas*   *yn*   *eidaw ef ehvn.*
      two sons and ____ PRT took   the kingdom PRD his   he himself
      '. . . and he warred with him and captured him and put him in prison and killed his two sons and took the kingdom as his own.'   (*BB*₁ 194. 15–16)

    (*c*) . . . *a*   *'r dryded chwech onadunt a*   *dodassant liein ar y*   *byrdeu*
      and the third   six   of-them PRT put-3p   cloth on the tables
      ac ____ *a*   *arlwyassant bwyt* . . .
      and ____ PRT prepared-3P food
      '. . . and the third [group of] six put cloths on the tables and prepared food . . .'   (*Owein*, 67–9)

(d) ... ar   brenhin agynnullawd ygyt   ylu   ac _____
and-the king   PRT+gathered together his-army and _____
adoeth   hyt yn   Rudlan.
PRT+came as-far-as Rhuddlan.
'... and the king gathered his army together and came to Rhuddlan.'

(*BTy*₁ 167a. 9–12)

Example (3) shows the same with an expletive subject, and (4) with a direct object (see also *FfBO* 54. 25; *YCM* 4. 12).

(3) Expletive subject
    (a) *A   gwedy y   ollwng y mywn, ef a   vuwyt   lawen*
    and after   3SM-GEN let-VN in   it PRT was-IMPERS happy
    wrthaw, ac _____ a   gymerwyt   y uarch o 'e   ystablu ...
    at-him   and _____ PRT took-IMPERS his horse to 3SM-GEN stable-VN
    'And after he had been let in, people were happy towards him, and his horse was taken to be stabled ...'   (*YSG* 1770–1)

    (b) *Ac yn ol y twrwf ef a   daw cawat adoer,   ac   _____ a*
    and after the noise it PRT come shower very-cold and _____ PRT
    vyd   abreid ytti   y   diodef   hi yn vyw ...
    be-FUT scarcely to-you 3SF-GEN suffer-VN it PRD alive
    'And after the noise there will come a very cold shower and it will be scarcely (possible) for you to withstand it alive ...'   (*Owein*, 152–3)

(4) Direct object
    (a) *... a   gauas o achenogyon yn y holl lu   a   wisgwys*
    REL found of needy   in his whole host PRT clothed
    yn hard   ac _____ a   borthes yn enrydedus o vwyt a   diawt.
    beautifully and _____ PRT fed   honourably   of food and drink
    '... those needy people that he could find in his whole host he clothed beautifully and fed honourably with food and drink.'

(*YCM* 21. 32–22. 2)

    (b) *Ac y gyt a hynny yr arderchavc urenhin Arthur a   urathvt*
    and with   that   the munificent king   Arthur PRT wounded-IMPERS
    yn agheuavl, ac   odyno _____ a   ducpvt   hyt yn   enys
    mortally,   and thence _____ PRT took-IMPERS as-far-as island
    Auallach y yachau y   welioed.
    Avalon   to heal-VN his wounds
    'And with that the munificent King Arthur was mortally wounded and thence was taken to the Isle of Avalon to have his wounds healed.'

(*BD* 185. 23–5)

In (5) we have an adverbial topic in the first clause. In this case the preverbal particle in the second clause is *y(d)*, as required for agreement with an adverbial topic. In (5a) it is quite clear that the adverbs *peunyd* 'every day' and *pob hanner dyd* 'every midday' in topic position in the first clause have scope over the second — for instance, conditioning the aspect of the verb (imperfect). Uncertainties with adverbial scope in the other examples in (5) will be returned to below.

(5) Adverbial topic

(a) *A   gwedy bod   hynny yn   barawt gantunt,   peunyd   pob*
And after   be-VN that   PRD ready   with-them, every-day every
hanner dyd y   kymerei   y   deu amherawdyr eu   bwyt, ac ____
midday   PRT took-IMPF the two emperor   their food and ____
y   peidynt   ac ymlad o   bop   parth . . .
PRT stopped-IMPF-3P with fight-VN from every side
'And after that was ready with them, every day at midday the two emperors had their food, and they stopped fighting on every front . . .'

(*BM* 11. 5–8)

(b) *Ac yna y   kyhoedes   y   gyfreith yn gwbyl y 'r pobyl, ac ____*
and then PRT proclaimed the law   entirely to the people and ____
y   kadarnhawyt   y   awdurdawt vdunt   ar y   gyfreith honno,
PRT confirmed-IMPERS his authority   to-them on the law   that
ac ____ y   dodet   emelltith Duw . . . ar y   neb
and ____ PRT put-IMPERS curse   God   on the anyone
nys   katwei . . .
NEG+3S-ACC kept-COND
'And then he proclaimed the law in its entirety to the people, and his authority over that law was confirmed to them and the curse of God . . . was put on anyone who did not keep them . . .'   (*LlB* 2. 8–12)

(c) *. . . ac eno y   gvastataus ac y   gorvu   ar y   Freinc o*
and then PRT subjugated and PRT overcame on the French from
emlad,   ac ____ e   goresgynnvs rann vaur o Freinc . . .
fight-VN and ____ PRT conquered   part large of France . . .
'. . . and then he subjugated and overcame the French by fighting and conquered a large part of France . . .'   (*HGK* 4. 5–6)

(d) *Ac yna yr   anuonet   Pompeius yn erbyn Tigranes, vrenhin*
and then PRT sent-IMPERS Pompeius against   Tigranes   king
Armenia, ac ____ y   lladawd hwnnw Scaurus . . .
Armenia and ____ PRT killed   that   Scaurus
'And then Pompeius was sent against Tigranes, King of Armenia, and he killed Scaurus . . .'   (*BY* 46. 8–9)

Certain standard assumptions are generally made with regard to coordination. First, with a few exceptions (see Bayer 1996), the conjoined elements (conjuncts) must be constituents of the same category and level of projection (Chomsky 1957:

35–6; Dougherty 1970: 864; Gazdar 1981: 157; Wunderlich 1988: 292, etc.). This rules out sentences such as those in (6) and (7). The ungrammaticality of (6) is due to the fact that the two conjuncts do not constitute single constituents of the sentence. In (7), coordination of a Noun Phrase (DP) and Prepositional Phrase is ruled out by the condition that only like categories can be conjoined.

(6)   *John rang up his mother and up his sister.*   (Radford 1988: 75)

(7)   *John wrote [$_{DP}$ a letter] and [$_{PP}$ to Fred]*   (Radford 1988: 76)

Furthermore, where a single constituent bears some relation to both conjuncts, as in (8) where *John* is a subject of both clauses, that constituent must lie outside both conjuncts.

(8)   [$_{IP}$ *John* [$_{VP}$ *came in*] and [$_{VP}$ *looked around*]]

Finally, if an element is extracted from one conjunct, it must also be extracted from the other (Across-the-Board extraction (Burton and Grimshaw 1992; McNally 1992; Ross 1967; Edwin Williams 1977, 1978; Wunderlich 1988: 292)). This accounts for the difference in grammaticality between (9a) and (9b). In (9a) *who* is extracted from the subject position of both conjuncts, whereas in (9b) it is extracted only from the first conjunct. Hence (9b) is an Across-the-Board Violation and therefore ungrammatical.

(9) (a)   *Who$_i$ [t$_i$ wrote the book] but [t$_i$ did not produce the film]?*

    (b)   *Who$_i$ [t$_i$ wrote the book] but [someone else produced the film]?*

4.2.2.   *Against C′-coordination*

The cases in (2)–(5) above can be dealt with straightforwardly without violating these assumptions by adopting an analysis with coordination of the clauses at a level below the topic. Thus, for the case in (2a), there would be C′-coordination with Across-the-Board extraction (topicalization) of the identical subject in the two clauses:

(10)   [$_{CP}$ *mi*$_i$
         I

         [$_{C'}$ *a   rodaf*$_v$ [$_{IP}$ t$_i$ t$_v$ [$_{VP}$ t$_i$ t$_v$ *Pryderi a   Riannon   it*]]]
              PRT give-1s   Pryderi and Rhiannon to-you

         ac
         and

         [$_{C'}$ *a   waredaf*$_v$ [$_{IP}$ t$_i$ t$_v$ [$_{VP}$ t$_i$ t$_v$ *yr   hut . . . y   ar Dyuet*]]]]
              PRT remove-1s   the spell   from on Dyfed

The apparent gap in the topic position of the second conjunct can easily be accounted for. Since the two conjuncts share a single SpecCP position, there is in fact no gap—the topic position for both clauses is filled by the extracted subject *mi*, hence the appearance of the particle *a* on both main verbs. The obligatory gap in subject position is the usual *wh*-trace left by topicalization.

Other cases of coordination in Middle Welsh, however, present problems that cannot be handled in this way. For instance, it is possible to conjoin V2-clauses even if they do not share the same topic. In the most usual case, two clauses share a subject but this subject is not topicalized in the first conjunct, and hence occupies the postverbal subject position, SpecIP (SpecTP). Examples of this construction are given in (11). Throughout, the constituent in the first clause that acts as antecedent of the topic gap in the second clause is given in bold.[4]

(11) (a) A   thri ugein mlyned y   bu **ynteu**   yn   y   llywav hi
And sixty   years   PRT was he-CONJ PROG 3SF-GEN rule-VN it
yn vravl, ac ____ a   adeilvs dinas ar auon Soram, ac   ____
manfully and ____ PRT built   city   on river Soram and ____
a'e   gelwis o   'e enw ehun   Caer Llyr . . .
PRT+3S-ACC called from his name his-own Leicester
'And for sixty years he ruled it manfully, and built a city on the River Soram and called it from his own name Leicester . . .' (BD 26. 11–13)

(b) A   phan ymwahaneist di   y wrth Galaath, y'th   gafas
and when parted-2s   you from Galâth   PRT+2S-ACC took
y gwas drwc ac ____ a   aeth ynot.
the servant bad   and ____ PRT went into-you.
'And when you parted from Galâth the Devil took you and went into you.' (YSG 980–1)

(c) . . . ac yna y   kyuodes **sabot** ac ____ a   elwis ar bown ac
and then PRT arose   Sabot and ____ PRT called on Bown and
____ a   erchis idaw   talu   teyrnget yr   brenhin . . .
____ PRT asked to-him pay-VN homage to-the king
'And then Sabot arose and called on Bown and asked him to pay homage to the king . . .' (YBH 2825–8)[5]

(d) Ac yna yn gyflym yd   eynt   **[pro]** am benn yr honn a
and then quickly   PRT went-IMPF-3P [pro] against   the one   REL
vynnynt   ac ____ a   darostyngynt   hi vdunt.
wanted-IMPF-3P and ____ PRT subjugated-IMPF-3P it to-them
'And then quickly they would attack the one that they wanted and they would subjugate it to them.' (SDR 485–7)

Suppose we try to treat this as C'-coordination, analysing (11a) as in (12).

(12)   [$_{CP}$ A   *thri ugein mlyned*
       And sixty   years

      [$_{C'}$ *y*   *bu* [$_{IP}$ **ynteu**$_i$ [$_{VP}$ *yn y llywav hi . . .*]]]
         PRT was he   ruling-it

      ac
      and

      [$_{C'}$ *a*   *adeilvs*$_V$ [$_{IP}$?$_i$ t$_V$ [$_{VP}$ t$_V$ *dinas . . .*]]]]]
         PRT built   city

On the assumption that coordination requires the shared element to lie outside both conjuncts, this analysis is problematic, since the status of the subject of the second clauses, marked here with a question mark, is unclear.

Furthermore, in all cases the missing topic of the second clause is its subject, as can be seen from the appearance of the preverbal particle *a*, which agrees only with topicalized subjects and objects. If we take these cases to involve C'-coordination, there is no reason to expect the particle *a* to occur, since the common SpecCP position for both clauses is filled by an adverb. Given our account of the preverbal particles as topic agreement, the subject gap in the second clause must be preverbal, and some other account must be sought.

This construction is reminiscent of so-called SLF-coordination (*Subjektlücke Finit/Frontal*) in German conjoined V2-clauses (Höhle 1990), illustrated in (13).

(13)   *In Mainz fährt Karl am   Abend   los   und kommt am   Morgen*
      in Mainz goes Karl in-the evening away and comes in-the morning
      in Bonn an.
      in Bonn to.
      'Karl will leave Mainz in the evening and will arrive in Bonn in the
      morning.'   (Heycock and Kroch 1994: 258)

As in the Middle Welsh examples in (11), the two conjuncts have a shared subject, but not a shared verb. Therefore, the two verbs must lie below the level of coordination—that is, coordination must be above C. The shared subject *Karl* must occupy a position above the level of coordination. However, the subject has not topicalized in the first clause, so remains in SpecIP. Hence coordination must be below SpecIP. Clearly, it is impossible for the level of coordination to be both above C and below SpecIP.

The standard analysis of the German construction involves coordination at a sub-clausal level (Heycock and Kroch 1994; Kathol 1992). However, there are important differences between the German and Middle Welsh data, to which we return below and which suggest that a common analysis is not possible. The German data nevertheless turn out to be highly significant when we examine later developments in Welsh.

Similar data are also found in Breton V2-clauses. There, in addition to straight-forward cases of symmetric coordination below a topicalized subject (14a) and a topicalized object (14b), we find SLF-type coordination in (15).

(14) (a) *Me a   yelo   di   hag ____ a   gavo   an teñzor.*
          I   PRT will-go there and ____ PRT will-get the treasure.
          'I will go and get the treasure.'   (Press 1986: 204)

     (b) *Brezhoneg a   lennan hag ____ a   skrivan.*
          Breton   PRT read-IS and ____ PRT write-IS
          'I (can) read and write Breton (Breton I read and I write).'

                                                          (Jouin 1984: 29)

(15)   *Me am eus gwelet un den hag ____ a   deue din.*
          I   have-IS seen   a   man and ____ PRT came to-me
          'I saw a man and (he) came towards me.'   (Le Clerc 1908: 198)

Given these data, a number of interrelated questions arise:

1. What is the relationship between the gap in topic position in the second conjunct and its antecedent?
2. What is the nature of the gap?
3. What is the categorial status of the second conjunct?

The situation in Middle Welsh (and also in Breton) is complicated by additional information provided by the presence of the topic-agreement particle *a*.

The phenomenon in general is less restrictive in Middle Welsh than in German. Although the most usual situation is for the gap in the second conjunct in Middle Welsh to be coreferential with the subject of the first conjunct, this is not always the case. The antecedent of the gap may in fact fulfil any grammatical function in the first conjunct whatsoever. So, in (16a), the topic in the second conjunct corresponds to the direct object of the first. In (16b) it corresponds to the object of a preposition in the first conjunct (cf. *YSG* 1368, 1538, 2369, 2381, 2496, 3748, 4405, 4965, 5045); in (16c) to the subject of an embedded clause (cf. *YCM* 25. 13); and in (16d) to the implicit subject of an impersonal verb.

(16) (a) *Ac   yn yr vn   wythnos ef a   gyfaruu ac ef   vn marchawc ar*
          And in the same week   it PRT met   with him one knight   on
          bumthec, ac a   uyrywys **pob un,** *ac ____ a   doethant racdunt*
          fifteen   and PRT threw   every one, and ____ PRT came-3P onward
          lys   Arthur . . .
          court Arthur
          'And in the same week there met with him sixteen knights and he threw every one, and (they) came onward to Arthur's court . . .'

                                                          (*Peredur*, 16. 20–3)

(b) A   phan weles y   kythreul, drwc vu   ganthaw   **[pro]**, ac
   and when saw   the devil,   bad   was-PERF with-3SM [pro] and
   ____ a   vedylyawd ar wneuthur iawn itt   pan   weles y   gyflwr
   ____ PRT thought   on do-VN   right to-you when saw   his chance
   'And when the devil saw (that), he was displeased, and thought of paying
   you back when he saw his chance . . .'   (*YSG* 960–1)

(c) Ac yna yd   ysgawnhaawd y   dolur ual   y   gallei **[pro]**
   and then PRT eased   the pain so-that PRT could [pro]
   gysgu   a   cherdet, ac ____ a   dywawt . . .
   sleep-VN and walk-VN and ____ PRT said
   'And then the pain eased so that he could sleep and walk, and (he)
   said . . .'   (*YSG* 1301–2)

(d) Ac o 'r   diwed efo   a   delit   o gedernyt,
   and of the end   he-REDUP PRT caught-IMPERS of force,
   ac ____ a   'e   dugassant ____ y 'r fforest.
   and ____ PRT 3S-ACC took-3P   ____ to the forest.
   'And in the end he was caught by force, and (they) took him to the
   forest.'   (*YSG* 2756–7)

It is also not necessary for the topic to correspond to any single grammatical
position in the first conjunct. There are cases of split antecedents, as in (17*a*)–(17*c*)
and partial antecedents as in (17*d*) (cf. also *BB*₁ 90. 8; *Owein*, 768; *YSG* 4130,
5599, 5647).

(17) (a) *Iosep*ᵢ a   gymerth Meir ⱼ a   phymp or   guerydon ₖ y gyt a hy. ac
      Joseph PRT took   Mary and five of-the virgins   with   her, and
      ____ ᵢ₊ⱼ₊ₖ a   doethant y ty   Iosep.
      ____   PRT came-3P to house Joseph.
      'Joseph took Mary and five of the virgins with her and (they) came to
      Joseph's house.'   (*MIG* 216. 7–8)

   (b) *Mivi*ᵢ, . . . a   ymrodaf y gyt a thydi ⱼ   yn y   gwassanaeth
      I-CONJ   PRT engage-1S with   you-REDUP in the enterprise
      hwnn . . . ac ____ ᵢ₊ⱼ a   gymerwn, vi a   thi, arnam hediw
      this   and ____   PRT take-1P   I and you on-us today
      gostwg   syberwyt Rolond . . . hyt ar   dim.
      reduce-VN arrogance Roland   as-far-as nothing
      'I . . . shall engage with you in this enterprise . . . and (we) shall take (it)
      upon ourselves today, me and you, to reduce Roland's arrogance down
      to nothing.'   (*YCM* 139. 16–20)

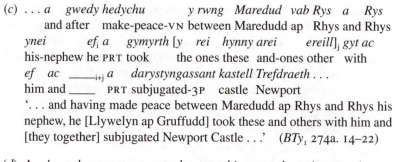

(c) . . . *a*   *gwedy hedychu*   *y rwng*   *Maredud*   *vab Rys*   *a*   *Rys*
         and after   make-peace-VN between Maredudd ap   Rhys and Rhys
ynei   *ef*ᵢ *a*   *gymyrth* [*y*   *rei* *hynny arei*   *ereill*]ⱼ *gyt ac*
his-nephew he PRT took   the ones these and-ones other   with
ef *ac* _____ᵢ₊ⱼ *a*   *darystyngassant kastell Trefdraeth* . . .
him and _____   PRT subjugated-3P   castle Newport
'. . . and having made peace between Maredudd ap Rhys and Rhys his
nephew, he [Llywelyn ap Gruffudd] took these and others with him and
[they together] subjugated Newport Castle . . .'   (*BTy*₁ 274a. 14–22)

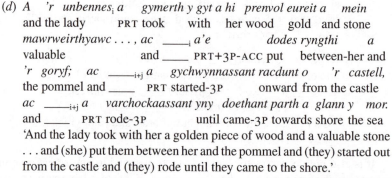

(d) *A*   *'r unbennes*ᵢ *a*   *gymerth y gyt a hi*   *prenvol eureit a*   *mein*
    and the lady   PRT took   with   her wood   gold   and stone
mawrweirthyawc . . . , *ac* _____ᵢ *a'e*   *dodes ryngthi*   *a*
valuable   and _____ PRT+3P-ACC put   between-her and
'r goryf; *ac* _____ᵢ₊ⱼ *a*   *gychwynnassant racdunt o*   *'r castell,*
the pommel and _____   PRT started-3P   onward from the castle
ac _____ᵢ₊ⱼ *a*   *varchockaassant yny* *doethant parth a* *glann y*   *mor.*
and _____   PRT rode-3P   until came-3P towards shore the sea
'And the lady took with her a golden piece of wood and a valuable stone
. . . and (she) put them between her and the pommel and (they) started out
from the castle and (they) rode until they came to the shore.'

(*YSG* 3981–4)

Notice that at this point the Middle Welsh and German constructions diverge
sharply. In German SLF-coordination, partial and split antecedents are completely
ungrammatical:

(18)   **In Berlin besprach Clinton die Krise mit Kohl und fuhren   dann*
        in Berlin discussed Clinton the crisis with Kohl and went-3P then
        zusammen weiter nach New York.
        together   on   to   New York.
        'Clinton discussed the crisis with Kohl in Berlin and then (they) went on
        together to New York.'

This evidence emphatically confirms that in Middle Welsh the second conjunct
cannot be a C′ with its topic in an external shared specifier position. In fact it
confirms that we are not dealing with a subject shared between the two clauses,
since the subject of the second conjunct does not even have to be a single
constituent of the first conjunct. Consequently, the second conjunct must contain
an empty category in topic position.[6]

Furthermore, the mechanism for coindexing between the gap in topic gap and its
antecedent must be pragmatic rather than syntactic, since there is no constant
feature of the syntactic relationship between them. The antecedent may or may not

c-command the topic gap, and it may or may not correspond to a single syntactic entity.

4.2.3. *The nature of the empty category*

We have already seen that the coordination structures in German are more restricted than in Middle Welsh, and that this may suggest a purely syntactic approach for German coordination. This approach is not, however, appropriate for Middle Welsh. Two other languages display a system more similar to the Welsh one—namely, Old French and Old Icelandic. There are two proposals for what the empty category might be, either a null operator (Sigurðsson 1993) or a null pronominal (Vance 1993). I turn first to the Old French evidence discussed by Vance, before engaging in more general discussion of the nature of the empty category, returning eventually to Sigurðsson's proposals for Old Icelandic.

4.2.3.1. *Topic gaps as* pro

Vance (1993) discusses Old French constructions of this type as in (19). The third-person-plural DP in the existential construction in the first clause is the antecedent of a gap in subject position of the second clause.

(19) *Et devant   les paveillons avoit bien cinc cent   chevaliers . . . et*
     and in-front-of the pavillions had   well five hundred knights   and
     avoient comencié un tornoiment trop merveillex.
     had-3P begun   a   tournament very marvellous
     'And in front of the pavillions there were five hundred knights . . . and (they) had begun a very marvellous tournament.'   (Vance 1993: 288)

The French construction is like the Middle Welsh one in allowing a split or unexpressed antecedent to the gap in the second conjunct.

Vance suggests that the empty element in the second conjunct is a null subject *pro*. The obvious approach would be to adopt an analysis of the second conjunct as a full clause with *pro* in the topic position SpecCP. This would give an account of why the second conjunct is apparently verb-initial. However, in Old French *pro* is licensed only in postverbal position. Hence Vance is led to reject this approach, adopting instead an analysis in which the second conjunct is a partial clause, I′. In her analysis *pro* is licensed postverbally in SpecVP by being governed by rich Infl. The fact that the second conjunct is an I′ explains why it does not manifest verb-second effects. V2 is a result of movement to the CP-level. Since this level does not exist in these clauses, the movement that leads to V2 can never occur.

It is not clear from Vance (1993) whether the second conjunct I′ is intended to conjoin with the whole of the first conjunct or simply with the I′ of the first conjunct. The two possible structures for (19) are shown in (20). In (20*a*), CP is conjoined with I′, in (20*b*), I′ with I′.

(20) (*a*) [$_{CP}$ [$_{CP}$ *devant les paveillons avoit*$_{V1}$ [$_{IP}$ pro [$_{I'}$ t$_{V1}$ . . . *500 chevaliers*$_i$]]]
        in front of the pavillions had   500 knights

    et
    and

    [$_{I'}$ *avoient*$_{V2}$ [$_{VP}$*pro*$_i$ [$_{V'}$ *comencié un tornoiment* . . .]]]]
    had-3P   begun   a tournament

(*b*) [$_{CP}$. . . *devant*   *les paveillons avoit*$_{V1}$ [$_{IP}$ pro [$_{I'}$ [$_{I'}$ t$_{V1}$ . . . *500 chevaliers*$_i$]
        in front of the pavillions had   500 knights

    et
    and

    [$_{I'}$ *avoient*$_{V2}$ [$_{VP}$*pro*$_i$ [$_{V'}$ *comencié un tornoiment* . . .]]]]]]
    had-3P   begun   a tournament

                           (adapted from Vance 1993: 295)

The main objection to the structure in (20*a*) is that it involves coordination of non-like constituents. A similar approach is defended for German in Heycock and Kroch (1994), but it is difficult to see how it could be constrained in the present instance.

The structure in (20*b*), on the other hand, avoids this objection by coordinating exclusively I′.[7] However, according to this analysis, one would expect Binding Condition B violations if *pro* in the second conjunct is bound by the subject of an unergative verb in the first conjunct. Such a configuration is shown in (21). The governing category for *pro* is IP. This contains a DP subject in SpecIP which A-binds *pro* in SpecVP, a Condition B violation.

(21)   [$_{CP}$ XP V$_{V1}$ [$_{IP}$ DP$_i$ [$_{I'}$ [$_{I'}$ t$_{V1}$ . . .]

            et

          [$_{I'}$ V$_{V2}$ [$_{VP}$*pro*$_i$ [$_{V'}$ t$_{V2}$ . . .]]]]]]

Even if these objections are disregarded, there are further difficulties with this approach that arise specifically from a consideration of Middle Welsh.

The Welsh data in (11) and (16)–(17) appear to be very similar to the Old French data. As in Old French, preverbal *pro* is not normally licensed in Middle Welsh. This suggests that Vance's analysis should be transferable to Welsh. In Welsh, however, there are preverbal particles, the distribution of which proves that this is not possible. Indeed, since the situation in the two languages is otherwise very similar, it casts doubt on the original analysis itself.

Transferred directly to Welsh, this analysis would give the structure of (16*a*) as (22), ignoring for the moment the question of precisely at which level coordination takes place.

(22)   [CP *ef*ᵢ ... *a*   *uyrywys* [IP tᵢ t_V [VP tᵢ t_V *pob*   *un*]]]
         he   PRT threw   every one

      ac
      and

      [I' *a*   *doethant* [vP pro *racdunt lys*   *Arthur*]]
        PRT came-3P   onward court Arthur

The biggest problem with this is the preverbal particle *a* in the second conjunct. It has been assumed so far that this particle is base-generated in C as a reflex of Spec-head agreement within CP. The second conjunct here has no CP, so this account would have to be revised. However, even if it were revised to allow *a* to be the reflex of Spec-head agreement within IP, the form of the particle would still fail to be predicted correctly. The particle in I of the second conjunct would agree with its Specifier position. Depending on what the second conjunct is taken to conjoin with, there is either no specifier of IP (if CP conjoins with I') or the specifier is filled by the subject of the first conjunct or its trace. In this particular example this second option happens to produce the correct particle *a* in the second conjunct in agreement with a nominal element in SpecIP.

However, the approach predicts that *y*(*d*) can never occur in the second conjunct, since the specifier position of the particle in the second conjunct will always be SpecIP, the subject position of the first conjunct. This is not true. We find frequent examples in Middle Welsh of sentences such as those in (23), where the particle in the second conjunct is *y*(*d*).

(23) (*a*) *Dyuot*   *a*   *wnaeth Gwalchmei attaw heb*   *arwyd creulonder*
        come-VN PRT did   Gwalchmai to-him without sign   cruelty
        gantaw, ac y   dywawt wrthaw . . .
        with-him and PRT said   to-him
        'Gwalchmai came to him without any sign of cruelty and said to him . . .'
                                         (*Peredur*, 33. 13–15)

    (*b*) *Arthur a   deuodes   dala   llys yg Kaer Llion ar Vysc ac*
        Arthur PRT was-accustomed hold-VN court in Caerleon   on Wye and
        y   dellis ar un tu   seith Pasc a phymp Nadolic.
        PRT held consecutively seven Easters and five   Christmases
        'Arthur was accustomed to holding court at Caerleon-on-Wye and held it (there) consecutively for seven Easters and five Christmases.'
                                          (*ChCC* 57. 1–2)

    (*c*) *Ac yna gyntaf y   dywetpwyt   y geir hwnnw, ac y*
        and then first   PRT said-IMPERS the word that   and PRT
        diharebir   etwa ohonaw.
        use-as-proverb-IMPERS still of-it
        'And then for the first time that expression was said, and it is still used as a proverb.' (*PKM* 41. 1–2)

(d) *Ac   yn olaf y   doeth Chyarlymaen a   Rolant ac   eu   lluoed. Ac*
     and last   PRT came Charlemagne and Roland and their forces and
     yd   achubassant yr holl   dayar . . .
     PRT saved-3P   the whole earth
     'And last came Charlemagne and Roland and their forces. And they
     saved the whole earth . . .'   (*YCM* 16. 20–2)

Note that (23c)–(23d) cannot be analysed like (8) above—that is, with C′-coordination and the adverb in a single SpecCP position—since the adverb clearly does not have scope over the second clause. Sentences such as those in (23), parallel to our original problem example in (1), have in recent works been classified as V1. It should by now be clear that they fit into a wider phenomenon of coordination rules which are intimately bound up with the V2-constraint.

Again notice the direct parallel with coordination in Breton. In (24) the order particle–VSO appears in the second of a pair of conjoined clauses despite the fact that clause-initial VSO is not normally possible in main clauses in Breton.

(24)   *He bizied   a   c'hoarie   lentik gant va blev . . . Hag e*
        her fingers PRT played-IMPF slowly with my hair   and PRT
        lavare   din   geriòu-mamm ha   kariadez.
        spoke-IMPF to-me words-mother and love
        'Her fingers played slowly with my hair . . . and (she) spoke to me
        mothering and loving words.'   (Le Gléau 1973: 79–80)

One syntactic difference between the Welsh sentences with *y(d)* in the second conjunct and those with *a* is clear. With *y(d)*, the subject in the second conjunct may be overt in postverbal position, as it is in the examples in (25), whereas postverbal subjects, with one class of exceptions to be discussed below, are not permitted if the particle in the second conjunct is *a*.

(25) (a) *Pan deuthum i yma gyntaf, y   cwm   mawr a   welwch glynn coet*
         when came-1S I here first,   the valley big   REL see-2P dale wood
         oed, ac y   deuth kenedlaeth o dynyon idaw ac y
         was, and PRT came race   of men to-it and PRT+3S-ACC
         diuawyt.   Ac y   tyuwys yr eilcoet   yndaw . . .
         destroyed-IMPERS. And PRT grew the second-forest in-it
         'When I came here first, the big valley that you see, it was a wooded
         dale, and a race of men came to it and it was destroyed. And the second
         forest grew in it . . .'   (*CO* 875–7)

(*b*) *Haralld Harfagyr . . . a   damgylchynus holl Ywerdon gan*
Harald Harfagri   PRT surrounded   all Ireland   with
greulonder, . . . a   'e   goresgyn   ar hyt   ac ar llet.
cruelty   and 3SF-GEN conquer-VN on length and on breadth
Ac yd adeilws enteu   dinas Dulyn a   llawer o dinassoed
and PRT built   he-CONJ city Dublin and many of cities
eraill . . .
other
'Harald Harfagri surrounded the whole of Ireland cruelly, and conquered
it completely. And he built the city of Dublin and many other cities . . .'

(*HGK* 3. 18–22)

(*c*) *. . . a   Pheredur a   gyfodes ac a   wiscawd y arueu ymdanaw*
     and Peredur PRT arose   and PRT wore   his arms on-him
ac ymdan y   varch, ac ef a   deuth y 'r weirglawd. Ac y
and on   his horse and he PRT came to the meadow   and PRT
deuth [*y*] *wreic   ohen   a   'r vorwyn at y   gwr llwyt.*
came the woman very-old and the maiden to the man grey
'. . . and Peredur arose and put his arms on himself and on his horse, and
he came to the meadow. And the very old woman and the maiden came
to the grey man.' (*Peredur*, 38. 7–10)

(*d*) *A   thu ac yno y   kyrchawd, ac y   kyfaruu ac ef gwr*
and towards there PRT headed   and PRT met   with him man
prud . . .
solemn
'And he headed towards there and a solemn-looking man met with
him . . .' (*YSG* 1009–10)

As already noted, the cases with *a*, on the other hand, alternate with a subject
pronoun in preverbal rather than postverbal position. These facts suggest that the
difference between the cases in (16)–(17) and those in (23) is that in (23) the null
subject *pro* occupies (postverbal) SpecIP (SpecTP), whereas in (16)–(17) SpecIP
(SpecTP) is filled by the trace of the subject *pro* which has topicalized to SpecCP.
The structure of (23*a*) and (16*a*) would therefore be as in (26) and (27) respectively.

(26)   *. . . ac* [$_{CP}$ *y   dywawt*$_V$ [pro$_i$ t$_V$ [$_{VP}$ t$_i$ t$_V$ *wrthaw . . .*]]]
        and   PRT said   to-him

(27)   *. . . ac* [$_{CP}$ pro$_i$ *a   doethant*$_V$ [$_{IP}$ t$_i$ t$_V$ [$_{VP}$ t$_i$ t$_V$ *racdunt lys   Arthur*]]]
        and   PRT came-3P   onward court Arthur

In (27), *pro* is topicalized to SpecCP, and the particle *a* in C agrees with it. SpecIP contains its trace, which cannot alternate with an overt DP. In (26) there is no such topicalization, hence *pro* is postverbal and may alternate with an overt DP subject. I leave for the moment the question of how *pro* is licensed in preverbal position in (27).

This leaves us with the question of what occupies SpecCP in (26). One possibility is nothing at all. If so, we need an account of why the particle *y(d)* appears on the verb. One solution would be to redefine *y(d)* as the default particle in C, but this solution would force us to modify the otherwise strong V2-constraint for Middle Welsh requiring SpecCP to be filled.

This would also give an inadequate account of the semantics and peculiar distribution of V1-clauses, since it would imply that leaving SpecCP empty is a general possibility. We would expect general VSO. It therefore fails completely to address the question of why we should find V1-clauses in the second conjunct of pairs of conjoined clauses, when they are so rare everywhere else in the language. V1-main clauses in Middle Welsh may not begin a narrative. Fife (1988: 104) notes the converse of this—namely, that topic-initial structures are associated with or perhaps required at the beginning of a narrative. Why should this be?

The parallels with the symmetric Germanic V2-languages and with Breton are revealing in this respect. Of the Germanic V2-languages, Icelandic (28*a*) and Yiddish (28*b*) permit declarative verb-initial main clauses.

(28) (*a*) *Kom Ólafur seint heim.*
            came Olaf late home.
            'Olaf came home late.'   (Thráinsson 1986: 173)

     (*b*) *Hot men geheysn shisn.*
            has one ordered shoot
            'They ordered to shoot.'   (Santorini 1989: 61)

According to Diesing (1990: 56 n.14), V1 in Yiddish is possible when 'the sentence has a corollary status with respect to the narrative that precedes'. Sigurðsson (1990: 45) gives a similar description of the function of V1-clauses in Icelandic. They indicate strong discourse cohesion, and cannot initiate a discourse. V1 is also dominant in Icelandic in conjoined clauses introduced by *ok* 'and' (Sigurðsson 1990: 51).

In Middle Welsh, restrictions on V1 are of a similar nature. As implied above, the usual use is in the second conjunct of a pair of conjoined clauses, or in a longer sequence of conjoined clauses. A good example of this is the passage in (29). VSO clauses introduced by *y(d)* are marked in bold.

(29) *A'r marchawc a ossodes arnaw, ac nyt ysgoges ef o'r lle yr hynny. Ac ynteu* **Peredur a ordinawd** [1] *y varch* **ac a'e kyrchawd** [2] *yn llityawcdrut engiryawlchwerw awydualch, ac a'e gwant* [3] *dyrnawt gwenwyniclym,*

tostdrut, milwreidffyryf y dan y dwyen, **ac y drechefis** [4] *o'e gyfrwy* **ac y byryawd** [5] *ergyt mawr y wrthaw.* **Ac yd ymchoelawd** [6] *trachefyn* **ac yd edewis** [7] *y march a'r arueu gan y gweisson mal kynt.*

'And the knight attacked him, but he did not move him from the place despite this. And on the other hand **Peredur spurred** [1] his horse **and attacked** [2] him angrily, ferociously and ardently, **and struck him** [3] an incisive, hard, bellicose blow under his mouth, **and raised him** [4] from his saddle **and struck** [5] him a great blow. **And (he) turned** [6] back **and left** [7] the horse and the arms with the servants as before.'   (*Peredur*, 41. 27–42. 6)

The three actions [1]–[3] performed initially by Peredur are expressed using an SVO clause conjoined with two clauses each with an empty subject in topic position coreferential with *Peredur*. The consequence of these actions, the knight rising up from his saddle [4], is expressed using a verb-initial clause. Peredur's subsequent actions [5]–[7] are also expressed using verb-initial clauses. These actions follow on from the SVO clauses, either causally or temporally.

With the example in (29), as with those in (23*c*)–(23*d*), there is no possibility that the topic of an earlier clause has scope over the V1-clause(s). In perhaps the majority of cases of V1-clauses in Middle Welsh, however, the scope of the adverb is ambiguous for the modern reader to a greater or lesser extent. The interpretation of these cases is a matter for the judgement of the researcher. A number of studies of Middle Welsh word order mention this problem (Poppe 1989: 45, 49; Poppe 1990: 448, 452; Watkins 1983–4: 155), generally taking such adverbs to have scope over subsequent conjuncts wherever this is semantically at all conceivable, thereby reducing the number of V1-clauses. For instance, Poppe's (1991*a*: 163) policy is that 'sentences in which more than one finite verb is syntactically dependent on a fronted constituent which governs the choice of relative pronoun or particle are counted as one example of a word-order pattern'. The same policy is applied implicitly by Watkins (1977–8, 1983–4, 1993). However, this is by no means an obvious conclusion. The typical case in Middle Welsh prose is with a first conjunct with *yna* 'then' in topic position. Examples are given in (30).

(30) (*a*) *Ac yna y   messurassant wynteu   hyt nos uchet y   gaer, ac*
           and then PRT measured-3P they-CONJ at night height the castle and
           yd ellygassant eu   seiri   y 'r koet, ac y   gwnaethpwyt
           PRT let-out-3P   their carpenters to the forest and PRT made-IMPERS
           yscawl y   pob petwar gwyr onadunt.
           ladder for every four   men of-them
           'And then by night they measured the height of the castle, and let their carpenters out into the forest and a ladder was made for every four men of them.'   (*BM* 11. 2–5)

(b) *Ac yna y   kerdawd racdaw, ac y   deuth y dyffryn yr afon. Ac*
and then PRT walked onward and PRT came to valley the river and
y   kyfaruu ac ef nifer   o wyr yn   mynet y hela . . .
PRT met   with him number of men PROG go-VN to hunt-VN
'And then he walked onward and came to the river valley. And (there)
met with him a number of men going hunting . . .' (*Peredur*, 62. 23–5)

(c) *Ac yna y   kyfaruu y llog a   chreigawl garrec . . . Ac y*
and then PRT met   the ship with craggy   rock   and PRT
torres y llog genti yn drylleu; ac y   bodes   y meibon a
broke the ship with-it in pieces   and PRT drowned the sons   and
phawb   o 'r nifer . . .
everyone of the company
'And then the ship came up against a craggy rock . . . And the ship broke
into pieces because of it; and the sons and everyone in the company
drowned . . .' (*BTy₂* 104. 12–15)

(d) *Ac yna y   gelwis ynteu y uerch   yeuhaf   idav   attav, a*
and then PRT called he   his daughter youngest to-him to-him, and
gouyn idi   hitheu pa ueint y   carei ef. Ac y   dywavt
ask-VN to-3SF her   how-much PRT loved him and PRT said
hitheu ry   garu   ef eryot mal y   dylyei uerch   caru
she   PERF love-VN him always as PRT should daughter love-VN
y   that . . .
her father
'And then he called his youngest daughter to him, and asked her how
much she loved him. And she said that she had always loved him as a
daughter should love her father . . .' (*BD* 27. 1–3)

The examples given in (5b)–(5d) as possible instances of C′-coordination below an
adverb could also be included here.

There are three interpretations of the scope of the adverb in such sentences. The
adverb may have scope over the two events viewed as a single action, or over each
of the events individually, or over the first event only. These possibilities are given
schematically in (31).

(31) (a) then (x and y)

(b) then (x) and then (y)

(c) (then x) and (y)

The natural assumption to make would be that these interpretations correspond to
distinct syntactic representations like those in (32).

(32) (a) [*then* [[$_{C'}$] *and* [$_{C'}$]]]

(b) [*then*$_i$ [[$_{C'}$ . . . t$_i$ . . .] *and* [$_{C'}$ . . . t$_i$ . . .]]]

(c) [$_{CP}$*then* [$_{C'}$]] *and* [$_{CP}$]

The most likely semantic interpretation for the examples in (30) seems to be that in (31c). However, with an adverb like *yna* in first position it is quite difficult to distinguish between them. The difference comes out more clearly if another time adverb is substituted, as in (33) with *tranoeth* 'on the next day'. The interpretation of this is surely 'On the next day (*x*), and (then) (*y*) and (then) (*z*) . . .' rather than 'On the next day (*x* and *y* and *z* . . .)'. That is, in (33), there is surely no implication that the company did homage to Arthur on the same morning that they set out for his court.

(33)   *Tranoeth y   bore   yd aeth y   gwr llwyt a   'e nifer*
       next-day the morning PRT went the man grey and his company
       *gantaw   y   lys   Arthur, **ac   y   gwrhayssant**   y Arthur **ac   y***
       with-him to court Arthur and PRT did-homage-3P to Arthur and PRT
       parawd Arthur** eu   bedydyaw. **Ac   y   dywawt y   gwr llwyt
       caused Arthur 3P-GEN baptize-VN and PRT said   the man grey
       y Arthur . . .
       to Arthur
       'The next morning the grey man went with his company to Arthur's
       court and did homage to Arthur and Arthur had them baptized and the
       grey man said to Arthur . . .'   (*Peredur*, 39. 28–40. 1)

This view is supported by the independent existence of cases such as (23c) and (23d) where *y(d)*+VSO orders cannot be syntactically dependent on adverbial topics in preceding clauses.

Diesing (1990) posits a non-overt adverb, with a semantic interpretation roughly equivalent to 'therefore' in topic position, to account for the parallel verb-initial orders in Yiddish. A similar proposal is made for Old Icelandic by Sigurðsson (1990: 62; 1993: 261), who suggests instead a null topic operator in SpecCP.[8] This non-overt continuity adverb/operator seems to be the most satisfactory way of accounting for the interpretation of sentences such as those in (30) and (33). It also accounts for the restrictions on their use. If such clauses require a non-overt adverb/operator, they can be used only in contexts where that adverb/operator has something appropriate to refer back to—that is, where it can be licensed by the discourse. Accordingly, I conclude that the structure of the first two clauses of (33) is as given in (34).

(34) $[_{CP}$ *tranoeth* $[_C$ *yd   aeth*$_{V1}]$ $[_{IP}$ *y   gwr*$_i$ t_{V1} $[_{VP}$ t_i t_{V1} *y   lys*$]]]$
               next-day   PRT went   the man   to court
       ac
       and

       $[_{CP}$ Op$_j$ $[_C$ *y   gwrhayssant*$_{V2}]$ $[_{IP}$ pro$_k$ t_{V2} $[_{VP}$ t_k t_{V2} *y   Arthur*$]$ $t_j]]$
               PRT did-homage-3P   to Arthur

Finally, in support of the non-overt adverb hypothesis, it should be noted that in many of the cases of VSO in second conjuncts the subject is highly topical (cf. for instance (30c) and (30d)). It would therefore seem odd to argue that SpecCP in such clauses is empty. If it is empty, and Middle Welsh has a productive topicalization rule, why does a topical constituent not front? If a non-overt continuity adverb occupies SpecCP, we have a (syntactic) answer. This adverb is the topic constituent *par excellence*, and therefore has greater topicality, and therefore a greater claim to occupy SpecCP, than even a topical subject.

4.2.3.2. *Other V1 in Middle Welsh*

It should be noted that not all instances of V1 in Middle Welsh are in series of conjoined clauses. Some examples are found in a clause introduced by *ac* 'and' even when there is no preceding clause with which it could be conjoined, as in (35). Both of these are immediately preceded by direct speech. A few examples are even found without *ac* at all, although these are exceedingly rare.[9] Examples are given in (36). As with the comparable examples in conjoined clauses, the preverbal particle is always *y(d)*. If we assume that these clauses too contain the null topic adverb/operator, the presence of *y(d)* is not surprising. It follows from the general rule that *y(d)* appears as the head of C when SpecCP is occupied by an adverbial element.

(35)　(a)　*Ac　y　doethant parth a　llys　yr iarlles . . .*
　　　　　and PRT came-3P towards court the countess
　　　　　'And they came towards the court of the Countess . . .' (*Peredur*, 50. 7)

　　　(b)　*Ac　y　gwledychwys Peredur gyt a 'r　amherodres pedeir blyned ar*
　　　　　and PRT ruled　　　Peredur with the empress　four　years　on
　　　　　dec . . .
　　　　　ten
　　　　　'And Peredur ruled with the empress for fourteen years . . .'
　　　　　　　　　　　　　　　　　　　　　　　　　(*Peredur*, 56. 14–15)

(36)　(a)　*Osla Gyllelluawr, yn　redec　yn ol y　twrch, y　dygwydwys y*
　　　　　Osla Gyllellfawr, PROG run-VN after the boar　PRT fell　　　the
　　　　　gyllell o　'e wein　ac　y　　　kolles.
　　　　　knife　from his sheath and PRT+3S-ACC lost
　　　　　'Osla Gyllellfawr, (as he was) running after the boar, the knife fell from his sheath and he lost it.' (*CO* 1193–5)

　　　(b)　*Y　rodet　　　y　march y 'r　mab, ac　y　deuth hi　at y*
　　　　　PRT gave-IMPERS the horse　to the son　and PRT came she to the
　　　　　guastrodyon . . . y　orchymyn synyeit wrth y　march . . .
　　　　　grooms　　　　to order-VN attend to　the horse
　　　　　'The horse was given to the son and she came to the grooms . . . to order (them) to attend to the horse . . .' (*PKM* 24. 4–6)[10]

(c) *E   doeth im . . . y gan wr   a   uu   y 'th   wlat   ti.*
PRT came to-me from man REL was-PERF in your country you
'It came to me . . . from a man who had been in your country.'

(*PKM* 35. 3)

(d) *Yd   af   i yn   agel y gyt ac wynt . . .*
PRT go-IS I PRD angel with   them
'I shall become an angel with them . . .'   (*Peredur*, 8. 18)

Such examples also rule out another possible approach—namely, one in which the possibility of V1 order is related to language-specific lexical properties of the coordinating conjunction *ac*, for instance, a feature marking it as optionally a subordinating complementizer.

A handful of examples of VSO where there is no preverbal particle at all are found in Middle Welsh. Note that replies to questions and responses to requests always follow this pattern in Middle and Modern Welsh. The only exceptional examples are therefore those instances of absolute VSO which do not belong to these categories. Those in *Culhwch ac Olwen* have already been discussed (Section 3.7). Remaining examples are given in (37) and (38).

(37) (a) *"Dygaf   y Duw uyg kyffes,"   heb ef . . .*
bring-IS to God my confession said he
' "I confess to God . . . ," he said . . .'   (*PKM* 79. 4)

(b) *"Dygaf   y Duw vyng kyffes,"   heb yr iarll . . .*
bring-IS to God my   confession said the earl
' "I confess to God," said the earl . . .'   (*KAA* 545–6)

(c) *Diolchaf inheu   y Duw . . .*
thank-IS I-CONJ to God
'I thank God . . .'   (*Peredur*, 39. 24)

(38) (a) *Buassei   well   itti   bei roessut   nawd y 'r maccwy*
be-PLUPERF better to-you if   give-COND-2S mercy to the squire
kyn   llad   dy   deu vab . . .
before kill-VN your two sons
'It would have been better for you if you had granted mercy to the squire before your two sons were killed . . .'   (*Peredur*, 38. 30–39. 1)

(b) *Archaf   i oet   ulwydyn . . .*
request-IS I delay year
'I request a year's delay . . .'   (*Peredur*, 61. 6)

(c) *Gwelsont hagen,   or kaffei   veddic y   gyuanhei   y   ascwrn*
saw-3P   however if found-COND doctor REL heal-COND his bones
ac   a   rwymei   y   gymaleu yn da, na   hanbydei   waeth.
and REL bind-COND his joints   well, NEG fare-COND worse
'They saw, however, that, if he found a doctor who would heal his bones
and bind his joints well, then he would not be any the worse.'

(*Peredur*, 31. 28–30)

(d) *A   vynnei,   hagen,   arbenhicrwyd clot   ac etmyc,*
REL want-COND however honour   praise and admiration
gwn   y   lle   y   kaffei.
know-1S the place REL+3S-ACC find-COND
'Anyone, however, who would like the honour of praise and admiration,
I know the place that he might find it.' (*Peredur*, 57. 30–58. 1)

Those in (37) appear to be formulaic, and their appearance might be related to the
use of VSO in replies and responses. Those in (38) appear to be genuine violations
of V2.

To summarize, we have looked at the possibility that apparent instances of V1
in conjoined clauses in Middle Welsh can be reduced to the existence of two empty
categories in these clauses—namely, *pro* and a null continuity adverb or operator.
We can now proceed to examine whether these two elements might be united in
some way, as different manifestations of the same element.

4.2.3.3. *Null operators*

One possibility for uniting the two is to suggest that, in Welsh conjoined clauses,
the SpecCP position of the second clause is always occupied by a phonetically
null topic operator. Such operators have been proposed both as adverbial elements
and as arguments. As examples of the use of null topic operators to account for
gaps in argument (particularly direct-object) position, we may cite Huang's (1984)
proposals for Chinese and Raposo's (1986) proposals for European Portuguese.

European Portuguese permits sentences where a transitive verb lacks a lexically
realized direct object, shown as [e] in (39). Such sentences may not be uttered in
isolation: the content of the direct object must be recoverable from the linguistic
or extralinguistic context.

(39)   *A Joana viu* [e] *na TV ontem.*
Jane   saw [e] on TV yesterday.'
'Jane saw [that] on TV yesterday.'   (Raposo 1986: 373)

Evidence from a number of sources indicates that such sentences must contain
some null element in sentence-initial position, and that this element restricts the
distribution of this type of sentence. One such piece of evidence is given in (40),
which shows that a null object may not appear in a *wh*-question.

(40)   *[Para qual dos filhos]ⱼ é que a Maria comprou [e] tⱼ?*
        for which of-her children is that Mary bought [e]
        'For which of her children did Mary buy [that]?'   (Raposo 1986: 383)

In order to account for this strange restriction, it must be suggested that some aspect of the *wh*-question interferes with the mechanism for licensing a null object. Raposo suggests that null objects in Portuguese are licensed by the presence of a phonetically unrealized element (null operator) in SpecCP. The null operator receives its interpretation from the discourse topic, and fills in the value for the null object, which it binds in an operator-variable chain parallel to that in *wh*-constructions. Since the *wh*-element *para qual dos filhos* 'for which of her children' must move from postverbal position to SpecCP, SpecCP cannot house the operator and the null object cannot be licensed.

A much closer parallel to Middle Welsh is Old Icelandic, where there is evidence for a null topic operator in both argument and non-argument positions in conjoined clauses (Sigurðsson 1993). The linguistic facts are similar to those of Old French and Middle Welsh. In an example like (41), the subject of the second clause is non-overt. It has a split antecedent corresponding to the subject plus object of the first conjunct, just as in the Middle Welsh case the gap could have a split or partial antecedent.

(41)   *... **Olaf konungr**ᵢ hafþi stefnv   við **lið** **sitt**ⱼ oc við **bøndr**ₖ oc*
        Olaf king   had meeting with men his and with farmers and
        reðv   _____ᵢ₊ⱼ₊ₖ landraðvm.
        considered-3P _____   land-matters
        'King Olaf had a meeting with both his men and the farmers, and (they all) considered government policy.'   (Sigurðsson 1993: 252)

Sigurðsson suggests that cases like (41) involve conjunction of full clauses (CPs), with a null topic operator in the second clause binding a variable in subject position.

The crucial support for this hypothesis is that null objects are licensed in Old Icelandic coordination structures, as in (42). The gap cannot contain *pro* since null objects are not otherwise possible in the language.[11]

(42)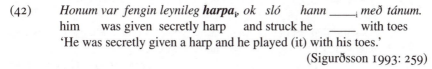
        *Honum var fengin leynileg **harpa**ᵢ, ok sló   hann _____ᵢ með tánum.*
        him   was given secretly harp   and struck he _____ with toes
        'He was secretly given a harp and he played (it) with his toes.'
                                                    (Sigurðsson 1993: 259)

In a language like Welsh, if we find instances of null objects in second conjuncts in contexts where null objects are not licensed normally, then this is good evidence for the existence of a null topic operator binding a variable in object position. The evaluation of this evidence is complicated somewhat by the fact that Welsh licenses omission of object pronouns anyway in the presence of accusative or genitive clitics on the verb or preverbal particle. Null objects in these environments cannot be taken as evidence for a null operator. However, in the absence of these clitics, null objects are not permitted. A null object in a second conjunct in the absence of these clitics would be strong evidence for a null topic operator. Such examples are attested exceedingly rarely. One example from Middle Welsh is given in (43*a*). In (43*a*) there is a gap in object position of the third conjunct not licensed by an object clitic on *a* (that is, we do not find *a'i* or *y'i*).[12] The same is true in the second conjunct in (43*b*). This example occurs in this form only in one manuscript. In the other a pronoun appears after *Duw*. This is probably a resumptive pronoun acting as a variable to indicate the extraction site, given that otherwise the sentence is ambiguous between '(he) called God' and 'God called (him)'. These are the only examples that I have found in Middle Welsh. A similar example from the sixteenth century is given in (43*c*).

(43) (*a*) *Ac   yna y   kanhatwyt   y Chyarlys bot   yn Ager **gawr**ᵢ,*
    And then PRT reported-IMPERS to Charles be-VN in Ager giant
    Ffarracut y   enw, o   genedyl Goliath, ac   ____ᵢ a
    Fferracud his name, from race   Goliath, and ____ PRT
    *dathoed   ____o   eithauoed Sirya **ac**   ____ᵢ **a   anuonassei***
    had-come-3s ____from extremes Syria and ____ PRT had-sent
    Amilald vrenhin Babilon ____ᵢ, y ryuelu   ar Chyarlys ac
    Amilald king   Babylon ____ to make-war-VN on Charles and
    ugein mil   o 'e genedyl gantaw.
    twenty thousand of his race   with-him.
    'And then it was reported to Charles that there was in Ager a giant named Fferracud from the race of Goliath, and (he) had come from the ends of Syria and Amilald King of Babylon had sent (him) to make war on Charles with twenty thousand of his people with him.'

                                             (*YCM* 25. 12–16)

(*b*) *Yr   hynny ual kynt   llawer dyn*ᵢ *a   drigyawd mywn tywyllwch*
    Despite that   as before many man PRT dwelt   in   darkness
    *pechodeu, a   gwedy hynny ____ᵢ a   **elwis** Duw ar oleuni a*
    sins   and after   that ____ PRT called God to light   and
    thrugared . . .
    mercy
    'Despite that, as before, many a man dwelt in the darkness of sins and later God called (him) to light and mercy . . .'

                                            (*YSG* 2590–1 (B MS only))

(*c*) *. . . ac fo a   ddalied   Ioacim*ᵢ *ac ____ᵢ a*
    and it PRT caught-IMPERS Joachim and ____ PRT
    ddyged   *at Nabugodonosor ynn gaeth i Vabilon . . .*
    brought-IMPERS to Nebuchadnezzar PRD captive to Babylon
    '. . . and there was caught Joachim and was brought (him) captive to Nebuchadnezzar in Babylon . . .'   (*RhG* ii. 126. 5–7 (1589–90))

Two possible representations for (43*a*) are given in (44). In (44*a*), we continue the earlier analysis by generating *pro* in object position and topicalizing it to SpecCP, thereby inducing *a* as the agreeing particle. However, object *pro* in the example is not licensed by rich-agreement morphology in the form of object clitics, and it is hard to see how else it could be licensed. The alternative approach is that in (44*b*), where a topic operator in SpecCP binds a variable in object position.

(44) (*a*) . . . *ac* [$_{CP}$ pro$_i$ *a*   *anuonassei* [$_{IP}$*Amilald* t$_i$ *y ryuelu   ar Chyarlys*]]
    and   PRT had-sent   A.   to make-war on C.

  (*b*) . . . *ac* [$_{CP}$ Op$_i$ *a*   *anuonassei* [$_{IP}$*Amilald* t$_i$ *y ryuelu   ar Chyarlys*]]
    and   PRT had-sent   A.   to make-war on C.

Suppose the data in (43) are representative and provide evidence for (44*b*) as the correct analysis of null object topics. It would obviously be uneconomical to have to posit three empty elements in topic position—namely, topic *pro*, a null adverbial topic, and a null operator for objects. Is it possible to generalize the null operator analysis back to the cases of subject gaps like those in (11) and (16)–(17)? For these cases, the answer would seem to be yes. We can simply replace *pro* in SpecCP with a null operator binding a trace in subject position. With the cases involving a null adverbial, as in (23), we can simply assume that this adverbial is in fact a null topic operator, a possibility that has already been entertained above. The null topic operator, just like overt operator, will have a category specification, appearing as a nominal when base-generated in subject or object position, or as an adverbial elsewhere. The correct forms of the preverbal particles will follow straightforwardly from agreement with this category specification. Accordingly, (11*a*) will have the structure in (45) with the operator marked as nominal inducing *a* as the preverbal particle.

(45)   [$_{CP}$*A   thri ugein mlyned* [$_C$ *y   bu*$_{V1}$] [$_{IP}$ *ynteu$_i$* t$_{V1}$
      And sixty   years   PRT was   he
    [$_{VP}$ t$_i$ *yn y llywav hi*]]]
        ruling-it
    ac
    and
    [$_{CP}$ Op$_j$ [$_C$ *a   adeilvs*$_{V2}$] [$_{IP}$ t$_j$ t$_{V2}$ [$_{VP}$ t$_i$ t$_{V2}$ *dinas* . . .]]]
      [+DP]
            PRT built   city
    'Sixty years he ruled it . . . and built a city . . .'

Postulation of a null topic operator also provides a way out of the question posed earlier—namely, why *pro* is licensed in preverbal position in conjoined clauses in Middle Welsh (and in Old French), when it is not licensed in preverbal position elsewhere. Under the general null topic operator analysis, *pro* is not involved in the representation of these clauses, therefore questions of licensing do not arise. Instead the null topic operator is discourse licensed in contexts of narrative continuity, but not in isolated non-conjoined clauses.

However, there is a problem for this analysis in cases where SpecCP in the second conjunct is filled by a null expletive subject. Examples of this occur in Middle Welsh, as in (46). Their distribution is exactly like that of overt expletive subjects (cf. example (3) in Chapter 3). Like overt expletive subjects (see Chapter 5), they are rare in early texts and restricted to unaccusative contexts, whereas in later texts they are common and not restricted in this way. This confirms their status as involving an expletive subject.

(46) (*a*) *Ti   a   geueist veichogi.   ac ____a   vyd   mab*
you PRT got-2S become-pregnant-VN and ____PRT will-be son
ytt . . .
to-you
'. . . you have become pregnant and (there) will be a son (born) to you . . .'   (MIG 216. 30)

(*b*) *A   guedy daruot   henne, Hu   yarll Caer . . . a   gynullus*
and after happen-VN that   Hugh earl Chester PRT assembled
llynges a   llu   diruaur anryued   y 'r wlat . . . Ac ____a
fleet   and force mighty wondrous to the country and ____PRT
gytduvnvs ac   ef   Hu   arall . . .
allied   with him Hugh other
'And after that had happened, Hugh Earl of Chester assembled a fleet and a mighty, wondrous force into the country . . . And (there) became allied with him another Hugh . . .'   (*HGK* 23. 10–14)

(*c*) *. . . ni   a   gollwn ynn kyuoeth ac ____a'n*
       we PRT lose-1P our lands   and ____PRT+1P-ACC
carcherir   yny vom   ueirw neu ____a'n
imprison-IMPERS until be-SUBJ-1P dead or   ____PRT+1P-ACC
lledir.
kill-IMPERS
'. . . we shall lose our lands and (we) shall be imprisoned until we die or are killed.'   (*BTy₂* 66. 13–14)

(*d*) *A   'r marchogyon urdolyon a   welsant hynny ac a'e*
and the knights   noble   PRT saw-3P that   and PRT+3S-ACC
darlleassant, ac ____a   vu   ryued   ganthunt hynny . . .
read-3P   and ____PRT was-PERF marvellous with-them that
'And the noble knights saw that and read it and it was marvellous to them . . .'   (*YSG* 5442–3)

Assuming that expletive elements cannot undergo A′-movement, being unable to form operator-variable chains (Cardinaletti 1990*b*: 82–3), then the second conjunct of the sentences in (46) cannot involve a null operator binding a variable in subject position. This would amount to vacuous quantification ruled out by the principle of Full Interpretation (Chomsky 1995: 151–2). So it seems that we must retain the analysis with *pro* for these cases.

This difficulty is not insurmountable, however. It is part of the wider problem of the status of SpecCP raised in Section 3.5 above. In this instance, if SpecCP is an A′-position, it is not clear why expletive elements in general should be allowed to appear there in V2-languages. This general phenomenon suggests that the topic position in some V2-languages may be an A-position for (some) subjects, but an A′-position for non-subjects (Diesing 1990: 48). If this is the case, a general analysis of gaps in Middle Welsh coordination as involving empty operators can be pursued. The only proviso required is that when SpecCP is an A-position, (expletive) *pro* may appear there; when it is an A′-position, empty operators are licensed there.

4.2.4. *Conclusions about coordination*

If the above discussion is on the right lines, then Middle Welsh does not have verb-initial clauses in the syntax. Even if we consider only the surface ordering, we must accept that verb-initial ordering is highly marked, occurring only in contexts of narrative continuity. It is thus entirely different in nature from the neutral VSO order of Contemporary Welsh. Once we have posited a null topic operator in the topic position of apparent instances of V1, it is possible to maintain a strict V2-requirement for Middle Welsh.

The earliest reliable evidence we have for spoken Welsh provides further support for this conclusion. An examination of the depositions of witnesses in slander cases for the years 1570–1650 (Suggett 1983; the material essentially covers Denbighshire, Flintshire, Montgomeryshire, Cardiganshire, Pembrokeshire, and Brecknockshire) shows no signs of V1 with full lexical verbs at all.[13] The data consist almost entirely of isolated sentences reporting alleged slanderous statements verbatim.[14] If VSO is limited to contexts of 'narrative continuity' with a null operator in Middle Welsh, this is precisely the result we expect.

Pursuing our general line of enquiry into the relationship between acquisition and linguistic change, we may ask how an element such as a null topic operator could be acquired. The null topic operator is a language-specific device and there is no reason to link it to any parameter setting. Instead, it can be treated as an item in the lexicon. Given strong enough evidence for a positive setting of the V2-parameter, a child is left with little option but to posit some element in the SpecCP of clauses which otherwise appear to lack anything there. The existence of agreeing preverbal particles in C would provide a further pointer to the existence of the relevant null element(s). Given a rule that $y(d)$ is an agreement marker signalling an adverbial topic in SpecCP, a child who is confronted with sentences like (23) in which $y(d)$ appears in clause-initial position can either reject the agreement rule or posit a non-overt adverbial in

SpecCP. The former is clearly the 'simpler' option, for instance, in terms of the Least Effort Strategy (cf. Section 2.2.2). However, if the evidence in favour of the existence of overt agreement between the topic in SpecCP and the preverbal particle head of C is solid, as it is in Middle Welsh, the latter option will nevertheless be chosen.

4.3. OTHER EVIDENCE FOR V1-CLAUSES IN MIDDLE WELSH

In addition to coordination, one other factor correlates with absolute verb-initial orders in Middle Welsh tales. Verb-initial orders are very frequent with the non-copular uses of the present and imperfect tenses of the verb *bot* 'to be' (the MAE- and OED-paradigms). For instance, four of the eight instances of verb-initial main clause declarative statements in *Pwyll* are with the verb *bot* (Watkins 1993).[15] In *Breuddwyd Maxen (BM)*, it is three out of fourteen (Poppe 1989: 45).[16] Examples are given from dialogue, where such examples are more frequent than in narrative, in (47), and from narrative passages in (48).[17] Notice that, whereas instances of V1 with other verbs are normally in environments of 'narrative continuity' covered by the null topic operator analysis, instances of V1 with *bot* are not so restricted. This emerges clearly from the examples in (48) and in particular (47).

(47) (a) *"Yd wyf", heb ynteu,   "yn   dyuot   o   edrych gwas*
         PRT am   said he-CONJ PROG come-VN from look-VN boy
     yssyd ym   yn glaf yn y fforest yma."
     is-REL to-me PRD ill   in the forest this
     '"I have come," he said, "from looking at a boy who is ill in this forest."'   (*YSG* 3191–3)

   (b) *Yd wyt   yn y lle   y   perthyn arnat llonydu   eircheit*
       PRT are-2S in the place REL is-fitting on-you satisfy-VN supplicants
       a   cherdoryon.
       and musicians
       'You are in a position where it is incumbent upon you to satisfy supplicants and musicians.'   (*PKM* 17. 20–2)

   (c) *Y   mae ettwa galanas y   gwyr hynny heb   y   dial.*
       PRT is   still murder the men those without 3SM-GEN avenge-VN
       'The murder of those men is still unavenged.'   (*YCM* 116. 4–5)

   (d) *"Yd oedut,"   hep ef, "ynn wastat ynn   keissaw gennyf rann o*
       PRT were-2S said he continually PROG seek-VN from-me part of
       tir   y   Bryttannyeit. ..."
       land the Britons
       '"You were," he said, "continually seeking from me a part of the territory of the Britons. ..."'   (*BTy₂* 72. 1–2)

(48) (*a*) *Ac   yd   oed ynteu   yn   gorffowys wrth paladyr y   wayw ac*
and PRT was he-CONJ PROG lie-VN   by   shaft   his spear and
yn   medylyaw yr vn   medwl.
PROG think-VN the same thought
'And he was lying by the shaft of his spear and thinking the same
thought.'   (*Peredur*, 33. 11–13)

(*b*) *Yd   oed ganthav   hagen   etwa o 'e lu   chue guyr a*
PRT was with-him however still of his force six   men and
chuech canwr   a   thriugein mil.
six   hundred-men and sixty   thousand
'He still had, however, sixty thousand six hundred and six men of his
force left.' (*BD* 184. 14–15)

(*c*) *Yd   oed gynt yn Rufein marchawc . . .*
PRT was once in Rome knight
'There was once a knight in Rome . . .'   (*SDR* 135)

(*d*) *Yd   oed rei   hagen   a   oed hoff   ganthunt hynny . . .*
PRT was some however REL was pleased with-them that
'There were some, however, who were pleased about that . . .'
(*YSG* 378–9)

Again the slander-case evidence provides corroborating evidence that this was
indeed the case even in the early spoken language. Although VSO is generally
unattested there in the earliest period (1570–1650), verb-initial clauses are
common, in fact normal, with the verb 'to be'. A selection of the earlier examples
is given in (49).[18]

(49) (*a*) *Yeroyte   tee in   cadowe ac in   mentino   mortherers*
PRT+are-2S you PROG keep-VN and PROG maintain-VN murderers
a   lladron.
and thieves
'You keep and maintain murderers and thieves.'
(Slander case (Radnor Sessions 1576))

(*b*) *. . . ag y   may rhoyde lledrad worth y   di   le/fo . . .*
and PRT is   net   stolen by   his house him
'. . . and there is a stolen net by his house . . .'
(Slander case (Pembroke Sessions 1608))

This seems to be an exceptional fact about the verb *bot*, rather than anything
following from general principles involving verb-second in Middle Welsh.
Ultimately, it may be that it follows from some other fact about the syntax or
morphology of *bot*. In the present instance though, it can be assumed to be a
marked lexical property of that verb.

4.4. THE GRADUALIST ACCOUNT RECONSIDERED

Recall from Section 4.1 that the previous approach to the rise of VSO in Welsh has been to claim a kind of syntactic drift with VSO gradually increasing in frequency in the language. In this scenario, it is important that the frequency of VSO in Middle Welsh be low but not zero, with a steady rise in Early Modern Welsh through to Modern Welsh. Most of this chapter has concentrated on challenging the first part of this scenario by denying the existence of general unmarked VSO in Middle Welsh. If general VSO did not exist, then some grammatical innovation must have brought it about, and the gradualist approach begins to weaken.

We can now turn briefly to the later evidence cited in favour of the gradualist approach. This can be challenged on purely empirical grounds. Fife (1991) finds that V1 is common and growing in frequency in sixteenth- and seventeenth-century literary texts. Compare for instance the figures 16, 15, and 20 per cent that he gives for the frequency of V1 in Elis Gruffydd's *Castell yr Iechyd* (*CI*) (1540s) and Ephesians and Galatians in the 1620 Bible. Immediately we notice a contradiction between this and the absence of lexical VSO in the slander material noted above. How can the two be reconciled? One possibility would be that the literary and spoken language had diverged on the point of word order. In fact, however, a closer look at the data from the literary texts reveals a pattern fully in accord with the data from slander-case depositions. Consider, for instance, the text of Galatians. Fife (1991: 255) bases his description on an examination of every finite clause in the text, categorized into those in main, relative, and other subordinate clauses. He thus includes imperatives and interrogatives in his figures for V1. Once the numerous examples of these, which have always been verb-initial in Welsh and do not form part of the V2-system, are excluded, we are left with thirteen examples of absolute sentence-initial V1 in affirmative matrix declarative clauses in the text. Of these, six have main verb *bod*, and six have auxiliary *bod*. The only instance of a full lexical verb in a V1 structure is that given in (50).

(50)   *Eithr cydgaeodd yr ysgrythur bob   peth dan   bechod, fel   y*
        but   shut-away the scripture every thing under sin   so-that PRT
        rhoddid   yr addewid trwy   ffydd Iesu Grist i 'r rhai sydd
        gave-IMPERS the promise through faith Jesus Christ to the ones REL
        yn   credu.
        PROG believe-VN
        'But scripture shut everything away under sin, so that the promise was
        given through the faith of Jesus Christ to the ones who believe.'
                                                                    (Gal. 3. 22)

Fife states that the text contains 174 affirmative main clauses. Excluding imperatives and interrogatives, there turn out to be only thirteen absolute V1 clauses, forming only 7 per cent of the total. Excluding *bod*, even that percentage will fall considerably. Thus V1 is not nearly as common in what is termed

'Classical Welsh' as Fife would have us believe.[19] All but one of these V1 clauses begin with a form of the verb *bod*. This distribution is virtually indistinguishable from that found in the Middle Welsh tales.[20]

In half of the clauses with initial *bod*, *bod* is acting as an auxiliary in the periphrastic form of the present tense. The periphrastic present is less frequent in Middle Welsh than in Modern Welsh (see Watkins 1960). The spread is apparently due to a narrowing in the semantics of the synthetic forms (see Poppe 1996). One consequence of the spread of this construction in late Middle Welsh and Early Modern Welsh is necessarily an increase in the recorded frequency of absolute verb-initial clauses in the sixteenth and seventeenth centuries. Since the periphrastic tenses were more frequently verb-initial than the synthetic tenses, an increase in their use naturally results in an increase in V1. The rest of the apparent increase in V1 in Fife's Classical Welsh texts can be attributed to the high incidence of (rhetorical) questions and exhortations in the Renaissance prose examined.

This is not to say that there was no word-order change at all in Early Modern Welsh. In fact there is other evidence that true instances of verb-initial orders were about to appear. I return to this point in Chapter 6.

4.5.   CONCLUSION

The above discussion suggests that the instances of apparent V1 in Middle Welsh can be considered to be the result of construction-specific phenomena. The lexicon will include a null topic operator, acquirable from particle agreement evidence. Exception features on the lexical entries for certain paradigms of the verb *bod*, and on the negative marker *ny(t)* (cf. Section 3.6) will allow peripheral instances of VSO in other circumstances. However, despite these lexical exceptions, the core positive parameter setting for a general verb-second can be acquired and maintained on the basis of robust data in Middle Welsh.

5. Subject Pronouns and the Expletive Construction

In this chapter I investigate the development of preverbal subject pronouns, arguing that in the course of Middle Welsh they became clitics. This had repercussions for the whole pronominal system, and in particular for the expletive subject construction. It is suggested that phonological reduction of preverbal subject pronouns led to a number of exceptions to the verb-second rule. At first these exceptions could be incorporated into the peripheral grammar. In Chapter 6, I argue that these exceptions, along with other features of the grammar beyond the pronominal system, led to a switch in the V2-parameter and the innovation of VSO word order in Modern Welsh.

5.1. THE WELSH PRONOMINAL SYSTEM

Middle Welsh has three series of pronouns that may appear in preverbal subject position. Traditionally these are termed simple, conjunctive, and reduplicated. Their forms are given in Table 5.1 (see D. Simon Evans 1964: 49). Examples of their use as preverbal subjects are given in (1)–(3).

TABLE 5.1. *Forms of Middle Welsh preverbal subject pronouns*

Person	Simple	Conjunctive	Reduplicated
Singular			
First person	*mi*	*minneu*	*miui*
Second person	*ti*	*titheu*	*tidi*
Third-person masc.	*ef*	*ynteu*	*efo*
Third-person fem.	*hi*	*hitheu*	*hihi*
Plural			
First person	*ni*	*ninneu*	*nini*
Second person	*chwi*	*chwitheu*	*chwichwi*
Third person	*wy*	*wynteu*	*wyntwy*

(1)   *Mi a   af . . . y 'r orssed y eisted.*
       I   PRT go-IS to the hillock to sit-VN
       'I shall go . . . to the hillock to sit.'   (*PKM* 9. 10–11)

(2)   *A   mi ui   a   rodaf   y   wled y 'r teulu   a   'r niueroed . . .*
       and I-REDUP PRT give-IS the feast to the retinue and the company
       'And *I* shall give the feast to the retinue and the company . . .'

                                                           (*PKM* 14. 26)

(3)   *Minheu . . . a   baraf . . . na   bydei   launach no chynt.*
       I-CONJ   PRT cause-IS that+NEG would-be fuller   than before
       'I (for my part) shall cause (it to happen) that it should not be any fuller
       than before.'   (*PKM* 15. 5–7)

As can be seen from the translations in (1)–(3), the three series reflect distinctions of contrastive and emphatic stress. Simple pronouns are the weak pragmatically unmarked forms. Reduplicated pronouns are their emphatically stressed counterparts. Conjunctive pronouns are used to set the pronoun against a previous noun or pronoun (Mac Cana 1990; Morris-Jones 1913: 273). For instance, the first-person-singular conjunctive pronoun may typically be translated as 'I, on the other hand' or 'I too'.

5.1.1. *Preverbal subject pronouns in Middle Welsh*

The preverbal conjunctive and reduplicated subjects are clearly full nominal subjects in Middle Welsh. For the first part of this chapter I concentrate on the status of the simple series.

Standard tests for clitic status (cf. Roberts 1993*b*: 112–17) indicate that simple preverbal subject pronouns in Middle Welsh were not clitics. This evidence suggests that they can be treated exactly as full nominal (DP) subjects, topicalizing to SpecCP in the usual manner. The pronouns will therefore be heads of a complement-less DP. Evidence for this interpretation comes from the placement of adverbs and emphatic reflexives, from absolute and verbless constructions, and from coordination facts.

The first evidence comes from the behaviour of pronouns with respect to adverb placement. Preverbal subject pronouns may be separated from the verb by interposed adverbs in the same way that a full lexical topic may be (cf. Section 3.3.2). Examples are given in (4).[1]

(4)   (*a*) *Ef heuyt a   arvaethassei torri   yr holl goedyd a   'r llwyneu . . .*
            he also PRT intended   cut-VN the all   forests and the woods
            'He also intended to cut down all the forests and the woods . . .'

                                                           (*HGK* 22. 14–15)

(b) *Ac ef, wedy kleuychu ohonaw, a   gauas   arwyd yechyt y*
and he PERF fall-ill-VN of-him   PRT received sign   health from
gan Ysaias . . .
with Isaiah
'And he, having fallen ill, received a sign of health from Isaiah . . .'

(BY 34. 25–6)

This is expected if subject pronouns behave like full lexical subjects, topicalizing
to SpecCP. Since interposed adverbs adjoin to C′, they will follow the subject, but
precede the particle and verb, just as was argued to be the case with full nominal
subjects in Section 3.3.3. A typical property of clitic pronouns, on the other hand,
is that no non-clitic material may intervene between them and their host.

Pronouns may furthermore be modified by emphatic elements like the emphatic
reflexive *ehun* 'himself'. This reflexive may follow a simple subject pronoun,
thereby intervening between it and the verb. This can be seen in (5) (cf. *BTy₁*
183a. 27; *BTy₂* 88. 21, 194. 8; *BY* 28. 20; see also Emrys Evans 1958: 31).

(5) (a) *. . . ac ef ehun   yn y   priawt person a   'e   gwylwys.*
          and he himself in his own   person PRT 3S-ACC watched
          '. . . and he himself watched it in person . . .'   (*CLlLl* 141–2)

    (b) *. . . ac ef ehun   adodes tan yny   kastell ac ay*
          and he himself PRT+put fire in-the castle and PRT+3S-ACC
          llosges . . .
          burned
          '. . . and he himself put fire in the castle and burned it . . .'

(BTy₁ 222a. 22–4)

A plausible assumption about the structural position of emphatic reflexives is
that they right-adjoin to the top of DP.[2] If so, adopting the structure of preverbal
pronouns as full DPs rather than as clitics leads us to expect that emphatic
reflexives will be able to adjoin to them and therefore to intervene between them
and the verb.

Subject pronouns may also appear in two types of construction containing no
verb. The first type is the absolute construction, illustrated in (6) (cf. example (29)
in Section 1.5).

(6) (a) *Os arhoy   ditheu efo, a   thi yn varchawc, ef a   'th   edeu*
          If wait-2S you   him and you PRD knight   he PRT 2S-ACC leave
          yn   bedestyr.
          PRD standing
          'If you wait for him when you are on horseback, he will leave you on
          foot.' (*Owein*, 162–3)

(b) *nyt ami yn uyw yd aho ef y Gernyw*
not and-I PRD alive PRT go-SUBJ he to Cornwall
'He will not go to Cornwall with me alive (while I am alive).'

(*W.* 504. 3–4)

The second is their independent use in sentences like (7).

(7) *"Mi Ereint uab Erbin. . . ." "Mi Edern uab Nud."*
I Geraint son-of Erbin I Edern son-of Nudd
' "I am Geraint son of Erbin. . . ." "I am Edern son of Nudd." '

(*ChCC* 69. 10–11)

In these cases the pronoun clearly does not require any verbal host, and hence must be a full DP.

Finally, perhaps the most convincing evidence that preverbal subject pronouns are not clitics comes from their behaviour with respect to coordination. Cross-linguistically, clitic pronouns typically do not participate in coordinate structures at all. This is the case with French subject clitics, as shown in (8).

(8) **Je et tu irons à Paris.*
I-CL and you-CL will-go-1P to Paris
'You and I will go to Paris.' (Roberts 1993*b*: 113)

In Middle Welsh, in contrast, preverbal subject pronouns can conjoin freely, and the agreement which results is between the verb and the whole subject DP. So, in (9*a*) the preverbal conjoined pronominal subject *ef a hi* 'he and she' causes third-person-plural agreement on the verb. In (9*b*) a singular personal pronoun is conjoined with a singular lexical DP, again resulting in third-person-plural agreement on the verb, and so on (cf. *BTy₂* 82. 30; *LlB* 31. 9; *YCM* 59. 32, 81. 7).

(9) (a) *A phan vu barawt bwyt, ef a hi a aethant y eisted*
and when was ready food he and she PRT went-3P to sit-VN
y gyt . . .
together
'And when food was ready, he and she went to sit together . . .'

(*YSG* 3279–80)

(b) *. . . ac am hynny ef a Aram y vab yr hynaf a diffodassant*
and for that he and Aram his son the eldest PRT put-out-3P
y tan . . .
the fire
'And for this reason he and Aram his eldest son put out the fire . . .'

(*BY* 13. 5–6)

Such evidence proves conclusively that simple preverbal subject pronouns are not syntactic clitics in Middle Welsh. Their behaviour can thus be assimilated to the general pattern for all preverbal subjects. This involves movement of a maximal projection to SpecCP, where the pronoun can fulfil the V2-requirement.

The acquisitional evidence for the non-clitic status of preverbal subject pronouns is probably phonological rather than syntactic. That is, children hear them stressed and conclude that they are not clitics. It is important to note that the syntactic evidence cited above, although crucial for the historical linguist, is not frequent enough to be of much use to a child acquiring Middle Welsh, and, given the rich phonological information, is in any case not necessary for acquisition of the correct lexical characterization of the pronouns as non-clitics.

5.1.2. *Subject pronouns in Early Modern Welsh*

By the end of the sixteenth century, the evidence on the status of preverbal subject pronouns has changed radically, and a number of pieces of evidence point to the conclusion that the pronouns had become clitics hosted by the following verb by this time. The evidence comes mostly in the form of syntactic changes in the Early Modern period which remove the constructions which were used above to confirm their independent status.

The first piece of evidence comes from adverb placement. In low-style texts of the sixteenth century, the frequency of adverbs intervening between a preverbal pronominal subject and the verb appears to drop considerably.[3] This can best be illustrated by citing 'missed opportunities', examples where an intervening adverb would appear to have been a reasonable option, but where that option is not taken. For instance, in (10) the necessity of placing an adverb between a simple pronominal subject and the verb is avoided by the left dislocation of a reduplicated pronoun, and then using a simple pronoun directly before the verb.

(10)   *Ond dydi,   gan na fynni   wneuthur da, Di a   fedri*
         but   you-REDUP since NEG want-2S do-VN   good you PRT can-2S
         ac   a   fynni   wneuthur drwg.
         and PRT want-2S do-VN   evil
         'But you, since you do not want to do good, you can and want to do evil.'
                                                        (*LITA* 18. 29–31 (1653))

This evidence is suggestive although not conclusive, since instances of adverbs following pronouns are not particularly common in Middle Welsh either. We cannot be completely sure whether the scarcity of examples in the later period is due to the loss of the construction or is merely due to chance. Taken with other evidence, however, this does suggest that something systematic is taking place.

The evidence from emphatic reflexives goes in the same direction. By the seventeenth century preverbal pronouns cease to appear in preverbal position modified by emphatic elements. So examples like those above with *ehun* 'himself' are not found. Instead the emphatic element usually follows the verb as in (11).

(11) (a) *Je di weli dy hunan ein bôd ni yn cael agos bôb peth*
yes you see-2S yourself IP be-VN we PROG get-VN almost everything
ar yr ydym ni yn i ofyn . . .
REL PRT are we PROG 3SM-GEN ask-VN
'Yes, you yourself see that we get almost everything that we ask for . . .'
                                                      (*LITA* 22. 2–3 (1653))

(b) *Mi wn fy hun, fôd llawer o lwynogod cyfrwys . . . rhyd y*
I know-1S myself be-VN many of foxes cunning across the
gwledydd . . .
lands . . .
'I know myself that there are many cunning foxes . . . across the lands.'
                                                      (*LITA* 29. 29–31 (1653))

(c) *Mi wn fy hyn pa beth iw wneythyd.*
I know myself what to+3SM-GEN do-VN
'I know myself what to do.'   (IYCA 85. 27, *c*.1758)

Again the evidence is suggestive of phonological weakening of the pronouns, but the scarcity of examples makes firm conclusions difficult to draw.

I now turn to the behaviour of pronouns in conjoined structures. Conjoined preverbal subjects containing pronouns are still found in the sixteenth century, as in (12).

(12)   *. . . velly ti a 'th eppil a gwaad ag a fforward . . .*
        thus you and your descendants PRT arise and go forward
        'Thus you and your descendants will arise and go forward . . .'
                                                      (*RhG* ii. 85. 6–7 (*c*.1588))

There are three other parallel examples in the same passage (*RhG* ii. 84. 21–7).

However, these seem to be amongst the last examples of this kind, and such examples do not seem to be found after the sixteenth century.

Finally, developments in the complementizer system suggest that a closer phonological relationship was developing between preverbal pronouns and their verbs. The particle *a* may not generally be omitted in Middle Welsh, except in three cases. In its use as a relative particle, *a* may be omitted before the third-person singular of the verb *bot* 'to be' (D. Simon Evans 1964: 61). There are also instances of *a* being omitted before verbs beginning with /a/ (Emrys Evans 1958: 24). Finally, *a* is not found following a fronted predicate (cf. example (2) in Chapter 3).

In the late sixteenth century, however, we find omission of the particle in all contexts on a wide scale. In (13) early examples are given of the omission of *a* before a consonant after a simple subject pronoun.[4]

(13) (*a*) *Chwi wyddoch yr ymadrodd a   ddanuones Deo i plant   yr*
you know-2P the words   REL sent   God to children the
Israel . . .
Israel
'You know the words that God sent to the children of Israel . . .'
(*KLlB* 82. 19–20 (1551))

(*b*) *chi vynwch roi   gwr gwirion j varfolaeth ar y groes*
you want-2P put-VN man innocent to death   on the cross
'You want to put an innocent man to death on the cross.'
(*TWRP, Y Dioddefaint*, 122–3 (MS 1552))

(*c*) . . . *ef godes y bore   heb   wybod   yr   llew* . . .
he rose   the morning without know-VN to-the lion
'. . . he got up in the morning without the lion knowing . . .'
(DFf 172. 2–4 (1550–75))

(*d*) . . . *ag ty ddygaist   trays   ar Mauld v[er]ch Morgan* . . .
and you brought-2S violence on Maud ferch   Morgan
'. . . and you raped Maud ferch Morgan . . .'
(Slander case, Brecon Sessions (1580))

The examples in (14) are equivalent cases with a reduplicated pronoun.[5]

(14) (*a*) . . . *y vo   gymerth lywenydd mawr* . . .
he-REDUP took   happiness great
'. . . he became very happy . . .' (*RhG* I. 25. 17 (*c*.1530))

(*b*) *nyni   dynwn gytysav am i   pyrssav yforv*
we-REDUP draw-1P lots   for their purses tomorrow
'We shall draw lots for their purses tomorrow.'
(*TWRP, Y Dioddefaint*, 295–6 (MS 1552))

(*c*) *efo   ddyw[od] lasswyre* . . .
he-REDUP said   psalms
'He said psalms . . .'
(*TWRP, Yr Enaid a'r Corff*, 145 (MS 16th c. [1500–20]))

(*d*) . . . *ag myfi   brifa   hyn arnad ti.*
and I-REDUP prove-1S that on-2S you
'. . . and I shall prove that of you.'
(Slander case, Brecon Sessions (1577))

Examples of omission of *a* following full lexical constituents are rarer, but are found, for instance, in DFf 156. 14; *RhG* i. 14. 20, 16. 9, 85. 16, ii. 79. 16.

In Contemporary Welsh *a* is not in general use in speech (Morgan 1952: 174), and the evidence of the sixteenth-century texts suggests that this is the period to which we should date its disappearance.

It seems reasonable to conclude that the loss of *a* begins in the position after pronominal subjects, an indication that these were becoming phonologically dependent on the following verb. The fact that reduplicated pronouns participate fully in this development alongside simple pronouns may indicate that they too were undergoing weakening, a possibility to which we shall return in Section 5.2.2.1.

Further evidence for the loss of *a* comes from instances of hypercorrection. In Middle Welsh a clause-initial adjectival or nominal predicate is followed consistently by mutation of the verb, but no preverbal particle, as in the example in (15).

(15)   *Llawen uu   pob   un wrth y   gilid o honunt.*
        happy   was-PERF every one to   each other of-them
        'Every one of them was happy towards each other.'   (*PKM* 6. 17–18)

In the sixteenth century examples are found where the preverbal particle *a* follows such predicates. The most plausible explanation for this phenomenon is that *a* in environments where it was historically correct was being elided in speech, and being reinstated in writing. The most straightforward rule for reinstating this *a* would be to write it wherever the verb had undergone soft mutation. However, such a rule would wrongly result in *a* being written after predicative adjectives, and this is precisely what we find. The examples in (16) are from literary texts of the late sixteenth and early seventeenth centuries. For further examples from the same period see D. Simon Evans (1968: 318 n. 1, 326–7).

(16) (*a*) ... *llawen a   vyddai   ganto   ddyfod allan oe   amod.*
              happy PRT would-be with-him come   out   of-his obligation
         '... he would be happy to be released of his obligation.'
                                        (DFf 109. 15 (1550–75))

    (*b*) *Cymwys a   fuasse   gymeryd llwybr vniownach ...*
          fitting   PRT would-be take-VN path   straighter
          'It would have been fitting to take a straighter path ...'
                                        (*DFfEL* 9. 28–9 (1595))

    (*c*) *Addas   a   fyddai   i wragedd argraphu   yr ymadrodd hwn*
          appropriate PRT would-be to women   imprint-VN the expression that
          yn eu   meddyliau ...
          in their thoughts
          'It would be appropriate for women to imprint that expression on their thoughts ...'   (Edward James, *Llyfr y Homiliau*, 3. 173. 6 (1606), (D. Simon Evans 1968: 327))

(d) *Canys pa amlaf   y   byddai   'r moddion, posiblach*
    for   the more-abundant PRT would-be the means,   more-possible
    a   fyddai   'r bobl   i'w   dysgu . . .
    PRT would-be the people to+3P-GEN teach-VN
    'For the more abundant the means would be, the easier the people
    would be to teach . . .'   (*HG* 27. 20–1 (1651))

Parallel hypercorrect insertion of a particle is also found occasionally after the negative marker *ni(d)*, as in (17). In this case the particle is spelt *y*, but the soft mutation indicates that this represents preverbal *a*.

(17)   *Ny   y   ddygais i *ddim* yn lleddrad . . .*
        NEG PRT took-IS I nothing thievishly
        'I stole nothing . . .'   (Slander case, Pembroke Sessions (1611))

Other evidence for the loss of this particle comes from an instance like (18), where the 'wrong' particle is found.

(18)   *Deu wr o   Ddeheubarth, a 'r naill ohanyn y   laddasse wr*
        two men from South-Wales and the one of-them PRT had-killed man
        o   Wynedd, a   ddayth ar negessau y Wynedd . . .
        from Gwynedd PRT came   on errands   to Gwynedd
        'Two men from the South, one of whom had killed a man from
        Gwynedd, came on business to Gwynedd . . .'
                                          (*RhG* ii. 5. 6–7 (?1502–55))

The particle before *laddasse* 'had killed' is *y*, but, since the verb is preceded by the subject, *a* is expected. The mutation, however, is the historically correct soft mutation that normally follows *a*. There are two possible interpretations of this, both of which suggest a development towards the loss of the particle *a*. One possibility is again hypercorrection. The writer knows that particles that are omitted in speech must be used in writing, so adds *y* for the *a* that has been lost in his speech. Another is that we are witnessing an intermediate stage in the loss of *a*, during which it weakens to schwa, thereby merging with the other preverbal particle *y(r)*. For further examples, all dating from the sixteenth and seventeenth centuries, see Morgan (1952: 174).

Taken together, these various pieces of evidence mean that there is little evidence in the Welsh language around 1600 that the preverbal pronouns were any longer independent of the verb. It seems best to regard them as verbal clitics. Note that, as this happens, one property of preverbal subjects remains. In Middle Welsh SVO (and indeed V2 generally) was restricted to main clauses, a fact which was linked in Chapter 3 to the presence of a filled C-position in embedded clauses which blocked movement to C and SpecCP. Even after the development of preverbal clitic pronouns, the restriction of SVO order to main clauses remains. Any analysis of the clitic phenomena must also be consistent with this fact.

5.1.3. *Subject pronouns as clitics*

We can now move on to provide an explicit formulation of this change. There are broadly two approaches to pronominal clitics in the generative literature. The central point of disagreement concerns whether clitics are full arguments of the verb or are agreement markers.

One approach regards them as verbal-agreement elements licensing an empty category (*pro*) in an argument position. This would mean that subject clitics were essentially agreement morphology—that is, AgrS-heads licensing *pro* in subject position. This has been argued to be the case for subject clitics in some Italian dialects (Brandi and Cordin 1989; Rizzi 1986). The crucial evidence in favour of such an analysis is the existence of doubling constructions—that is, constructions where a subject clitic must appear even though there is another subject, as for instance in (19) from the Fiorentino dialect of Italian.

(19)   *Te   tu   parli.*
         you you-CL speak-2s
         'You speak.'   (Brandi and Cordin 1989: 113)

Brandi and Cordin present evidence that the non-clitic subject here is not left dislocated, hence *it* rather than the subject clitic must occupy the subject position. If the clitic does not occupy the subject position, the obvious solution is to suggest that it is an agreement element.[6]

The other approach regards clitics as being base-generated in an argument position and subsequently moving to adjoin to (or incorporate into) a verbal head, leaving a trace in the argument position (Baker and Hale 1990; Kayne 1989*b*, 1991). Since the argument position is filled by the trace of the clitic, doubling is ruled out. Such a case is found in a number of languages, notably with object clitics in French and Standard Italian.

Although often proposed as competing analyses of clitic phenomena, the two seem to reflect two classes of clitics represented in different languages (cf. Rizzi's 1986 contrastive analysis of Italian dialects and French). One possibility is to view them as different degrees on a scale of grammaticalization from full nominal elements (DPs) to reduced nominal elements (D-heads) to fully grammaticalized agreement elements (Agr-heads). In fact, the history of Welsh seems to exemplify the full course of this possible grammaticalization process.

In the current instance, an analysis of sixteenth-century Welsh subject clitics as full arguments correctly generates the grammatical structures. The subject pronoun is base-generated as the head of a DP, and moves via Head Movement to incorporate into the verb (cf. Baker and Hale 1990: 293). In doing so, it leaves a trace that is antecedent-governed in accordance with the Empty Category Principle. IP is not a barrier to this government under any standard definition of barrierhood. Under this approach, as the subject pronouns (diachronically) acquire the status of clitics, the structure in which they participate undergoes the Diachronic Reanalysis indicated in (20), illustrating the simple sentence *mi a af* 'I shall go'. The move to clitic status is realized in the lexicon by a change in the lexical specification of the pronouns, now marked as affixes that must adjoin to a verb in C.

(20) (*a*)

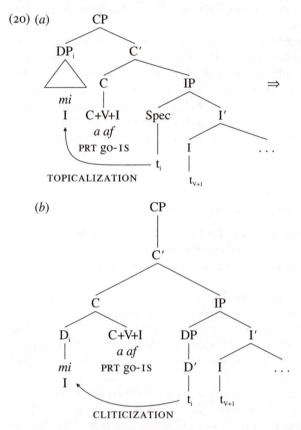

In the new structure, the verb raises to C, and the pronominal head raises to left-adjoin to it. This naturally has a number of consequences.

First, the pronoun is now necessarily adjacent to the verb. An adverbial adjoined to C′ will now precede a pronominal clitic, rather than intervene between it and the verb.

Movement of the pronoun is incorporation into C, rather than the A′-movement of earlier Welsh, hence only the pronoun itself moves. Any modifying material remains behind in the subject DP. Hence emphatic reflexives adjoined to DP remain in postverbal position as in (11).

Analysing clitics in Early Modern Welsh as D-heads originating in an argument position also allows us to account for the fact that we do not find doubling of subject pronouns at this stage of the language. That is, the grammar continues to exclude the construction in (21), even though it is parallel to the grammatical Fiorentino example in (19).

(21)   *Mi feddyliais   i . . .
        I   thought-1s I
        'I thought . . .'

A (referential) pronominal subject is base-generated as an argument of the verb in SpecVP. There it is assigned a theta-role by the verb. It raises to SpecIP (SpecTP) to receive Nominative Case under government from AgrS in the verbal complex in C. It thus 'uses up' AgrS's Nominative Case and, more significantly, the verb's theta-role. Consequently, there can be no other subject position in the structure, and (21) is ruled out because there is no theta-marked position available for the second pronominal subject.

Finally, preverbal subjects still occupy a position within CP. Hence, assuming that the presence of overt material in C is sufficient to block antecedent government of the trace of the clitic by minimality, preverbal subjects cannot co-occur in subordinate clauses with an overt complementizer.

The proposed structure of main clauses with subject clitic subjects in Early Modern Welsh is summarized in (22).

(22)

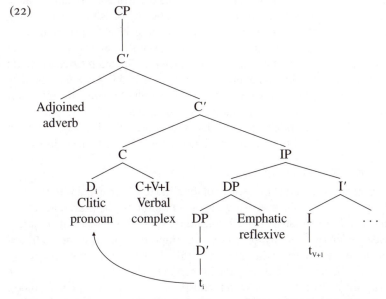

If we attempt to pursue the alternative possible analysis of (subject) clitics as agreement elements, a number of problems arise. On this analysis the clitic would attach to the verb in the same way as other agreement morphology as the verb raises to C. Since this attachment is a feature of the agreement projection, there is no reason why it should be restricted to main clauses. Furthermore, such an account requires that the agreement clitic license a non-overt element in the true subject position. It would be expected that this null subject would alternate with a full subject pronoun in some cases. Doubling constructions like (21) should therefore appear. The fact that they do not is a strong piece of evidence leading us to reject such an analysis for subject clitics in sixteenth-century Welsh.

5.1.3.1. *Is a lowering rule necessary?*

There are two difficulties with the head-movement account of Welsh clitics, either of which might suggest that clitics in sixteenth-century Welsh raise to SpecCP before cliticizing onto the verb.

Before examining the evidence for such a process, we should first consider why it would be undesirable. In the first instance cliticization of a D-head in SpecCP onto the verb in C would constitute a lowering rule. Lowering rules in general violate the ECP, since the moved element does not antecedent-govern its trace (cf. McCloskey 1996: 76, 97).

Furthermore, allowing clitic pronouns to raise to SpecCP before cliticization might create difficulties for the account of the changes above. For instance, how would it follow that the clitic pronoun must be adjacent to the verb? If clitics moved to SpecCP and then lowered onto the verb in C, the movement would presumably be a phonological process—that is, one occurring at PF rather than in the syntax. In order to account for the ungrammaticality of adverbs intervening between the clitic and the verb, we would have to require the clitic to cliticize onto the verb, and put an extra restriction on this process, stating that it is blocked by an intervening adverb or indeed any intervening material. Such a restriction would also have to account for the loss of emphatic reflexives in this position. Emphatic reflexives in postverbal position would then be the result of floating the reflexives off—that is, moving them to right-adjoin to some maximal projection. It is, however, not clear that a cliticization rule that is sensitive to the difference between a verb and a non-verb could be accommodated at a non-syntactic level like PF.

5.1.3.2. *Cliticization and verb-second*

The first difficulty with direct movement of the clitic to adjoin to the verb involves the verb-second rule. Even after its change to clitic status, the preverbal subject pronoun still suffices to satisfy the V2-constraint. We shall see below that there is some evidence for a move away from the use of simple pronouns, but the continued grammaticality of clauses with preverbal simple subject pronouns remains unexplained if the pronoun fails to pass through SpecCP.

The same difficulty is found in West Flemish, as analysed in Haegeman (1990). West Flemish has a V2-constraint that may be satisfied by a preverbal subject clitic

(Haegeman 1990: 351–4). Since (23) is grammatical, the subject clitic *ze* must satisfy the constraint. Assuming that the V2-constraint directly or indirectly requires that SpecCP be filled, this suggests the clitic moves through SpecCP before adjoining to the verb in C.

(23)   *Ze*   *werkt zie.*
        she-CL works she
        'She's working.'   (Haegeman 1990: 338)

Furthermore in West Flemish, a subject clitic prevents an adverb from appearing in preverbal position, as can be seen from the ungrammaticality of (24).

(24)   **Morgen   ze   werkt.*
        tomorrow she-CL works
        'Tomorrow she's working.'   (Haegeman 1990: 354)

Preverbal adverbs in West Flemish must occupy SpecCP—that is, there are no pre-topic adverbs as there are in Middle Welsh. This strongly suggests that the clitic passes through SpecCP.[7] Haegeman suggests that the subject clitic satisfies the V2-constraint by topicalizing to SpecCP, and cliticizing and thereby receiving case at PF. The sixteenth-century Welsh case is parallel: we are faced with the problem of why a sentence where only a subject clitic precedes the verb is grammatical if the derivation of such a sentence leaves SpecCP empty.

In the Welsh case, I shall not attempt to suggest that the subject clitic in the structure in (22) actually satisfies the V2-constraint. Instead, it seems that the clitic is a marked exception to the constraint given in the peripheral grammar. In Section 5.2.2 I shall present evidence that Welsh went through a stage where, as we expect with features marked as exceptional, use of the exception rule was reduced by the replacement of the clitic with elements that did satisfy the V2-constraint. However, I shall argue that the eventual loss of V2 allowed the preverbal subject clitics to survive.

5.1.3.3. *Clitics and clausal coordination*

A second problem is found in the behaviour of clitic pronouns in conjoined structures. It might be expected that, in a language with subject clitics, the clitic would have to be repeated in conjoined clauses. In (22), the verb and object do not form a single constituent excluding the subject, hence coordination at a level below the subject but above the verb should be ruled out.

There seems to be some cross-linguistic variation with respect to whether subject clitics must be repeated in conjoined clauses. For instance, omission of the subject clitic in the second conjunct is fully acceptable in Dutch, less so in French, and ungrammatical in northern Italian dialects (cf. Rizzi 1986: 402–7).

However, in Early Modern Welsh, even after the subject pronouns become clitics, conjoined clauses involving shared subject pronouns do not require the subject to be repeated in the second conjunct. Examples from sixteenth-century texts are given in (25).[8]

(25) (a) *A   phan welodd vorwyn dec . . . ef ai   herfynniodd ac*
        and when saw   maiden fair   he PRT+3S-ACC asked   and
        ai   duc   adref at ei arglwydd ai   veistyr.
        PRT+3S-ACC brought home to his lord   and-his master
        'And when he saw a fair maiden . . . he asked for her and brought her
        home to his lord and master.'   (CHSS 118. 21–2 (1574–1604))

     (b) *A   hwy a   gawsant wenwyn ag a'ü   roesant yddo   ef.*
        and they PRT took-3P poison and PRT+3S-ACC gave-3P to-3SM him
        'And they took poison and gave it to him.'
                                        (YAL 284. 37 (MS *c.*1590 [post-1515]))

There are two possible views of this construction. On one view, it raises considerable difficulties. As discussed in Section 4.2.1, it is standardly assumed that only like constituents may conjoin. The second clause is a C′, since it apparently shares its topic with the first clause. If so, we must conclude that in each case the first conjunct below the pronoun (*ai herfynniodd* 'asked for her' in (25*a*)) is a C′-constituent. However, if the subject clitic *ef* raises at S-structure to left-adjoin to the verb in C, then C′ includes the subject clitic. Such an analysis would require a solution along the lines of West Flemish subject clitics, involving a lowering rule at PF.

There is another possibility, however. If we continue with the analysis developed in Section 4.2 and assume that the second conjunct has the ability to host a null topic operator, then conjoined structures like (25) actually involve coordination of full clauses (CPs). The second conjunct has its own separate topic position (SpecCP), occupied by an operator binding a variable in subject position. This operator is coindexed with the subject of the preceding clause. The proposed structure is given in full in (26).

(26)   . . . [[$_{CP}$ [$_C$ *ef$_i$ ai*   *herfynniodd$_V$*] [$_{IP}$ [$_{DP}$ t$_i$] t$_V$ [$_{VP}$ t$_i$ t$_V$ pro]]]
                    he PRT+3S-ACC asked

              ac
              and

              [$_{CP}$ Op$_j$ [$_C$ *ai*   *duc*] [$_{IP}$ t$_j$ t$_V$ [$_{VP}$ t$_j$ t$_V$ pro *adref*]]]]
                    PRT+3S-ACC brought   home

If this representation is correct, then the first conjunct involves only the single violation of V2 that has already been noted. Beyond this, however, there is no need for any other exceptions, whether to V2, to the clitic status of subject pronouns, or to the ban on lowering rules.

Having dealt with these apparent difficulties, we can continue to maintain that pronominal subjects in Early Modern Welsh may move at S-structure to cliticize onto the verb by adjoining to C. We conclude that this is an exception to V2, and must be marked as such in the peripheral grammar.

5.2. CONSEQUENCES OF THE CHANGE IN STATUS OF SUBJECT PRONOUNS

It seems reasonable to assume that a move to clitic status is essentially a phonological change. In the process of language acquisition, children register the lack of stress generally placed on the pronouns and interpret them as being dependent upon the head to which they are habitually adjacent. The most 'robust' evidence regarding their status is thus phonological, and any syntactic indications are of marginal value at best. In this sense, all of the syntactic changes discussed so far are in fact trailing changes. In other words, the disappearance of these constructions is itself a consequence of the reanalysis of the pronouns as clitics rather than a cause of it. They were dealt with above because they were useful diagnostics for clitic status. I now go on to examine other changes, not diagnostic of clitic status, but which can be interpreted as following on from that change of status. I distinguish between the syntactic changes below and those above not for theoretical reasons, since both sets are reflections of a phonological change, but because the changes discussed so far are straightforward diagnostics of clitic status. The changes that follow involve somewhat more involved argumentation.

5.2.1. *Expletive subjects*

I now turn to the development of the expletive construction in the history of Welsh, examining and evaluating the possibility that syntactic change in the restrictions on this construction can be derived from the appearance of clitic pronouns. One major cause of the spread of verb-initial word order at lower stylistic levels is the spread of the expletive construction beyond the environment to which it is restricted in the Middle Welsh tales. The construction is discussed and exemplified further by D. Simon Evans (1968: 328–35), from where a number of the following examples have been taken. I also draw on examples from *Geiriadur Prifysgol Cymru (GPC)*.

Recall from Section 3.1 that in V2 main clauses, Middle Welsh has the option of inserting an expletive subject *ef* in topic position. An example is (3*a*) in Chapter 3, repeated here as (27).

(27) *Ef a   doeth makwyueit a   gueisson ieueinc y*
      it PRT came squires   and lads   young   to+3SM-GEN
      diarchenu . . .
      disrobe-VN
      'There came squires and young lads to disrobe him . . .'   (*PKM* 4. 8–9)

Before changes in this construction can be discussed, it is first necessary to justify the assumption that *ef* in sentences like (27) is an expletive subject at all, since this is not the dominant position in the literature. D. Simon Evans (1964: 172) lists this use of *ef* alongside preverbal particles, whilst describing it as a personal pronoun. Lewis and Pedersen (1937: 145) call it a preverbal particle. This terminology seems to derive from too heavy a reliance upon the status of the cognate 'presentential particle' *fe* in Contemporary Welsh. Instead I shall show that *ef* is an expletive subject showing similar properties to the expletive subjects *it* and *there* in English, as illustrated in (28) and (29).

(28)   *It seems that Mary will be late.*

(29)   *There will be a meeting tomorrow.*

In order to do this, I shall examine the syntactic properties of the construction in Middle Welsh in some detail, showing that its behaviour is very different from that expected of a verbal particle. For instance, unlike Contemporary Welsh *fe*, *ef a* in Middle Welsh is restricted to co-occur with third-person-singular verb forms, suggesting that the verb in fact agrees with it.

5.2.1.1. *Expletive subjects in Middle Welsh*

Middle Welsh of the thirteenth and fourteenth centuries manifests a number of restrictions on the use of the expletive construction. These restrictions are paralleled by expletive constructions in other languages. The system to be described is based on exhaustive searching of a number of early Middle Welsh texts—namely, *Culhwch ac Olwen* (*CO*), *Owein*, *Pedeir Keinc y Mabinogi* (*PKM*), *Peredur*, and *Ystorya de Carolo Magno* (*YCM*). Examination of some later, fifteenth-century texts—notably, *Chwedleu Seith Doethon Rufein* (*SDR*) and *Ffordd y Brawd Odrig* (*FfBO*)—shows that it also holds there. It may also be valid for a number of other Middle Welsh texts—for instance, *Brut Dingestow* (*BD*), *Chwedlau Odo*, *Historia Gruffud vab Kenan* (*HGK*), and 'Mabinogi Iessu Grist' (*MIG*) (Peniarth 14, Part II version).

In this system expletive *ef* is permitted exclusively in three contexts. First, it may be used to fill the empty subject position before a well-defined set of verbs, all of which are intransitive change of state verbs (unaccusatives), and most of which are verbs of motion. Examples are found with the verbs *bot* 'to be' (*FfBO* 51. 31; *HGK* 22. 8; *Owein*, 546), *kerdet* 'to walk' (*Peredur*, 36. 6), *kyuaruot* 'to meet, come across, come towards' (*Peredur*, 16. 21, 28. 12; *SDR* 572), *kyuodi* 'to arise' (*PKM* 18. 27; *Peredur*, 69. 6), *kyhwrd* 'to hit upon' (*Peredur*, 52. 21), *daruot* 'to finish, come to an end' (*SDR* 98, 892, 924; *YCM* 66. 11), *dyuot* 'to come' (*CO* 6; *Owein*, 152; *MIG* 189. 12; *Peredur*, 11. 22, 26. 16, 27. 6, 27. 21, 31. 15, 41. 9, 48. 26, 51. 8; *PKM* 4. 8, 65. 1; *SDR* 381, 740, 907; *YCM* 78. 14, 84. 18, 132. 24), and *mynet* 'to go' (*ChCC* 60. 7; *YCM* 105. 31). The following examples are typical of this use of the expletive subject in these texts:

(30) (a) *Ac yn yr vn   wythnos ef a   gyfaruu ac   ef   vn   marchawc ar*
     and in the same week   it PRT met   with him one knight   on
     bumthec . . .
     fifteen
     'And in the same week there met with him sixteen knights . . .'

                           (*Peredur*, 16. 20–2)

    (b) *Ac yn ol y   twrwf   ef a   daw cawat adoer . . .*
       and after the commotion it PRT come shower very-cold
       'And after the commotion there will come a very cold shower . . .'

                            (*Owein*, 152–3)

This pattern is typical of expletive subjects in other languages. In English, expletive *there* appears with unaccusative verbs (31) but not with transitive verbs (32).

(31)   *There arrived three ships in the harbour.*

(32)   **There ate Steven the apples.*

Secondly, expletive *ef* is found with impersonal verb forms, glossed below using passives, from whatever verb they are derived, as in (33).[9]

(33) (a) *Ef a   dywetpwyt idaw.*
      it PRT was-said to-him
      'It was said to him.'   (*PKM* 80. 9–10)

    (b) *. . . ac eissoes ef a   anet   meibon idaw   ef . . .*
       and yet   it PRT was-born sons   to-3SM him
      '. . . and yet sons were born to him . . .'   (*YCM* 30. 6–7)

Again, this is a typical environment for an expletive construction to appear cross-linguistically. In German, expletive *es* 'it' appears in impersonal constructions as in (34).

(34)   *Es wurde   getanzt.*
      it became danced
      'There was dancing.'

And thirdly *ef* is found in the topic position of some main clauses containing postposed clausal arguments. Postposed clausal arguments are found with a number of verbs such as *bot agos* 'to be almost' (*Owein*, 546), *dywedut* 'to say' (*Peredur*, 45. 22; *YCM* 158. 6), *gallael* 'to be possible' (*PKM* 6. 1, 83. 10, 68. 28; *YCM* 31. 2, 73. 30), *peri* 'to cause' (*YCM* 116. 2) and *tebygu* 'to suppose', and with the present subjunctive of the verb *gwneuthur* 'to do' (*YCM* 141. 10, 142. 8).[10] Examples are given in (35). Evidence of later texts suggests that we should add at least *damweinaw* 'to happen' to this list.

(35) (a) *Ac ef a   tebygei   Owein bot   yr awyr yn   edrinaw*
and it PRT supposed Owain be-VN the air   PROG reverberate-VN
rac meint y   gweidi . . .
from amount the shouting
'And Owain supposed (it seemed to Owain) that the air was reverberating
with the noise of the shouting . . .'   (*Owein*, 346–7)

(b) *Nyt ef a   wnel   Duw . . . tybyaw   Gwenwlyd o 'e*
NEG it PRT do-SUBJ God   suspect-VN Gwenwlydd of 3SM-GEN
vot   ynn anffydlawn ymi . . .
be-VN PRD unfaithful   to-me
'Let not God suspect Gwenwlydd of being unfaithful to me . . .'
(*YCM* 140. 20–1)

These verbs parallel the common use of extraposed clausal arguments linked to
an expletive subjects in other European languages as with the English verb *happen*
in (36).

(36)   *It (so) happened that Matthew won.*

Superficially, there are two counter-examples to these rules, namely the cases in
(37), whereas an expletive subject appears with the transitive verbs *darogan* 'to
foretell' and *gwanu* 'to strike'.

(37) (a) *Ac ef a 'e   gwant y Sarassin ef yn y   daryan dyrnawt*
and it PRT+3S-ACC struck the Saracen him in his shield blow
mawr . . .
great
'And the Saracen struck him a great blow in his shield . . .'
(*YCM* 71. 21–2)

(b) *Ef a 'e   daroganvs Merdin ef ynni val hynn . . .*
it PRT+3S-ACC foretold   Merlin it to-us like this
'Merlin foretold it to us like this . . .'   (*HGK* 5. 22–3)

Note that in both cases the direct object of the verb is a masculine third-person-
singular pronoun. An analysis of these examples in harmony with the restrictions
described above could be attempted if *ef* in topic position could be interpreted as
a direct object pronoun rather than an expletive. Initially this seems to be ruled out
by the presence of another object pronoun *ef* in the object position itself. However,
other evidence from Middle Welsh suggests that such configurations, with a
resumptive object pronoun acting as a variable A'-bound from SpecCP, are possible
even where the distance between the two is very short.

If this were the case, the structure of (37a) would be as in (38), with the pronoun
ef in SpecCP binding a resumptive pronoun variable in object position.

(38) [_{CP} *ef*_i [_{C'} *a'e*   *gwant* [_{IP} [_{VP} *y*   *Sarassin* t_V *ef*_i . . .]]]]
          him PRT+3S-ACC struck   the Saracen   him

Recall from Section 3.4.3 that there are other examples in Middle Welsh of such resumptive pronouns occurring in the extraction site of topicalization. Examples are frequent in *Y Bibyl Ynghymraec*, from which the following is taken:

(39)   *Davyd, kyt   bei   lleiaf   o 'y vrodyr   a   yeuaf,   a*
          David although was-SUBJ smallest of his brothers and youngest PRT
          detholes Duw yn   vrenhin ef . . .
          selected God PRD king   him
          'Although he was the smallest of his brothers and the youngest, God
          selected David as king . . .'   (*BY* 27. 22–3)

Such examples would generally be ambiguous without the resumptive pronoun. For instance, in (39) the nominal topic could have been extracted from either subject or object position, and there is no other evidence to show which. It would, therefore, be ambiguous between 'David chose God as king . . .' and 'God chose David as king . . .'. The resumptive pronoun marks out the extraction site as being after the Noun Phrase *Duw* 'God', and therefore makes it clear that, since the subject must precede the object, *Duw* is in subject position, and *Davyd* has been extracted from object position. The sentences in (37) can be reduced to fairly unexceptional examples of this construction.

The conditions on the use of *ef* in topic position therefore reduce to three environments—unaccusative verbs, impersonal verbs, and constructions with clausal arguments. Expletive constructions are widespread in European languages, occurring in all the Germanic languages and in French. These environments are all ones in which expletives typically appear in these languages. Added to the internal evidence, this comparative evidence confirms our identification of *ef* in Middle Welsh as an expletive subject.

5.2.1.2. *A comparative account of Middle Welsh expletives*

In this section I shall review some of the cross-linguistic differences in the properties of expletives, discussing the base-position and categorial status of the Middle Welsh expletive in this comparative context. The discussion is based mainly on Belletti (1988), Cardinaletti (1990a), Christensen (1991), Rögnvaldsson and Thráinsson (1990), Sigurðsson (1990), and Tomaselli (1986).

Expletive subjects in V2-languages divide into those that disappear in embedded and inversion contexts and those that do not. For instance, the German expletive *es*, as in (40a), is ungrammatical in an inversion context (40b) (Cardinaletti 1990a: 136–7; Tomaselli 1986: 175–7). The situation is similar with the Icelandic expletive *það* (Zaenen 1983: 492–4).[11] Contrast this with the expletive *det* in Norwegian (41) and in Swedish (42), which must be retained under inversion.

(40) (*a*) *Es ist ein Junge gekommen.*
      it is a   boy   come
      'There came a boy.'

   (*b*) *Gestern   ist (*es) ein Junge gekommen.*
      yesterday is (it) a   boy   come
      'Yesterday there came a boy.'   (Vikner 1994: 132)

(41) (*a*) *Det har kommet lingvister hit   i dag.*
      it   has come   linguists here today
      'There have come linguists here today.'

   (*b*) *I dag har det kommet lingvister hit.*
      today has it   come   linguists here
      'Today there have come linguists here.'   (Christensen 1991: 141, 149)

(42) (*a*) *Det kom   många studenter till mötet.*
      it   came many   students to the-meeting
      'There came many students to the meeting.'

   (*b*) *Igår   kom det   många studenter till mötet.*
      yesterday came there many   students to the-meeting
      'Yesterday there came many students to the meeting.'

In this respect, Middle Welsh follows the German pattern. The expletive is possible neither in inversion contexts nor in subordinate clauses, and we find no sentences like (43) to parallel (27).

(43)   **Yna y   doeth ef makwyueit a   gueisson ieueinc y*
      then PRT came it squires   and lads   young to+3SM-GEN
      diarchenu . . .
      disrobe-VN
      'Then there came squires and young lads to disrobe him . . .'

There is nevertheless evidence for a postverbal null expletive subject. In (44), the subject *ef* 'he' appears after a PP-complement, rather than in the immediately postverbal subject position. The obvious conclusion to draw is that the subject position is occupied by a null expletive subject marked as [e]. Whereas, in preverbal topic position, this expletive subject has overt form as *ef*, in postverbal position it is always null.

(44)   *. . . ac yn y   deudecuet dyd wedy Calan Mei yd   aeth* [e]
         and in the twelfth   day after May   Day PRT went
      [$_{PP}$ *o   'r byt   hvn*] *ef y tragywyd*[avl] *teyrnas   wlat nef . . .*
         from the world this   he to eternal   kingdom land heaven
      'And on the twelfth day after May Day he went from this world to the eternal kingdom of the land of heaven . . .'   (*BD* 207. 22–3)

There is, furthermore, variation with respect to whether the expletive imposes an unaccusative restriction. As has been seen, Middle Welsh, along with English, imposes such a restriction. German (marginally) (45a) and Icelandic (fully) (45b) allow expletives to co-occur with transitive verbs.

(45) (a) *Es stieß   ihn ein Soldat von   der Brücke.*
           it pushed him a   soldier from the bridge
           'A soldier pushed him from the bridge.'   (Cardinaletti 1990a: 139)

      (b) *Það hafa einhverjir stúdentar sennilega stolið smjörinu.*
           it   have some   students   probably stolen the-butter
           'Some students have probably stolen the butter.'   (Sigurðsson 1990: 50)

The comparative data are summarized in Table 5.2.

TABLE 5.2. *Cross-linguistic properties of expletive constructions*

Syntactic feature	English	German, Icelandic	Swedish, Norwegian	Middle Welsh
Verb-second?	no	yes	yes	yes
Expletive in inversion contexts?	yes	no	yes	no
Transitive expletives?	no	yes	no	no

Let us first consider how the distribution of the expletives in inversion and subordinate contexts can be accounted for. Clearly in languages of the type exemplified by Swedish and Norwegian, the expletive is base-generated in a postverbal (post-C) position, say SpecIP, where it remains in embedded and inversion contexts. In other cases it moves to SpecCP. This accounts for its presence in both types of clause.

A natural way to account for the different behaviour of German *es* would be to make a difference in the lexical specification of *es*, base-generating it in SpecCP, rather than SpecIP as specified for *det* (Tomaselli 1986). In German clauses lacking inversion, as in (46a), *es* occupies the topic position SpecCP. In an inversion context in (46b) the topic position is filled by an adverb, leaving SpecIP as the only position for the expletive. If the German expletive is base-generated in SpecCP, it is no surprise to find that (46b) is ungrammatical. Similar reasoning applies to the embedded context in (46c).

(46) (a) [$_{CP}$ *es wurde*$_i$ [$_{IP}$ [$_{VP}$ *getanzt*] t$_i$]]
           it became   danced

      (b) *[$_{CP}$ *heute wurde*$_i$ [$_{IP}$ *es* [$_{VP}$ *getanzt*] t$_i$]]
           today became   it   danced

      (c) *. . . [$_{CP}$ *daß* [$_{IP}$ *es* [$_{VP}$ *getanzt*] *wurde*]]
              that   it   danced   was

If, on the other hand, *es* appears in SpecIP and then raises, the obligatory nature of this raising is not motivated. Neither (46*b*) nor (46*c*) violates any other constraint. The example in (46*b*) is a perfectly well-formed verb-second clause in all respects other than the expletive. In order to rule these out while maintaining that expletives raise from SpecIP, some special appeal has to be made—for instance, to the Avoid Pronoun Principle (Cardinaletti 1990*a*; Chomsky 1981). On this account, C in German licenses (but does not identify) a null subject in SpecIP. This allows a null expletive subject in SpecIP, but nowhere else. Indeed there can be no other null subjects in German. Since a null expletive is possible in SpecIP, according to the Avoid Pronoun Principle, it must be used if it can be. Only pragmatic factors could prevent the use of a null pronoun. Since the pronoun in this case is expletive, however, pragmatic factors cannot require an overt pronoun, so the null subject must be used. However, such special pleading is not necessary on the SpecCP account. In the absence of good evidence to the contrary, it seems reasonable to conclude that lexical differences in the base-position of the expletives provide the best account of variation in their behaviour in inversion and embedded contexts.

For an answer to the question of why there should be restrictions on the type of verb compatible with expletives in some languages, we can start from Belletti's (1988) analysis of unaccusatives. Belletti's principal aim is to derive an account of Definiteness Effects in expletive constructions. Almost all of the Germanic and Romance languages with expletive subjects show such effects: the postverbal DP may be indefinite but not definite.[12] In the examples in (47) from English (47*a*) and German (47*b*), the sentence is ungrammatical if the definite article is added.

(47) (a) *There sailed (*the) two ships into the harbour.*

    (b) *Es hat ein/*der Mann die Marie geküßt.*
       it has a   the man   the Mary kissed
       'A/The man kissed Mary.'   (Belletti 1988: 14)

Belletti (1988) derives Definiteness Effects from an account of Case-assignment. Following the Unaccusative Hypothesis (Burzio 1986; Perlmutter 1978) she assumes that the surface subject of an unaccusative verb (*two ships* in (47*a*)) is actually its internal argument, to which a theme theta-role is assigned. It has generally been assumed that unaccusative verbs lack the ability to assign Accusative Case to this argument, hence it raises to subject position to receive Nominative. Belletti argues that unaccusative verbs, although unable to assign Accusative, may assign inherent Partitive case to their internal arguments. This Case carries a meaning of 'part of, any' and is thus incompatible with a definite Noun Phrase (DP). So, the English sentence in (47*a*) would have a structure something like that in (48*a*).

(48) (a) [$_{CP}$ [$_{IP}$ *there* [$_{VP}$ *sailed two ships into the harbour*]]]

    (b) [$_{CP}$ [$_{IP}$ *two ships* [$_{VP}$ *sailed into the harbour*]]]

The verb assigns Partitive to its internal argument *two ships*, and Infl assigns Nominative to *there*. Partitive Case assignment is optional. If the option of assigning it is not taken, then the internal argument must raise to SpecIP to receive Nominative Case as in (48*b*).

Middle Welsh expletive constructions show no Definiteness Effect, although there is a 'thematic' effect—namely, a requirement that the associate DP be new information in the discourse (cf. the examples in (30)). The restriction on subject type has been described in a similar way for Icelandic, as a restriction against topical subjects (Sigurðsson 1990: 47). In languages such as Middle Welsh and Icelandic, the thematic effect associated with expletive constructions is clearly not a syntactic phenomenon, and an account in terms of Case Theory seems inappropriate. Definiteness Effects in other languages may also turn out actually to be of the same order. However, the central idea remains—namely, that unaccusative verbs may assign Case to their internal arguments, freeing them from the need to raise to receive Case. This allows an expletive to appear in the usual subject position and receive Case there. I shall ignore the question of Partitive Case here, supposing for the moment simply that unaccusative verbs assign Case (of an unspecified kind) to their internal arguments. This provides us with the basis of an account of a subset of the cross-linguistic differences in the behaviour of expletives.

Having examined the types of variation associated with expletive constructions, we can now consider how the differences can be accounted for, and see how Middle Welsh fits in to the general pattern.

Consider first the English situation in (49). English is not V2, so the expletive subject must be in the highest specifier position of IP. This is also the only position to which Nominative Case can be assigned. In an unaccusative construction, the internal argument receives Case under theta-marking from the verb. In the transitive construction, the external argument *a boy* cannot receive the Case reserved for assignment to internal arguments, nor can it raise to SpecIP to receive Nominative Case, since SpecIP is already occupied by *there*. The transitive expletive construction in (49*b*) is therefore ungrammatical.

(49) (a)   [$_{CP}$ [$_{IP}$ *there* [$_{VP}$ *arrived*$_V$ *a ship in the harbour*]]]

    (b) *[$_{CP}$ [$_{IP}$ *there* [$_{VP}$ *ate* [$_?$ *a boy*] *an apple*]]]

In Icelandic, transitive expletive constructions are possible. We can assume, given that it disappears in inversion contexts, that expletive *það* in Icelandic is base-generated in SpecCP (Rögnvaldsson and Thráinsson 1990: 19–20). In the unaccusative construction, the internal argument receives Case directly from the verb. This leaves two possibilities for *það*. Either it receives Nominative in SpecCP (under agreement with Infl in C); or it does not require Case, and Nominative is left unassigned.[13]

In the transitive construction, the internal argument receives Accusative. The external argument can raise to SpecIP to receive Nominative Case from C under government (cf. Platzack 1986). Since *það* is base-generated in SpecCP, and neither it nor its trace occupies SpecIP, this raising is not blocked. The relevant structures are given in (50).

(50) (a) [$_{CP}$ *Það eru*$_V$ [$_{IP}$ t$_V$ [$_{VP}$ *komnir gestir hingað*]]]
            are   arrived guests here
            'There have arrived some guests.'

      (b) [$_{CP}$ *Það hafa*$_V$ [$_{IP}$ *einhverjir stúdentar* t$_V$ [$_{VP}$ *stolið smjörinu*]]]
              have   some   students   stolen the-butter
             'Some students have stolen the butter.'   (Sigurðsson 1990: 48, 50)

There remains the question of Case-assignment to *það*. If it is assumed that *það* does not need Case, there is no problem (cf. Thráinsson 1994: 158). If *það* does need Case, then it is not clear how it can be assigned to it in the transitive construction, where Nominative is assigned to the external argument of the verb. If this alternative were chosen, we would need to propose a new mechanism for Case-assignment in this configuration.

As currently formulated, the ability of the internal argument to raise to SpecIP voids any Definiteness Effects imposed by Case-assignment within the VP. A DP that raises to SpecIP receives Nominative Case, and should not therefore be subject to Definiteness Effects. If, however, these effects are not syntactic in nature, this is in fact a welcome result.

Like Icelandic, Swedish and Norwegian are V2-languages, but, unlike Icelandic, they do not allow transitive expletive constructions. The Swedish situation is illustrated in (51). The expletive *det* must in any case be base-generated in SpecIP, since it, unlike the expletive subject in Icelandic and German, does not disappear in inversion contexts (cf. (40)–(42) above). If so, then when *det* appears in sentence-initial position, it must have raised there from SpecIP. This allows an unaccusative expletive construction (51a) in the usual way, with the internal argument of the verb receiving Case from the unaccusative verb in a VP-internal position.

(51) (a)   [$_{CP}$ *det*$_i$ *kom*$_V$ [$_{IP}$ t$_i$ t$_V$ [$_{VP}$ t$_V$ *många studenter till mötet*]]]
                came   many   students   to   the-meeting
            'There came many students to the meeting.'

      (b) *[$_{CP}$ *det*$_i$ *köper*$_V$ [$_{IP}$ t$_i$ t$_V$ [$_{VP}$ *många studenter* t$_V$ *böcker*]]]
               buy   many   students   books
             'There buy many students books.'

      (c) *[$_{CP}$ *igår*   *köpte*$_V$ [$_{IP}$ det t$_V$ [$_{VP}$ *många studenter* t$_V$ *böcker*]]]
               yesterday bought   many   students   books
            'Yesterday there bought many students books.'

In a transitive expletive construction, the trace of *det* in (51*b*) or, in an inversion context (51*c*), *det* itself prevents the external argument from raising to SpecIP. It is thus deprived of Case, resulting in ungrammaticality. It makes no difference in fact whether the expletive itself requires Case or not. If it does, the external argument could not receive Case if it raised to SpecIP. But even if *det* does not need Case, it still prevents the external argument from raising to the only Case-marked position SpecIP.

In many respects, Middle Welsh is like Swedish. It is a V2-language in which expletive subjects are found with unaccusative verbs, but not with transitive verbs. The crucial difference is that, in inversion contexts, the expletive subject disappears in Middle Welsh but not in Swedish. In Icelandic, such behaviour was attributed to the fact that the Icelandic expletive subject *það* was base-generated in SpecCP. We can generalize this to Welsh, and say that the expletive subject in Middle Welsh is base-generated in SpecCP. However, if we suggest this, we cannot argue that the expletive prevents the external argument from raising to SpecIP. Instead, we must suggest that, even if it raises to SpecIP, it will not be saved. This will be the case only if the expletive subject *ef* itself requires (Nominative) Case. This is a reasonable conclusion, especially given that *ef* is itself the third-person-singular masculine pronoun, and thus clearly a DP, rather than, say, an AP. If it is base-generated in SpecCP, it receives Nominative from Infl in C under agreement.[14] Having assigned Case to SpecCP, Infl cannot assign it also to SpecIP. Therefore, raising of the external argument to SpecIP will not help. The external argument in a transitive expletive construction will therefore always fail to receive Case. The structure proposed for Middle Welsh expletives is given in (52), the grammatical unaccusative structure in (52*a*), the ungrammatical transitive one in (52*b*).

(52) (*a*) [$_{CP}$ *ef a-doeth* [$_{IP}$ t$_V$ [$_{VP}$ t$_V$ *gwr*]]]
         came   man
         'There came a man.'

    (*b*) *[$_{CP}$ *ef a-welodd* [$_{IP}$ *Arthur* t$_V$ [$_{VP}$ t$_V$ *farchawc*]]]
         saw   Arthur   knight
         'There saw Arthur a knight.'

We can generalize our conclusions for Welsh back to Swedish, suggesting that it is preferable to analyse Swedish *det* as a Case-marked element.[15]

This then leaves us with the question of how Middle Welsh differs from Icelandic. We have concluded that, in both languages, the expletive is base-generated in SpecCP. How then do we account for the presence of transitive expletives in Icelandic but not in Middle Welsh? In the light of the two possibilities that we suggested for Icelandic above, the difference can be accounted for in one of two ways. The first possibility is that Middle Welsh *ef* is nominal, a DP requiring Case, whereas Icelandic *það* is adverbial, an *AP* not requiring Case. Alternatively, if both are Case-marked, then Icelandic must possess some additional case-assigning mechanism not found in Middle Welsh, with which to assign Case to *það*.[16] I shall assume the first, since it requires the postulation of lexical rather than parametric differences between the two languages.

In this section I have sketched out an account of the differences in behaviour of expletive constructions in which they are derived from differences in lexical properties of the expletive elements themselves, specifically whether the expletives are DPs requiring Case or APs not requiring Case, and the structural position in which they are required to base-generate. Specifically for the Welsh case, I have argued that the Middle Welsh expletive *ef* is a DP base-generated in SpecCP. The cross-linguistic findings are summarized in Table 5.3.

TABLE 5.3. *Cross-linguistic variation in the lexical properties of expletive subjects*

Language	Expletive subject	Lexical entry	
		Category	Base-position
English	*there*	DP	SpecIP
Icelandic	*það*	AP	SpecCP
Middle Welsh	*ef*	DP	SpecCP
Swedish	*det*	DP	SpecIP

This account of the unaccusative restriction on the expletive construction in Middle Welsh transfers to cases of expletive subjects with impersonal verbs. The structure of an impersonal expletive construction is given in (53).

(53) $[_{CP}$ *ef a* *rodet* $[_{IP}$ t$_V$ $[_{VP}$ t$_V$ *vdvnt* *y* *llog oreu*$]]]$
      it PRT was-given   to-them the ship best
      'There was given to them the best ship.'

The impersonal verb, like the unaccusative verb, assigns Case to its internal argument, leaving Nominative Case free to be assigned to the expletive subject *ef*.

The impersonal construction provides further evidence on the nature of the Case assigned to internal arguments of unaccusative and impersonal verbs. In both Middle Welsh and Modern Literary Welsh, the pronominal internal argument of an impersonal verb appears with an accusative object clitic.[17] Examples are given from Modern Literary Welsh in (54). Example (54a) shows the third-person-singular accusative clitic *'i* (followed by absence of mutation) with a transitive verb. There is clitic doubling with the full pronoun *ef*, which is not marked for case. The same accusative clitic shows up in the impersonal construction in (54b).

(54) (a) *Fe'i*   *gwelais ef.*
         PRT+3S-ACC saw-1S him
         'I saw him.'

(b) *Fe'i*   *gwelwyd*   *ef.*
PRT+3S-ACC saw-IMPERS him
'He was seen.'

This suggests that, despite Burzio's Generalization (Burzio 1986: 178–9), impersonal verbs in Modern Literary Welsh and in earlier varieties of Welsh assign
Accusative Case to their internal arguments. We conclude that the case assigned
to the internal argument in (53), and presumably also in the parallel unaccusative
construction, is Accusative.

This leaves us only with the case of expletives in main clauses with clausal
complements in (35). The ability of expletive *ef* to appear there is not particularly surprising, given the analysis of the expletive that has been followed so far.
Clausal arguments are not DPs and do not, therefore, require Case. Provided
that such clausal arguments appear in a theta-marked position it is possible to
assign Nominative Case to the expletive subject regardless of whether the verb is
transitive or intransitive (unaccusative).

5.2.1.3.   *Expletives in later Middle Welsh and Early Modern Welsh*

Already in the early Middle Welsh period there are texts that contain the occasional
counter-example to the general rules on the distribution of expletive subjects
presented in Section 5.2.1.1. These cases are given in (55), where an expletive
subject appears in a transitive construction with *gwelet* 'to see' and *gouwyaw* 'to
visit'.

(55) (a) *Ac ef a   weles yr ebestyl y   heneit en   wynnach nor   eiry.*
and it PRT saw   the apostles her soul PRD whiter   than-the snow
'And the apostles saw her soul whiter than snow.'

(GWV 10. 31. 5–6 (c.1250))

(b) *Ef a   ovwynha Duw y bobyl o   lau tramwy . . .*
it PRT visit   God his people from hand passing
'God will visit his people with a passing hand . . .'

(MIG 212. 21 (1300–25))

In later texts we find many more cases of expletive subjects with transitive verbs.
Early examples of texts in which such constructions are found regularly are the
Cotton Cleopatra B. v. version of *Brut y Brenhinedd* (*BB₁*) (15th c.) and *Y Bibyl
Ynghymraec* (*BY*) (MS P (c.1350–1450)), and to a greater extent in *Ystoryaeu Seint
Greal* (*YSG*) (end 14th c.) and the Peniarth 20 version of *Brut y Tywysogyon* (*BTy₁*)
(15th c.). Exceptions of a similar type are found later also in *Buchedd Sant Martin*
(*BSM*) (MS 1488–9) and 'Buchedd Collen' (1536). This having been said, in most
of these texts the expletive construction is not particularly common. Examples of
expletives in transitive constructions are given in (56).[18]

(56) (a) "*Ef a   danuon Duw,*" *heb yr Arthur,* "*taryan itt . . .*"
         it PRT send   God   said the Arthur   shield to-you
         ' "God will send a shield to you", said Arthur.'   (*YSG* 247–8)

   (b) . . . *ef a   rodes Duw glaw ar y   byd   deugeinn niwarnawt a*
            it PRT put   God rain on the world forty   day   and
        deugeinn nos . . .
        forty   night
        '. . . God put rain on the world for forty days and forty nights . . .'
                                                    (*BY* 9. 4–6 (MS P))

By the sixteenth century, we find a number of innovative texts, in which the
expletive subjects are not only possible with transitive verbs, but are in fact
extremely common in all uses. Such texts include 'Darnau o'r Efengylau' (DE)
(1550–75), 'Darn o'r Ffestival' (DFf) (1550–75), *Y Bibyl Ynghymraec* (MS A
(1594)), 'Mab y Fforestwr' (MFf) (MS *c.*1600), the slander-case depositions
for 1570–1630, and *Llyfr y Tri Aderyn* (*LlTA*) (1653). Consider the examples in
(57) with the verbs *dwyn* 'to steal', *creu* 'to create', *cymeryd* 'to take', and *clywed*
'to hear'.[19]

(57) (a) *Fo ddygodd Lewys ap Nicholas fuch yn lledrad . . .*
         it stole   Lewis ap Nicholas cow thievishly
         'Lewis ap Nicholas stole a cow . . .'
                                    (Slander case, Denbigh Sessions (1593))

   (b) *Ac ef a   greodh Dûw morûeirch . . .*
        and it PRT created God whales
        'And God created whales . . .'   (*BY* 4. 26–7 (1594))

   (c) *A   chwedy diweddy y   wledd, ef a   gymerth pawb   i   kennad*
        and after   end-VN the feast it PRT took   everyone their leave
        oddi wrth yr amherawdr . . .
        from   the emperor
        'And after the feast had ended, everyone took their leave of the emperor.'
                                            (*RhG* i. 126. 25–7 (*c.*1600))

   (d) *Ond os dywedaf wrthyt gyfrinach, fe a   glyw 'r golomen.*
        but if say-IS to-you secret   it PRT hear the dove
        'But if I tell you a secret, the dove will hear.'   (*LlTA* 27. 27–8 (1653))

Other texts from the same period keep to a more conservative usage. In 'Ystori
Alexander a Lodwig' (YAL) (*c.*1590), for instance, although violations of the
Middle Welsh rule are found (for instance, YAL 281. 20, 284. 38, 288. 37), the
usual environment for the expletive remains the unaccusative construction. The
same is true of *Ystoria Taliesin* (*YT*) (1540s).
    The development is seen more clearly from the results of an investigation into

TABLE 5.4. *Frequency of expletive subject constructions in Welsh texts, 1200–1700*

Text	Date	Expletives (%)	Transitive expletives (%)	Sample size
Historia Gruffud vab Kenan	*c.*1250	2	0	50
Pwyll	end 13th c.	2	0	50
Peredur	end 13th c.	4	0	50
Ystoryaeu Seint Greal	end 14th c.	14	4	50
Y Bibyl Ynghymraec (MS P)	*c.*1350–1450	2	2	50
Buchedd Sant Martin	1488–9	10	2	50
'Buchedd Collen'	1536	4	2	50
'Darnau o'r Efengylau'	1550–75	18	8	50
'Ystori Alexander a Lodwig'	*c.*1590	8	0	50
Y Bibyl Ynghymraec (MS A)	1594	44	32	50
'Mab y Fforestwr'	*c.*1600	26	8	50
Slander cases	1577–1631	40	20	25
Llyfr y Tri Aderyn	1653	64	18	50

the frequency of the expletive construction shown in Table 5.4. This is based on a sample of the first fifty affirmative main clauses with synthetic verb forms and full lexical subjects from thirteen Middle and Early Modern Welsh texts. The first column gives the approximate date of the text in question. The second column shows the percentage of these clauses that contain expletive subjects of any description; the third column shows the percentage which contain an expletive

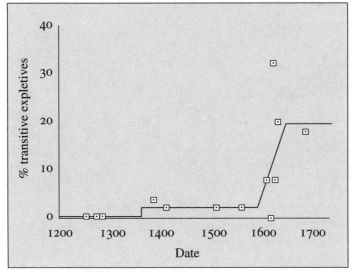

FIGURE 5.1. Frequency of transitive expletive constructions in Welsh, 1200–1700

subject in a transitive construction violating the Middle Welsh rule. The latter set of data is represented graphically in Figure 5.1.

It seems that two points of change need to be accounted for. The first change is the newly found grammatical status of transitive expletives in the fourteenth century. The second is a sudden and quite dramatic rise in the frequency of expletives at the end of the sixteenth century.

5.2.1.4.   *Clitic pronouns and the spread of expletive subjects*

I shall first offer an account of the emergence of the transitive construction, linking it to the change in status of preverbal pronominal subjects. Intuitively, the idea is that the move to clitic status for the expletive subject *ef* permits another true subject (external argument) to appear in the clause.

Once preverbal pronouns become clitics, the expletive *ef* construction is reanalysed, with a sentence like (58) being assigned the structure in (59), in conformity with the structure of all other clauses involving preverbal pronominal subjects (cf. (20)). In this structure, the expletive subject receives Nominative Case by incorporating into the verbal complex as in (59).[20]

(58)   *Ef ddoeth yno   marchawc.*
        it came   there knight
        'A knight came there.'

(59)

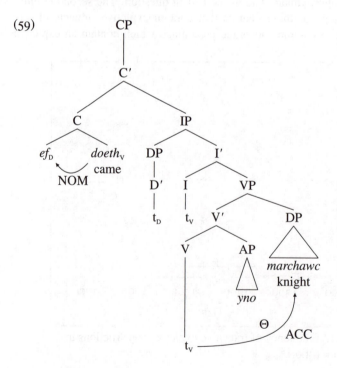

Suppose, following Rizzi and Roberts (1989: 7), that the biunique relation between Case-assigners and Case-assignees holds only within each mode of Case-assignment. That is, a Case-assigner may assign Case twice provided the modes of association are different in each instance—namely, once by association of Case features with a nominal and once by incorporation. Recall that the ungrammaticality of the transitive expletive structure in (52*b*) was due to the fact that the expletive subject prevents the lexical subject from receiving Nominative Case. Once preverbal subject pronouns can cliticize onto the verb, they no longer prevent this assignment. The sentence in (52*b*), repeated in Early Modern Welsh form as (60), can thus be assigned the structure in (61).

(60) *Ef welodd Arthur farchog.*
  it saw Arthur knight
  'Arthur saw a knight.'

(61)

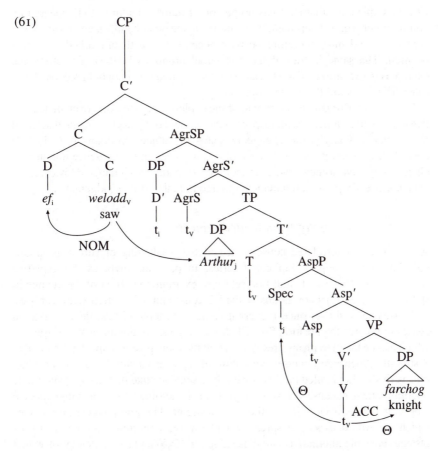

The expletive subject *ef* receives Case by cliticizing onto the verb. *Arthur*

receives Nominative in SpecTP under government from AgrS in C. The structure therefore becomes grammatical as a result of the change in status of the preverbal subject pronouns.

Although *ef* is allowed to co-occur with another true subject from the fourteenth century onwards, the same does not happen with other personal pronouns. That is, we do not find sentences like those in (62).

(62) (*a*) *Mi a   weleis i uarchawc.*
       I   PRT saw-IS I knight
       'I saw a knight.'

   (*b*) *Wynt a   welsant wy   uarchawc.*
       they PRT saw-3P they knight
       'They saw a knight.'

Ef is an expletive—that is, it has no person or number features and appears in a non-argument (non-theta-marked) position. On the other hand, *mi* and *wynt* are not expletives, and must therefore be base-generated in a theta-marked argument position. The same is true of the postverbal pronouns in (62). Therefore, the examples in (62) are ruled out because the two pronouns cannot both receive theta-roles. They thus fail the Theta Criterion.

It is difficult to evaluate the spread of the expletive construction from unaccusative to transitive contexts with respect to the account of syntactic change discussed in Chapter 2. Clearly, the change in status of subject pronouns is lexical. It nevertheless involves the appearance of a new construction, evidence that lexical change may have some of the characteristics of parametric change. However, the data at this early period are not clear enough to make further judgements.

5.2.2. *The rise of reduplicated subjects*

A second and interrelated consequence of the weakening of simple pronouns concerns the 'strong' reduplicated series. In part this involves the expletive construction. However, I shall first return to examine the effect of the change in status of simple subject pronouns on the V2-constraint (cf. Section 5.1.3.2 above).

As was seen above, once preverbal subjects become clitics, their derivation ceases to involve the position SpecCP. If the language maintains a V2-constraint, which can be taken to mean a restriction that the topic position SpecCP be filled at S-structure, then main clauses consisting of a preverbal simple subject pronoun plus verb should be ruled out. Accordingly, a sentence like that in (63*a*) should be ungrammatical because the subject pronoun is adjoined to C, leaving SpecCP empty. It is thus a violation of the V2-constraint. The grammatical alternatives which we would expect to spread would involve non-clitic pronominal forms instead. Possible alternatives are those given in (63*b*) and (63*c*), neither of which violate V2, since a non-clitic preverbal pronoun occupies SpecCP.

(63) (a) *Mi feddyliais.*
     I   thought-1s

   (b) *Myfi   feddyliais.*
       I-REDUP thought-1s

   (c) *Minnau feddyliais.*
       I-CONJ thought-1s
       'I thought.'

There is some evidence that effects of this nature *are* attested in Late Middle and Early Modern Welsh. This is predominantly in the form of changes made during copying of manuscripts which suggest change in usage of the different pronoun series over time. In the earlier period (14th–15th centuries) there may be a move towards conjunctive forms. In the later period, reduplicated forms come to dominate in preverbal subject position. This can be interpreted as a move to maintain V2 in the earlier period, replacing the V2-violation in (63a) with the orthodox (63c). The development in the later period is more problematic, since it must be linked to the fact that the reduplicated pronouns themselves undergo phonological reduction. One possibility is that the spread of reduplicated pronouns begins as a way of maintaining V2, but that, with their phonological reduction, and the loss of V2 generally, they too end up as preverbal subject clitics.

The first evidence comes from the manuscript history of the Red Book Version of *Brut y Tywysogyon (BTy₂).* In this case the evidence suggests a move away from simple pronouns as preverbal subjects primarily in favour of conjunctive forms. In a number of places the earliest manuscript P (Peniarth 18), dated to the first half of the fourteenth century, differs from all or some of the later manuscripts in having a simple preverbal pronominal subject where they have a conjunctive one. Consider, for instance, (64), given according to manuscript P. In manuscript T (last decade of the fourteenth century/c.1400), the simple pronoun *mi* is replaced as subject of the first clause at this point in the text by reduplicated *myui*, and as subject of the second clauses by conjunctive *minneu* (datings from *BTy₂*, pp. xxii, xxix).

(64)   *Mi a   af   y Normandi, ac o deuy   di gyt a mi, mi a*
       I PRT go-1s to Normandy and if come-2s you with me I PRT
       gywiraf   it   pop peth o 'r a edeweis   it.
       arrange-1s to-you everything of REL promised-1s to-you
       'I shall go to Normandy, and if you come with me, I shall arrange for
       you everything that I promised you.' (*BTy₂* 82. 3–4)

This is not an isolated case, but happens repeatedly in the manuscript tradition of this text. For other similar examples, see *BTy₂* 50. 3, 54. 27, 66. 23, 68. 14, 108. 3, 126. 7, 266. 28.

Somewhat later, there is evidence for movement towards reduplicated pronouns in preverbal position, rather than conjunctive ones. From the very earliest slander cases available (1577), reduplicated pronouns are the most common form for preverbal pronominal subjects. Examples are given in (65). Note that in these examples there can be no question of a contrastive or cleft reading ('It is I who will prove that', etc.). This is ruled out both by the presence of subject–verb agreement, which is generally incompatible with this reading, and on general grounds of plausibility in the examples cited.

(65) (a) ... *ag my fy   a   brova   hynny.*
        and I-REDUP PRT prove-1s that
        '... and I will prove that.'   (Slander case, Denbigh Sessions (1593))

    (b) *Ty di   a   osodaist   arna vi ar y   ffordd vawr ...*
        you-REDUP PRT attacked-2s on-1s me on the road   big
        'You attacked me on the highway ...'
                                        (Slander case, Flint Sessions (1600))

    (c) *Ty dy   a   gai   dy   grogi.*
        you-REDUP PRT get-2s 2s-GEN hang-VN
        'You will be hanged.'   (Slander case, Pembroke Sessions (1604))

    (d) *Ty dy   a   fiddy   in   vakrupt* [sic] ...
        you-REDUP PRT will-be-2s PRD bankrupt
        'You will be bankrupt ...'
                                        (Slander case, Montgomery Sessions (1588))

Full details of the frequency of reduplicated pronouns as preverbal subjects in the slander cases up to 1650 are given in Table 5.5. The table shows the frequency of the various pronominal forms as preverbal subject pronouns. This evidence clearly suggests that, by the end of the sixteenth century, the reduplicated forms

TABLE 5.5. *Frequency of reduplicated pronouns as preverbal subjects in slander-case depositions, 1570–1650*

	1 sing.		2 sing.			3 sing. masc.			Reduplicated forms (%)
	mi	*myfi y fi*	*ti*	*di*	*tydi*	*ef*	*fo fe*	*efo/efe y fo/fe*	
Anglesey	0	0	1	0	1	0	1	0	—
Brecknockshire	0	2	2	1	0	1	0	0	—
Cardiganshire	2	4	2	6	3	0	3	0	35
Denbighshire	4	3	3	3	4	0	10	2	31
Flintshire	6	2	2	10	7	2	10	0	26
Montgomery	1	7	1	1	20	0	9	7	74
Pembrokeshire	5	5	8	13	10	0	9	0	29
All Wales (%)	44	56	19	35	46	6	78	17	—

were well represented as unmarked preverbal subject pronouns in speech. Overall, unambiguously reduplicated forms account for 56 per cent of all first-person-singular preverbal pronouns, 46 per cent in the second person, and 17 per cent in the masculine third person. One complication is the appearance of forms such as *fi*, *di*, *fe*, and *fo*, neither obviously simple nor reduplicated. I shall return to these below.

Evidence from other texts is less clear. A number of texts have widespread use of pragmatically neutral preverbal reduplicated subject pronouns. Such texts include *Ystoria Taliesin* (*YT*), 'Ystorya Erkwlf' (both part of Elis Gruffydd's chronicle, 1540s), 'Ystoriau Digrif' (1582), 'Ystoriau o Ddyfed' (*c*.1588), and *Three Welsh Religious Plays* (*TWRP*) (16th c.). On the other hand, there is no evidence of this spread in many other texts of the sixteenth century.

The reverse development, apparent phonological strengthening, is found in the textual tradition of *Ystoryaeu Seint Greal* (*YSG*). The B manuscript (NLW 3063E, end of fifteenth to early sixteenth century) frequently has simple pronouns in preverbal subject position where the much earlier A manuscript (Peniarth 11, end 14th century) has reduplicated forms (datings from *YSG*, p. xi). Examples are given in (66). In (66a) a conjunctive form *ynteu* 'he' is replaced by a simple form *ef*, and in (66b) a reduplicated form *efo* 'he' is replaced.[21]

(66) (*a*) *Ac ynteu* (MS A) *a   henyw   o   vrenhined.*
              ef (MS B)
          and he   PRT is-descended from kings
          'And he is descended from kings.'   (*YSG* 396–7)

    (*b*) *A   bit   dieu   ytti,   Efo* (MS A) *a   allei gael y*
                                              ef (MS B)
          and be-IMPER doubtless to-you, he-REDUP PRT could get   the
          meirch goreu, pei as mynnei.
          horses best   if it wanted-COND
          'And you may be sure, he could have got the best horses if he had wanted it.'   (*YSG* 3109–10)

The best explanation for this contradictory evidence may lie in the standardization of the language, which was beginning in the sixteenth century (Dafydd Glyn Jones 1988: 128–31). By this time, the reduplicated forms of the pronouns were being 'devalued' in speech—that is, used in less marked contexts. It can only be concluded that there was normative pressure in the literary language against this use of reduplicated pronouns as neutral (non-emphatic, non-contrastive) subjects. For this reason, we lack evidence for them in many texts of the period, and, in copying texts such as *Ystoryaeu Seint Greal*, copyists would tend to replace any 'non-standard' reduplicated forms in their original by standard simple ones. Of course, when these texts were first compiled, the use of the reduplicated pronouns had not been stigmatized, since they were still restricted to marked, emphatic environments. However, in some less literary texts, and in material like the slander cases, which reflect spoken usage, we find extensive use of these pronouns as preverbal subjects.

Something like this phenomenon is expected if late Middle Welsh maintains a V2-constraint, whilst marking its preverbal simple subject pronouns as clitics. Inasmuch as the V2-rule is maintained, a full DP must occupy the initial position. Once simple pronouns become clitics, they are no longer full DPs, and cannot satisfy V2. Reduplicated and conjunctive pronouns, on the other hand, remain as DPs, and therefore can fulfil the V2-constraint when they occur as preverbal subjects. The reduplicated series, being emphatic but not contrastive, are preferred for this purpose, since the contrastive semantics of conjunctive series prevents them from being used on a wide scale.

5.2.2.1.   *Weakening of the reduplicated pronouns*

As mentioned above, the commonest form for third-person-masculine preverbal pronoun is *fo*, which, along with its variant *fe*, occurs in 78 per cent of cases. This form is neither clearly simple nor reduplicated in form (the simple form is *ef*, the reduplicated *efo*). The same is true of a common second-person-singular form *di* (simple *ti*, and reduplicated *tydi*). This form cannot merely be the mutated form of the simple pronoun, since there is no evidence for any period of Welsh for preverbal subjects undergoing mutation.

How can these forms be accounted for historically? I shall argue here that they are clitic forms of the reduplicated series of pronouns. I consider first how such a view can be integrated into an account of the development of expletives presented above. Subsequently, I turn to philological evidence that supports this view.

5.2.2.2.   *Reduplicated pronouns and the expletive construction*

There is one apparent problem for the analysis of the spread of expletive subjects that has not been mentioned so far. The problem is the appearance of the reduplicated third-person-singular masculine pronoun *efo* as an expletive. This usage is attested from the sixteenth century onwards. Early examples are given in (67).[22]

(67) (*a*) . . . *ac yvo   a   ddywedir mai   ynGhaer Wyrangon y   mae*
        and it-REDUP PRT is-said   CLEFT in-Worcester   PRT is
        y   lili hwnw eto.
        the lily that   still
        'And it is said that (it is) in Worcester (that) that lily is still.'

                                                    (RhG i. 39. 2–4 (1536))

    (*b*) . . . *y vo   a   uu   y kyuriw dymesdyl ynGymhrv y   dethwn*
           it-REDUP PRT was the such   storm   in-Wales the day
           yma . . .
           that
           '. . . there was such a storm in Wales that day . . .'

                                             (RhG i. 32. 16–17 (1540s))

(c) *efo   wyr   pawb . . .*
it-REDUP knows everyone
'Everyone knows . . .'

(*TWRP, Yr Enaid a'r Corff*, 46 (MS 16th c. [1500–20]))

(d) *Ac yvo   a   ellir   ydnabod   gwaed mallinckoliws . . .*
and it-REDUP PRT can-IMPERS recognize-VN blood melancholic
'And melancholic blood can be recognized . . .'   (*CI* 143. 6 (1540s))

As (67c) shows, the reduplicated expletive is like the simple expletive by this period in being fully compatible with transitive verbs.

The slightly later example in (68) confirms that this does indeed reflect spoken usage of at least some parts of Wales.

(68)   *Efo   ddyg dy   wr   di naw o wyn   yn lledrad . . .*
it-REDUP took your husband you nine of lambs thievishly
'Your husband stole nine lambs . . .'

(Slander case, Montgomery Sessions (1619))

Given the analysis developed above that fully productive expletive subjects were possible only once the expletive pronoun became a clitic, this seems problematic. However, if the reduplicated pronouns were themselves being reduced to the point where they became clitics, the same logic as applied to the spread of the simple pronouns as expletives would allow reduplicated pronouns to fulfil the same function.

There is both internal and cross-linguistic evidence that suggests that strong (for instance, reduplicated) pronouns could not function as expletives unless they became clitics. First, note that the parallel construction in Early Modern Welsh in (69), with the other strong pronoun series—namely, the conjunctive series—is completely unattested.

(69)   **Yntau   welodd Arthur y   gaer.*
it-CONJ saw   Arthur the fortress
'Arthur saw the fortress.'

Furthermore in other languages with both expletive subjects and a weak/strong distinction in the pronominal system, the strong pronoun cannot normally function as an expletive. For instance, in French, a strong pronoun may double a referential subject clitic subject in (70), but not an expletive subject in (71).

(70) (a) *Je   sais.*
I-CL know

    (b) *Moi   je   sais.*
I-STRONG I-CL know
'I know.'

(71) (a) *Il   pleut.*
      it-CL rains

  (b) **Lui   il   pleut.*
      it-STRONG it-CL rains
      'It's raining.'

In the light of this evidence it would be odd to find the reduplicated pronoun *efo* functioning as an expletive subject if it remained a stressed pronoun. It therefore seems appropriate to try to pursue an account according to which *efo* became a clitic at the same time that it began to participate in the expletive construction. Such a change would on the evidence presented so far be dated to the sixteenth century.

5.2.2.3.   Fe *and* fo

The clearest evidence for such a weakening of the reduplicated pronouns is the loss of the first (unstressed) syllable in the pronoun *efo*, well attested as *fo* from the mid-sixteenth century.[23]

(72) (a) *Vo aeth oddiwrth   yr holl gythrelied . . .*
      he went away-from the all   devils
      'He went away from all the devils . . .'
                               (*TWRP, Y Dioddefaint*, 777 (MS 1552))

  (b) *. . . vo dyvei   yn   vwy   ei swmp na   'r ddarn arall ir*
      it grow-COND PRD bigger its size   than the part   other to-the
    llyfr hwn.
    book this
    '. . . it would grow bigger than the rest of this book.'
                                   (*TN* c.i^{v}. 22 [1567])

  (c) *Vo gaiff pawb   o hyn o le   ar hynt   glowed   newydd*
      it   gets everyone of this of place in course hear-VN new
    chwedley.
    tales
    'Everyone from this place will in due course get to hear new tales.'
          (*TWRP, Yr Enaid a'r Corff*, 115–16 (MS 16th c. [1500–20]))

  (d) *. . . fo ddaeth Dam   Ffolineb a   Wyllys Drwg gyda hi . . .*
      it came Madam Folly   with Will   Bad   with her
    '. . . Madam Folly brought Ill will with her . . .'
                        (*RhG* i. 102. 31–103. 1 (*c*.1575))

Note that the form appears simultaneously in both referential uses in (72*a*) and (72*b*) and in expletive uses in (72*c*) and (72*d*). The form is also attested in a number of slander cases for north-east Wales (Denbighshire, Flintshire, and Montgomeryshire—Denbigh Sessions (1593, 1604×2, 1626, 1631, 1633×3); Flint

Sessions 1612, 1621, 1622, 1631×2; Montgomery Sessions (1592, 1608, 1626, 1644)), for Anglesey (Anglesey Sessions (1652)) and Pembrokeshire (Pembroke Sessions (1633)) from the earliest records in the late sixteenth and early seventeenth century.

Morgan (1952: 368) points out this variation in form, and gives two quite early examples of *fo* from poetry:

(73) (a) *I 'r dafarn, fo 'i   barn   y   byd.*
     to the tavern   he 3S-ACC judges the world
     'He condemns the world to the tavern.'   (*DGG* 8. 24)

 (b) *vo[w]na honn   vy nihennydd.*
     it does   that-one my death
     'That one will cause my death.'   (*ID* 12. 24 (MS 1527–47 [*fl.* 1460]))[24]

The difference in date between composition and the manuscript of (73*b*) means that there is no compelling evidence to seek the appearance of this form any earlier than the mid-sixteenth century. Example (73*a*) is perhaps the earliest evidence for the weakening process.

At approximately the same time, the third-person-masculine-singular pronoun appears as *fe*, along with a new full form of the reduplicated pronoun *efe*. The new form *efe* is found both as a fully referential pronoun (74*a*, *b*), and as an expletive subject (74*c*, *d*).[25]

(74) (a) *Ag velly gwedy dibeny   'r stori a   ddechressey ef o'r blaen,*
         and so   after   finish-VN the story REL had-started   he before
         efe   gwsgodd.
         he-REDUP slept.
         'And so having finished the story that he had begun before, he slept.'
                                         (*RhG* ii. 83. 5–6 (MS *c.*1588))

 (b) *Wrth hynny Noe . . . efe   a   ellyngodd allan gigfran . . .*
     upon this   Noah   he-REDUP PRT let   out   raven
     'Upon this, Noah . . . he let out a raven . . .'
                                         (CHSS 114. 25–8 (1574–1604))

 (c) *efe   a   all Duw wneuthur hynny*
     it-REDUP PRT can God do-VN   that
     'God can do that.'
                         (John Davies, *Llyfr y Resolusion*, 5 (1632) (*GPC* 1170))

 (d) *efe a   ddywedir . . . fal hyn*
     it   PRT is-said   like this
     'it is said . . . like this . . .'   (Siôn Treredyn, *Madrvddyn y Difinyddiaeth Diweddaraf*, 239 (1651) (*GPC* 1170))

The traditional view is that this new form was the 'invention' of William

Salesbury, and was adopted by the translators of the Welsh Bible in 1588 as 'a self-imposed rule' (Morris-Jones 1913: 272; cf. Morris-Jones 1921: 85). Morris-Jones cites as support for this view the fact that *efe* in the Bible translation may occur as the object of a preposition, where reduplicated pronouns are not possible in (Modern Literary) Welsh. First, Emrys Evans (1959) shows that the older form *efo* also occurs as the object of a preposition in Middle Welsh. The distribution of *efe* in the Bible is thus identical to that of earlier *efo* in Middle Welsh. This casts doubt on its supposed artificiality.

Furthermore, the earliest cases of *efe* in other texts cited in (74) are roughly simultaneous with the Bible translation, and it therefore seems unlikely that Bible translation was the model for these other texts. Most probably, the innovation of *efe* for *efo* is a case of natural language change.

The form *efe* undergoes similar phonological reduction to that found with *efo*. So, from the mid-sixteenth century, the form *fe* is found in both referential uses (75*a*, *b*) and expletive uses (75*c*, *d*) of the pronoun.[26]

(75) (*a*) *Ve ai   galwe i hvn   brenin gwar . . .*
he PRT+3S-ACC called himself king   civilized
'He called himself a civilized king . . .'

(*TWRP, Y Dioddefaint*, 237 (MS 1552))

(*b*) *Ar foregwaith teg fe aeth alhan or   fynachlog . . .*
on morning   fair he went out   of-the monastery
'One fair morning he went out of the monastery . . .'

(*DC* 61. 5–6 (1585))

(*c*) *vei   gwyr   pawb   ar a aned*
FE+3S-ACC knows everyone REL was-born
'Everyone who was born knows it.'

(*TWRP, Y Dioddefaint*, 466 (MS 1552))

(*d*) *. . . ag o bydd   rhai yn   gistwng, fe gyfyd rhai ereill . . .*
and if will-be some PROG fall-VN   it rises ones other
'. . . and if some fall, others will rise . . .'   (*RhG* ii. 85. 7 (MS c.1588))

If it is suggested that the reduplicated pronouns undergo phonological weakening, we also have a better account of the historical origin of the particle *fe* than the traditional view which saw it as deriving historically from *ef a* (D. Simon Evans 1968: 329; Morris-Jones 1913: 428). *Efe a* becomes *efe* by the general loss of preverbal *a*, then *efe* becomes *fe* as part of the general loss of unstressed syllables in weakened reduplicated forms. The traditional account has to rely on the postulation of *ad hoc* phonological changes (*ef a > fe*), and is even harder to understand in the light of the loss of the particle *a* in the sixteenth century. Also, on the traditional account, the existence of *fe* in the same clause as the particle *a*, as in (75*a*), is inexplicable (see also the examples of *fe a* given in D. Simon Evans 1968: 330).

Such clear evidence for the phonological weakening of the third-person-masculine pronouns *efo* and *efe* to *fo* and *fe* justifies the claim that the appearance of transitive expletives in Welsh is linked to the appearance of subject clitics.

It is important that all these phonological changes in the forms of the pronoun affect both referential and expletive uses simultaneously. This suggests that both uses form a single lexical item in the grammar of this period. This change is thus simply the addition of an extra phonetic form in the lexical entry for the third-person-singular-masculine pronoun.

5.2.2.4. *The remains of* ef

Finally, we should note that, although the weak pronouns *fo* and *fe* develop from reduplicated pronouns in the sixteenth century, the simple pronoun *ef* (by this time frequently *e*) does not disappear. It continues in use in preverbal position both as an expletive and as a referential pronoun.[27]

(76) (*a*) *Os byddai   vn yn   chwennychu digrifwch,   e gai*
       if would-be one PROG desire-VN   entertainment he would-get
      buror   a   'i delyn i ganu   mwyn bynciau . . .
      melody with his harp to play-VN gentle tunes
      'If someone were to desire entertainment, he would get a melody on his harp to play gentle tunes . . .'   (*RhG* ii. 10. 23–4 (1567))

   (*b*) *Ac e ddechreodd* [*ym*] *Moysen ar   oll prophwti . . .*
      and he started   in Moses and-the all prophets
      'And he started with Moses and all the prophets . . .'
                              (*KLlB* 84. 10–11 (1551))

   (*c*) *A   phan scrivenont   "a Soldan", yn y fan   e fudd   y peth*
      and when write-3P-SUBJ a Soldan in the place it will-be the thing
      a   fvnnont . . .
      REL want-3P-SUBJ
      'And when they write "a Soldan", immediately there will appear what they want . . .'   (*RhG* i. 74. 33–75. 1 (1578–85))

   (*d*) *Ac e vydd   vn gorlan ac vn bugail.*
      and he will-be one paddock and one shepherd.
      'And there will be one pen and one shepherd.'
                         (*TN* 150ʳ. 2–3 (John 10. 16) [1567])

Since the forms have entirely merged in function by this period, there are thus apparently three variant forms of the preverbal third-person-masculine-singular pronoun, *fe*, *fo*, and *e*. The referential/expletive contrast plays no part in distinguishing them.

5.2.2.5. Di

A similar phenomenon, without the complication of the expletive, is well attested early on with the second-person-singular pronoun. The form *di* appears as a preverbal subject pronoun at the end of the sixteenth and start of the seventeenth century. Following the logic of the account developed so far, this must be a reduced form of the reduplicated pronoun *tydi*, with loss of the unstressed first syllable. The earliest example is in a slander case at the Brecknockshire Sessions in 1577. First attestations in other county Courts of Sessions are: Flintshire (1604), Pembroke-shire (1607), Cardiganshire (?1611), Montgomeryshire (1620), Denbighshire (1626), data being absent for the rest of Wales. This means that its use cannot be associated with any particular area. The earliest examples from the slander cases are given in (77):

(77) (a) ... *di   a   ddigest o   siope Ph[ilip]e Capp yngevenny*
           you PRT stole   from shop Philip   Capp in-Abergavenny
         ... *hatt yn lledrad* ...
         hat thievishly
         '... you stole a hat from Philip Capp's shop in Abergavenny ...'
                                  (Slander case, Brecknock Sessions (1577))

     (b) ... *ag di   a   ddwygest yn lledrad bedole* ...
          and you PRT stole-2S   thievishly horseshoes
          '... and you stole horseshoes ...'   (Slander case, Flint Sessions (1604))

     (c) *Dy gymmerest ffurth yn neved y* ...
          you took-2S   away my sheep me
          'You took away my sheep ...'
                                    (Slander case, Pembroke Sessions (1607))

     (d) ... *ag di   a   ddygaist yn lledrad fyngwregis.*
          and you PRT stole-2S   thievishly my-belt
          '... and you stole my belt.'   (Slander case, Flint Sessions (1609))

Examples in literature appear slightly later, mainly from the 1640s onwards.[28]

(78) (a) *Bett vayd   ti   yn   kyddnabod   anregion duw* ...
         if   were-2S-IMPF-SUBJ you PROG recognize-VN gifts   God
         di a   vynnyd   erchi iddaw ef ddiod ...
         you PRT want-2S-COND   ask-VN to-3SM him drink
         'If you recognized God's gifts ... you would ask him for drink ...'
                                      (DE 392. 3–6 (1550–75))

     (b) *Noa, di a   wyddost modd i   gwnauthost* ...
         Noah you PRT know-2S how   PRT did-2S
         'Noah, you know what you did ...'   (HGC 12. 21 (c.1640))

     (c) *Di wyddost (ô Gigfran) i 'r golomen ddychwelyd yn ôl* ...
         you know-2S (o raven)   to the dove   return-VN back
         'You know (o Raven) that the dove returned ...'
                                    (LITA 7. 18–19 (1653))

(*d*) *Di ae   'n   union   i   Baradwys* ...
    you go-2s PRD straight to Paradise
    'You shall go straight to Paradise ...'

                        (Rees Prichard, *Gwaith*, 2. 4 (1672))

The obvious conclusion to draw is that, like *fo*, the form *di* represents a phonological reduction of the reduplicated pronoun *tydi*. This reduction may have been a fairly general phenomenon. For the other persons, an intermediate stage with loss of only the initial consonant is attested (Morgan 1952: 453). Thus, the process of phonological reduction might be a general one for all the reduplicated pronouns. The three stages hypothesized for this development are shown in Table 5.6.[29]

TABLE 5.6. *Development of reduplicated subject pronouns in Early Modern Welsh*

Person	Stage 1	Stage 2	Stage 3
Singular			
First person	*myfi* /mə'vi/	*y fi* /ə'vi/	*fi* /'vi/
Second person	*tydi* /tə'di/	*y di* /ə'di/	*di* /'di/
Third-person masc.	*efo* /e'vo/	*y fo* /ə'vo/	*fo* /'vo/
Third-person fem.	*hyhi* /hə'hi/	*y hi* /ə'hi/	*hi* /'hi/
Plural			
First person	*nyni* /nə'ni/	*y ni* /ə'ni/	*ni* /'ni/
Second person	*chwchwi* /χu'χwi/	*y chwi* /ə'χwi/	*chi* /'χi/
Third person	*hwyntwy* /huin'tui/	*yntwy* /ə'nhui/	*nhw* /'nhu/

Only in the singular, and possibly in the third-person-plural form, would such a phonological reduction produce a form distinct from the simple pronoun. Note that the evidence of Table 5.5 suggests that in the singular this phonological reduction occurs most quickly in the third person masculine form, then in the second person, whilst the first person is most resistant to change.

5.2.2.6.   *A paradox?*

We were faced earlier with the problem that reduplicated pronouns seemed to spread because strong pronouns were needed in order to preserve V2, but the fact that *efo* was a clitic allowed it to act as a fully productive expletive subject. These two suggestions need to be reconciled with each other.

This can only be done if, as seems reasonable, the cliticization processes were lexical and gradual. The evidence of Table 5.5 suggests that the phonological reduction of the reduplicated pronouns was more advanced in the third person in the slander cases. This may well suggest that the phonological reduction began in the third-person-masculine singular and spread only later to the first and second persons. If so, it could well be the case that the third-person-singular reduplicated pronoun *efo* spread to expletive construction when this pronoun became a clitic, whilst at the same time the first- and second-person-singular reduplicated pronouns *myfi* and *tydi* were full pronouns satisfying the V2-constraint.

5.2.2.7.   *The status of expletive* fe

One question remains. It has been established that the spread of the expletive construction to transitive contexts can be linked to a change in a lexical entry of a personal pronoun. This accounts for the increase in use of expletive subjects in the fourteenth century (cf. Figure 5.1). However, the sudden increase in the use of the expletive construction in the sixteenth century has not been fully accounted for.

According to the parametric model of change, we would expect such a sudden change to reflect a parametric change. However, in this case, the only plausible candidate for a change in the grammar seems to be a lexical change rather than a parametric one. This instance seems to provide good evidence that at least some lexical changes can exhibit the properties associated with parametric change.

The possible lexical change is as follows. Once the expletive construction is available with all verbs, the expletive pronoun *fe* (along with *fo* and *e*) is liable to reanalysis as a main-clause affirmative complementizer, occurring with default (non-agreeing) forms of the verb. Before this time, the fact that it is found only with unaccusative verbs, coupled with the knowledge that complementizers (universally) do not select for unaccusativity, allows the child to establish that it is an expletive element.

Consequently, the structure of the expletive construction undergoes the Diachronic Reanalysis in (79)–(80). Instead of raising from the base-position for expletive subjects, SpecAgrSP, *fe* is base-generated in C, where it selects for a verb in the default third-person form. Such a reanalysis is favoured because it allows a reduction in the amount of movement generated by the grammar. It can thus be motivated as a reduction in the number of chain positions in the sense of Roberts's Least Effort Strategy (cf. Section 2.2.2). Before the reanalysis, there are two chains, one headed by *fe* (fe_D, t_D) and one headed by the verb ($welodd_V$, t_V, t_V, t_V), with a total of six chain positions. The reanalysis reduces this to four by the elimination of the chain involving *fe*.

(79)   *Fe welodd Arthur farchog.*
         FE saw   Arthur knight
         'Arthur saw a knight.'

This reanalysis has no particular repercussions in the output of the grammar, and as such it is not possible to demonstrate its effect in terms of new constructions or in obsolescence. However, it does result in a fundamental change in the status of the construction. Once *fe* is reanalysed as a complementizer, the construction in which it participates is no longer an expletive construction in any sense. We therefore expect the sorts of restrictions (for instance, in terms of discourse structure and topicality) typically found with expletive constructions to be dropped

(80) (*a*)

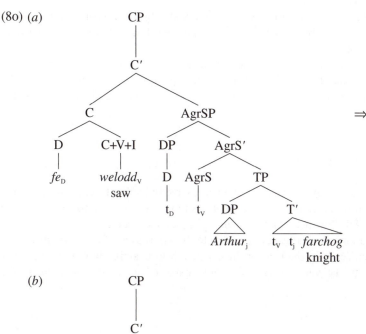

$\Rightarrow$

(*b*)

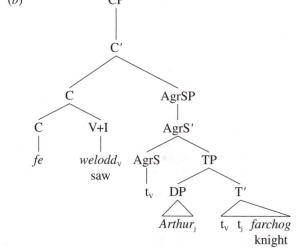

immediately. This new-found unmarked status accounts for the sudden rise in the use of the *fe*-construction in the sixteenth century.

Such a reanalysis is effected in the grammar through a change in the lexical entry for *fe*. At the earlier stage the lexical entry for *fe* had specified it as a pronoun—that is, a Determiner (D) head—with third-person-singular-masculine features. With the change, *fe* splits into two lexical items, one, *fe₁*, a complementizer selecting an AgrS-head (and therefore a verb) in the default (third-person-singular) form; the other, *fe₂*, a pronoun with third-person-singular-masculine features as before. Thus the reduction in movement is at the cost of the addition of one additional item in the lexicon. Note that the complementizer *fe₁* selects for a verb in the default form, and is therefore not compatible with pronominal subjects. It is, however, compatible with nominal subjects, whether singular or plural, since these require a verb in the default form.

In addition to the evidence of the sudden rise in frequency of the construction, any evidence that the two lexical items subsequently develop differently is evidence in favour of the reanalysis. Such evidence does exist, and will be presented in Chapter 7.

5.3.   CONCLUSION

In this chapter we have seen that the successive reduction to clitic status of the subject pronouns creates a set of exceptions to the verb-second constraint. These exceptions fall into two classes—namely, exceptions due to the clitic status of preverbal pronouns, and exceptions due to the innovation of *fe* as an affirmative complementizer. We shall go on in Chapter 6 to examine how this and other exceptions to the verb-second rule could have led to its abandonment in the grammar.

6. The Loss of Verb-Second

The V2-system described in Chapters 3 and 4 began to break down in Late Middle Welsh. Some aspects of this have already been noted, in particular, exceptions to the V2-rule with subject pronouns and the affirmative complementizer *fe*. In this chapter other sources of the loss of the V2-rule are examined. Particular attention will be paid to the role of language acquisition in this process. This chapter begins with an examination of how V2-systems, and the Middle Welsh V2-system in particular, may be acquired. It is subsequently argued that, during the period when topicalization was lost, the three typical V2-structures—SVO, AdvVSO, and OVS —ceased to be acquired as a single, unified V2-phenomenon. In so far as these orders were replicated in successive generations of speakers, they were generated using grammatical rules unconnected with verb-second. The V2-parameter was thus reset to a negative value and V2 was lost from the grammar. Textual evidence suggests that this change does indeed show the characteristics usually associated with parametric change. In particular, sudden changes in the output of the grammar are manifested—in this case, the sudden innovation of unmarked VSO, and the obsolescence of a number of minor syntactic structures.

6.1. LEARNABILITY AND THE LOSS OF V2

As we saw in Chapter 2, much recent research on syntactic change has focused on what evidence children could use to acquire the grammars postulated for their language. Children have the task of producing a grammar whose output approximates to the language that they hear around them. In accounting for syntactic change, the linguist faces (amongst others) two tasks: first to explain how children acquired the conservative linguistic system, and, secondly, to show what aspects of that system were acquisitionally ambiguous—that is, prone to a different syntactic analysis.

6.1.1. *Acquiring verb-second in Germanic and Welsh*

In answering the first of these questions with reference to Welsh, the example of the Germanic languages is instructive. Lightfoot (1991: 50–6) has suggested that Dutch and German children establish the V2-nature of their language in the following way. They first observe that sentences begin with an arbitrary phrasal category (subject, object, adverbial). Since it is a phrasal category, it must be either a specifier or a complement. Since it is sentence-initial and therefore not preceded by a head, it cannot be a complement, so must be identified as a specifier.[1] This specifier position has no fixed thematic or functional role, so cannot be identified as, say, IP or VP, hence it must be a higher projection, which Lightfoot labels YP (under the standard analysis, CP). The child therefore concludes that its language has obligatory topicalization to a sentence-initial specifier position.

A number of empirical studies of the acquisition of verb-second in German take a similar view. These show that German children go through an early stage of dominant SXOV word order, followed by a later stage when a verb-second rule is established (Clahsen 1988: 53–4; Clahsen and Muysken 1986: 97–102; Clahsen and Smolka 1986; Weissenborn 1994: 219). Later, when the earliest subordinate clauses appear, they are correctly SXOV, and children do not overgeneralize main-clause word order into them. This has been interpreted as meaning that children first establish underlying SOV order, producing bare VPs with the structure $[_{VP} NP_{subj} NP_{obj} V]$ (Weissenborn 1994: 220). Then, on the basis of cases of observed XVSO word order, they establish the higher functional projections IP and CP, along with a rule moving the verb leftwards to C and topicalization of an arbitrary constituent to SpecCP. In Clahsen and Muysken's formulation the crucial evidence for the child is essentially the observation that the dominant alternation in German is between SXOV orders and XVSO ones. The optimal grammar that gives this alternation is one in which SXOV is basic, and there is leftward movement of the verb across the subject, and of an arbitrary constituent XP to the clause-initial position (Clahsen and Muysken 1986: 111–12). As in Lightfoot's account (see Section 2.2.1), the 'separable particles' play an important role in the establishment of underlying OV order inasmuch as verb-final order is established first with verbs with separable particles (Clahsen 1988: 53; Clahsen and Muysken 1986: 98; Clahsen and Smolka 1986: 146–7).

Returning to the Middle Welsh system, we need to establish what evidence there is parallel to that in German for the acquisition of V2. It is difficult to be sure of what sort of input children acquiring Middle and Early Modern Welsh would have received. However, the results of statistical studies on Middle Welsh prose tell us that Adverb–*y(d)*–Verb–Subject–Object was the most frequently attested order in writing, followed by Subject–*a*–Verb–Object (cf. Table 3.1).

Let us take the SVO order first. SVO main clauses provide the child with clear data, but they are compatible either with a V2-analysis or with subject-raising to SpecIP, as in English, and are thus acquisitionally ambiguous. When confronted with such sentences, the child will be given no particular reason to opt for the more complex V2-grammar. The evidence of these clauses is therefore irrelevant. The same is true of clauses of the form AdvSVO. The adverb might be adjoined to IP, and the SVO order might simply be the result of subject raising.

The child will also come across clauses of the form Adv–$y(d)$–V–S . . . Even if we suppose that this order was less frequent in speech than in writing, children would still have come across it frequently. What is to stop the child from analysing the adverb here as adjoining to AgrSP and the subject as occupying SpecTP? First, if it does, case-assignment in Welsh would have to be bidirectional to allow for the variation between SVO and VSO orders. This is found in other languages, hence cannot be ruled out on universal grounds, although it may represent a complication of the grammar. Secondly, and far more significantly, the evidence of the preverbal particles *a* and *y(d)* will confirm to the child that the preverbal position is a specifier position. The child sees that certain preverbal elements require the verb to be preceded by *a* whilst others require the verb to be preceded by *y(d)*. This is clearly an agreement process, so the element triggering agreement must be in a Spec-head relation with the head showing agreement. Some adverbs trigger this agreement, hence they must be in a Spec-head relation with the preverbal particle. The agreeing elements are complementizers, thus the position of the adverb must be SpecCP. This also gives the child a reason why not all preverbal adverbs trigger a preverbal particle. The difference can be reduced to whether or not the adverb occupies a specifier position or an adjoined position.

The child will also come across sentences containing fronted objects, in which the subject follows the verb. This construction triggers the same agreeing particle *a* found with a preverbal subject. The child is therefore led to infer that preverbal objects and subjects occupy the same structural position, and the grammar with preverbal elements in SpecCP is given further support.

Hence, the child can hypothesize a general agreement process between the head of C and an arbitrary XP in SpecCP. This is sufficient for the V2-parameter to be set positively.

6.1.2. *Acquisitional ambiguity*

The Middle Welsh child is at two disadvantages when compared with a child learning a typical V2-language, say German. In two parts of the acquisition process, a 'simpler' analysis is plausible, but must be rejected by the child in constructing the V2-rule.

First, as we have seen, Middle Welsh is not a strict V2-language. It allows preverbal adverbs to occur in positions other than SpecCP, some being adjoined to CP or C'. The most straightforward hypothesis would be that all preverbal adverbs occupy an adjoined position. The evidence of the preverbal particles is therefore crucial in telling the child that when the only preverbal element is an adverb, it occupies SpecCP.

Secondly, AgrS-to-C movement is not transparent in Middle Welsh as it is in Germanic. Consider a German child who wrongly hypothesizes that, in a V2-structure beginning with an adverb, the adverb occupies an IP-adjoined position, that is:

(1)   [$_{IP}$ *Morgen* [$_{IP}$ *wird* [$_{VP}$ *Peter nach Hause kommen*]]]
       tomorrow will   Peter home   come
       'Tomorrow Peter will come home.'

The German child has plenty of word-order evidence to prove that this is wrong and that the inflected verb does not occupy I. In particular the child will come across evidence showing that IP is head-final in German—for instance, embedded clauses with compound tenses, as in (2), where the inflectional element, the auxiliary *ist*, is in clause-final position.

(2)   . . . [$_{CP}$ *daß* [$_{IP}$ *Peter heute* [$_{VP}$ *nach Hause gekommen*] *ist*]]
       that   Peter today   home   come   is
       '. . . that Peter came home today.'

It should therefore be clear that, if the sentence in (1) really did have the structure hypothesized, the word order would be as in (3), which is not the case.

(3)   *[$_{IP}$ *Morgen* [$_{IP}$ [$_{VP}$ *Peter nach Hause kommen*] *wird*]]
       tomorrow   Peter home   come   will
       'Tomorrow Peter will come home.'

Suppose the Early Modern Welsh child makes a similar 'mistake', and hypothesizes a structure like (4).

(4)   [$_{AgrSP}$ *Yfory* [$_{AgrSP}$ *y*   *gwel*$_V$ [$_{TP}$ *Arthur*$_i$ t$_V$ [$_{VP}$ t$_i$ t$_V$ *y*   *Greal*]]]]
       tomorrow PRT sees   Arthur   the Grail
       'Tomorrow Arthur will see the Grail.'

There is no comparable word-order evidence to correct the mistake, since embedded word order is identically VSO. Once again, the only evidence to lead the child to correct the hypothesis is the agreement relationship between the adverbial and *y(d)*, which suggests that they are in a Spec-head configuration within the same XP.

In both cases, evidence other than the word order of the construction under consideration shows the child that the more complex V2-structure is the correct one. If such evidence falls in frequency, the simpler analyses may become available.

6.2. REDUCTION IN THE EVIDENCE FOR V2

In Chapter 5, change in the system of pronouns and complementizers was examined. The changes discussed there had a significant effect on the quality of the trigger experience in that they reduced the frequency with which children were exposed to V2-structures and therefore the ease with which the V2-parameter could be set correctly. They also increased the number of lexical exceptions to V2. Whereas in Middle Welsh there were only two major classes of exceptions to V2—

namely, negative main clauses and clauses containing auxiliary and copular *bot* 'to be'—by the sixteenth century there were four such classes. Both the affirmative complementizer *fe* and the subject pronoun clitics had to be acquired as lexical exceptions to V2. Since the affirmative complementizer was very frequently used, its effect in impoverishing the triggering evidence for V2 must have been particularly significant.

I now turn to two other aspects of the trigger experience which became signif- icantly less favourable to the acquisition of a positive setting of the V2-parameter during the course of Middle Welsh. First, the status of object topicalization in the trigger experience is considered. Secondly, I examine the preverbal particles.

6.2.1. *The decline of object topicalization*

Object topicalization is frequent in Welsh texts of the thirteenth and fourteenth centuries. In Contemporary Welsh, on the other hand, object topicalization is possible only with a contrastive reading, as in English. Exposure to unmarked OVS structures gives the child evidence for a fronting rule, and, taken together with other word-order possibilities, is evidence for a V2-rule. The frequency of this evidence seems to have declined gradually in the course of Middle Welsh. It is, of course, not possible to equate the textual evidence with the trigger experience itself, since questions of narrative style interfere in the texts. However, the kind of drift away from OVS in texts is at least suggestive of a similar drift away from OVS in the trigger experience.

I shall demonstrate this effect quantitatively by looking at a number of Middle and Early Modern Welsh texts. One way to look at the development is to ask to what extent the possibility of object topicalization was in fact utilized where it was syntactically available. Table 6.1 shows the frequency with which direct objects are

TABLE 6.1. *Frequency of object topicalization in Welsh texts, 1200–1700*

Text	Date	Objects topicalized (%)	Sample size
Historia Gruffud vab Kenan	*c.*1250	42	50
Pwyll	end 13th c.	34	50
Peredur	end 13th c.	46	50
Ystoryaeu Seint Greal	end 14th c.	8	50
Y Bibyl Ynghymraec (MS P)	*c.*1350–1450	8	50
Buchedd Sant Martin	1488–9	10	50
'Buchedd Collen'	1536	16	25
'Darnau o'r Efengylau'	1550–75	8	24
'Ystori Alexander a Lodwig'	*c.*1590	4	50
Y Bibyl Ynghymraec (MS A)	1594	27	22
'Mab y Fforestwr'	*c.*1600	0	50
Llyfr y Tri Aderyn	1653	12	50

topicalized in a number of texts from the thirteenth to seventeenth centuries. In each case a quota of the first fifty instances of nominal (non-clausal and non-pronominal) direct objects is considered, or the whole text if there are fewer than fifty relevant cases. Excluded are the direct objects of imperative verbs, negative verbs, and nonfinite verbs, and direct objects in questions. That is, attention is focused on the direct object in a typical main clause with subject, synthetic verb, and direct object. This is a standard position in which topicalization may be expected to take place, and excludes environments which inhibit or prohibit topicalization.

It can be seen from Table 6.1 that object topicalization was on the decline in the medieval period, and that it became rare quite early, perhaps as early as the fourteenth century. A closer examination of the ways in which object topicalization is used is also supportive of such claims. In the early texts object-fronting is most commonly the fronting of the direct object of a personal form of the verb. For instance, of the seventeen examples of object topicalization in the sample from *Pwyll*, fifteen are direct objects of personal verbs, and in *Peredur* it is twenty-two out of twenty-three. Admittedly, in *Historia Gruffud vab Kenan* (*HGK*) it is only eleven out of twenty-one, but in general in early texts it is clear that the great majority of instances of object topicalization are with personal verbs. Data from quantitative textual studies support this. For instance, Poppe (1989: 47) states that, out of thirty instances of object topicalization in *Breuddwyd Maxen* (*BM*), all but two are in clauses with personal forms of the verb. In *Breudwyt Ronabwy* (*BR*) it is seven out of thirteen (Poppe 1990: 449), and in *Branwen* nine out of twelve object topicalizations are with personal verbs (Watkins 1983–4: 152).

In the later texts, object-fronting is much more frequently associated with impersonal (pseudo-passive) forms of the verb, the objects of which may have syntactic and pragmatic similarities with subjects. One of the later texts examined, *Y Bibyl Ynghymraec* (*BY*) (MS A (1594)) seems to fall outside the general pattern of decreasing frequency of object topicalization in having an unexpectedly high frequency. Yet, even in this text object topicalization is more closely associated with impersonal forms of the verb than it is in texts of the earlier period. Only three out of the six cases of object topicalization are with personal verbs.

Other studies also provide support for the claim that there is a marked decline in the frequency of direct-object-fronting in late Middle Welsh and Early Modern Welsh. Studies of Middle Welsh word order give the frequency of clauses with topicalized objects as a percentage of all declarative main clauses at between 4 per cent (*Cyfranc Lludd a Llefelys* (*CLlLl*) (Poppe 1991*a*)) and 20 per cent (*Breuddwyd Maxen* (Poppe 1989)), averaging out at around 10 per cent. Data from studies of texts from later periods suggest that the frequency of object topicalization had settled down to something approaching the low level of contrastive object-fronting in Contemporary Welsh by the sixteenth century at the latest. Fife (1991) puts the frequency of nominal object topicalization in main clauses in Elis Gruffydd's

Castell yr Iechyd (*CI*) and the 1588 Bible translation at between 1 and 4 per cent. This is close to the Contemporary Welsh situation, where object topicalization is statistically negligible, as described in Fife (1993). Even allowing for differences in the counting procedures between studies, these data support the claim that there was a significant drop in the use of object topicalization already in the medieval period.

D. Simon Evans (1968) provides copious examples of fronting in religious texts of the late sixteenth and early seventeenth centuries. From the examples given it is impossible to determine the frequency of object topicalization. Certainly, there are some examples of non-contrastive direct object topics. In the main, however, the examples given there in these texts involve either a contrastively topicalized object, or the object of an impersonal verb.

The evidence discussed above points towards the general conclusion that non-contrastive direct-object topicalization, with the exception of the direct object of impersonal verbs, was rare, although not ungrammatical, by the Early Modern Welsh period. There is every reason to suppose that, in terms of the theory of syntactic change discussed in Chapter 2, this is a step—namely a performance change affecting the frequency with which a particular construction is chosen in actual use. Inasmuch as object topicalization was good evidence for V2, this represents an impoverishment of the triggering data for the acquisition of a positive setting of the V2-parameter.

Most importantly, this gradual decline in the use of object topicalization is not part of a wider reduction in the use of V2-structures. That is, there is no gradual drift from V2 to VSO in the medieval period, as Fife (1991) implies (see Section 4.1). By the seventeenth century, when object topicalization is rare, there is good evidence that subject topicalization was still productive in all, including spoken, varieties of Welsh. For instance, there are numerous examples of subject topicalization in slander-case records of the sixteenth and seventeenth centuries. Examples are given in (5).

(5) (a) *Thomas ap Madock aeth am   hanneyr i   yn lledraddaidd.*
         Thomas ap Madog went with-my heifer   me thievishly
         'Thomas ap Madog stole my heifer.'
                                        (Slander case, Brecon Sessions (1577))

     (b) *John ap Robert a   ddygodd yd   Bryn yr Odyn yn lledrad.*
         John ap Robert PRT took   grain Bryn-yr-Odyn thievishly
         'John ap Robert stole the Bryn-yr-Odyn grain.'
                                         (Slander case, Flint Sessions (1618))

It can, therefore, be concluded that object topicalization ceased to be common at a date when topicalization of nominal subjects was still common, and that this is true even in non-literary varieties of Welsh. On the other hand, true VSO

structures—that is, those with the verb in absolute initial position not preceded by
y(d) or *fe*—remain virtually non-existent up to the sixteenth century.

6.2.2.   *The loss of the preverbal particles*

Topic-complementizer agreement realized on the preverbal particles is a good
guide to the correct placement of preverbal adverbs in SpecCP rather than in an
adjoined position. Any phonological reduction of these particles will necessarily
obscure a crucial piece of evidence for acquisition of V2.

We saw above (Section 5.1.2) that the preverbal particle *a* was lost after
pronominal subjects in the sixteenth century. The loss of *a* is observed with full
lexical elements soon afterwards. Examples are given in (6) (see also DFf 156. 14,
and perhaps *RhG* i. 14. 20, 16. 9).

(6)   (*a*) . . . *a   jessu gwnnwys yolwc   y vynydd* . . .
            and Jesus raised   his-look up
            'And Jesus looked up.'   (DE 402. 10–11 (1550–75))

    (*b*) *A   chwedy kinio   mynegi   wnaeth gwraig y   ty   gwbl o 'r*
        and after   dinner indicate-VN did   woman the house whole of the
        matter y 'r   gwr . . .
        matter to the husband
        'And after dinner, the woman of the house indicated the whole matter
        to the husband . . .'   (*RhG* ii. 79. 15–17 (MS *c*.1588))

From the sixteenth century *y(r)* in preverbal position begins to be dropped too.[2]
D. Simon Evans (1968) suggests that, with this loss, the syntactic connection
between the preverbal adverb and the rest of the sentence would be lost, and 'the
adverb would no longer be confined by the syntax of the sentence to the position
which it occupied in the "abnormal order"' (D. Simon Evans 1968: 335). In
generative terms, this can be equated with a claim that the position occupied by the
preverbal adverb had changed from a specifier position to an adjoined position.
This position must be modified somewhat, in that some adverbs already occupied
adjoined positions even in Middle Welsh. However, it seems essentially correct that
the loss of the particle *y(r)* is the single most important development precipitating
the breakdown of verb-second.

D. Simon Evans (1968: 335) gives examples of omission of *y(r)* in the sequence
yma gellir 'here it can be . . .' from Morys Clynnog's *Athravaeth Gristnogavl*
(1568). He also gives a larger number of more varied examples from Roger
Smyth's *Theater du Mond* (1615).

Earlier examples of the loss of *y(r)* after a sentence-initial adverbial from the late
fifteenth century and the sixteenth century are given in (7). Omission of *y(r)* after
adverbs in the written language was certainly widespread by the second half of the
sixteenth century.[3]

(7) (a) A   phann oedd ddec blwydd o oedran aeth yr   eglwys o
         and when was ten   years of age   went to-the church from
         anvodd   i   rieni   i geisio   bedydd . . .
         disapproval his parents to seek-VN baptism
         'And when he was ten years old, he went to church against his par-
         ents' wishes to seek baptism.' (*BSM* I. 10–11 (MS 1488–9))

     (b) *Ac ynna gouynno*[*dd*] *hi   Jddo   ef   pa ddelw J   gollyngei   ef*
         and then asked   she to-3SM him how   PRT released-IMPF he
         J   veisdyr ynhrydd.
         his master PRD+free
         'And then she asked him how he had released his master.'
                                                              (*YT* 74. 9–10 (1540s))

     (c) *Yn vffern peraist   gyffro* . . .
         in hell   caused-2S commotion
         'In hell you caused a commotion . . .'
                                         (*TWRP, Y Dioddefaint*, 825 (MS 1552))

     (d) . . . *os kwys   lydan a   erddy,   a   gado   y   tir yn vyw*
             if furrow broad PRT plough-2S and leave-VN the land PRD alive
         rwng   y   kwysay, twyllaist   y   tir a   chollaist yr had.
         between the furrows, deceived-2S the land and lost-2S the seed
         '. . . if you plough a broad furrow, and leave the land alive in between
         the furrows, you have deceived the land and you have lost the seed.'
                                         (*RhG* i. 57. 32–58. 1 (before 1561))

At this early stage there is evidence that the omission of *y(r)* is a purely phonological phenomenon—that is, the particle is still present at an underlying level. This
evidence comes from the observed forms of *a(c)* 'and', which in general appears
as *a* before a consonant and as *ac* before a vowel. In 'Darn o'r Ffestival' (DFf)
(1550–75), a text in which *y(r)* is sometimes omitted, the form is *ac* in contexts
where the following word begins with a consonant but where *y(r)* would have been
expected to occur. An example is given in (8) (see also DFf 165. 23).

(8)   . . . *ef aeth anyssbrydoedd ac   ef   yr   poenav tragwddawl, ac*
                 it went evil-spirits   with him to-the pains   eternal   and
             yr   agores y ddayar, ac llyngkawdd y wyr ef oll.
             PRT opened the earth   and swallowed his men him all
             '. . . evil spirits took him to eternal torment, and the earth opened and it
             swallowed all his men.' (DFf 162. 3–5 (1550–75))

Therefore, we must posit the presence of *y(r)* at whatever level of representation
the form of *a(c)* is determined.

6.3. A PARAMETRIC CHANGE

With respect to the evidence outlined in Section 6.1 as crucial for children's acquisition of a V2-system, the changes sketched out above represent a significant impoverishment of the trigger experience. 'Simpler' analyses of V2-structures are available to the child which do not require a full V2-system.

Consider first the case with an adverb in the topic position SpecCP. Preverbal adverbials had always had to be licensed, with variations according to adverb type, either in SpecCP or in an adjoined position. With the loss of the preverbal particle $y(r)$, the motivation for separating these two structural positions was lost. The possible patterns for simple sentences containing a subject, verb, and non-argument adverb before and after the loss of preverbal particles are those in (9)–(11).

	Middle Welsh		Early Modern Welsh
(9) (a)	*Arthur a welodd gaer.*	→ (b)	*Arthur welodd gaer.*
	Arthur PRT saw fort		Arthur saw fort
	'Arthur saw a fort.'		'Arthur saw a fort.'

(10) (a)	*Yna y gwelodd Arthur gaer.* → (b)	*Yna gwelodd Arthur gaer.*
	then PRT saw Arthur fort	then saw Arthur fort
	'Then Arthur saw a fort.'	'Then Arthur saw a fort.'

(11) (a)	*Yna Arthur a welodd gaer.* → (b)	*Yna Arthur welodd gaer.*
	then Arthur PRT saw fort	then Arthur saw fort
	'Then Arthur saw a fort.'	'Then Arthur saw a fort.'

Given the knowledge that agreement is between a head and specifier position, the Middle Welsh child can easily establish from the evidence of the preverbal particles that in (9a) and (11a) the subject occupies SpecCP, and that in (10a) *yna* occupies SpecCP. The child is thus led away from adopting the same position for *yna* in both (10a) and (11a). With the loss of the particles in Early Modern Welsh, the child has no reason to suppose that *yna* in (10b) occupies SpecCP. On the other hand, the adverb cannot be in a specifier position in (11b) but must be adjoined, since the specifier position is filled by the subject *Arthur*. The simplest hypothesis is therefore that *yna* always occupies an adjoined position. This hypothesis is supported by the presence in the trigger experience of instances of multiple sentence-initial adverbs (cf. the examples in (13) in Chapter 3). The child is likely to conclude that *yna* in (10b) does not occupy SpecCP but rather some adjoined position. Furthermore, given that there is now no overt element in C, the child has no reason to infer raising of the verb to C to give support to the particle.[4] The reanalysis indicated in (12) can therefore take place. The adult grammar produces representations like that in (12a), with the preverbal particle deleted in speech. The child infers a grammar that generates the representation in (12b), which does not contain a preverbal particle at any level. The reanalysed structure is preferred by the Least Effort Strategy because it allows the rejection of a representation with chains (*Arthur*$_i$, t$_i$) and (*gwelodd*$_V$, t$_V$, t$_V$, t$_V$) with six chain positions in favour of one with shorter chains (*Arthur*$_i$, t$_i$) and (*gwelodd*$_V$, t$_V$, t$_V$). For concreteness it is assumed that, in the new structure, preverbal adverbs adjoin to C′.

(12) (*a*)

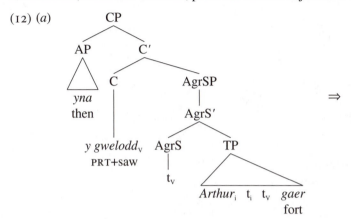

(*b*)

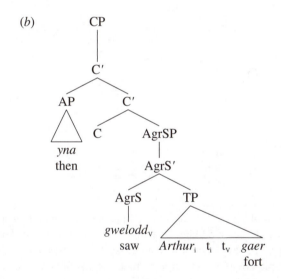

To a child who rejects the possibility that the language is verb-second, surface SVO orders are also amenable to a non-V2 analysis, involving subject-raising to SpecAgrSP. That is, in the adult grammar, SVO orders are subsumed under general verb-second. However, they are also open to an analysis parallel to SVO in English or French, with subject-raising to a preverbal position. With the loss of preverbal particles, this analysis becomes quite attractive. Thus (13), analysed in the adult grammar and by earlier generations of Welsh speakers as (14*a*), can be acquired by the innovating generation of children as (14*b*).

(13)   *Arthur (a) welodd gaer.*
        Arthur PRT saw   fort
        'Arthur saw a fort.'

(14) *(a)*

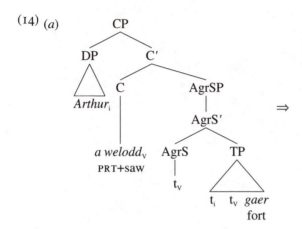

(b)

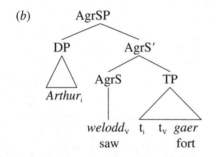

Suppose that under normal circumstances, these analyses are ones that are adopted by children, only to be rejected later in acquisition by a full V2-system. By the sixteenth century, the evidence for the V2-system, particularly the evidence in the form of topic-complementizer agreement, is insufficient to cause the new analysis either of preverbal adverbs or of SVO structures to be rejected. As soon as the new structures are accepted, however, the evidence for V2 in the form of variation in the order of element drops virtually to nil. The language contains virtually no sentences that are being analysed as V2 or that need to be analysed as V2. Children will, therefore, begin to set the V2-parameter to a negative value. Whatever the precise nature of the V2-parameter, this has the effect that SpecCP is no longer obligatorily filled, and general A'-movement to SpecCP is lost.

Of course there remain some sentences in the trigger experience that are not so easily amenable to a non-V2 analysis. The relevant constructions are non-contrastive topicalizations of non-subjects and possibly instances of adverbs intervening between the subject and verb. However, none of these occurs with sufficient frequency to force rejection of the non-V2 analyses.

Let us now turn to examine the effects of the parametric change on Case-assignment. The change in the structure assigned to SVO main clauses requires that Nominative Case be assigned by Infl (AgrS) optionally either under government or agreement. In the Middle Welsh system, Infl (AgrS) assigns Nominative Case mainly under government to SpecTP. The innovation of the affirmative comple-mentizer *fe* did nothing to alter this. However, if our account of agreement and of expletive subjects is correct, and SpecCP can under some circumstances be an A-position (cf. Sections 3.5 and 5.2.1), then unfocused preverbal subjects and expletive subjects must have received Case in SpecCP even in Middle Welsh—that is, under agreement from a Nominative Case-assigner in C. Some instances of Case-assignment under agreement must therefore also have existed.

Once the analysis of SVO in (14*b*) is adopted, the possibilities for Case-assignment under agreement must be extended to permit general assignment of Nominative by Infl under agreement. This change in the configuration for Case-assignment may be a parametric change, although one which seems to have had little effect on the output of the grammar.

If we consider the different word-order possibilities now permitted by the language, the configurations for Case-assignment become clear. Three word-order possibilities are given in (15). Since no A′-chains are ever formed, it must be assumed that Nominative Case is assigned to the surface position of the subject in each instance. That is, Case may be assigned to SpecAgrSP in the AdvSVO order, but to SpecTP in the AdvVSO order. In order to allow for this, it has to be assumed that Case-assignment by Infl (AgrS) is possible under government to SpecTP and under agreement to SpecAgrSP, and that it is always entirely optional. Accordingly, for a sentence like (15*a*) to be generated, the verb must fail to assign case rightwards to the subject in SpecTP, even though it could have assigned case to that position, and indeed does so in the VSO counterparts in (15*b*) and (15*c*).

(15) (*a*) $[_{CP} [_{C'} yna [_{AgrSP} Arthur_i welodd_V [_{TP} t_i t_V [_{VP} t_i t_V gaer]]]]]$
      then   Arthur saw   fort

   (*b*) $[_{CP} [_{C'} yna [_C fe-welodd_V] [_{AgrSP} t_V [_{TP} Arthur_i t_V [_{VP} t_i t_V gaer]]]]]$
      then   PRT-saw   Arthur   fort

   (*c*) $[_{CP} [_{C'} yna [_{AgrSP} gwelodd_V [_{TP} Arthur_i t_V [_{VP} t_i t_V gaer]]]]]$
      then   saw   Arthur   fort
   'Then Arthur saw a fort.'

Given the subsequent historical preference for structures such those in (15*b*) and (15*c*), it may be that this possibility should be allowed for. However, it is worth noting that, under minimalist assumptions, the structure in (15*a*) involving the unnecessary raising of the subject violates Procrastinate (Chomsky 1995: 198). The presence of the complementizer *fe* may be sufficient to cause (15*a*) and (15*b*) to involve distinct derivations, involving distinct numerations in the sense of Chomsky (1995: 227). However, it is hard to see how this could be the case with (15*a*) and (15*c*), which seem to differ solely in the fact that the subject has raised above the verb in (15*a*) but not in (15*c*).

I shall, however, assume that Nominative Case may be assigned by Infl (AgrS) either under government or agreement after the loss of V2 in Welsh.

If the presence of topic-complementizer agreement was so crucial for the retention of V2 in Middle Welsh, it is reasonable to ask why other V2-languages, most of which lack an equivalent for the preverbal particles of Welsh, have not lost V2 also. There are three reasons: first, strict V2-languages like German do not allow preverbal adverbs that do not count for V2—that is, they do not license C′-adjunction at all, and do not freely license CP-adjunction. Consequently, a child learning a language like German will never be exposed to sentences like the Welsh one in (11), which confirms the possibility of adjoining an adverb to CP. Given this, the optimal hypothesis for the structure of a sentence parallel to (10*b*) in German will always be with the adverb in SpecCP.

Secondly, other word-order evidence—notably, object and VP-topicalization—supports a V2-analysis in these languages. This had originally also been the case for Middle Welsh children. They would encounter instances of OVS order in main clauses, and from this would have to infer the existence of a preverbal A′-position to which topicalization may take place. The frequency with which this piece of evidence is encountered falls in late Middle Welsh, and the child is thus unable to use it to construct a grammar containing A′-topicalization to SpecCP.

Finally, there is word-order evidence for AgrS-to-C movement in most V2-languages—for instance, in asymmetries between main and subordinate clauses or between synthetic and periphrastic verb construction. No such evidence for AgrS-to-C movement ever existed in Welsh.

6.4.   CONSEQUENCES OF THE PARAMETRIC CHANGE

If a parametric change is posited, it is reasonable to ask what changes it produced in the output of the grammar in terms of 'trailing' changes. In the case of the resetting of the V2-parameter, changes are manifested in one new word-order type—namely, true VSO—and also in obsolescence of a number of other structures. I now turn to these changes.

6.4.1.   *The null topic operator and true VSO*

The loss of the positive setting for the V2-parameter creates serious difficulties for the acquisition of the null topic operator posited for Middle Welsh surface VSO main clauses in Chapter 4. Since the null topic operator has no phonological exponent, it cannot be acquired directly from the trigger experience. Instead it has to be acquired using indirect evidence.

The child must infer a null element in these clauses by generalizing from the standard cases of V2 with overt elements. A null operator had to be posited in VSO conjoined clauses like (16a) because of the presence of the particle $y(d)$, which required its specifier position to have an appropriate agreeing constituent. The loss of $y(d)/y(r)$ creates acquisitional ambiguity with conjoined clauses. Once it is lost, these clauses contain no evidence in favour of general V2, and can be analysed satisfactorily as VSO. They thus appear to give the child firm evidence that VSO is in fact generally possible. The adult grammar analyses (16a) as (17). A child hearing (16b) no longer has any reason to reject the analysis in (18). In the course of this reanalysis the null topic operator necessarily fails to be acquired in the child's lexicon.

(16) (a) *Arthur a   ddaeth ac y   gwelodd ef gaer.*
       Arthur PRT came   and PRT saw   he fort $\rightarrow$

   (b) *Arthur ddaeth a   gwelodd ef gaer.*
       Arthur came   and saw   he fort
       'Arthur came and saw a fort.'

(17) $[_{CP}$*Arthur*$_i$ *a ddaeth*$_{V1}$ $[_{IP}$ t$_i$ t$_{V1}]]$

       ac

       $[_{CP}$ Op$_j$ *y gwelodd*$_{V2}$ $[_{IP}$ *ef* t$_{V2}$ *gaer*$]$ t$_j]$

(18) $[_{CP}$ $[_{IP}$*Arthur*$_i$ *ddaeth*$_{V1}$ $[_{VP}$ t$_i$ t$_{V1}]]]$

       a

       $[_{CP}$ $[_{IP}$*gwelodd*$_{V2}$ $[_{VP}$ *ef* t$_{V2}$ *gaer*$]]]$

With the loss of V2, the null topic operator should therefore drop out of the language. It is difficult to find reliable data to prove this with reference to conjoined clauses in the sixteenth and seventeenth centuries. Better data are available from the eighteenth-century corpus. Discussion of these is deferred until consideration of the eighteenth-century material in Chapter 7 (Section 7.9).

The more important case, however, is the one in non-conjoined clauses. The null topic operator was restricted to conjoined clauses and similar contexts because of a requirement that it be discourse-licensed. Once the contexts in which it was formerly used are analysed in a different way, there is no reason for this discourse requirement to continue. To look at it another way, since the core grammar no longer requires movement of some element to SpecCP, cases should appear quite generally where such movement has not taken place. If, as a result of the new negative setting of the V2-parameter, SpecCP is permitted to be actually empty (rather than apparently empty but filled by a null topic operator), then it should be possible for there to be no complementizer at all in C. Furthermore, assuming that movement of the verb to C is motivated solely by the need to give morphological support to the complementizer, the verb itself should also now be free to remain in AgrS. It is, therefore, expected that structures of the type in (19) will become possible. This is a major departure from the Middle Welsh system, but is precisely the structure that has been assumed for VSO in Modern Welsh (cf. (25), (36), and (38) in Chapter 1).

(19) $[_{CP} [_{AgrSP}$ verb$_V$ $[_{TP}$ subject$_i$ t$_V$ $[_{VP}$ t$_i$ t$_V$ object]]]]

It is thus expected that the parametric change will lead to the introduction into the language of unmarked absolute verb-initial sentences, without the particle $y(r)$ and without the need for the null operator. A few examples of these were given for Middle Welsh in (37) and (38) in Chapter 4, but these were only isolated, and often formulaic, examples. They appear on a wide scale only from the second half of the sixteenth century. Early examples are given in (20).[5]

(20) (a) *Gorvüost   ar dy   elynion . . .*
         overcame-2s on your enemies
         'You overcame your enemies . . .'   (*RhG* i. 22. 28–9 (*c*.1514))

     (b) *Gellwch wybod   yn hysbys am   bob peth   y   fo*
         can-2P   know-VN publicly about everything REL be-SUBJ
         kyfiownys na   wnaf   i yn erbyn ych wllys.
         just   COMP+NEG will-do-1s I against   your will
         'You may know publicly that, regarding everything that is just, I shall not act against your will.'
                                      (*TWRP, Yr Enaid a'r Corff*, 139–41 (MS 16th c.))

     (c) *Jessu dywedaist di   dy   vod   yn   vrenin ar yn defod.*
         Jesus said-2s   you 2s-GEN be-VN PRD king   on our custom
         'Jesus, you said that you were king according to our custom.'
                                      (*TWRP, Y Dioddefaint*, 197–8 (MS 1552))

     (d) *Gofynnasoch ym . . . ae   i briodi   Mrs Watkins y*
         asked-2P   to-me whether-CLEFT to marry-VN Mrs Watkins PRT
         doethwn . . .
         had-come-1s
         'You asked me . . . whether it was to marry Mrs Watkins that I had come . . .'   (*RhG* ii. 52. 17–18 (1582–3))

This change shows all the signs of being parametric in origin. Specifically, the discourse-marked VSO construction of Middle Welsh is replaced in the sixteenth century by general unmarked VSO. As was suggested in Section 4.4, it is therefore possible to reject the idea (Fife 1991) that there was a gradual drift towards VSO order. Instead, we find little evidence for true VSO up to the sixteenth century, but rapid innovation during the century. The conservative pattern is maintained in some sixteenth-century texts, notably in the 1588 Bible translation which paradoxically Fife uses as evidence for the drift to VSO.

6.4.2. *The loss of minor topicalization types*

In Section 3.4.3 the existence of minor topicalization types was used to justify the claim that V2 in Middle Welsh involved A'-movement. Specifically, these types involved topicalization from embedded nonfinite clauses and from Prepositional Phrases. It is clear that, unlike, say, object topicalization, these would never have been sufficiently frequent to have provided acquisitional evidence in favour of V2. However, once V2 is lost, these types should disappear silently from the language.[6] Their disappearance is thus a change in a trailing feature (cf. Section 2.3.3).

First, let us consider topicalization of the object of a preposition, an unmarked construction in Middle Welsh. Some examples of this can still be found in sixteenth-century texts.

(21) (*a*) *Gwr o   'r Deheûbarth Cymrû a   latratesit   dwy hepher*
         man from the South   Wales PRT was-stolen-IMPERS two heifer
         y   arnaw ____ . . .
         from on-3SM ____
         'Two heifers were stolen from a man from the south of Wales . . .'
                                (*RhG* ii. 183. 8–9 (MS *c*.1600))

(*b*) . . . *a   hwnnw a   hapiodd iddo   ____ glefychy a   marw* . . .
         and that-one PRT happened to-3SM ____ fall-ill-VN and die-VN
         '. . . and he happened to fall ill and die . . .'   (DFf 87. 1–2 (1550–75))

(*c*) . . . *a   'r brenin a   fu   drist ganddo   ____.*
         and the king   PRT was-PERF sad with-3SM ____
         '. . . and the king became sad.'
                           (Matt. 14: 9 (1588) (Richards 1938: 109))

However, these seem to be some of the last examples of this construction. The disappearance of this construction is to be expected if unmarked topicalization is reanalysed as A-movement, and therefore restricted to subjects.

Similarly, (non-contrastive) topicalization from embedded positions had been quite possible in fourteenth-century texts. In Early Modern Welsh literary texts topicalizations from positions which might be considered to be embedded are still attested. D. Simon Evans (1968) gives some examples with topicalization of objects across modals (*dyl-* 'should' and *gallael* 'to be able') and the verbs *darfod* 'to happen, finish', *mynnu* 'to want', and *gorfod* 'to have to' in religious texts of the later sixteenth and early seventeenth centuries. There are no examples anywhere, however, of topicalization from complement clause with overt subjects —for instance, from complements of verbs of saying, thinking, or knowing, the typical cases in Middle Welsh. It is reasonable to suppose that in the literary language topicalization remained as a feature of high style. Outside literary texts, such topicalizations are very rare and also restricted to the same sorts of verbs—for instance, *RhG* i. 24. 28, (?) 25. 32, 130. 4.

I conclude that the topicalizations that are attested reflect a literary phenomenon. The fact that such constructions were no longer possible in the core grammar is shown by the complete absence of unmarked topicalizations from complement clauses with overt subjects. It is, therefore, possible to view the absence of unmarked topicalization from embedded contexts as a consequence of the loss of V2.

6.4.3. *Topicalization across negation*

Topicalization of a subject across a negative continues to be attested in the fifteenth and sixteenth centuries.[7]

(22) (*a*) *A   Chollen nid   aeth.*
          and Collen   NEG went
          'And Collen did not go.'   (*RhG* i. 39. 28 (1536))

      (*b*) . . . *kanys yntwy   ni   wyddant beth i   maent yn   i*
              for   they-CONJ NEG know-3P what PRT are   PROG 3SM-GEN
              wnythyr.
              do-VN
              '. . . for they do not know what they are doing.'
                            (*TWRP, Y Dioddefaint*, 327–8 (MS 1552))

D. Simon Evans (1968: 322) cites a number of examples from texts of the late sixteenth and early seventeenth centuries, although the texts are all highly literary, and as such of dubious value as to the status of this construction in the spoken language of the time. In particular, these texts contain a number of examples of topicalization across *nid yw*, *nid ydynt*, and *nid ynt* 'is, are not', forms which do not allow topicalization over them (even in the affirmative) in Middle Welsh. Such cases point to hypercorrect literary usage in these texts, suggesting that their testimony is in fact not relevant to the question of spoken usage on this point.

Topicalization of a direct object over a negative is attested in these same texts (D. Simon Evans 1968: 323) and also in the 1588 Bible translation (Richards 1938: 107), but not elsewhere in the sixteenth century.[8] It is difficult to be sure whether this reflects the general decline in the frequency of object topicalization, or is a development specific to the negative. I shall assume the former on the grounds that the latter interpretation is not especially well supported by the evidence, and would involve an unnecessary complication of the analysis.

Most importantly, however, topicalization of any kind across a negative is not attested in non-literary texts from around 1600 onwards, even though preverbal subjects are well-attested in affirmative main clauses at this period.[9]

This is no surprise given the analysis of negation presented in Section 3.6 and the changes in topicalization suggested above. If the negative marker *ni(d)* originates in C, then given a rule of topicalization that consists of A′-movement to SpecCP, the grammar will permit strings of the form [$_{CP}$ XP$_i$ Neg+V [$_{IP}$ . . . t$_i$ . . .]]. This is the case in the earlier period. However, once topicalization is reanalysed as Subject-raising to SpecAgrSP, this is not possible. The negative marker C will necessarily precede the subject, whether it is in the topicalization position (SpecAgrSP) or in the lower position (SpecTP). It can be assumed either that the negative marker attracts the verb to C for morphological reasons, or that, because it is a (PF-)clitic, it must be adjacent to the verb. Under either assumption, movement of the subject to a position between the negative marker and the verb is ruled out. The scenario envisaged (under the latter assumption) for a negative main clause like (23) is shown in (24).

(23) *Ni thyciodd hynny.*
      NEG availed   that
      'That did not work.'

(24)

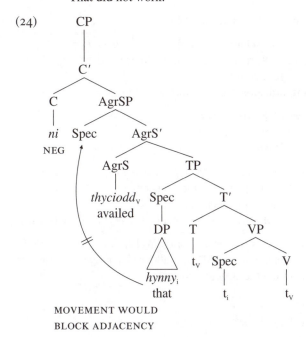

6.4.4. *Embedded clauses*

One might expect from the fact that the CP-projection is no longer involved in the derivation of SVO structures in Early Modern Welsh that SVO should spread to embedded clauses. That is, we expect structures of the type in (25).

(25) $[_{CP}$ comp $[_{AgrSP}$ subject$_i$ verb$_V$ $[_{TP}$ t$_i$ t$_V$ $[_{VP}$ t$_i$ t$_V$ object]]]

In general this does not occur, except with complementizers like *canys* 'since' that already allowed V2 in Middle Welsh. That this does not in general happen may be attributed to the fact that almost all complementizers are clitics on the verb. One may surmise that the cliticization process is disrupted by the presence of an intervening subject.

However, one change in the structure of embedded clauses is suggestive in this respect, although doubt as to the status of the complementizer involved makes it unclear precisely what conclusions should be drawn. The change is in the syntax of *os* 'if'. Richards (1938: 181) and Stephen J. Williams (1980: 159) note, citing examples mainly from the Bible translation, that unmarked SVO order with agreement (the abnormal order) can be found after this complementizer. In Contemporary Welsh the construction is archaic at best. Examples are given in (26).

(26) (*a*) . . . *os ti   ai   hesceulusi* . . .
        if you PRT+3S-ACC neglect-2S
        '. . . if you neglect it'   (*LlTA* 74. 29 (1653))

     (*b*) . . . *os y ni   a   ddychwelwn atto êf   a   gwîr ofid.*
        if we-CONJ PRT return-1P to him with true fear
        '. . . if we return to him with true fear.'
                (John Langford, *Holl Ddledswydd Dyn*, 13 (1672), (*GPC* 2604))

     (*c*) . . . *os ni a   wrandawn ar S. Paul* . . .
        if we PRT listen-1P to St Paul
        '. . . if we listen to St Paul . . .'   (*RhG* ii. 213. 24–5 (1606))

     (*d*) *Ac os myfi   a   af . . . mi a   ddeuaf   drachefn* . . .
        and if I-CONJ PRT go-1S I PRT come-1S back
        'And if I go . . . , I shall come back . . .'
                (John 14: 3 (1588) Stephen J. Williams 1980: 159))

Since *os* is independent of the verb in Contemporary Welsh, it is possible that in this construction the verb remains in AgrSP, and allows the subject to raise to SpecAgrSP, thereby instantiating the structure in (25).

6.5. RESIDUAL V2 IN CONTEMPORARY WELSH

Despite what has been said so far about the loss of V2 in Early Modern Welsh, some instances of V2, involving a filled SpecCP position and a particle in C, nevertheless survive into Contemporary Welsh. Residual V2 is a phenomenon common in other languages that have lost a verb-second system (cf. Rizzi 1990;

Vikner 1995: 48–51). The contexts in which V2 survives in Contemporary Welsh parallel what is found in these languages.

Mostly these involve contrastive focus in the mixed sentence. A Contemporary Welsh example with contrastively focused subject is shown in (27*a*); (27*b*) has contrastively focused object; and (27*c*) a contrastively focused adjunct.

(27) (*a*) *Afon Teifi a   orlifodd   ei glannau.*
     river Teifi PRT overflowed its banks
     '(It was) the River *Teifi* (that) overflowed its banks.'

   (*b*) *Ci   a   welodd y   ffermwr.*
     dog PRT saw   the farmer
     '(It was) a *dog* (that) the farmer saw.'

   (*c*) *Y   prynhawn yma y   byddaf   fi 'n   mynd.*
     the afternoon this PRT will-be-1S I PROG go-VN
     '(It's) *this afternoon* (that) I'll go.'   (Thorne 1993: 370–3)

I assume that these are instances of V2. Although, as ever in Welsh, verb-raising to C is not visible, the presence of a particle agreeing with the preverbal element is evidence enough that a Spec-head relationship is formed between the head of C and a fronted constituent in SpecCP (cf. Tallerman's 1996 analysis of the mixed sentence as A'-movement to SpecCP).

Wh-questions in Contemporary Literary Welsh are formed in the same way, in (28).

(28) (*a*) *Beth a   barodd iddo greu   'r fath effaith?*
     what PRT caused to-it create-VN the sort effect
     'What caused it to create such an effect?'

   (*b*) *Pa   effaith gafodd dy   bregeth di?*
     what effect had   your sermon you
     'What effect did your sermon have?'

   (*c*) *Sut   y   gwyddoch chi hynny?*
     how PRT know-2P you that
     'How do you know that?'   (Thorne 1993: 187–9)

Once again the particle in C agrees with the *wh*-element in SpecCP.

Clearly, the loss of the positive setting of the V2-parameter must not be allowed to rule out such structures. We should, therefore, envisage the shift in the V2-parameter to be from a situation where fronting is virtually although decreasingly obligatory to one where it is merely permitted, presumably triggered by features of a more specific nature (focus features, interrogative features). Any movement must remain A'-movement, and the mechanisms for it (preverbal particles, agreement patterns) remain the same. In a language in which such movement is not syntactically required, it must be associated with some marked stylistic effect. This is in fact simply the situation required for languages like English which have fronting of *wh*-elements and contrastively focused constituents.

We can assume a structure for (27*b*) as in (29) (cf. (90) in Chapter 3).

(29) $[_{CP} ci_j [_C a$ *welodd*$_V] [_{AgrSP} t_V [_{TP} y$ *ffermwr*$_i t_V [_{VP} t_i t_V t_j]]]]$
        dog PRT saw   the farmer
        '(It was) a *dog* (that) the farmer saw.'

Since the movement in question is identical to A′-movement in relative clauses and in *wh*-questions, there is no reason why the lexical mechanisms that accompany it—namely, the agreeing forms of the preverbal particles on the verb in C— cannot be acquired easily by children even after the loss of V2. It seems likely that the distinctive intonational prominence associated with the contrastive mixed sentence prevented it from following the same historical path as the verb-second abnormal sentence.

A second type of residual V2 occurs with a fixed set of modal adverbs, including in Contemporary Welsh *braidd* 'scarcely', *diamau* 'certainly', *diau* 'certainly', *dichon* 'perhaps', *efallai* 'perhaps', *gobeithio* 'hopefully', *hwyrach* 'probably', *odid* 'probably not, can hardly', and *prin* 'hardly' (cf. King 1993: 260–2; Richards 1938: 103–4). These are all modal adverbs modifying the clause as a whole.

These adverbs must be analysed as occupying SpecCP rather than adjoining to C′ or CP. Compare their distribution to that of an adverb like *yfory* 'tomorrow'. This can appear in sentence-initial position either before a bare verb as in (30*a*) or before a presentential particle *mi* or *fe* as in (30*b*). Its use before the particle *y(r)* is marginal.[10]

(30) (*a*) *Yfory*   (?*y*) *bydd   Ifan yn   mynd adref.*
            Tomorrow (PRT) will-be Ifan PROG go-VN home

     (*b*) *Yfory   fe fydd   Ifan yn   mynd adref.*
            tomorrow PRT will-be Ifan PROG go-VN home
            'Tomorrow Ifan will be going home.'

This follows if *yfory* adjoins to C′. Y(*r*) needs to be in a Spec-head relationship with an agreeing phrasal constituent in SpecCP. An adverb adjoined to C′ does not fulfil this requirement. On the other hand, if C is generated empty or with an affirmative presentential particle *mi* or *fe*, there is no such agreement requirement, and adjunction of the adverb to C′ makes no difference to the grammaticality of the sentence.

The behaviour of residual V2-adverbs is strikingly different, and suggests a typical V2-scenario with a phrasal constituent in SpecCP and V-to-C movement. In (31), *hwyrach* 'probably' may appear before the particle *y(r)* or before a bare verb but not before the particles *mi* or *fe*.

(31) (*a*)   *Hwyrach* (*y*)   *bydd*   *Ifan yn*   *mynd adref yfory.*
probably (PRT) will-be Ifan PROG go-VN home tomorrow.

(*b*) *Hwyrach fe   *fydd*   *Ifan yn*   *mynd adref yfory.*
probably PRT will-be Ifan PROG go-VN home tomorrow.
'Ifan will probably be going home tomorrow.'

This follows if *hwyrach* is base-generated in SpecCP. An element in SpecCP needs to be in a Spec-head relationship with an appropriate element in C. The only appropriate element is the particle *y(r)*, which is now optionally (although generally) omitted in speech. *Mi* and *fe* are ruled out because they are inappropriate agreeing elements for a filled SpecCP.

Similar sets of adverbs triggering residual V2 are found in English and French, and the Welsh particle data are paralleled in those languages by differences in the position of the verb. For instance, obligatory V2 with auxiliary-raising to C (inversion) is found with clause-initial negative adverbs in English, as in (32).

(32)   [$_{CP}$ *Never had* [$_{IP}$ *Mary seen such a mess*]]

Both can be seen as consequences of the presence or absence of a feature on the adverb in SpecCP. This feature must be in an agreement configuration with a matching element in C. In Welsh this element is an agreeing preverbal particle; in French and English there is presumably an equivalent non-overt element which forces verb-raising to C (cf. Rizzi 1990; Roberts 1993*b*: 201; Vikner 1995: 48–51).

How and why such elements survive as V2-triggers even after the loss of V2 is not entirely clear. However, the parallelisms in the class of adverbs that trigger residual V2 in Modern Welsh, English, and French are sufficiently striking to suggest that the maintenance in the lexicon of such a class of adverbs with a V2-feature is a normal part of the loss of V2.

Two other instances of residual V2 in Modern Welsh are worth mentioning. We find unemphatic fronting of the complements of verbs of motion as in (33) with the structure in (34).

(33)   *I 'w waith yr/*fe aeth.*
to his work PRT   went
'To work he went.'   (Thorne 1993: 371)

(34)   [$_{CP}$ [*i'w waith*]$_j$ *yr aeth*$_V$ [$_{AgrSP}$ t$_V$ [$_{TP}$ pro$_i$ [$_{VP}$ t$_i$ t$_V$ t$_j$]]]]

Again this has a direct parallel in a non-V2 language, English, as the translation of (33) shows. The fronted constituent must be base-generated as a complement of the verb, and then raise. Assuming that movement is possible only to SpecCP (rather than, say, to a C′-adjoined position), the obligatory presence of *y(r)* rather than *mi* or *fe* follows in the same way as for V2-adverbs.

We also find non-focus fronting of the VP-complements (but not lone verbnouns) of auxiliaries, in (35).

(35) (*a*) . . . *digwydd   troi   i 'r Swyddfa wnes i* . . .
　　　　happen-VN turn-VN to the office　did-1S I
　　　　'. . . I happened to turn into the office . . .'

　　(*b*) *Disgrifio   bywyd yn America a   wna 'r llyfr sydd*
　　　　describe-VN life   in America PRT does the book be-REL
　　　　o'm blaen.
　　　　in-front-of-me
　　　　'The book in front of me describes life in America.'

(Watkins 1991: 344, 347)

Again the parallel English case in (36) (albeit without inversion) suggests that such clauses can be generated without requiring a positive setting of the V2-parameter.

(36)　　*Richard wanted to finish in time and finish in time he did.*

I shall leave open the question of the precise nature of the V2-trigger in sentences like (35).

To summarize, residual V2 in Modern Welsh is triggered by movement of phrasal constituents to SpecCP, particularly in focus constructions and *wh*-questions, and by a closed class of adverbial triggers base-generated in SpecCP. This behaviour is typical of languages that have lost V2. The V2-parameter must, therefore, be taken as representing a choice between global V2, forced by some feature requiring C and SpecCP to be lexically filled, and the lack of any such requirement. Languages which have a negative setting for the V2 parameter may nevertheless have residual V2-structures triggered in other ways. After the loss of general V2, Welsh retains a number of such structures.

6.6. CONCLUSION

In this chapter a historical development has been presented and justified for Welsh word-order patterns. It has been argued that the evidence in the trigger experience for the correct acquisition of the V2-rule was gradually eroded by a number of processes, specifically the gradual evolution of a marked status for object topicalization; the relaxation of the constraints on expletive topics to a point where a non-V2 general complementizer *fe* is introduced into the lexicon; the development of subject clitics; and in particular the phonological erosion of the preverbal particles. This reduction of evidence reached such a point in the seventeenth century that verb-second failed to be acquired by children learning Welsh. Instead they reanalysed the language as being VSO with optional raising of subjects to preverbal position and free placement of adverbs in a preverbal adjoined position. SVO and AdvVSO order were sufficiently common in the trigger experience that a new grammatical structure had to be assigned to them. Other minor syntactic structures, on the other hand, could be ignored, and were dropped from the language. As in other former V2-languages, some cases of residual V2, many of them lexically specific, survive the loss.

By this stage, it is fair to characterize Welsh as a VSO language. However, SVO structures appear far more frequently in the Welsh of the seventeenth century than in that of the twentieth. In the next chapter I turn to those syntactic innovations of the eighteenth century which removed the remaining instances of SVO from the language, concentrating specifically on grammaticalization in the pronominal system.

7. Pronouns and Complementizers

The focus of discussion now returns to the status of the preverbal subject pronouns. During the eighteenth century, a series of changes in the syntax of these pronouns takes place. In this chapter I show that these changes represent a shift away from SVO orders in Welsh, and help to ensure the dominance of the VSO pattern in Contemporary Welsh. In order to do this, I look at a substantial body of texts from the eighteenth and early nineteenth centuries. For the first time in this study, it will be possible to distinguish sharply the separate development of the literary language and the vernacular, and also the emergence of regional syntactic variation within the vernacular. In presenting the divergent evidence of the different stylistic levels, I concentrate on the developments in the dialects rather than the literary language, in the belief that these allow an investigation into the mechanisms of natural linguistic change in a way that changes in the essentially artificial literary language do not. Before looking at the syntactic changes in detail, I shall begin by discussing the sources of evidence in general, and the texts used in this chapter in particular.

7.1. SOURCES OF LINGUISTIC EVIDENCE

Sources of evidence for the historical development of the Welsh language are significantly richer and more diverse in the eighteenth century than earlier. This is reflected in both published and manuscript sources. The potential audience for books in Welsh had increased substantially as a result of increased literacy produced by the Circulating Schools, reflected, for instance, in the growth in the 1750s in the number of people from lower social classes on lists of subscribers (Richards 1966). The spread of subjects on which books are published in Welsh had increased, and in particular several types of more populist works were beginning to appear on a large scale. These developments inevitably have an effect on the nature of the evidence for linguistic change, introducing a number of new types of potential sources that can be put together to build up a more reliable picture of the state of the language at this period.

The discussion of syntactic change in this chapter uses a corpus of texts selected from a number of the available genres in the period 1760–1825. The total size of the corpus is approximately 300,000 words. For convenience, the corpus is divided into six sections, namely interludes, political texts, personal letters, ballads, trial proceedings, and miscellaneous texts. I now introduce the texts in each of these sections, giving available biographical information about their authors. Unless otherwise stated, biographical details derive from the *Dictionary of Welsh Biography*.

7.1.1. *Interludes*

Interludes, popular plays in verse, are an important source of information about informal Welsh, extant from the start of the seventeenth century. They are described by Bishop Percy in a letter of 1762 to Evan Evans (Ieuan Fardd) as 'Dramatic Pieces, on Scripture and Moral Subjects, which are even yet acted by the vulgar at wakes and festivals on Stages, &c.' (Panton MS 74 (Watkin-Jones 1928: 108)). Evans's reply that they 'deserve only the attention of clowns and rustics' is typical of the dismissive attitude of the literati, and in part this represents an antipathy towards their language, which differed radically from the literary standard. From the early eighteenth century, interludes appear in abundance, in the first half of the century mostly in manuscript. With increased general literacy, an interlude could be made more profitable by publishing it once the performing company had finished touring (G. G. Evans 1950; Watkin-Jones 1928). The earliest datable printed interlude is William Roberts, *Ffrewyll y Methodistiaid* (*FfM*) ('The Scourge of the Methodists' (1745)), the height of production being reached between 1765 and 1790.

Five interludes are included in the corpus, namely Edward Thomas, *Cwymp Dyn* (*CD*) ('The Fall of Man' (*c.*1767–8)), Ellis Roberts, *Gras a Natur* (*GN*) ('Grace and Nature' (1769)), Hugh Jones, *Protestant a Neilltuwr* (*PN*) ('A Protestant and a Non-conformist' (1783)), Thomas Edwards, *Tri Chryfion Byd* (*TChB*) ('The Three Strongmen of the World' (?1789)), and *Ystori Richard Whittington* (*YRW*) ('The Story of Richard Whittington' (1812)).

The authors of all these texts are, or appear to be, from the north-east. This reflects the general concentration of interlude-production in the Vales of Conwy and Clwyd. Of Edward Thomas, very little is known—his home is given on the frontispiece of *Cwymp Dyn* as Rhydwen, Flintshire. Ellis Roberts (d. 1789), as well as writing seven extant interludes, was a prolific writer of ballads and religious 'letters'. He was sexton at Llanddoged, Denbighshire (Watkin-Jones 1926), although he may originally have come from Merionethshire to the west (G. G. Evans 1995: 9–10). Hugh Jones, a farm labourer of Llangwm, Denbighshire, and author of *Protestant a Neilltuwr*, was similarly a prominent figure in the popular literature of the period, writing two other interludes and many ballads and editing two collections of poetry, *Dewisol Ganiadau yr Oes Hon* ('Selected Verses of this Age' (1759)) and *Diddanwch Teuluaidd* ('Family Entertainment' (1763)). Thomas Edwards (Twm o'r Nant) (1739–1810) was born at Llannefydd, Denbighshire, although he worked for most of his life as a haulier in Denbigh, and spent several years in south Wales at Llandeilo, Carmarthenshire. He is the author of eight surviving interludes, as well as numerous ballads and an autobiography.

Ystori Richard Whittington poses several textual difficulties which need to be borne in mind when using it as evidence. Although the author is not named directly, he identifies himself as 'R. a P.' towards the end (*YRW* 70. 20). Although the work was published in 1812, the author also gives the date of composition as 'un mil a saith can mlwydd, | Tri deg sydd yn dygwydd, | Yn wych, heblaw chwe' blwydd, | Am oedran yr Arglwydd' (*YRW* 70. 23–6)—that is, 1736. The initials and date suggest that the author is quite likely to be Richard Parry (1665–1749), author of a manuscript interlude *Cyndrigolion y Deyrnas Hon* (*CDH*) (1737) and of the lost *Hypocristia* upon which Twm o'r Nant based one of his own interludes (G. G. Evans 1950: 90; 1995: 24). Watkin-Jones states that Richard Parry was from Dyserth, Flintshire, apparently basing this on the frontispiece of Thomas Edwards's reworking of *Hypocristia* (Watkin-Jones 1928: 107, 110). The text itself was published in Carmarthen in 1812, and consequently might include some southern linguistic features introduced by the printer.

7.1.2. *Political texts*

The eighteenth century sees the first writings of an explicitly political nature and the first periodicals in Welsh. The earliest Welsh periodicals are Lewis Morris's short-lived *Tlysau yr Hen Oesoedd* ('Jewels of the Former Ages' (1735)), and *Trysorfa Gwybodaeth/Eurgrawn Cymraeg* ('The Treasury of Knowledge'/'The Welsh Magazine' (1770)) (see J. Ifano Jones 1902; T. Llechid Jones 1932; Phillips 1937). A particularly vigorous period of activity is the 1790s, when a number of radically minded journals come and go in the wake of the French Revolution: *Y Cylchgrawn Cynmraeg* ('The Welsh Magazine' (1793–4)), *Y Drysorfa Gymmysgedig* ('The Miscellaneous Treasury' (1795)), and *Y Geirgrawn* ('The Magazine' (1796)). A number of political pamphlets appear at about the same time debating the ideas of the Revolution.

The corpus contains seven political texts: William Richards, *Cwyn y Cystuddiedig* (*CwyC*) ('The Complaint of the Afflicted' (1798)), extracts from *Y Cylchgrawn Cynmraeg* (*CylC*), Thomas Jones, 'Gair yn ei Amser' (GA) ('A Word in Time' (1798)), *Meddyliau yr Esgob Watson* (*MEW*) ('Thoughts of Bishop Watson' (1793)), Walter Davies, *Rhyddid* (*Rhy*) ('Freedom' (1791)), John Jones, *Seren tan Gwmwl* (*StG*) ('Cloud-hidden Star' (1795)), and *Toriad y Dydd* (*TD*) ('The Break of Day' (1797)).

Y Cwyn y Cystuddiedig is a report of the trial of two Pembrokeshire Nonconformists acquitted of conspiring with the French attack near Fishguard in February 1797 (see Davies 1926: 231–5; John James Evans 1928: 177–8; Salmon 1937).

Y Cylchgrawn Cynmraeg is a political periodical, first published in February 1793 in Trefeca. Possibly as a result of government persecution, publication was soon moved in August 1793 to Machynlleth, then in November to Carmarthen. Five issues were published in total (see Davies 1926: 29–40; John James Evans 1928: 73; David Oswald Thomas 1989: 70–9). The editor was Morgan John Rhys (1760–1804), minister and native of Llanfabon (*DWB*) or Llanbradach (Stephens 1986), Glamorgan. The extracts in the corpus consist mainly of news reports, plus Rhys's translation of parts of Volney's *Ruins of Empires*.

Revd. Thomas Jones's 'Gair yn ei Amser' is a quietist response to the radical anti-government pamphlets of the 1790s. The author was a native of Denbigh (see Davies 1926: 84–90; John James Evans 1928: 180–2; Jonathan Jones 1897).

Meddyliau yr Esgob Watson is a translation of Bishop Watson's visitation charge, promoting greater religious tolerance, delivered at Llandaf in June 1791. John James Evans (1928: 58–9) reports Thomas Shankland as claiming that Morgan John Rhys was the translator, but a note in the copy in the Cardiff Free Library says that 'Timothy Davis has in J. D. Lewis's (Llandysul) copy written that the Translation was done by his father', that is Revd. David Davies (Castellhywel, Cardiganshire) (1745–1827) (Davies 1926: 74–5; John James Evans 1935: 125). The English version was published in London in 1792, and the Welsh is a translation of this.

The essay entitled *Rhyddid* by Walter Davies (Gwallter Mechain) (1761–1849) won the essay prize at the eisteddfod held by the Gwyneddigion society at Llanelwy in 1790 (Davies 1926: 194). It is highly conservative in outlook. The author was from Llanfechain, Montgomeryshire.

John Jones (Jac Glan-y-gors) (1766–1821), from Cerrigydrudion, Denbighshire, was the leading radical writer in Welsh of the 1790s. The corpus contains two of his works, *Seren tan Gwmwl* (1795) and *Toriad y Dydd* (1797). *Seren tan Gwmwl* is based on Tom Paine's *Rights of Man*, aiming, as its subtitle 'written for the monolingual Welsh' ('wedi ei ysgrifennu er mwyn y Cymru uniaith') indicates, to make it accessible to a Welsh audience. *Toriad y Dydd* additionally shows the influence of Theophilus Evans's history of the Welsh people *Drych y Prif Oesoedd*. In the discussion which followed the publication of his first work, Jones was criticized by 'Antagonist' (Edward Charles, according to Ifano Jones and Davies) in the periodical *Y Geirgrawn* for his ignorance of the classics and unpolished style. In *Toriad y Dydd* the need to know the classics is specifically rejected (*TD* 15. 22–16. 27). However, other criticism seems to have been accepted, resulting in a more literary style (Davies 1926: 186; John James Evans 1928: 154). For general discussion of John Jones's work, see Davies (1926: 148–86); John James Evans (1928: 148–61); Foulkes (1883); Albert E. Jones (1967); David Oswald Thomas (1989: 82–9).

7.1.3. *Personal letters*

Literary activity and political discussion were also fostered by the various literary societies founded in London. The earliest Welsh society in London was the *Society of Ancient Britons* (1714), but flourishing literary and political activity came only later, with the founding of the Cymmrodorion (1751), and especially of the Gwyneddigion (1770) and Cymreigyddion (1794). In particular, the Gwyneddigion promoted Welsh culture and poetry by holding a series of eisteddfodau in the 1790s, notably at Corwen (1789), Bala (1789), St Asaph (1790), and Llanrwst (1791) (see J. Ifano Jones 1902).

Much of the correspondence of the literary figures involved in the societies survives, and in general much more personal correspondence is available than from the seventeenth century. Although much of this is from highly literate individuals associated with the literary societies (the Morris brothers, Goronwy Owen, and others), there is also a small number of letters from non-literary individuals.

This literary activity provides the bulk of the personal letters included in the corpus—namely, letters relating to the eisteddfodau of the Gwyneddigion society (Eist.), and collections of letters by hymn-writer Ann Griffiths (LAG) (1776–1805, Llanfihangel-yng-Ngwynfa, Mont.), poets David Thomas (LDT) (Dafydd Ddu Eryri, 1759–1822, Waunfawr, Caerns.) and Evan Evans (LEE) (Ieuan Fardd, 1731–88, Lledrod, Cards.), political pamphleteer and balladeer John Jones (LJJ) (see above), and interlude-writer and balladeer Thomas Edwards (LTE) (see above).

In presenting quantitative data from the letters relating to the eisteddfodau, I have split them into groups according to author. The most substantial body of data in fact consists of letters by Thomas Jones (Corwen). Data for other writers are used where there is sufficient material.

Non-literary letters are a particularly valuable source of information about change in the spoken language. Two groups of letters relating to Welsh settlers in the United States have therefore been included (LUSS). The A group relates to settlers from south Merionethshire, the B group to settlers from south-west Carmarthenshire. For translations, summaries, and background information on these letters, see Conway (1961: 55–63) and Dodd (1955). There are also two miscellaneous letters from Caernarfonshire (Misc).

Each of the settlers' letters and miscellaneous letters has been treated as an individual text except in one instance, where there are several letters in the B group by the same individual—namely, Samuel Thomas. This approach creates difficulties because the amount of data for each writer is small, but it allows us to see differences between speakers. In some cases, the amount of data is so small that, although undesirable, it has been necessary to amalgamate each group of letters into a single text. The letters are extremely valuable sources of information about the language of less well-educated speakers, and it is vital to include them in the corpus despite the difficulties.

7.1.4. *Ballads*

Printed ballads are also an important new source of evidence (see Watkin-Jones 1926), appearing at about the same time as the printed interludes. Again, these were despised in literary circles, partly for their linguistic form. Although a useful source for non-literary forms of Welsh, these often have the disadvantage that, unless internal evidence—for instance, references to real events—is available, they are difficult to date with any accuracy. In some cases, even authorship is difficult to establish, and even where the author of a ballad is identified, other biographical details needed for a full interpretation of the evidence, such as date of birth or place of origin, may be lacking.

Three collections of ballads are included, all by authors well-known in other fields, Ellis Roberts (BER), Hugh Jones (BHJ) (Llangwm), and John Jones (BJJ) (Jac Glan-y-gors). For biographical details, see above.

7.1.5. *Trial proceedings*

The records of witnesses' depositions in defamation cases have already been used extensively. These continue in abundance in the eighteenth century. Included in the corpus are all the depositions in Welsh in the cases in Suggett (1983). The biggest quantities of material are from the Bangor Consistory Court, the Caernarfon Sessions, the Denbigh Sessions, Flint Sessions, Glamorgan Sessions, and Pembroke Sessions. Small amounts are available also from the Anglesey Sessions, the Archdeaconry of Brecon, and St David's Ecclesiastical Court. Coverage is thus better for north Wales than for south Wales, and the slander cases provide virtually no information for most of the Midlands, including Merionethshire, Cardiganshire, Montgomeryshire, and Radnorshire.

7.1.6. *Miscellaneous texts*

Finally, there are a number of miscellaneous texts, including almanacs, mixed religious prose, historiography, and autobiography.

Late in the seventeenth century we find the first almanac in Welsh, *Y Cyfreith-lawn Almanac Cymraeg* (published from 1680) (Watkin-Jones 1926: 191). During the next century, almanacs in Welsh containing varying amounts of literary, non-literary, and astronomical material were being produced on a fairly regular basis, with three or four appearing each year by the second half of the century. The corpus contains the prose sections of a selection of almanacs by two prominent almanac-writers, Mathew Williams (AMW) (1732–1819, of Llangadog and Llandeilo, Carms.) and John Prys (AJP) (1739?–86?, of Bryneglwys, Denbs.).

The first original novels in Welsh do not appear until the mid-nineteenth century, but, by the start of the nineteenth century, translations of English novels have already appeared. A Welsh translation of *Robinson Crusoe* appears in Wrexham in 1795, with further editions in Carmarthen in 1810 and 1816. Three novels by Legh Richmond appear somewhat later in Welsh: *Crefydd mewn Bwthyn* ('Faith in a Cottage') (Bala, 1819; 2nd edn. 1829), *Hanes Merch y Llaethwr* ('The Tale of the Dairyman's Daughter') (Bala, 1821), and *Hanes y Bachgen Du* ('The Tale of the Black Boy') (Bala, 1821). *Crefydd mewn Bwthyn (CMB)* is included in the corpus.

The other miscellaneous texts are Ellis Roberts, *Ail Lythyr Hen Bechadur (ALHB)* ('The Second Letter of an Old Sinner' (1772)), a populist religious work;

Robert Jones (Rhos-lan, Caerns.) (1745–1829), *Drych yr Amseroedd* (*DA*) ('Mirror of the Times'), a history of the Methodist Revival in North Wales; the autobiography of Thomas Edwards (Twm o'r Nant) (*Hanes Twm o'r Nant* (*HTN*) (1805)); and Mathew Williams, *Hanes Holl Grefyddau'r Byd* (*HHGB*) ('The History of All the Religions of the World' (1799)).

7.2. PREVERBAL PRONOUNS AS AGREEMENT MARKERS

The corpus texts having been introduced, we can now return to the linguistic developments. Recall from Chapter 5 that preverbal subject pronouns were preverbal clitics by the sixteenth century. In the eighteenth century, they undergo further syntactic changes which lead towards the loss of SVO as a productive pattern in Welsh. We can now investigate these changes, using in particular the evidence of the corpus.

7.2.1. *Pronoun-doubling*

In the seventeenth and eighteenth centuries, new syntactic patterns are found with overt pronominal subjects. Let us consider the first-person-singular pronoun *mi* to begin with. In main clauses with the preverbal pronoun *mi*, a postverbal pronoun appears optionally for the first time. The two earliest examples are given in (1).

(1) (*a*) *Mi wn   fi mai   gwell gan Noah faddeu   i vn a*
     I   know-1S I CLEFT better with Noah forgive-VN to one REL
     edifarhao   na   difa   cant.
     repent-SUBJ than destroy-VN hundred.
     'I know that Noah prefers to forgive one who might repent than to
     destroy a hundred.'   (*LlTA* 38. 21–2 (1653))

   (*b*) *mi fynne   fi ei   chrogi   hi*
     I   want-1S I 3SF-GEN hang-VN her
     'I want her hanged' (Slander case, Caernarfon Sessions (1730))

The earliest attestation is from Morgan Llwyd's *Llyfr y Tri Aderyn* (*LlTA*) (1653). A difficulty is raised by the appearance of the postverbal pronoun as *fi*, rather than *i* as would normally be expected after a verb ending in a consonant. However, this use of the form *fi*, although unknown in Contemporary Welsh, is attested in the seventeenth century (see also *PN* 4. 21; *YRW* 57. 26):

(2)   *Miwn fi   'n ddi gwestiwn   ei   fod   ê 'n bur*
     I   know-1S I PRD without-doubt 3SM-GEN be-VN he PRD very
     gostus.
     costly
     'I know without doubt that he's very costly.'   (*TChB* 22. 40)

The earliest instance of pronoun-doubling with a conjunctive subject is also from *Llyfr y Tri Aderyn* (see below).

Examples of pronoun-doubling are relatively frequent in the interludes of the early part of the eighteenth century. Examples from seven eighteenth-century interludes are given in (3).[1]

(3) (*a*) *Mi â   fi tu ag   adre* . . .
　　　　I   go-1s I towards home
　　　　'I shall go homeward . . .'   (CDH 42. 13 (18th c. [1737]))

　　(*b*) *Mi af   fi 'n   feichiau trosti*
　　　　I   go-1s I PRD surety   for-her
　　　　'I shall act as surety for her.'   (YDG 50. 6 (18th c. [1744]))

　　(*c*) *Mi wna   fi eitha   ngallu* . . .
　　　　I   do-1s I extreme my-power
　　　　'I shall do everything in my power . . .'   (*FfM* 22. 13 ([1745]))

　　(*d*) *Mi ddo   fi rowan iw   fferiodi* . . .
　　　　I   come-1s I now   to-3SF marry
　　　　'I shall come now to marry her . . .'   (FfBD 29. 3 (*c*.1700–50))

　　(*e*) *mi dewes i fy   spectol gartre*
　　　　I   left-1s I my glasses at-home
　　　　'I left my glasses at home.'   (BLl 8. 22 (*c*.1700–50))

　　(*f*) *mi daria   fi yma rai   mynude*
　　　　I   stay-1s I here a-few minutes
　　　　'I shall stay here for a few minutes.'   (IYCA 88. 12 (?*c*.1758))

By the time of the late-eighteenth-century corpus this pattern is found relatively frequently. Table 7.1 gives the frequency of patterns like *mi welais i* 'I saw' with a first-person postposed pronoun in addition to preverbal *mi*. This is given as a percentage of the total affirmative main declarative clauses with first-person-singular synthetic verbs. Only texts containing ten or more tokens are listed. In addition to the incidence in the texts listed, there is also one example in *Meddyliau yr Esgob Watson*.

It can be seen from Table 7.1 that the innovation is found in all the interludes, in the letters of about half of the Welsh settlers in the United States, two out of the three sets of ballads, the slander cases for all of Wales except for the south-east, and in a number of other texts.

Pronoun-doubling of this kind is not restricted to the first-person singular, although it is much more common there than in any other person. A selection of examples in other persons from the corpus is given below. Note especially (4*c*), where it is the postverbal pronoun that conjoins with another pronoun. There are no examples in the third-person plural.[2]

TABLE 7.1. *Frequency of pronoun-doubling in the first-person singular, 1760–1825*

Text	Frequency of pronoun-doubling (%)	Sample size
Cylchgrawn Cynmraeg	0	11
Rhyddid	0	17
Letters of Ann Griffiths	0	48
Letters of David Thomas	0	96
Letters of Evan Evans	0	46
Letters of John Jones	0	12
Letters of Samuel Thomas (B settler)	0	14
Ballads of Hugh Jones	0	22
Almanacs of Mathew Williams	0	13
Crefydd mewn Bwthyn	0	84
Drych yr Amseroedd	0	24
Hanes Twm o'r Nant	0	127
Slander cases (south-east)	0	24
Gras a Natur	3	153
Letters of Thomas Edwards	3	74
Ballads of John Jones	3	30
Settlers' letters (B group)	4	28
Cwymp Dyn	5	155
Ystori Richard Whittington	5	121
Ballads of Ellis Roberts	5	21
Letters of Thomas Jones	7	44
Letters of Owen Jones	8	12
Seren tan Gwmwl	8	13
Protestant a Neilltuwr	9	144
Tri Chryfion Byd	14	93
Slander cases (south-west)	21	19
Slander cases (north-west)	23	30
Slander cases (north-east)	26	23
Settlers' letters (A group)	28	32
Settlers' letters (A2)	38	21

(4)   Second-person singular

    (a) *Ti elli   di fyn'd lle   gwelech   di 'n dda.*
        you can-2S you go   where see-2S-SUBJ you PRD good
        'You can go where you please.'   (*PN* 13. 19)

    (b) *Di gei   di wel'd y boreu foru,   Y rhai'n yn gwplws*
        you shall-2S you see-VN the morning tomorrow those   PRD pair
        tan   dy   gablu.
        under 2S-GEN curse-VN
        'You shall see those tomorrow morning in a pair cursing you.'
                                        (*YRW* 13. 24–5)

(c) *di   ddysgest* [sic] *di   a   minneu ddigon o bechod hefo ni ir*
you brought-2s   you and I-CONJ enough of sin   with us to-the
bŷd   ini   edifarhau ei   blegid . . .
world to-us repent-VN 3SM-GEN because-of
'You and I brought enough sin with us to the world for us to repent of . . .'
                                                                    (*ALHB* 8. 3–4)

(5)   Third-person singular

(a) *fo gaiff ef eu   gwerthu a   derbyn   arian am danynt, os na*
he can he 3P-GEN sell-VN and receive-VN money for-them   if NEG
wêl y   Subscribers yn   dda
see the subscribers PRD good
'He can sell them and receive money for them if the subscribers don't
approve.'   (LEE 253. 12–13)

(b) *Fe fu   Ef ddwy flyned a   hanner yn   lled afiach . . .*
he was-PERF he two   years and half   PRD quite ill
'He was quite ill for two-and-a-half years.'   (LUSS B2. 1. 14–15)

(6)   First-person plural
Ni ddawn   i   rhawg i ben a   henwi,   Faint   mae natur
we come- IP we soon   to end with name-VN how-many is   nature
yn   i   golli . . .
PROG 3SM-GEN lose-VN
'We shall soon manage to name how many nature is losing . . .'
                                                                    (*GN* 32. 36–7)

(7)   Second-person plural
Beth gaf   innau   am eu   cario,   Siwr   chwi rowch   chwi
what get- I s I-CONJ for 3P-GEN carry-VN, certainly you   give-2P you
ran o 'ch   cinio.
part of your dinner
'What shall I get for carrying them? Certainly, you'll give (me) part of
your dinner.'   (*YRW* 53. 9–10)

The geographical distribution of pronoun-doubling (in all persons) is also
revealed by the corpus. It is clear that, although primarily a feature of northern
dialects, being found in slander-case depositions from north Wales and in northern
interludes and other texts, pronoun-doubling is found also in the south. Note in
particular its presence in low-style texts from parts of the South: the B group of
settlers' letters from south-west Carmarthenshire; slander cases from Pembrokeshire; and the letters of Evan Evans and *Meddyliau yr Esgob Watson* from
Cardiganshire. However, the evidence for the south-east, particularly the slander
cases, suggests that the innovation did not occur in or spread to the language of this
part of Wales.
     What change in the grammar could have brought about this innovation? Before

the appearance of pronoun-doubling, a pronominal subject was generated in the same position as any other subject and cliticized to the left of the verb, leaving a postverbal trace (see Section 5.1.3). This trace left no position empty for a second subject pronoun; hence we find no alternation between a null element and a full pronoun. On the other hand, we can take the alternation between a null element and a full pronoun to indicate that the null element is the null pronominal *pro*, rather than a trace.

If this is so, then these examples reflect a reanalysis of the status of the preverbal pronoun from a subject which raises to left-adjoin to the verb into some kind of agreement marker. In other words, the pronoun is reanalysed from being a pronominal D-head into the head of some other functional category.

The question remains as to which functional category the preverbal 'pronoun' instantiates. The obvious possibilities are C and AgrS. The fact that pronoun-doubling is essentially an agreement process initially suggests that the agreeing element might be the head of an agreement phrase, say AgrSP (cf. the analysis of pronoun-doubling in Italian dialects by Brandi and Cordin 1989 and Rizzi 1986; Section 5.1.3). However, the other facts about the distribution of pronoun-doubling seem to point to CP as the phrase that the agreeing pronoun heads. That is, the preverbal element in a pronoun-doubling construction is a complementizer which agrees with the subject of its clause.

Three facts about the distribution of pronoun-doubling provide evidence on this question. First, pronoun-doubling, just like topicalization before it, is, with the minor exception of a well-defined group of conjunctions that allow general SVO, restricted to main clauses. Furthermore, it is always optional—that is, the alternative pattern Verb + Pronoun is always available. Finally, we should prefer an analysis that treats the preverbal element in the pronoun-doubling construction and *fe* in *fe* + verb + NP subject orders as parallel. I shall now deal with each of these in turn.

Pronoun-doubling is not possible in embedded clauses. We do not find the innovation of sentences like (8*b*) alongside the innovation of pronoun-doubling.

(8) (*a*)   *Mi wn   y   gwelaf i Ifan.*
        I   know-1s COMP see-1s I Ifan

  (*b*) **Mi wn   (y)   mi welaf i Ifan.*
        I   know-1s (COMP) I   see-1s I Ifan
        'I'll see Ifan.'

That is, the presence of an overt complementizer prevents the preverbal element from appearing. This suggests that both are members of the same category— namely, C.

The preverbal element (*mi*, etc.) is never required. Accordingly, alongside the pronoun-doubling construction in (9*a*) it is equally possible to have a lone verb or a verb-plus-postverbal pronoun sequence as in (9*b*) or (9*c*).

(9) (*a*) *Mi wn*   *i.*   (*b*) *Gwn.*   (*c*) *Gwn*   *i.*   'I know.'
         I   know-IS I   know-IS   know-IS I

These facts again suggest that we are not dealing with a standard subject–verb agreement phenomenon. Such agreement is not usually optional in languages which have it. If *mi* were an instantiation of AgrS, we would have no account of why the sentences in (9) should be equally well formed with or without this agreement. On the other hand, complementizers are frequently optional. If *mi* were to be a complementizer, it would be analogous to the English subordinator *that*, which is optional in sentences like *I know (that) Mary will arrive soon.*

Finally we have analysed *fe* as an instantiation of C, marked as occurring solely with verbs in the default third-person-singular form (Section 5.2.2.7). The language thus already has a main-clause complementizer restricted in its distribution by an agreement requirement. The creation of other items in the same category and with the same type of distribution seems entirely reasonable.

If this is the case, then the preverbal subject clitics had been reanalysed as a series of main-clause complementizers in many dialects by the early decades of the eighteenth century. The reanalysis is given below in (11), representing the structure of (10).

(10)   *Mi welais gaer.*
         MI saw-IS fort
         'I saw a fort'.

Before the change preverbal pronouns originate in the usual subject position SpecVP, and raise and then cliticize onto the verb. After the change, they are base-generated in C. I shall assume that agreement between the complementizer and the verb is enforced by selectional restrictions imposed by the lexical entry for each of the complementizers. That is, in their lexical entry, each of the complementizers

(11) (*a*)

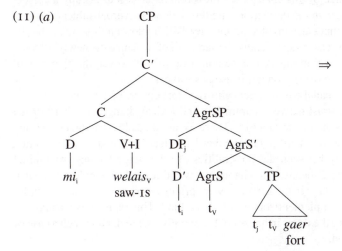

(*b*)

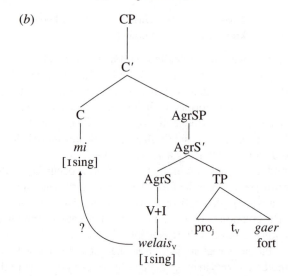

selects for an IP (AgrSP) headed by person and number features of the required type. As in Chapter 6, it is unclear whether raising of the verb to C to adjoin to the complementizer takes place, since this has no effect on word-order possibilities.

Once the subject position in clauses of the *mi welais* type is occupied by *pro*, overt pronouns may follow the verb, resulting in pronoun-doubling structures. In the data above, we must conclude that, even where the *mi welais* pattern remains, *mi* is always a complementizer rather than a pronoun.

Cross-linguistically, complementizers of this kind are found in a number of languages. For instance, in West Flemish the subordinating complementizer *da* 'that' agrees with the subject of its clause (Haegeman 1990: 334; Shlonsky 1994).

As a consequence of this change, the preverbal *mi* ceases to occupy a subject position at any stage in the derivation, and thus a new postverbal subject position is created. Given that early eighteenth-century Welsh allows null subjects freely, the result is in most cases superficially the same as before, since the newly licensed postverbal subject will in most cases be non-overt *pro*. However, the change will reveal itself when an overt pronoun is used as subject.

How does this reanalysis interact with our conception of syntactic change? In terms of the contrast between parametric and lexical change, it is hard to see how the change can be parametric. There is no plausible candidate for the changed parameter. It is hard to believe that Universal Grammar could contain a parameter choosing between the possibilities of a language having pronominal D-head or agreeing C-heads. The change is instead lexical. A number of lexical items which at one stage in the language were pronouns are reanalysed as complementizers, albeit complementizers of a specific kind. This represents a change in the lexical entry for the items in question. Essentially we are dealing with a case of grammaticalization.

Why should this reanalysis have taken place? In acquisitional terms, the analysis of *mi* as a complementizer was attractive because it meant that it could be assimilated to a pre-existing class of presentential particles. In particular *mi*, etc., could be seen as the affirmative counterpart of the negative complementizer *ni*, and as a pronominal counterpart to the affirmative complementizer *fe*.

As with earlier reanalyses, note that this reanalysis reduces the amount of movement in the derivation. For instance, in (11) above, three chain positions are removed by base-generating *mi* in C, rather than having it raise there from subject position.

If such an analysis was so attractive, what had prevented earlier generations of children from adopting it? Earlier generations of children had had three reasons to reject it.

First, as long as the particle *a* was present in speech, children had to hypothesize an agreement process which required *mi* to be a DP in a specifier position. Secondly, as long as pronouns were not clitics, examples with material intervening between the pronoun and the verb indicated that the pronoun did not adjoin to C. Finally, it may be supposed that a positive setting of the V2-parameter forces the child to choose analyses of data which do not violate that parameter setting. That is, children will avoid language-specific devices wherever possible. To choose to analyse *mi*, etc., as complementizers will inevitably result in a marked violation of V2. Accordingly, as long as a V2-rule is maintained, children must prefer the lesser violation of V2 that arises if they analyse *mi*, etc., as pronouns. Once V2 is lost, the more attractive analysis of the preverbal pronoun clitics as complementizers may, in time, be chosen.

Note that this case also suggests that indirect negative evidence (Chomsky 1981: 8–9) is not relevant in syntactic change. Children could have established that the analysis of *mi* as a complementizer was incorrect simply by the absence of sequences like *mi welais i* with pronoun-doubling. This should have been a fairly common pattern if *mi* was a complementizer. Its absence, however, clearly did not alert children to the fact that *mi* was a pronoun.

7.2.2. *Doubling with conjunctive pronouns*

A natural consequence of this reanalysis is a change in the distribution of the contrastive series of conjunctive pronouns (*minnau*, etc.). In the earlier grammar, the preverbal position is occupied by a full phrasal head, whereas in the later grammar the preverbal position is occupied merely by an inflected complementizer. It can be assumed that, since they are phonologically strong, conjunctive pronouns are full pronominal D-heads throughout, and that they are not liable to undergo reanalysis as inflecting complementizers. Once the new grammar is in place, preverbal pronouns are no longer possible, and conjunctive pronouns will automatically begin to occupy the postverbal position where the new pronominal subject surfaces. The new structure is given in (12).[3]

(12)   [$_{CP}$ [$_C$ agreeing comp.] [$_{AgrSP}$ verb [$_{TP}$ conjunctive pronoun$_i$ t$_V$ [$_{VP}$ t$_i$ t$_V$]]]]

Evidence for this development appears already in the late seventeenth and early eighteenth century. The traditional pattern is illustrated from a literary text in (13).[4] In certain interludes of this period, examples of this older pattern with preverbal conjunctive pronoun remain, suggesting that at this time it was indeed a living form. Such examples are given in (14) (see also BL1 15. 15, 15. 21).

(13) (*a*) *pettwn   perchen traed a   dwylo fel y   bûm,   minneu*
         if-I-were owner   feet   and hands as PRT was-IS I-CONJ
         awn   i garu   neu addoli   y rhain.
         go-COND-IS to love-VN or   worship-VN the these
         'If I were the owner of feet and hands as I was, I too would go courting
         or worship these.'   (*GBC* 10. 27–9 (1703))

    (*b*) *Felly nineu   aethom i weled   y 'Lecsiwn.*
         so   we-CONJ went-IP to see-VN the election
         'So we too went to see the election.'   (*GBC* 20. 7–8 (1703))

(14) (*a*) *Ac fel yr   adwaenai Solomon ddail y   ddaiar, minneu*
         and as PRT recognized Solomon leaves the earth,   I-CONJ
         adwaen   y Danadl Poethion, sy   'n   tyfu   yn y
         recognize-IS the nettles hot   be-REL PROG grow-VN in the
         Muriau . . .
         walls
         'And as Solomon recognized the leaves of the earth, I too recognize the
         stinging nettles that grow in the walls . . .'   (*FfM* 56. 14–16 ([1745]))

    (*b*) *fine   addownsia   n   ddigon sionk*
         I-CONJ PRT+dance-IS PRD enough nimble
         'I shall dance nimbly enough.'   (BL1 25. 18 (*c.*1700–50))

    (*c*) *. . . a   mine   arhosa yma i orffwyso*
            and I-CONJ stay-IS here to rest-VN
         '. . . and I shall stay here to rest.'   (FfBD 9. 4 (*c.*1700–50))

The more usual pattern even at this date in the interludes is that shown in the examples in (15), where an agreeing complementizer precedes the verb, and the conjunctive subject pronoun follows.[5]

(15) (*a*) *Mith   friŵŵn   ine   dithe   oni   bae*
         MI+2S-ACC wound-COND-IS I-CONJ you-CONJ if-not be-IMPF-SUBJ
         rhag ofn dy   gledde . . .
         for fear your sword
         'I (too) would wound you if it weren't for fear of your sword . . .'
         (CDH 51. 8–9 (18th c. [1737]))

(b) *Mi af   innau 'n feichiau sadlon syth   Na   thalith*
 MI go-1S I-CONJ PRD surety   steadfast straight NEG-COMP will-pay
 hi byth mor   arian
 she ever NEG+the money
 'I will act as guarantor against her failing to pay the money.'

(YDG 49. 20–1 (18th c. [1744]))

(c) *... Mi dynga   finne ...*
    MI swear-1S I-CONJ
    '... I swear ...'   (*FfM* 52. 7–8 [1745])

(d) *mi dora   fine   ngalon*
 MI break-1S I-CONJ my-heart
 'I shall break my heart.'   (BLl 53. 20 (*c*.1700–50))

The same development is attested also outside the interludes. The examples in (16) include the earliest example of this order, from *Llyfr y Tri Aderyn* (1653).

(16) (a) *Mi henwaf finnau hênrai   eraill.*
    MI name-1S I-CONJ old-ones other
    'I shall name some other old ones.'   (*LlTA* 34. 19–20 (1653))

(b) *Os lleddis   i fy mab fy hun Mi af   inne   i run*
 if killed-1S I my son my own MI go-1S I-CONJ to the-same
 ddihenudd.
 death
 'If I killed my own son, I (too) shall go to the same death.'

(HGC 35. 19–20 (*c*.1716))

The development is clearest in the first-person singular, but, as the examples in (17) demonstrate, it is found in other persons *simultaneously*.

(17) (a) *Di grogit   dithe   y rhan fwya Sydd yn y*
    you hang-COND-2S you-CONJ the part largest be-REL in the
    gwledydd yma ...
    lands here
    'You (on the other hand) would hang most of those who are in these lands ...'   (CDH 32. 21–2 (18th c. [1737]))

(b) *Ped fei   ti 'n   darllen yr un   Llyfrau ... Di*
 if   be-IMPF-SUBJ-2S you PROG read-VN the same books   DI
 ddwedit   titheu ... yr un   pethau.
 say-COND-2S you-CONJ the same things
 'If you were to read the same books ... you (too) would say the same things.'   (*FfM* 8. 17–20 ([1745]))

(c) *Ac yno di gei   dithe   ddechre pregethu ...*
 and then DI may-2S you-CONJ begin-VN preach-VN
 'And then you may begin to preach ...'   (*FfM* 33. 19 ([1745]))

(d) *Fe a   gaiff   yntau . . . Yn yr hidill ddal   yr adar*
FE PRT will-be-able he-CONJ in the sieve catch-VN the birds
'He will be able to catch the birds in the sieve.'

(YDG 31. 10 (18th c. [1744]))

Data from the late-eighteenth-century corpus clearly show the innovative construction in an overwhelmingly dominant position in colloquial texts. Once we abstract away from the issue of the presence or absence of preverbal *a*, there are four possible syntactic patterns in a main clause with a conjunctive subject and finite verb:

A. Conjunctive Pronoun+Verb
B. Agreeing Simple Pronoun/Complementizer+Verb+Conjunctive Pronoun
C. Other Particle+Verb+Conjunctive Pronoun
D. Verb+Conjunctive Pronoun

In pattern A the subject precedes the verb. In all the other patterns it follows. In B the preverbal pronoun/complementizer agrees with the postverbal conjunctive pronoun subject; in C preverbal *fe* or *mi* shows no agreement with the subject (see Sections 7.3 and 7.4). In D there is no preverbal element. Once the preverbal pronouns are reanalysed as complementizers, B should replace A. Pattern C requires another syntactic innovation which will be discussed below, but is otherwise compatible with the new grammar, but not with the old. D is compatible with either grammar. Thus the presence of pattern A in the text is indicative of the old grammar still being in place, whereas the appearance of B or C indicates the introduction of the new grammar.

The main difficulty in investigating the distribution of these patterns in the late eighteenth century is the lack of examples of conjunctive pronouns generally. Most texts in the corpus give either no examples at all or just a handful of them. This must be borne in mind in the analysis of the results.

Table 7.2 shows the extent to which the innovation described above is found in the corpus. It shows the B and C patterns as a percentage of the total instances of the A, B, and C patterns. That is, taking only those sentence types which differ in grammaticality between the old and new grammar, it shows the percentage of cases compatible with the new grammar but not the old. All texts containing one or more tokens are listed in the table. In view of the small number of examples, data for all persons are given together, although, in the vast majority of cases, the subject is first-person singular.

The innovating pattern with preverbal agreement marker and postverbal conjunctive pronoun is found in ten texts, including all of the interludes and five sets of letters. The lack of good data limits the conclusions that can be drawn. However, it is clear that, in four of the five interludes, the innovating pattern forms an overwhelming majority of the examples. In the more literary texts, the pattern is exceedingly rare.

TABLE 7.2. *The position of conjunctive pronoun subjects*

Text	Patterns B+C as % of patterns A+B+C	Sample size
Letters of Ann Griffiths	0	1
Crefydd mewn Bwthyn	0	1
Cylchgrawn Cynmraeg	0	1
Letters of David Thomas	0	1
Drych yr Amseroedd	0	9
Hanes Twm o'r Nant	0	32
Rhyddid	0	3
Seren tan Gwmwl	0	1
Tri Chryfion Byd	25	4
Letters of Edward Evans	33	3
Letters of Thomas Edwards	33	3
Letters of John Jones	50	2
Ystori Richard Whittington	90	10
Protestant a Neilltuwr	93	15
Cwymp Dyn	100	3
Gras a Natur	100	1
Letters of Samuel Thomas (B settler)	100	2
Letters of Thomas Jones	100	1

These data suggest that, outside the literary language, postverbal conjunctive subject pronouns ousted preverbal ones very quickly. The pattern of first attestation is similar to that of pronoun-doubling with simple pronouns, with the first attestation in *Llyfr y Tri Aderyn*, then attestations from the early part of the eighteenth century. By the time of the corpus, conjunctive subject pronouns are postverbal in virtually all cases in colloquial texts. However, there seems to have been strong pressure against the pattern in the literary language.

Some twentieth-century dialects of south Wales seem to have reached this stage of development and gone no further. In particular, the dialects usually characterized as retaining the abnormal sentence in the form of SVO with pronominal subjects actually seem to have agreeing affirmative complementizers rather than real preverbal subjects. This can be seen clearly from the fact that, in addition to preverbal subject markers, all such dialects seem to exhibit pronoun-doubling and postverbal conjunctive pronouns. Examples are given from the Ely Valley dialect (Glamorgan) in (18a) (pronoun-doubling) and (18b) (postverbal conjunctive pronouns).

(18) (a) *nu e'θön   nu   ta θre we'tin*
        they went-3P they home then
        'They went home then.'

    (b) *nu æʌn   nuntʌ*
        they will-go-3P they-CONJ
        'They (too) will go.'   (Phillips 1955: 301, 303)

The same applies to other southern dialects—namely, those of Nantgarw (Ceinwen H. Thomas 1993: ii. 44, ii. 309), and possibly also Cwm-ann (Brake 1981: 365, 564).

7.2.3. *Discrete and gradual innovation*

I have argued that the introduction of pronoun-doubling reflects a change in the status of the preverbal pronominal subject clitics from D-heads to C-heads. The most salient characteristic of the change is the discrete nature of the innovation. This is clearest in the development with the conjunctive pronouns. There are few texts where the old and new patterns exist side by side. The pattern with preverbal conjunctive pronoun disappears in low-style texts almost as soon as the innovation begins.

This is already apparent in the data for the interludes of the earlier part of the eighteenth century. Whilst we find a number of attestations of the older pattern concentrated in one interlude, namely, 'Y Brenin Llyr' (BLl), where it appears to be the dominant pattern, elsewhere ample evidence of the new pattern is found (cf. the examples in (15)). There are no intermediate or transitional texts—that is, texts where both old and new patterns are well represented.

TABLE 7.3. *Correlation between pronoun-doubling and postverbal conjunctive pronoun subjects*

Text	Pronoun-doubling?	Postverbal conjunctive pronouns?
Cylchgrawn Cynmraeg	–	–
Rhyddid	–	–
Letters of Ann Griffiths	–	–
Letters of David Thomas	–	–
Letters of Evan Evans	–	(+)
Letters of John Jones	–	(+)
Letters of Samuel Thomas (B settler)	–	+
Crefydd mewn Bwthyn	–	–
Drych yr Amseroedd	–	–
Hanes Twm o'r Nant	–	–
Gras a Natur	+	+
Letters of Thomas Edwards	+	(+)
Cwymp Dyn	+	+
Ystori Richard Whittington	+	+
Seren tan Gwmwl	+	–
Protestant a Neilltuwr	+	+
Tri Chryfion Byd	+	(+)

Notes:
+ Feature attested.
– Absence of feature attested.
(+) Conjunctive subject pronouns postverbal; preverbal ones also attested.

The same is also broadly true within the corpus. Furthermore, the two innovations have virtually parallel distribution in the corpus (cf. the notion of uniform diffusion of change in Section 2.4). If a text allows one of them, the other will also be permitted. This can be seen from Table 7.3, which summarizes the data already presented. The parallel distribution of the changes reinforces the conclusion made above that they reflect a single change in the lexical entry of the pronouns.

Furthermore, the discrete nature of the change and the lack of the two patterns coexisting suggest that the new grammar replaces the old grammar—the two do not coexist for a while. In any given text, preverbal elements like *mi* are treated either as C-heads or as D-heads, but not as both.

In terms of the distinction between parametric and lexical change, the change must be regarded as lexical. Yet, the hypothesis implied by the parametric account of change was that lexical change should be gradual, whereas parametric change would be sudden. Why should this lexical change be so sudden? An answer may lie in the nature of the grammatical change itself. The change is an instance of grammaticalization from the category of pronoun (D-head) to that of complementizer, categories that do not appear to have any features in common. It is hard to see how any lexical item could be both a pronoun and a complementizer, or unspecified between them. Hence, once the pronouns become complementizers, constructions compatible only with their status as pronouns disappear. We are thus led to modify somewhat our view of the distinction between lexical and parametric change.

7.3. THE SPREAD OF *MI* BEFORE NON-FIRST PERSON SINGULAR VERBS

From the middle of the eighteenth century, rather later than the appearance of pronoun-doubling, we find the first-person-singular complementizer ('pronoun') *mi* being used before verbs other that those in the first-person singular. Some of the earliest examples are given in (19).[6]

(19) (*a*) oni   buasae   hi efa 'r gwas   yn llofft y   gwair mi fuase
        unless be-COND she with the servant in the loft   the hay   MI be-COND
        heb   blant   etto
        without children still
        'If she hadn't been with the servant in the hayloft, she'd be childless
        still.'   (Slander case, Flint Sessions (1754))

    (*b*) *Mi welen   yno ffenest* . . .
        MI saw-3P there window
        'They saw there a window . . .'   (Ellis Roberts, *Dwy o Gerddi*
        Newyddion (1759) (D. M. Lloyd 1937: 98))

(*c*) *Mi ddylen   gyd gofio   'r amser   aeth heibio*
MI should-IP all   remember-VN the time (REL) went past
'We should all remember the time which has gone by'

(*W. Ballads*, 71B: 6 (*GPC*: 1267))

(*d*) *Mi awn   drwu   ffansi gwall gyfeillach, Un iw   faes ar   llall*
MI go-IP through fancy false friendship one to-his field and-the other
iw   fasnach
to-his market
'We shall go through the fancy of false friendship, one to his field and
the other to his market-place'   (*W. Ballads*, 106: 6 (*GPC*: 1267))

It seems to be reasonably secure that this occurs later than and separate from the
emergence of pronoun-doubling described above. Whereas pronoun-doubling is
extremely common in the interludes of the first half of the eighteenth century, the
use of *mi* beyond the first person singular does not seem to be attested there. The
fact that the two securely dated examples in (19) are from the 1750s whereas
pronoun-doubling is frequent already in the 1730s and 1740s suggests that the two
changes are separated in time by at least one generation.

A reasonable question to ask at this point is whether the use of *mi* spreads from
the first-person singular to other persons and numbers one by one or whether it
spreads indiscriminately to all persons and numbers. The evidence points to the
latter conclusion. *Mi* is well attested before non-third-person synthetic verbs of all
persons in a number of texts in the corpus. A full paradigm of cases is given in
(20)–(25).[7]

(20)   Second-person singular
        Lladrones wyt ti,   mi a   ddygaist fy nghaws i.
        thief   are you MI PRT stole-2S my cheese me
        'You are a thief, you stole my cheese.'

(Slander case, Flint Sessions (1779))

(21)   Third-person singular (pronominal)
        Mi gostiodd am fwud o gwmpas 10 punt   i   bôb   un   ohonom . . .
        MI cost   for food about   ten pounds for every one of-us
        'It cost about ten pounds for each one of us for food . . .'

(LUSS A2. 7. 12–13)

(22)   Lexical subject
    (*a*) *Mi fu   'r hen Jacob addfwyn, . . . Yn   gorwedd gyda ei*
        MI was-PERF the old Jacob mature   PROG lie-VN   with his
        forwyn . . .
        maid
        'Old mature Jacob lay with his maid . . .'   (BJJ 2. 1. 19–20)

(*b*) *mi Nai*   *William Lewis i   ffortiwn toc   iawn*
MI make-COND William Lewis his fortune soon very
'William Lewis would make his fortune very soon.'   (LUSS A2. 7. 32)

(23)   First-person plural
       Wel natur cyn   ymado,   Mi ganwn benill eto.
       well Nature before leave-VN MI sing-1P verse again
       'Well, Nature, before leaving, we shall sing another verse.'

                                                   (*GN* 53. 20–1)

(24)   Second-person plural
       . . . ag am hynny mi haeddech   eich   crogi . . .
       and for that   MI deserve-COND-2P 2P-GEN hang-VN
       '. . . and for that you'd deserve to be hanged . . .'
                         (Slander case, Flint Sessions (1794))

(25)   Third-person plural
       mi gant   bôb   chawre [sic] têg ag sudd bosibl . . .
       MI get-3P every play   fair as is   possible
       'They'll get every possible fair play . . .'   (LUSS A2. 8. 19–20)

The frequency of use of *mi* in preverbal position in the corpus is given in
Table 7.4 (singular verbs) and Table 7.5 (plural verbs). Texts where this use of *mi*
is not found are excluded, with the exception of *Toriad y Dydd*, which is included
for purposes of comparison with *Seren tan Gwmwl* by the same author. The data
are based on an examination of all main, affirmative declarative clauses containing
synthetic verb forms (including the BYDD, BYDDAI, BU, and BUASAI paradigms
of *bod* 'to be', but excluding the MAE and OEDD paradigms), and give the
percentage of these clauses for each person–number combination where the particle
mi is used. The columns for third-person singular and plural give data for clauses

TABLE 7.4. *Frequency of particle* mi *before singular verbal forms*

Text	Second-pers. sing.		Third-pers. sing.		Lexical subj.	
	mi (%)	Sample size	*mi* (%)	Sample size	*mi* (%)	Sample size
Ballads of Ellis Roberts	0	30	2	43	0	97
Ballads of John Jones	—	—	0	72	1	95
Cwymp Dyn	0	24	0	59	0	92
Gras a Natur	0	18	0	71	1	128
Letters of Thomas Jones	—	—	13	8	0	26
Seren tan Gwmwl	—	—	50	18	58	45
Settlers' letters (A group)	0	1	11	19	16	25
Slander cases (north-east)	25	16	28	18	27	11
Slander cases (north-west)	40	20	63	27	13	8
Toriad y Dydd	—	—	0	19	0	36

with pronominal subjects;[8] lexical subjects, which co-occur only with third-person-singular verbs, are treated separately.

From these tables, it can be seen there are no significant differences between persons. The variation that we do find between different persons is entirely random. This supports a conclusion that *mi* spread to all person–number combinations outside the first person in a single change.

What change in the grammar do these data reflect? It was suggested in Section 7.2.1 that the preverbal 'pronouns' in the pronoun-doubling constructions are in fact various forms of an agreeing complementizer. Let us assume, as suggested there, that this is enforced by selectional restrictions imposed by the complementizer heads.

What seems to be happening is that the selectional restrictions of the complementizer *mi* fail to be acquired by a generation of children learning Welsh in the mid-eighteenth century. The loss of the feature in the lexical entry for *mi* is consistent with the pattern of data found. The selectional restriction is either present or absent, hence we expect that *mi* should either be confined to first-person-singular verbs, or should be freely available as a general complementizer. The system of selectional restrictions envisaged does not allow for the possibility of intermediate stages. The other (agreeing) complementizers, *di*, *hi*, *ni*, etc., would of course remain in the lexicon and their grammaticality would remain unchanged. Unlike the case with preverbal conjunctive pronouns, we do not, therefore, expect the agreeing complementizers to become obsolete as soon as the innovation appears. However, since they have to 'compete' with the new general complementizer *mi*, their observed frequency will drop. Note that, on the assumption that the acquisition of these complementizers depends upon their frequency of use, this is potentially the first step towards their disappearance.

TABLE 7.5. *Frequency of particle* mi *before plural verbal forms*

Text	First-pers. plur.		Second-pers. plur.		Third-pers. plur.	
	mi (%)	Sample size	*mi* (%)	Sample size	*mi* (%)	Sample size
Slander cases (north-east)	—	—	33	3	—	—
Slander cases (north-west)	—	—	40	5	—	—
Ballads of Ellis Roberts	0	11	0	3	0	13
Letters of Thomas Jones	—	—	14	7	0	2
Seren tan Gwmwl	50	2	0	3	36	11
Toriad y Dydd	0	1	—	—	0	6
Ballads of John Jones	0	7	0	11	0	4
Gras a Natur	9	11	4	27	0	24
Settlers' letters (A group)	43	7	0	3	38	8
Cwymp Dyn	7	14	0	19	0	3

The data suggest that the introduction of *mi* is sudden in the sense that as soon as *mi* spreads beyond the first-person singular, it acquires the status of general complementizer without regard to person or number. On the other hand, the change is gradual in the sense that *mi* does not immediately oust the agreeing forms. This pattern of data follows naturally from the account of the change given here.

Unlike person–number variation, geographical variation in the use of *mi* is very much in evidence. *Mi* is found exclusively in texts from north Wales, being found in slander cases from across the north, and in other texts of northern provenance, including a number of interludes, ballads, and the letters of the Welsh settlers from Merionethshire. This suggests that the modern situation where *mi* is broadly characteristic of northern speech (King 1993: 138) was already well established by the start of the nineteenth century.

I shall return to an account of the dialect variation below. First, however, it is necessary to look at other changes in the complementizer system.

7.4. THE SPREAD OF *FE*

At approximately the same time as *mi* appears in all persons, the third-person-singular pronoun/complementizer *fe*, previously restricted to appear before third-person verbs with a lexical subject or a masculine-singular pronominal subject, spreads to all the other persons. Examples in interludes and ballads are found at least from the 1740s. Currie (1997) notes examples somewhat earlier than this in two translations by Thomas Williams of Denbigh, published in 1691 and 1712. The evidence suggests that the change originates in the north-east at a period after pronoun-doubling, and somewhat earlier than the generalization of *mi*. Examples from each person–number combination are given in (26).[9]

(26) (*a*) *Fe fydda   fi bôb   Boreu   yn   gorfod   gweiddi* ...
        FE will-be-1S I every morning PROG have-to-VN shout-VN
        'every morning I shall have to shout ...' (*BDGU* 16. 25–6 (*c*.1765))

(*b*) ... *Fe a   geit   wisgo   cyrfat o gowarch* ...
        FE PRT be-allowed-2S wear-VN cravat of hemp
        '... You shall be allowed to wear a cravat of hemp ...'
                        (YDG 38. 21–2 (18th c. [1744]))

(*c*) *Ond fe gawn   ymladd   ar   Cristnogion Etto   yn ymyl*
        but FE be-allowed-1P fight-VN with-the Christians   again near
        tre   Ifiangon[?] ...
        town I.
        'But we shall have the opportunity to fight again with the Christians
        near the town of Ifiangon [?] ... (YDG 37. 23–4, 18th c. [1744])

(d) *Fe wnaethoch chware cas a   nyni.*
FE made-2P game   evil with us-CONJ.
'You played an evil game with us.'

(*W. Ballads*, 77B: 6 (1760) (*GPC*: 1267))

(e) *. . . fe lyncan'   am y   cynta 'r byd   yma 'n   damaid . . .*
FE swallow-3P for the first the world this PRD mouthful
'. . . they'll race to be first to swallow this world in a mouthful . . .'

(Hugh Jones, *Daeargryn Lisbon*, 67. 25 (after 1755))

Even in the third-person singular, there is evidence in the corpus for a change in
the status of *fe* at about this time. In a number of cases, *fe* occurs before a verb
whose subject is a feminine pronoun, either null or overt. The examples are rare,
but give firm evidence of the change. In the two cases in (27), *fe* occurs before a
verb with an overt feminine pronoun as subject.

(27) (a) *. . . Fe sugne   hi mer   nhw am arian.*
FE suck-COND she bone-marrow them for money
'. . . she'd suck their bone-marrow for money.' (*GN* 45. 15)

(b) *Pan ddeuen   iw   holi   fe wadodd hi wedî . . .*
when came-COND-3P to+3SF-GEN ask-VN FE denied she afterwards
'When they came to ask her, she denied it afterwards . . .'

(BER 5. 3. 5–6)

In the cases given in (28), *fe* appears where context shows the subject to be
feminine (see also *CD* 62. 3, and perhaps *TChB* 22. 34). In (28*b*) the subject of the
verb is a ship referred to in the immediate context using the feminine noun *llong*.
The use of *fe* rather than feminine *hi gafodd* clearly does reflect an innovation in
its use in this case. It is thus clear that, in these cases, *fe* is no longer acting as a
pronoun.

(28) (a) *A   fe yfiff   Dea a   Choffi Jyst 'run   fath a Dyfrgi . . .*
and FE drink-FUT tea and coffee just the-same sort as otter
'And she'll drink tea and coffee just the same as an otter . . .'

(*CD* 18. 25–6)

(b) *Fe gafodd hir lwyddiant . . .*
FE had   long success
'It (fem.) had long success . . .' (BER 1. 3. 14–16)

As with *mi*, it seems reasonable to investigate whether the loss of agreement
proceeds in stages, or whether *fe* spreads to all person–number combinations
simultaneously. A selection of examples is given in (29)–(33).[10] The relative
frequency by person for those texts where this use of *fe* is found is given in
Tables 7.6 (singular verbs) and 7.7 (plural verbs). As above, only synthetic verbal
forms are included.

(29)   First-person singular
         Fe ddweŷda i   chwi . . . Pwy ydi   ymhedair Nain   yn union.
         FE say-1S   to you   who is   my-four   grandmothers exactly
         'I shall tell you . . . exactly who my four grandmothers are.'
                                                                    (*CD* 61. 9–10)

(30)   Second-person singular
         Leidr, fe ddygest y   gwair o'ng   cae   i
         thief FE stole-2s the hay   from-my field me
         'Thief, you stole the hay from my field.'
                              (Slander case, Flint Sessions (1809), two depositions)

(31)   First-person plural
         Fe ddylen   godi   i'w   gadw   'n   loew   lân,
         FE should-1P arise-VN to+3SM-GEN keep-VN PRD shining pure
         Trwy   ddarllain ei orch'mynion . . .
         through read-VN   his commandments
         'We should arise to keep it pure by reading His commandments . . .'
                                                                    (BHJ 4. 15. 29–30)

(32)   Second-person plural
         Fe glawsoch bersonied ar y   sulie,   Ymron chwdu   wrth son
         FE heard-2P parsons   on the Sundays almost vomit-VN at   talk-VN
         am   bechode . . .
         about sins
         'You have heard parsons on Sundays almost vomiting when talking
         about sins . . .'   (*GN* 11. 10–11)

(33)   Third-person plural
         Py rhoe   rhain   eu   Pennau ynghŷd, Fe a   gyrran
         if put-COND those-ones their heads   together FE PRT drive-COND-3P
         y   Bŷd   yn   Bowdwr.
         the world PRD powder
         'If they put their heads together, they would turn the world to powder.'
                                                                    (*CD* 71. 25–6)

It can be seen from Tables 7.6 and 7.7 that, in the texts in which it is found
outside the third person, the use of *fe* is not associated with any particular person–
number combination. Its distribution seems to be entirely random. We can therefore
say, as with *mi*, that, once the restriction on agreement is broken, *fe* spreads to all
persons simultaneously—there are no intermediate restrictions, nor any environment based on person or number which favours or inhibits the spread of *fe*.

There seems to be no reason not to extend our account of *mi* to cover the change
associated with *fe*. That is, we can claim that the selectional feature in the lexical
entry for *fe*, requiring it to co-occur with a third-person-singular-masculine verb,

TABLE 7.6. *Frequency of particle* fe *before singular verbal forms*

Text	First-pers. sing.		Second-pers. sing.	
	fe (%)	Sample size	*fe* (%)	Sample size
Ballads of Hugh Jones	0	22	0	9
Ballads of John Jones	0	30	—	—
Crefydd mewn Bwthyn	1	84	0	1
Cwymp Dyn	6	155	4	24
Gras a Natur	1	153	0	18
Protestant a Neilltuwr	0	144	0	14
Slander cases (north-east)	0	23	13	16

TABLE 7.7. *Frequency of particle* fe *before plural verbal forms*

Text	First-pers. plur.		Second-pers. plur.		Third-pers. plur.	
	fe (%)	Sample size	*fe* (%)	Sample size	*fe* (%)	Sample size
Ballads of Hugh Jones	13	8	0	3	33	6
Ballads of John Jones	0	7	9	11	0	4
Crefydd mewn Bwthyn	0	4	0	7	0	2
Cwymp Dyn	14	14	0	19	67	3
Gras a Natur	0	11	26	27	4	24
Protestant a Neilltuwr	0	11	3	29	0	16
Slander cases (north-east)	—	—	0	5	—	—

fails to be acquired, and that this change had been manifested by the mid-eighteenth century.

The geographical distribution of *fe* before non-third-person verbs deserves comment. In modern Welsh, *fe* is associated with southern dialects (King 1993: 138). The situation in the eighteenth century is considerably different. The only evidence for the use of non-agreeing *fe* comes from the north-east, in slander cases and in ballads and interludes from that region. Here its use is well entrenched. Its absence in the south is surprising. One possibility is that we simply do not have access to appropriate texts from the south in which to find evidence for *fe*. However, the corpus does contain a number of texts from the south of a non-literary nature, and other texts in which non-standard variants are attested. Particularly important in this respect are the letters from settlers from Carmarthenshire and the slander-case depositions. Neither of these sources provides any evidence for *fe* in the relevant contexts. This leads one to conclude, albeit tentatively, that, in the latter part of the eighteenth century, *fe* outside of the third person is restricted to the north-east, and that it is in this region of Wales that one should look for its origins. This suggestion, although surprising from a twentieth-century perspective, is consistent with the geographical provenance of the earliest attested examples too.

7.5. THE CAUSE OF THE LOSS OF COMPLEMENTIZER AGREEMENT

I have suggested that children may have failed to acquire the person and number features associated with the agreeing complementizers *mi* and *fe*. However, it is not yet clear that there was any confusion in the trigger experience which might have caused children difficulty in acquiring what was otherwise a perfectly straightforward agreement rule. I now turn to some evidence from the syntax of the verb *darfod* to suggest that confusion was possible.

The contemporary dialects of north Wales have a perfective auxiliary *ddaru*, shown in (34) (for discussion, see Tallerman 1993). This auxiliary is generally defective—it does not conjugate for person, number, or tense. In the dialects in which it occurs, it is the unmarked way of expressing the preterite.

(34)   *Ddaru mi/ti/o golli   'r trên.*
        DDARU I/you/he lose-VN the train
        'I/you/he missed the train.'

This auxiliary is a fossilized form of the third-person-singular past tense of the verb *darfod* 'to happen, finish'. The use of the construction as an unmarked past tense in main clauses goes back in speech at least as far as the seventeenth century. Examples of its use in the seventeenth century are given from slander-case depositions from north Wales in (35).

(35) (*a*) *Fo a   ddarfu   yt ti   dyngu   yn annudo[n]*
          it PRT happened to you swear-VN false-oath
          'You perjured yourself.'   (Slander case, Denbigh Sessions (1633))

     (*b*) *Fo ddarfu   i Joan Vaughan o Tredderwen yn   ysbeilio ni . . .*
          it happened to Joan Vaughan of Tredderwen IP-GEN rob-VN us
          'Joan Vaughan of Tredderwen robbed us . . .'
                                       (Slander case, Montgomery sessions (1644))

     (*c*) *. . . ag fo ddarfy   iddo fo   dwyn   keffyl John ap William*
            and it happened to-3SM him steal-VN horse John ap William
          David . . .
          David
          '. . . and he stole John ap William David's horse . . .'
                                       (Slander case, Anglesey Sessions (1652))

In its earliest form, that found in (35), the verb *darfod* selects for a Prepositional Phrase headed by *i* 'to', the agent being the object of the preposition. At this
stage, there is an expletive subject, *fo* in the examples in (35), although *fe* is also
found. This expletive subject is a masculine-singular pronoun with which the verb
agrees.

By the mid-eighteenth century at the very latest, phonological erosion had set in,
and the preposition *i* is omitted in a large number of cases. Examples of this
omission of *i* are given in (36) from corpus texts.[11] Once *i* is deleted in adult
speech, there is no longer any reason for children to analyse the structure as
involving a PP. Consequently the structure changes. With a full lexical agent,
erosion of the preposition makes it appear as though this were the subject, inviting
a reanalysis of *darfod* as an auxiliary with a referential subject. The *fe*/*fo* could
easily be made to fit into this analysis by treating it as a complementizer, rather
than as an expletive pronoun.

(36) (*a*) *Fe ddarfu   rhyw un, . . . lygad-dynnu 'r Cybydd.*
         FE DDARFU someone   bewitch-VN the Miser
         'Someone bewitched the Miser.'   (*PN* 55. 34)

    (*b*) *fe ddarfu   rheini   ddanfon llawer iawn o anwiredd.*
         FE DDARFU those-ones send-VN many very of untruth
         'Those ones sent very many lies.'   (LUSS A4. 5. 12–13)

    (*c*) *Ydw, fe ddarfu   hi ddwyn   y   blawd.*
         am   FE DDARFU she steal-VN the flour
         'Yes, she stole the flour.'   (Slander case, Denbigh sessions (1760))

Note that this is already a syntactic change and cannot by this time simply be
phonological reduction, as the form of the pronoun in (36*c*) shows. Under the
conservative system, an inflected form of the preposition—namely, *iddi*—would
have been required. The form that appears here—namely *hi*—must actually be a
subject pronoun, it cannot be a reduced form of this inflected preposition.

Other evidence supports the view that such a reanalysis had already occurred by
the second half of the eighteenth century.

First, since Welsh has subject–verb agreement between pronominal subjects and
verbs, speakers who allow *darfod* to have a referential subject should make the
auxiliary agree with this subject. Evidence for such agreement is impossible to find
insofar as the verb *darfod* is defective. However, some writers use new conjugated
forms of the verb which do show such agreement, creating a new first-person-
singular form *darfûm* and a second-person-plural form *darfych*:

(37) (*a*) *Fe ddarfy'm   I heddiw siarad am   Gadair Newydd . . .*
         FE DDARFU-IS I today   talk-VN about chair   new
         'I talked today about a New Chair . . .'   (Eist. B1. 113. 14)

(*b*) . . . *o herwydd ni   ddarfym   I ddim meddwl   fod   hynna yn*
          because   NEG DDARFU-IS I NEG think-VN be-VN that   PRD
      niwaid yn y byd . . .
      harm   at-all
      '. . . because I didn't think that that would do any harm . . .'

(Eist. B2. I14. 25)

(*c*) *Y   ddarfych   Screfenny yn   byr   Heleth.*
      FE [?] DDARFU-2P write-VN PRD quite extensive
      'You wrote quite extensively.'   (LUSS B5. 2. 27)

(*d*) *Ni   ddarfych   Son   am   farlys am   cyrch yn ych Llythyr.*
      NEG DDARFU-2P talk-VN about barley about oats in your letter
      'You didn't talk about barley or oats in your letter.'   (LUSS B5. 3. 21)

Moreover, if the postverbal Noun Phrase is indeed a subject, we expect it to display other subject-like behaviour. In eighteenth-century Welsh, subjects may move freely to preverbal position. The subject of *ddarfu* is no exception to this.[12]

(38) (*a*) *Yr Arglwydd a   ddarfu   eu   gwrando* . . .
            the lord   PRT DDARFU 3P-GEN listen-VN
            'The Lord listened to them . . .'   (BHJ 3. 4. 6)

     (*b*) *Hi ddarfu   eu   gadael   nhw 'i gyd* . . .
            she DDARFU 3P-GEN leave-VN them all
            'She left them all . . .'   (BJJ 3=BJJ I. 65. 20)

This suggests that, by the mid-eighteenth century, *darfod* had developed into a perfective auxiliary which could take a referential subject. In the generation that makes the leap between the expletive subject analysis of *darfod* and the referential subject analysis, a change in the lexical entry for the complementizer *fe* will occur. Consider the structure of a standard case of the *darfod* construction with a pronominal subject in (39).

(39)   *Fe ddar(f)u (i)chwi ddwyn   fy   nefaid.*
        FE DDARFU (to)-you steal-VN my sheep
        'You stole my sheep.'

The adult structure will be as in (40*a*) before preverbal subject pronouns are reanalysed as clitics, and (40*b*) afterwards. In (40*a*) *fe* is the expletive subject of *ddarfu*, and the verb agrees with it. In (40*b*) *fe* is a third-person-singular-masculine complementizer which requires a verb in the same form. The subject is a postverbal expletive null pronoun *pro*. It is assumed that *ddwyn fy nefaid* 'steal my sheep' is in both cases a clausal subject which obligatorily extraposes.

(40)   Adult structure

(a) $[_{CP}fe_i \ ddarfu_V \ [_{IP} t_i \ t_V \ [_{VP} t_j \ t_V \ [_{PP} (i)chwi]$
         it   happened   to-you

$[_{CP} ddwyn \quad fy \quad nefaid]_j]]]$ $\Rightarrow$
   steal-VN my sheep

(b) $[_{CP}fe \ ddarfu_V \ [_{IP} \ pro \ t_V \ [_{VP} t_j \ t_V \ [_{PP} (i)chwi]$
         it   happened   to-you

$[_{CP} ddwyn \quad fy \quad nefaid]_j]]]$
   steal-VN my sheep

For the child the structure will be as in (41) if the verb *darfod* remains morphologically defective, or as in (42) if the child introduces separate person and number forms for it.

(41)   Child structure
$[_{CP}fe \ ddarfu_I \ [_{IP} chwi_i \ t_i \ [_{VP} t_i \ ddwyn \quad fy \quad nefaid]]]$
FE DDARFU you   steal-VN my sheep

(42) $[_{CP}fe \ ddarfych_I \ [_{IP} chwi_i \ t_i \ [_{VP} t_i \ ddwyn \quad fy \quad nefaid]]]$
FE DDARFU-2P you   steal-VN my sheep

For the child, *fe* is a complementizer as in the adult grammar of (40*b*), but the subject is *chwi* 'you'. In the adult grammar the complementizer *fe* is marked as being restricted to co-occurring with verbs in the default third-person form or with verbs marked as third-person masculine. For the adult, this fact poses no problem, since the subject is a third-person-masculine expletive. However, for the child, (39) contains an auxiliary agreeing, whether overtly as in (42), or owing to morphological deficiency covertly as in (41), with a second-person-plural subject. If the child hypothesizes that *fe* is marked as occurring only with default verbs, the structures in (41) and (42) will be ruled out. The only option is to reject such a restriction, and acquire *fe* as a general non-agreeing complementizer. The other conceivable alternative, a return to the adult grammar, is presumably not available if the preposition is elided on a regular basis in the trigger experience.

The adult grammar had two homonymous lexical items. One, *fe*₁, had selected an AgrS-head (and therefore a verb) with the default third-person-singular features and was therefore compatible with nominal subjects, both singular and plural, but not with pronominal subjects. The other, *fe*₂, had selected a verb with third-person-masculine-singular features (morphologically identical with the default form, but conceptually distinct), and was therefore compatible only with a third-person-masculine-singular pronominal subject (see Section 5.2.2.7). Children who generalized *fe* by the process just described did not need two separate lexical items, and could merge them as a single complementizer *fe*, which imposed no restrictions on the subject-agreement features of the verb. The introduction into the grammar of one main-clause complementizer unmarked for person naturally provides a model for the reanalysis of the first-person-singular pronoun *mi* along the same lines.

If the reinterpretation of *fe* as a general complementizer was indeed driven by the reanalysis of the perfective *darfod* construction, then we have an account of why the affirmative complementizers should initially appear only in northern dialects of Welsh. Since the perfective auxiliary occurs only in the north, the basis for the reanalysis is present only there. Inasmuch as *fe* in particular appears at a later period also in southern dialects, its use there must be the result of diffusion from more northerly dialects.

7.6.   *MI* AND *FE* BEFORE FORMS OF *BOD* 'TO BE'

In Middle Welsh, there is a restriction that topicalization is not possible across the present and imperfect tenses of *bod* 'to be'. This means that the sequence Pronoun + Present/Imperfect of *bod* is not possible (see Section 4.3). This restriction is maintained into Early Modern Welsh.

What happens when the pronouns are reinterpreted as complementizers? The evidence of the corpus is clear. There are a number of cases where both *mi* and *fe* occur before these forms of the verb. Some of the earliest corpus examples of *mi* are from the letters of Thomas Jones. All the examples given in (43) are from letters dated 1789. Note that person seems to be irrelevant to the possibility of *mi* in this environment.[13]

(43) (*a*) *Mi 'rwyf fi ar fy ngorau . . . yn   ceisio rhwy[s]tro 'r Tân*
        MI am   I on my best   PROG try-VN stop-VN   the fire
        ddiffodd.
        go-out-VN
        'I'm trying my best to stop the fire from going out.'   (Eist. A3. 34. 15)

   (*b*) *. . . ac os oeddwn i yn   gloff, mi roedd yr Argraphwyr yn*
        and if was-1S I PRD lame, MI was   the printers   PRD
        gloffach . . .
        lamer
        '. . . and if I was lame, the printers were lamer . . .'   (Eist. A5. 38. 8)

More examples at a somewhat later date are found in the letters of the northern (Merionethshire) settlers.[14]

(44) (*a*) *. . . ag mi rydw i yn   meddwl na   budd fy siwrna*
        and MI am   I PROG think-VN COMP+NEG will-be my journey
        i   ddim yn ofar.
        me NEG in-vain.
        '. . . and I think that my journey will not be in vain.'
                        (LUSS A2. 4. 2 (1817))

(b) *mi roedd ganthom y llynedd o'ddeutu 20 Tynell o wair* ...
MI was   with-us last-year around   20 tons   of corn
'Last year we had around twenty tons of corn ...'

(LUSS AI. 3. 6 (1816))

Finally, *mi* before present and imperfect forms of *bod* is attested in the slander cases for Gwynedd. These cases include the earliest attestation of the development in the corpus, which dates from 1778.[15]

(45) (a) *Mi roedd hi   yn   discwyl   iddo   fo   ei   chymeryd hi* ...
MI was   she PROG expect-VN to-3SM him 3SF-GEN take-VN   her
'She was expecting him to take her ...'

(Slander case, Bangor Consistory Court (1778))

(b) ... *mi rydych yn   lleidr* ...
MI are-2P PRD thief
'... you're a thief ...'

(Slander case, Caernarfon Sessions (1825), two depositions)

It is not clear whether the (rare) spread to the third-person-singular form *mae*, morphologically distinct from the rest of the paradigm, occurs at this time. There are no examples in the corpus. I know of no other example earlier than the following from the late nineteenth century:

(46)   *mi mae yn   awal galad iawn ac yn   law mawr iawn.*
MI is   PRD wind harsh very and PRD rain big   very
'There's a very harsh wind and a great deal of rain.'

(John Evans, letter 153. 11–13 (1873))

Is the spread of *mi* to co-occur with *bod* a separate development or does it follow automatically from the reanalysis of *mi* as a particle? The distribution of the construction clearly suggests the former.

The earliest attestations of *mi* as a particle were in the late seventeenth century and early part of the eighteenth century. The earliest attestation for *mi* before forms of the verb *bod* is from 1778. It might be the case that paucity of evidence for the intervening period meant that cases of the particle before *bod* would not come to light anyway. However, it seems reasonable, if *mi* had spread to the position before *bod*, to expect examples to appear in the early eighteenth-century interludes, and even in the slander cases, although the relevant forms of *bod* are less common there.

Secondly, even within the corpus, there are a number of texts where *mi* is attested as a particle, but where it never occurs before *bod*. As Table 7.8 shows, the presence of *mi* before *bod* implies general use of *mi* as a particle, but the reverse does not hold.

Accordingly, it seems reasonable to suppose that the generalization of *mi* to all positions is a development separate from and subsequent to the reanalysis of the

TABLE 7.8. *Distribution of* mi *as an affirmative complementizer before* bod *'to be' and other verbs*

Text	particle *mi*?	*mi* before pres./impf. of *bod*?
Ballads of Ellis Roberts	+	−
Ballads of John Jones	+	−
Cwymp Dyn	+	−
Gras a Natur	+	−
Letters of Thomas Jones	+	+
Seren tan Gwmwl	+	−
Settlers' letters (A1)	+	+
Settlers' letters (A2)	+	+
Settlers' letters (A4)	+	+
Slander cases (north-east)	+	−
Slander cases (north-west)	+	+

pronoun as a particle. The evidence dealt with here suggests that this innovation had taken place by the 1770s.

Much the same development happens with *fe*. Once again there appears to be no evidence earlier than the corpus texts. The only text in which *fe* is firmly attested before present and imperfect forms of *bod* is the interlude *Cwymp Dyn*. It is not linked to the original person of the pronoun.[16]

(47) (*a*) *Fe roedd* Twm Bithel *ac* Wmffre Gabrel *Yn   byw   mewn Cenal*
      FE was   Twm Bithel and Wmffre Gabrel PROG live-VN in   kennel
      Ci . . .
      dog
      'Twm Bithel and Wmffre Gabrel were living in a dog-kennel.'
      (*CD* 61. 29–30)

    (*b*) *O achos hyn fe rydwi yn   gla' . . .*
      because this FE am   PRD ill
      'Because of this I am ill . . .' (*CD* 15. 34)

Outside this text, examples are scarce. One clear example comes from Thomas Edwards in *Tri Chryfion Byd*:

(48)   *. . . Ac fe roedd cyhoeddus weddus wâdd, . . . i ladd,   a   bwytta.*
        and FE was   public   fitting   invitation to kill-VN and eat-VN
        '. . . And there was a public fitting invitation . . . to kill and eat.'
        (*TChB* 6. 35–6)

Additionally, there is one example each in the letters of Thomas Jones (Eist. A5. 39. 29) and in the slander material (Pembrokeshire Sessions (1806)) and a possible example in the letters of Thomas Edwards (B5. 11. 1). Apart from the Pembrokeshire slander-case example, all these are in texts from the north-east, specifically Flintshire and eastern Denbighshire. This fact may help to explain the contrast between the eighteenth-century situation and the modern one. In modern Welsh dialects, *mi* is found in the north before all the present and imperfect forms, but in those southern dialects where *fe* occurs, it may not precede the relevant forms of *bod* (King 1993: 138; Thomas and Thomas 1989: 77; Thorne 1993: 348).

7.7. A SUMMARY OF THE DEVELOPMENT OF *MI* AND *FE*

It has been argued so far in this chapter that the syntactic changes in the status and distribution of weak pronouns (later complementizers) in the eighteenth century can be reduced to changes in the category and feature specifications of pronouns and related items. A number of stages have been identified. First, by 1730 at the latest, and probably rather earlier, preverbal clitic pronouns (Stage I below) become agreeing complementizers in all dialects except the south-east. This results in the introduction of pronoun-doubling structures with simple and conjunctive pronouns, and the obsolescence of preverbal conjunctive pronouns (Stage II). Next, two of the agreeing complementizers—namely, *mi* and *fe*—lose their feature specifications and become general main-clause complementizers (Stage III). I have suggested that this change was triggered by the reanalysis of the *darfod* construction, and supported by the existence already of a main clause-affirmative complementizer for use with nominal subjects (*fe*) and other negative and interrogative complementizers. These changes had occurred by the 1740s, with *fe* leading the way, and with the results varying from dialect to dialect. Subsequently, these affirmative complementizers are used from the 1770s with all verbs, losing a restriction against their use with certain forms of *bod* 'to be'. Again the results vary substantially from dialect to dialect. The final Stage IV represents the contemporary situation for most dialects, which, although not evidenced in the corpus, is worth noting. The non-agreeing complementizers (*mi* and *fe*) have ousted the agreeing ones completely. It seems reasonable to suppose that the increased use of the particles *mi* and *fe* was

TABLE 7.9. *Summary of the changes in the pronominal and complementizer systems of eighteenth-century Welsh*

Lexical item	Lexical entry			
	Stage I	Stage II	Stage III	Stage IV
mi	D [1S] [+cl]	C [$_{\text{AgrS}}$ 1S]	C	C
ti/di	D [2S] [+cl]	C [$_{\text{AgrS}}$ 2S]	C [$_{\text{AgrS}}$ 2S]	obsolete
*fe*₁	D [3SM] [+cl]	C [$_{\text{AgrS}}$ 3SM] ↘		
			C	C
*fe*₂	C [$_{\text{AgrS}}$ default]	C [$_{\text{AgrS}}$ default] ↗		
hi etc.	D [3SF] [+cl]	C [$_{\text{AgrS}}$ 3SF]	C [$_{\text{AgrS}}$ 3SF]	obsolete

a gradual one during the nineteenth century (a step in terms of the theory of syntactic change) mediated by standard sociolinguistic processes.

A summary of the changes in lexical entries postulated is given in Table 7.9.

By the late eighteenth century, four dialect patterns are discernible. The most conservative dialects are in the south-east. In these dialects, none of the postulated changes occurs: Subject–Verb order is found with pronominal subjects and there is no pronoun-doubling. In the south-west, pronoun-doubling is found, but agreement between the preverbal complementizer and the verb is strictly maintained. In the north complementizer–verb agreement is only sporadically maintained. In the north-west the general main-clause complementizer is *mi*. In the north-east there is alternation between *mi* and *fe* in this function.

7.8. VARIANT PRONOUN FORMS

The eighteenth century gives us our first real opportunity to examine the distribution of a number of variant pronominal forms. As well as allowing an account of the stylistic and geographical patterns of variation, this information offers another opportunity to test the account of phonological erosion of the stronger pronominal forms set out in Chapter 5 (Section 5.2.2). It was suggested there that in late Middle Welsh the reduplicated pronouns spread as a way of maintaining V2, and subsequently underwent phonological erosion at the same time that V2 was lost. Given this account, we would expect some evidence to remain in the language of the eighteenth and nineteenth centuries. An examination of the variant forms of the pronouns also provides support for the claim made there (Section 5.2.2.7) that the complementizer and pronominal uses of *fe* were distinct lexical items by the seventeenth century.

In this section, I review this evidence, concentrating on the development of the reduplicated and simple series of pronouns. I consider first the variation in the second-person singular between *ti* and *di*, familiar from Chapter 5. Subsequently I turn to variation in the first-person singular, which is attested much later. Finally, I return to the most significant case of variation in the form of the third-person-singular pronoun and complementizer *fe/fo*.

7.8.1. Ti *and* di

As was seen in Section 5.2.2.5, *di*, a reduced form of the second-person-singular reduplicated pronoun *tydi*, appears in preverbal environments from the sixteenth century onwards. If the development suggested for the sixteenth century is correct, some remains of this variation would be expected in the eighteenth century. This is indeed what we find in the corpus. Three forms coexist: *ti*, *di*, and *tydi*:

(49) (a) *Ti   gei   gymdeithion glân, cwrw, a   thwrw, a   thân*
  you have-2S companions fine beer   and noise and fire
  'You shall have fine companions, beer, and noise, and a fire.'

(BHJ 7. 2. 4)

  (b) *O Enaint   anwyl di   am   llygadynaist . . .*
  O ointment dear   you PRT+1S-ACC bewitched-2S
  'O dear Ointment, you have bewitched me . . .'   (*GN* 34. 28)

  (c) *. . . a   tydi   ai   dygaist . . .*
     and you-REDUP PRT+3S-ACC stole-2S
  '. . . and you stole it . . .'   (Slander case, Caernarfon Sessions (1797))

Table 7.10 gives the relative frequency of these forms in the corpus as preverbal subjects. Texts not listed contain no instances of the subject pronoun in preverbal position. Three of the texts in the table are by Ellis Roberts (ballads, *Ail Lythyr Hen Bechadur*, and *Gras a Natur*). They all consistently use *di*, and so show no evidence of style-shifting between them. The two by Hugh Jones both have *ti* consistently. There is virtually no variation within texts. With the exception of the slander cases, which do not reflect the output of any individual speaker, all other texts except the ballads of Ellis Roberts have only *di* or only *ti*.

How can this pattern be interpreted? The problem is to know to what extent the distribution reflects dialectal or stylistic differences. The variation cannot be entirely geographic. The slander cases for most of Wales show sporadic use of *di*. On the other hand, it cannot be entirely stylistic. We can assume that the interludes, part of a tightly defined and conscious genre, are all of approximately the same stylistic level, yet two of the four listed (*Gras a Natur* and *Ystori Richard Whittington*) have only *di* whilst the other two (*Cwymp Dyn* and *Protestant a Neilltuwr*) have only *ti*. Yet all these texts are from approximately the same part of Wales.

TABLE 7.10. *Variant forms of the second-person-singular preverbal pronoun/complementizer*

Text	di (%)	tydi (%)	Sample size
Ballads of Hugh Jones	0	0	4
Cwymp Dyn	0	0	11
Protestant a Neilltuwr	0	0	7
Rhyddid	0	0	2
Slander cases (north-east)	0	0	9
Slander cases (south-east)	25	13	8
Slander cases (north-west)	30	10	10
Slander cases (south-west)	57	0	7
Ballads of Ellis Roberts	86	0	14
Ail Lythyr Hen Bechadur	100	0	3
Gras a Natur	100	0	4
Ystori Richard Whittington	100	0	6

The evidence of modern dialect studies may be relevant in this respect too. Ceinwen H. Thomas (1993) deals with the dialect of Nantgarw (Glamorgan), in which, as we saw earlier, a form of SVO is still (partially) maintained with subject pronouns. Her work contains examples, such as (50), of the second-person-singular pronoun in this position. In all cases, its form is *di*.[17] Supporting evidence comes from Thorne (1993: 370).

(50)   *di gluasd əm   əni*
        DI heard-2s about this
        'You heard about this.'   (Ceinwen H. Thomas 1993: ii. 44)

The most plausible conclusion seems to be that, in most cases, *ti* is the standard variant and *di* the non-standard form across most of Wales. However, the presence of *ti* even in certain low-style texts suggests that it was the usual form in some dialects. *Ti* seems to have been usual in the north-east, as the evidence of the slander cases for the area and the usage of two of the authors (Hugh Jones from Denbighshire, and Edward Thomas from Flintshire) suggests. The evidence of the slander cases suggest that *ti* was found sporadically elsewhere in Wales too. The exact nature of the variation must be left open.

The conclusion that *di* was a common form in Welsh dialects of the eighteenth century is surprising given that, with the exception of south-east Glamorgan, it is virtually unknown in Welsh dialects of the present day. However, it seems to fit well with the conclusions about the early development of the pronominal system. If *di* is indeed a common form in Welsh dialects of the eighteenth century, then the survival of a form clearly derived historically from a reduplicated pronoun provides strong support for the argument presented earlier that the verb-second rule was maintained in late Middle Welsh by the spread of the reduplicated forms.

7.8.2.   Mi *and* fi

By the eighteenth century we find a first-person counterpart to the reduced forms of the reduplicated pronouns of the second and third person, *di* and *fe/fo*. The reduced form of reduplicated *myfi* appears as *fi*, used as a straightforward variant to the more common *mi*.

Confirmation that this is indeed a phonologically reduced form of the reduplicated pronoun may be provided by at least one case of an intermediate form, in the example in (51) *n'fi*, repeated in two depositions, from a slander case arising from a dispute at Newton Nottage, Glamorgan.

(51)   *Lleidir yw William Philly an fi y   prova fe o elman Jane Jones.*
        thief   is   William Philly and+I PRT prove it of elm   Jane Jones
        'William Philly is a thief, and I'll prove it of Jane Jones's elm tree.'
                                (Slander case, Glamorgan Sessions (1760))

In the corpus, *fi* occurs as a preverbal subject pronoun in the almanacs of

John Prys (three out of five instances of a preverbal first-person-singular subject pronoun) and in the slander cases for the south-east (eleven out of twenty-four instances) and south-west (one out of seventeen). An example of its use in the almanacs is given in (52) (also AJP 1. 5. 18, 2. 12. 17). Those in (53) are from slander cases from the Glamorgan Sessions and St David's Ecclesiastical Court (also Glamorgan Sessions (1762, 1768)). The evidence of the slander cases suggests very strongly that the use of *fi* is a dialect feature of the south-east. Why this variant should be found in the work of John Prys, a native of the north-east, is not entirely clear.

(52)   *Ond weithan fi Draethaf yn nes   at 'n Gwlad ein hunain . . .*
         but now   FI discuss-1S PRD nearer to our country our own
         'But now I shall discuss (matters) closer to our own country . . .'
                                                                    (AJP 1. 4. 38–9)

(53) (*a*) *. . . a   fi croga   fe   cyn   blwyddyn ei nawr.*
           and FI hang-1S him before year   to now
           '. . . and I'll hang him before the end of a year.'
                                    (Slander case, Glamorgan Sessions (1767))

    (*b*) *Putain yn gwr   i   iw dy   gwraig ti   fy dwnga.*
          whore my husband me is your wife   you FI swear-1S
          'Your wife is my husband's whore, I swear.'
                              (Slander case, St David's Ecclesiastical Court (1791))

Further suggestive evidence that *fi* might be associated in particular with the south-east comes the modern Nantgarw (Glamorgan) dialect (Ceinwen H. Thomas 1993). In this dialect, one of the few in Wales to retain agreeing preverbal pronouns/complementizers at all, the form of the first-person-singular pronoun preverbally is *fi*:

(54)   *vi eθɔ   ɘno.*
         FI went-1S there
         'I went there.'   (Ceinwen H. Thomas 1993: ii. 44)

The same form is reported for the Welsh of the Ely Valley (Glamorgan) by Phillips (1955: 298), and for Aberdare (Glamorgan) by Howell (1902).

7.8.3. Fo *and* fe

The nature of the variant forms in the third person is somewhat different from the first and second persons. In both these other persons, direct descendants of the Middle Welsh simple pronouns survive into Modern Welsh as preverbal pronouns —that is, MW *mi a* + verb > ModW *mi* + verb and MW *ti a* + verb > ModW *ti* + verb. However, the direct descendent in the third-person masculine, MW *ef a* + verb > ModW *e* + verb, had virtually died out by the eighteenth century. Instead both main variants are descended from reduplicated pronouns. The older *efo a* + verb gives *fo* + verb, whilst the later innovation *efe a* + verb gives *fe* + verb.

In Chapter 5 (Sections 5.2.2.3 and 5.2.2.7), it was suggested that the expletive use of *ef a*, *efe a*, and *efo a* resulted in the development of a main-clause complementizer *fe*/*fo*. It was also suggested there that this complementizer should be treated as a separate lexical item from the pronoun *fe*/*fo* from the sixteenth century. The variation in form between *fe* and *fo* was said to have been the result of phonological developments prior to the split into two lexical items. If this is the case, it is expected that, prior to the split, the variation between the forms will not be conditioned systematically by the distinction between expletive and referential uses. This is indeed what was found to be the case in the sixteenth century. After the split, however, it is expected that developments in the form of one of the items will not necessarily be shared by the other. In so far as later developments show this to be the case, our account of the split into two lexical items in the sixteenth century is supported. I present here a summary of the distribution of these forms in the corpus. This evidence supports the idea that the two underwent separate development.

In the eighteenth-century corpus both forms *fe* and *fo* are well attested in contexts where they could be analysed as preverbal pronouns rather than complementizers. Examples of *fe* are given in (55), and of *fo* in (56).

(55) (a) *Pan   oedd y   Publican yn   cwyno,   Fe aeth i 'r eglwys i*
     when was the publican PROG lament-VN FE went to the church to
     weddio . . .
     pray-VN
     'When the publican was lamenting, he went to the church to pray . . .'
                        (*PN* 17. 33–4)

   (b) *Os daw   fy Mrawd Hugh drosodd yn y   Gwanwyn fe all ei*
     if comes my brother Hugh over   in the spring   FE can 3SF-GEN
     chael.
     have-VN
     'If my brother Hugh comes over in the spring, he can have it.'
                        (LUSS A3. 3. 35–6)

(56) (a) *Fo huda   yn Nhâd i dorri   yr Gyfreth . . .*
     FO enchanted-3S-IMPF my father to break-VN the law
     'He enchanted my father to break the law . . .' (*CD* 29. 9)

   (b) *. . . ag fo fydd   yn   disgwyl   cael   rhyw atteb*
     and FO will-be PROG expect-VN receive-VN some answer
     ynghylch y   dosbarthiad.
     about   the distribution
     '. . . and he'll be expecting to get some answer about the distribution.'
                        (LEE 257. 8)

Fo is found as a pronoun in the interludes *Cwymp Dyn*, *Gras a Natur*, the letters of Evan Evans, the ballads of Ellis Roberts and Hugh Jones, and in slander cases from the north-east. With one exception, all the texts in which *fo* is found are from the north-east of Wales. The letters of Evan Evans, a native of Cardiganshire, are the only exception.

Although *fo* is found frequently in a referential function, its use as an expletive is extremely rare. There are only three examples in the entire corpus, all in the letters of Evan Evans.[18]

It seems that *fo* is restricted to function as a pronoun. This view is reinforced by the fact that it is not found in pronoun-doubling contexts (except once in the letters of Evan Evans), nor where the subject is a non-overt feminine pronoun.

This suggests that the north-eastern dialect must by this time have already begun to make a distinction between the referential use of the third-person-singular pronoun and its expletive use. This supports the attempt in Chapter 5 to relate the increase in the use of *fe/fo* in the sixteenth century to the splitting-apart of the expletive and referential uses of the pronoun into two separate lexical items. Morgan (1952: 367 n.) suggests that Edward Samuel (1674–1748) already makes a fairly consistent distinction between the form of the pronoun and that of the particle in his *Holl Ddyledswydd Dyn* (1718).

It can be concluded that, at an earlier stage, as suggested in Chapter 5, the referential pronoun split from the expletive pronoun, which was reanalysed as a complementizer. In the north-eastern dialect, the form of the complementizer changes to *fe* only, whereas variation in the form of the pronoun between *fe* and *fo* remains. Since they have separate historical developments, it can be concluded that they are distinct lexical items.

7.9. COORDINATION

The eighteenth-century data also give us the opportunity to test the analysis of coordination presented in Chapter 4. By the eighteenth century, the possible patterns of clause-level coordination had been reduced considerably. The new restrictions can be linked to the loss of the null topic operator strategy. Since the null topic operator could be acquired only on the basis of gaps in the V2-system, the breakdown of that system would necessarily mean that it would fail to be acquired by the next generation. I shall now examine the types of coordination found in the eighteenth-century corpus, presenting a syntactic analysis which accounts for these restrictions and showing how the possibilities are limited by the settings of the V2 and Case-assignment parameters at the time.

Clausal coordination with a gap is restricted virtually entirely to three types by the eighteenth century. The gap in the second conjunct, identified as the subject by the presence of the preverbal particle *a*, is nearly always coreferential with the subject of the first conjunct.

The first type can be accounted for fairly trivially. This is ordinary coordination with a raised nominal subject lying outside the coordination structure—that is, the type of coordination familiar from English and other SVO languages.[19]

(57) (a) ... *Griffith y Pandu*$_i$ *aeth ar ei ol e ac* ____$_i$ *a   ddaeth*
        Griffith y Pandy$_i$ went after-him and ____$_i$ PRT came
        i hyd ir   gwartheg.
        as-far-as-the cattle
        'Griffith y Pandy went after him and found the cattle.'
                    (Slander case, Caernarfon Sessions (1824), two depositions)

(b) [*Y   Wraig   a   roddaist etto   atta*]$_i$ *A   wnaeth i mi yn*
    [the woman REL gave-2S again to-me]$_i$ PRT made to me PRD
    ddifatter   fwŷta: Ag ____$_i$ *a   ddweydodd gwnn ar Goedd,*
    unconcerned eat-VN and ____$_i$ PRT said   indeed on public
    Mae   Siwgwr oedd y   Seigia.
    CLEFT sugar was the dishes
    'The woman that you gave to me made me eat unconcernedly and said indeed in public that the dishes were sugar.'   (*CD* 12. 8–11)

This type is expected from standard assumptions about coordination. Assuming that raised subjects by this time occupy SpecIP (or SpecAgrSP in a fully articulated Phrase Structure), it involves coordination at the I'-level (or AgrS'), with the subject having been extracted Across-the-Board from both conjuncts:

(58)   [$_{IP}$ *Griffith*$_i$ [$_{I'}$ *aeth*$_{V1}$ [$_{AspP}$ t$_i$ t$_{V1}$ *ar ei ol ef*]]
                went   after-him

        ac
        and

        [$_{I'}$ *a ddaeth*$_{V2}$ [$_{AspP}$ t$_i$ t$_{V2}$ *i hyd ir   gwartheg*]
        came   as-far-as-the cattle

The same construction is found with a pronominal subject lying outside the coordination.[20]

(59) (a) *Ti   a   ddygaist heffer ac ai   gwerthaist hi imi.*
        you PRT stole-2S heifer and PRT+3S-ACC sold-2S   it to-me
        'You stole a heifer and sold it to me.'
                    (Slander case, Caernarfon Sessions (1773))

(b) *fe aeth yn Glaf ar   Plurys ag a   fu   yn debig iawn*
    he went PRD ill   with-the palsy and PRT was-PERF PRD likely very
    yn ngolwg dinion i ymadel   ar   byd   hwn . . .
    in sight   men to leave-VN with-the world this
    'He became very ill with the palsy and was very likely in the eyes of men to leave this world . . .'   (LUSS B2. 2. 1)

In a grammar in which these are still pronouns, the structure of this, apart from the cliticization process, is identical with that found in Early Modern Welsh (for discussion, see Section 5.1.3.3). The structure is more complicated once the pre-verbal pronouns have been reanalysed as complementizers, since the true subject will actually be postverbal *pro*.

However, this will make them identical in structure to the third type, illustrated in (60).[21]

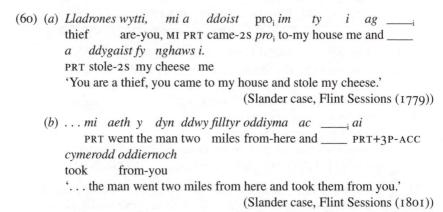

(60) (*a*) *Lladrones wytti,   mi a   ddoist   pro$_i$ im   ty   i   ag ____$_i$*
         thief   are-you, MI PRT came-2S *pro$_i$* to-my house me and ____
         a   ddygaist fy   nghaws i.
         PRT stole-2S my cheese me
         'You are a thief, you came to my house and stole my cheese.'
                                                (Slander case, Flint Sessions (1779))

     (*b*) *. . . mi   aeth   y   dyn   ddwy filltyr oddiyma   ac ____$_i$ ai*
              PRT went the man two   miles from-here and ____   PRT+3P-ACC
         cymerodd oddiernoch
         took   from-you
         '. . . the man went two miles from here and took them from you.'
                                                (Slander case, Flint Sessions (1801))

Here, the gap in the second conjunct is again coreferential with the subject of the first conjunct. However, the subject occupies a position in the first conjunct which is below a non-shared element—namely, the first verb.

In late-eighteenth-century and nineteenth-century written Welsh, a similar construction is used as a relative clause, with *ac a* as the relative marker (Richards 1938: 80). I take this to represent a misunderstanding and imitation of the coordinate construction that was becoming obsolete. Note that in most cases the examples given here of the coordinate construction cannot reasonably be interpreted as relative clauses. It is, therefore, not possible to argue that there are actually no coordination facts to account for.

Compare the coordination facts of eighteenth-century Welsh to those of Middle Welsh. In the eighteenth century the two clauses must share a common subject, whether that subject is preverbal in the first conjunct, as in the examples in (57) and in the conservative analysis of (59), or postverbal, as in the innovative analysis of (59) or as in (60). Other configurations are found only exceedingly rarely. This is a dramatic reduction in the possible types from Middle Welsh, where the antecedent of the gap in the second conjunct could fulfil any or no grammatical function in the first conjunct. Notice that this change results in the coordination possibilities in eighteenth-century Welsh being identical to those in Modern German (cf. Section 4.2.2). The main question that we have to deal with is why by the eighteenth century clausal coordination with a gap should require identical subjects when previously this had not been a requirement.

First, however, we also have to account for the appearance of the preverbal particle *a* in the second conjunct. This particle normally occurs only following a subject. We have assumed that this *a* is the result of agreement of the head of a functional projection (C) with a specifier position (SpecCP). Assume that after the reanalysis of subject-initial V2-structures as SVO, this process, if it takes place productively at all, operates as a Spec-head agreement relationship in AgrSP.

In the examples in (60), and potentially also those in (59), the subject in the first conjunct is postverbal, and apparently the absence of a subject in the second conjunct is licensed only by this subject. We can rule out the possibility that the second conjunct contains preverbal *pro*. First, preverbal *pro* is not otherwise licensed. Secondly, it should be possible for *pro* to have any antecedent, not simply the subject of the preceding clause. Hypothesizing postverbal *pro* fares just as badly, avoiding the licensing problem, but creating new difficulty in accounting for the appearance of the particle *a*, and still not accounting for the requirement that the subject be an antecedent.

The solution is to suggest that these sentences involve coordination at a level immediately below the subject of the first clause. On one interpretation, in a fully articulated Phrase Structure, this would be T′-coordination. The structure of (60*b*) would then be (61).

(61) $[_{CP}$ *mi* $[_{AgrSP}$ *aeth*$_{V1}$ $[_{TP}$ *y   dyn*$_i$
        PRT   went   the man
        $[_{T'}$ t$_{V1}$ $[_{VP}$ t$_i$ t$_{V1}$ *ddwy filltir oddiyma*]]
                            two   miles away

       ac
       and

       $[_{T'}$ *a'u*   *cymerodd*$_{V2}$ $[_{VP}$ t$_i$ t$_{V2}$ *oddiarnoch*]]]]]
          PRT+3P-ACC took   from-you

The subject undergoes Across-the-Board raising from SpecVP to SpecTP in each of the conjuncts. The particle *a* appears in the second conjunct as a result of Spec-head agreement between the verb in T, and its subject in SpecTP.

This presents one difficulty—namely, that in the second conjunct *a* appears in T, whereas the analysis of SVO assumes that the particle and verb end up in AgrS. It appears that this obliges us to revise the conditions under which *a* appears to include Spec-head agreement in TP. The structure may also present problems with regard to agreement. Alternatively it forces us to allow coordination of non-like projections. We could, for instance, claim that the second conjunct is an AgrS′, coordinating with a T′. The particle *a* would then head AgrSP rather than TP in the usual way, and agreement processes operating in AgrSP would not be affected. Heycock and Kroch (1994) propose that in German coordination structures of this type (SLF-coordination) the structure assigned to a sentence like (62) is that in (63).

(62)   *Das Gepäck ließ er fallen und rannte zum   Ausgang.*
     the   luggage let   he fall   and ran   to-the exit
     'He dropped the luggage and ran to the exit.'

(Heycock and Kroch 1994: 258)

(63) $[_{CP}$ *Das Gepäck*$_j$ $[_{C'}$ *ließ*$_{V1}$ $[_{IP}$ *er*$_i$ $[_{I'}$ t$_i$ *fallen* t$_j]$
     the   luggage   let   he   fall

und
and

$[_{C'/I'}$ *rannte*$_{V2}$ $[_{VP}$ *zum   Ausgang* t$_{V2}]]]]]$
ran   to-the exit

(Heycock and Kroch 1994: 264)

They argue that traces that are not needed to satisfy any licensing relations are deleted. So in (63) IP deletes because it contains two traces neither of which is required for Case- or theta-role assignment, leaving behind a hybrid category CP/IP which can coordinate with a full clause (CP).

The structure for eighteenth-century Welsh in (64) is simply a more articulated version of this idea. The traces in TP do not satisfy any licensing relations themselves—Nominative Case is assigned in AgrSP, and Accusative Case and theta-roles are assigned in VP. Therefore the traces in TP delete, causing TP to delete with them, thereby creating a hybrid category AgrSP/TP. The coordination is therefore coordination between T' and AgrS'/T', which counts as coordination of like categories.

(64) $[_{CP}$ *mi* $[_{AgrP}$ *aeth*$_{V1}$ $[_{TP}$ *y   dyn*$_i$
     PRT   went   the man
     $[_{T'}$ t$_{V1}$ $[_{VP}$ t$_i$ t$_{V1}$ *ddwy filltir oddiyma*$]]$
                 two   miles away

     ac
     and

     $[_{Agr'/T'}$ *a'u*   *cymerodd*$_{V2}$ $[_{\sout{TP} }$ t$_i$ t$_{V2}$ $[_{VP}$ t$_i$ t$_{V2}$ *oddiarnoch*$]]]]$
         PRT+3P-ACC took   from-you

The grammaticality of this construction in a non-V2 language depends crucially on the rules of Case-assignment.[22] Let us assume that Across-the-Board extraction entails that the moved element fulfil any Case requirements with respect to both conjuncts. With respect to the first conjunct, the subject is assigned Nominative Case under government from the verb in AgrS. With respect to the second conjunct, it is in the specifier position of the AgrSP/TP. It can therefore receive Case under agreement from the second verb in AgrS/T. This possibility does not therefore depend on V2, but rather the possibility of Case-assignment either under agreement or under government.

None of the clausal coordination structures in eighteenth-century Welsh discussed in this section requires the postulation of the null topic operator that was needed for earlier varieties of Welsh. This is a welcome result, given that it was argued in Section 6.4.1 that such a null operator could not be acquired outside a V2-system. It also allows us to relate the narrowing of possibilities for clausal coordination in eighteenth-century Welsh as compared to Middle Welsh to the loss of the V2-rule. The types of clausal coordination that remain can be generated by a non-V2 grammar. On the other hand, the types of coordination that are lost involve a discourse-bound gap that could only be generated using a null topic operator in a V2-language. It is, therefore, not surprising that the more restricted form of coordination should survive the loss of V2, as long as assignment of case to preverbal subjects remains a possibility, whereas the less restrictive coordination structure should not.

7.10. WORD-ORDER CHANGE SINCE THE EIGHTEENTH CENTURY

Our account of the development of Welsh word order has almost reached the stage of Contemporary Welsh. However, there is one way in which the word-order patterns found in the corpus differ substantially from those found in Contemporary Welsh. Synthetic verbs with full nominal subjects are found frequently in both SVO and VSO orders in eighteenth-century Welsh, whereas only VSO is found in unmarked contexts in Contemporary Welsh. I shall outline the sort of variation found in the corpus, and suggest a possible way in which the differences in word order and in coordination possibilities between eighteenth-century Welsh and Contemporary Welsh may be accounted for.

Table 7.11 gives the frequency of SVO as a percentage of affirmative declarative main clauses with synthetic verbs with full nominal subjects. As usual, texts with less than ten tokens are excluded.

Clearly, there is a very wide range of usage. Here, I shall limit myself to a few suggestions as to how this variation should be interpreted, concentrating on what conclusions can be drawn about the non-literary language, and the implications of the data for syntactic change.

Consider first what is happening in the literary language. There is a great deal of variation. A number of quite literary texts have very high frequency of SVO: the letters of Ann Griffiths (93 per cent), *Rhyddid* (69 per cent), *Meddyliau yr Esgob Watson* (60 per cent), 'Gair yn ei Amser' (50 per cent). On the other hand, other literary texts have a very low incidence of SVO: *Cylchgrawn Cynmraeg* (32 per cent), the letters of Owen Jones (23 per cent) and Evan Evans (18 per cent), *Drych yr Amseroedd* (16 per cent), *Seren tan Gwmwl* (16 per cent), *Crefydd mewn Bwthyn* (15 per cent), and *Cwyn y Cystuddiedig* (10 per cent).

A possibility worth considering is that there are two literary norms. The first norm has a high proportion of SVO clauses. The works which subscribe to this norm can be classified into two groups which may reflect the way in which the norm is transmitted. Some are highly conservative works, religious in outlook if not in content. Into this category fall the letters of Ann Griffiths, and two conservative political works, *Rhyddid* and 'Gair yn ei Amser'. The remainder are populist and technical works of types not traditionally written in Welsh, and as such heavily dependent on English sources. This is particularly the case with the almanacs and the translated work *Meddyliau yr Esgob Watson*. These texts are all in effect translated, whether directly or indirectly, from English. These have high levels of SVO too, and this may naturally be attributed to interference from the source language. In short, conservative and religious works adhere to an SVO-norm,

TABLE 7.11. *The frequency of SVO word order in eighteenth-century Welsh*

Text	SVO (%)	Sample size
Letters of Ann Griffiths	93	15
Almanacs of Mathew Williams	69	13
Rhyddid	69	114
Meddyliau yr Esgob Watson	60	15
Ballads of Hugh Jones	54	54
'Gair yn ei Amser'	50	12
Ballads of John Jones	51	95
Cwymp Dyn	43	92
Letters of Thomas Jones	42	26
Toriad y Dydd	42	36
Ystori Richard Whittington	39	72
Ballads of Ellis Roberts	38	97
Gras a Natur	38	128
Tri Chryfion Byd	38	80
Protestant a Neilltuwr	38	133
Letters of Thomas Edwards	37	30
Hanes Twm o'r Nant	34	58
Letters of David Thomas	34	38
Slander cases (south-west)	33	15
Cylchgrawn Cynmraeg	32	93
Letters of Owen Jones	23	13
Letters of Evan Evans	18	11
Slander cases (north-east)	18	11
Drych yr Amseroedd	16	120
Seren tan Gwmwl	16	45
Crefydd mewn Bwthyn	15	34
Cwyn y Cystuddiedig	10	52
Settlers' letters (A group)	8	25
Settlers' letters (A3)	0	12

maintained through the reading of the Bible, and are joined for different reasons by English-influenced texts.

Another competing norm uses predominantly VSO. The texts in this category can be seen more clearly from Table 7.12 which, using the same context as before, gives the frequency of absolute VSO clauses, that is those without the particles *fe* or *mi*.

A number of literary texts have very high levels of VSO: *Cwyn y Cystuddiedig* (85 per cent), *Drych yr Amseroedd* (80 per cent), *Crefydd mewn Bwthyn* (74 per cent), the letters of David Thomas (55 per cent), *Toriad y Dydd* (53 per cent), and *Cylchgrawn Cynmraeg* (51 per cent). The texts in question are either politically

TABLE 7.12. *The frequency of absolute verb-initial word order in eighteenth-century Welsh*

Text	VSO (%)	Sample size
Cwyn y Cystuddiedig	85	52
Drych yr Amseroedd	80	120
Crefydd mewn Bwthyn	74	34
Letters of David Thomas	55	38
Toriad y Dydd	53	38
Cylchgrawn Cynmraeg	51	93
Gras a Natur	49	128
Ballads of Ellis Roberts	45	97
Ystori Richard Whittington	36	72
Ballads of Hugh Jones	35	54
Ballads of John Jones	31	95
Rhyddid	29	114
Seren tan Gwmwl	27	45
Protestant a Neilltuwr	26	133
Tri Chryfion Byd	25	80
Letters of Owen Jones	23	13
Cwymp Dyn	23	92
Letters of Thomas Jones	23	26
Slander cases (south-west)	20	15
'Gair yn ei Amser'	17	12
Settlers' letters (A group)	16	25
Letters of Evan Evans	9	11
Almanacs of Mathew Williams	8	13
Settlers' letters (A3)	8	12
Letters of Thomas Edwards	7	30
Hanes Twm o'r Nant	3	58
Letters of Ann Griffiths	0	15
Meddyliau yr Esgob Watson	0	15
Slander cases (north-east)	0	11

radical (in the case of the three political publications *Cwyn y Cystuddiedig*, *Toriad y Dydd*, and *Cylchgrawn Cynmraeg*) or late in the period (*Crefydd mewn Bwthyn* (1819), *Drych yr Amseroedd* (1820)). A tempting conclusion is that in the last years of the eighteenth century, a VSO norm was competing with an SVO norm upheld by biblical usage. Writers who rejected traditional values were more likely to use the VSO norm. By the early years of the nineteenth century, the VSO norm had established itself for general use.

Compare this to non-literary usage. Most of the evidence in Table 7.11 points to fairly frequent but not overwhelming use of SVO order in colloquial texts. The interludes show remarkably consistent frequency of SVO at between 35 per cent and 45 per cent. The ballads are less consistent as a group, but still indicate that a good half of all affirmative main clauses with synthetic verbs are SVO. This evidence is confirmed by the prose of the slander material.

The only inconsistency in the non-literary material comes in the settlers' letters. In the letters of the A group of settlers SVO accounts for only 8 per cent of the clauses in question. The little evidence that we have from the B group is of the same order. In fact, the dominant pattern is *fe* + VSO. The somewhat later date of the settlers' letters compared to the other non-literary material may be significant in this regard.

In fact the most significant feature of colloquial texts seems to be a high frequency of the affirmative complementizers *mi* and *fe*. This is illustrated in Table 7.13, which shows the frequency of these complementizers in the texts, on the same basis as with the tables above. The interludes, settlers's letters, and slander-case depositions use the complementizers with a frequency that is generally higher than 30 per cent.[23]

It can be concluded that SVO was still a productive pattern in colloquial Welsh of the late eighteenth century.[24] It had to compete, however, with 'absolute' VSO and in particular with the increasingly frequent use of *fe/mi* + VSO. Contrast this with the situation in Contemporary Welsh, where preverbal non-contrastive subjects are at best marginal.

As was suggested in Section 6.3, once the non-V2 analysis of such sentences becomes established, the SVO pattern is derived from the VSO one by raising of the subject. This movement rule had to be justified there by claiming that Case-assignment by AgrS under government to the subject position in VSO structures—namely, SpecTP—was optional. A subject in this position could therefore raise to SpecAgrSP in order to receive Nominative Case. However, this movement is more costly in the sense that it involves an extra chain position, and it is difficult to see why such a system should be permitted.

This led to a situation, which presumably continued into the nineteenth century, where the SVO pattern competed with the more 'economical' VSO patterns. Under such circumstances it is reasonable to suppose that SVO would gradually be used less frequently in performance. Eventually the drop in frequency would be so great that the aspect of the grammar allowing SVO—namely, the possibility of Case-assignment to SpecAgrSP—was lost, and unmarked SVO became obsolete in Contemporary Welsh. This is the development that must be hypothesized as separating eighteenth-century Welsh from Contemporary Welsh.

The loss of Case-assignment by AgrS under agreement has interesting implications for the analysis of clausal coordination. The differences in coordination rules between eighteenth-century Welsh and Contemporary Welsh seem to support the idea that a change in the configuration for Case-assignment is involved.

Coordination rules in Contemporary Welsh are considerably more restrictive than even eighteenth-century Welsh. Coordination with a shared subject in post-

TABLE 7.13. *The frequency of* fe *and* mi *with nominal subjects in eighteenth-century Welsh*

Text	*fe/mi* (%)	Sample size
Cwyn y Cystuddiedig	2	52
Rhyddid	2	114
Drych yr Amseroedd	3	120
Letters of David Thomas	3	38
Toriad y Dydd	3	36
Ballads of Hugh Jones	4	54
Gras a Natur	6	128
Letters of Ann Griffiths	7	15
Ballads of Ellis Roberts	9	97
Crefydd mewn Bwthyn	12	34
Ballads of John Jones	15	95
Cylchgrawn Cynmraeg	16	93
Ystori Richard Whittington	19	72
Almanacs of Mathew Williams	23	13
'Gair yn ei Amser'	25	12
Cwymp Dyn	28	92
Tri Chryfion Byd	30	80
Letters of Thomas Jones	31	26
Protestant a Neilltuwr	31	133
Meddyliau yr Esgob Watson	33	15
Slander cases (north-east)	44	11
Letters of Owen Jones	46	13
Slander cases (south-west)	47	15
Letters of Thomas Edwards	50	30
Seren tan Gwmwl	58	45
Hanes Twm o'r Nant	59	58
Settlers' letters (A group)	60	25
Letters of Evan Evans	64	11
Settlers' letters (A3)	92	12

verbal position in the first conjunct in (65*a*) is now completely ungrammatical. The only possibilities for sentence-level coordination involve full CPs in (65*b*) and (65*c*).

(65) (*a*) **Daeth Siôn i'r   siop ac a   brynodd gaws.*
    came Siôn to-the shop and PRT bought   cheese

  (*b*) *Daeth Siôn i'r   siop ac mi   brynodd (e) gaws.*
    came Siôn to-the shop and PRT5 bought (he) cheese

  (*c*) *Daeth Siôn i'r   siop a   prynodd (e) gaws.*
    came Siôn to-the shop and bought   (he) cheese
    'Siôn came to the shop and bought cheese.'

The loss of the construction in (65*a*) reduces to the loss of the possibility of Case-assignment by AgrS under agreement. The alternatives in (65*b*) and (65*c*) both involve coordination of full clauses. In both cases the subject in the second conjunct is postverbal, as shown by the possibility of an overt pronoun there, and coordination is of full rather than partial clauses. In examples like (65*a*) the subject is extracted from both clauses. It is reasonable to assume that it must be case-marked with respect to both clauses. This was the case in eighteenth-century Welsh, where Nominative Case could be assigned either under agreement or under government. However, in Contemporary Welsh with Nominative Case assigned only under government, (65*a*) is ungrammatical because the shared subject cannot receive case with respect to the second conjunct (see (64) for the syntactic structure).

The result of the loss of Case-assignment under agreement is that coordination of the type in (65*a*) is ungrammatical under all conditions in Contemporary Welsh.

7.11.   CONCLUSION

In this chapter I have traced the development of Welsh word order from the loss of V2 up to the start of the nineteenth century, and offered some suggestions as to how its further development up to the present day is likely to have proceeded. The developments posited led to a decrease in the frequency of SVO structures in the language, and led ultimately to the complete loss of such orders. The data of this chapter have also provided us with more information about the mechanisms of syntactic change generally. Whilst the changes examined in the preceding chapter were thought of primarily as being parametric in nature, those examined here have been mostly lexical. As we have seen, the hypothesized differences between parametric and lexical change have not always conformed with the patterns found in actual historical cases.

8. Conclusion

This study has attempted to contribute to the understanding of a group of related questions in historical Welsh syntax, whilst at the same time investigating the ways in which syntactic change may universally operate. I shall now consider the main results of these enquiries.

8.1. VERB-SECOND IN MIDDLE WELSH

We first return to the question with which the investigation began: has Welsh word order really moved back from V2 (the abnormal sentence) to VSO since Middle Welsh? We are now in a position to judge the merits of the two accounts of the development of Welsh word order outlined there. Under the standard account of Mac Cana (1973), Watkins (1977–8), and Fife (1988), verb-second in Middle Welsh was a literary device introduced from an archaic form of the south-eastern dialects. Never a feature of the spoken language, it disappeared from the written language when the fashion for it abated in Early Modern Welsh (Sections 1.3.3.1–3). The alternative account treated the written evidence for Middle Welsh as essentially reliable. According to this account, the abnormal sentence was lost as a result of natural language change in the transition between (spoken) Middle and Early Modern Welsh.

The evidence presented in the course of this study allows us confidently to conclude that a verb-second rule (the abnormal sentence) was fully operative in spoken Middle Welsh. Evidence has been presented from three sources to support this view: from the internal structure of Middle Welsh itself, from comparative evidence both from the other Celtic languages and beyond, and from the subsequent historical development of Welsh syntax.

First, there is a substantial body of internal linguistic evidence from Middle Welsh itself to support this conclusion. The analysis of V2-structures in Middle Welsh in Chapters 3 and 4 showed that the V2-rule was manifested in a number of constructions in texts from all parts of Wales. It was seen that V2 incorporated rules of adverb placement in a natural way, distinguishing between several different classes of adverbs. The rules regulating the distance between the landing site of the topic and its base position exactly parallel those attested for a standard instance of A′-movement in Middle Welsh—namely, relative clauses. Specifically, topicalization from within embedded clauses and from within Prepositional Phrases is freely attested in both constructions. Finally, V2 was 'suspended' in contexts of narrative continuity, particularly in conjoined clauses. We can conclude that the abnormal sentence in Middle Welsh was a complex and fully developed V2-system, which interacted in a number of ways with other parts of the grammar. This is precisely the sort of behaviour that is expected if V2 was a naturally acquired part of the grammar of Middle Welsh. If, on the other hand, V2 was a consciously learned literary rule, it is hard to see how these complex interactions could have been devised or maintained.

The internal evidence of Middle Welsh is reinforced by the comparisons that we have made with other languages. We have seen that the rules for topicalization from Prepositional Phrases and coordination as they relate to V2 in Middle Welsh exactly parallel those found in Breton (see Sections 3.4, and 4.2.2 and 4.2.3.1). There is no reason to expect this if V2 was an imported literary addition in Middle Welsh prose. If, however, the connection between V2 in Middle Welsh and V2 in Breton is a natural genetic one, these similarities of detail are entirely to be expected. Similarities in detail have also been noted between Middle Welsh and languages where the V2-phenomenon is not genetically connected to that in Middle Welsh. Specifically, the limited use of V1-structures in Middle Welsh parallels V1 in Icelandic and Yiddish (Section 4.2.3.1). Furthermore, the interaction between V2 and coordination in Middle Welsh is virtually identical to that found in Old Icelandic and Old French, and shows parallels with coordination structures in German (Section 4.2.2–3). These similarities suggest that V2 in Middle Welsh makes use of a number of universally available options, and is therefore a natural linguistic pattern rather than a literary device.

The subsequent development of Welsh syntax points to the same conclusion. It has been shown that there is a substantial amount of evidence that remnants of the abnormal sentence survived into Modern Welsh. Certainly in the eighteenth century, SVO order is well attested in non-literary texts. This can be interpreted only as a residual form of the abnormal sentence. Similarly, residual V2 in Contemporary Welsh can be accounted for only if earlier stages of the language were verb-second.

Detailed evidence has also been presented regarding the development of the main-clause affirmative complementizers *mi* and *fe*. These must have developed from preverbal pronouns in the spoken language. Even without documentary evidence for Middle Welsh, we would on the basis of their development be forced to reconstruct the possibility of preverbal subject pronouns in Middle Welsh.

All this evidence points to V2 as a fully productive spoken pattern in Middle Welsh.

Finally, one of the central planks of the standard account, the Southern British Dialect Hypothesis, has been seriously undermined. According to this hypothesis, it is suggested that there was a major syntactic dialect split between the southern dialects of British, ancestors of Breton, Cornish, and south-eastern dialects of

Welsh, and northern dialects of British, ancestors of the remaining Welsh dialects. The main evidence was the existence of SVO in the former, but not the latter. We have seen (Section 7.2.2) that SVO in the south-eastern dialects of Welsh actually involves preverbal agreeing complementizers rather than true subjects. It therefore has little in common with the SVO found in Breton and Cornish, which is true topicalization as part of a full V2-system. In any case, the syntactic division between south-eastern Welsh and the other dialects seems likely to be of very recent origin, going back at most to the eighteenth century. In the light of this evidence, the Southern British Dialect Hypothesis cannot be maintained in any form, and a major part of the account of so-called literary word order in Middle Welsh disintegrates.

8.2.   HOW DID WELSH LOSE VERB-SECOND?

A related question that has been investigated is the question of how the verb-second rule came to be lost in the history of Welsh. Having established that verb-second was a rule of spoken Middle Welsh, we expect the answer to such a question to involve processes of natural language change, rather than, for example, recourse to explanations in terms of standardization or normative pressure. An account of the loss of verb-second in Welsh has been developed which focuses on the role of language acquisition and the nature of the trigger experience required to ensure transmission of the V2-rule from generation to generation. This account emphasizes that the main evidence allowing children to acquire V2 in Welsh was the presence of preverbal particles. These particles were the manifestation of an agreement rule between a head and a non-argument specifier position. This strongly suggested to children that movement of an arbitrary element to SpecCP was a part of their language. Additional evidence came from the alternation between the main variants of V2—namely, SVO, OVS, and AdvVSO word orders. On the other hand, children acquiring Middle Welsh V2 were hampered by the adverb-placement rules of their language, which created substantial potential for structural ambiguity (acquisitional ambiguity). Furthermore, unlike children acquiring Germanic V2, for example, they were not helped by a difference in position between a verb participating in V2 and one not participating in V2 (for instance, a nonfinite auxiliary or a verb in an embedded context). Whereas in German, raising of the verb from I to C creates alternations between SOV and XV(S)(O) orders, such raising in Middle Welsh made no difference to the position of the verb relative to the subject. In both cases the verb would precede the subject. The evidence allowing a child to acquire the V2-rule correctly in Middle Welsh was therefore noticeably different from that allowing the acquisition of V2 in Germanic.

It has been concluded that the crucial trigger for the loss of V2 in the sixteenth century was the phonological erosion of the preverbal particles. This, coupled with the presence of preverbal adverbs in V2-structures, obscured the evidence for V2, with the result that SVO patterns in the trigger experience were (re)analysed as non-V2 as in English, and AdvVSO patterns were (re)analysed as part of a general VSO rule that incorporated the freedom to place adverbs in a preverbal position. The OVS pattern, which might have provided the crucial evidence to maintain V2, had long since ceased to be a common feature of the language.

8.3.   SYNTACTIC CHANGE

As well as examining the historical syntax of Welsh, this study has provided a testing ground for a number of ideas in the theoretical study of syntactic change in general. Accounts of a number of syntactic changes have been presented in terms of the conditions of acquisition. Formal changes in the grammar have been related to changes in the trigger experience, the input available to the child during language acquisition.

The evidence of these changes forces us to revise aspects of the parametric model of syntactic change presented in Chapter 2, although in other ways it gives it support. I now turn to consider the implications of this evidence.

We shall first review the properties of the main syntactic changes proposed in the history of Welsh, concentrating specifically on their properties with respect to the theoretical notions of syntactic change raised in Chapter 2. Before doing so, however, it is worth clarifying the terms 'sudden' and 'gradual', since the notion of parametric change depends crucially upon defining a change as one or the other. These terms can be used in two ways. First, there is an intuitive sense: a change is sudden if the innovating syntactic pattern replaces the conservative pattern quickly, otherwise it is gradual. Secondly, in a more technical sense, a change is sudden if the patterns of data observed are consistent with the grammar having only either the old or the new setting of the feature undergoing change. It is gradual if the patterns of data require both old and new settings to be available for a considerable period of time. To avoid confusion, I shall use the terms **discrete** and **non-discrete** for the more technical sense, reserving **sudden** and **gradual** for the intuitive one.

The first major change that was noted in the development of Welsh syntax was a change in the status of preverbal pronouns from full elements to clitics (Section 5.1, esp. 5.1.2). In every sense this appeared to be gradual and non-discrete, taking several hundred years, and operating at different rates in different pronouns. The gradual nature of the change is probably connected to the fact that the feature to which it relates—namely [±clitic]—is phonologically gradual, in the sense that the ability of a pronoun to bear stress may vary by degree. The change had multiple effects, including the loss of various constructions where elements intervened between the pronoun and the verb, and the spread of expletive subject construction from unaccusative to transitive verbs. However, these were largely gradual in nature. Slow reductions were found in the frequency with which the non-clitic system was attested.

Somewhat later, we noted the reanalysis of the expletive subject, *ef*, *fe*, or *fo* from pronoun (D-head) to a default complementizer (C-head) (Section 5.2, esp. 5.2.2.7). This change is clearly lexical in that it represents a change in the category of a single word in the language. However, when the pronoun became a complementizer, the marked focus interpretation usually associated with expletive constructions was lost, and a sudden increase in the use of *fe* was observed in the sixteenth century. The change therefore exhibits the suddenness (and discreteness) associated with a parametric change, despite being lexical in nature.

The first parametric change to be observed was the resetting of the V2-parameter to a negative value, triggered in the first instance by the erosion of preverbal particles, and decline of object topicalization (Section 6.2.1), both gradual changes ('steps'). The loss of V2 led to a number of trailing changes, including the sudden innovation of VSO as an unmarked pattern in Early Modern Welsh. Additionally it resulted in the obsolescence of some minor topicalization types (Section 6.4.2) and topicalization across negation (Section 6.4.3), and a reduction in the possible types of clausal coordination (Section 7.9). The patterns of data, insofar as the relevant detail was available, were consistent with this change being discrete. In particular, frequent use of unmarked VSO orders appears in sixteenth-century texts. There is, therefore, every reason to believe it to be in accord with a parametric account of syntactic change.

In the early eighteenth century, preverbal subject pronoun clitics (*mi*, *ti/di*, *fe/fo*, *hi*, etc.) were reanalysed as agreeing complementizers (Section 7.2.1). This was clearly a lexical change, since it involved a change in the categorial status of the relevant items from pronouns (determiners) to complementizers. It was primarily reflected in the appearance of pronoun-doubling. This was gradual in the sense that the non-doubling pattern survived. However, since the non-doubling pattern could be generated even if the preverbal element was a complementizer, this gradualness does nothing to prevent the change from being discrete. Additionally, the change had the striking effect that, within the space of a generation or two, preverbal conjunctive pronouns were lost completely from the colloquial language of most of Wales (Section 7.2.2). This sudden aspect of the syntactic change suggests strongly that it was discrete. Again, this is slightly surprising given that this is clearly a change in a lexical feature rather than a parameter, and that our initial hypothesis was that a defining property of parametric changes was their discreteness.

Slightly later in the eighteenth century, two of the agreeing complementizers—namely, *mi* and *fe*—spread from their initial environments (first-person singular and third-person-singular-masculine respectively) to other environments. These changes were found to be sudden in that the complementizers spread to all persons and numbers simultaneously, but gradual in the sense that non-agreeing *mi* or *fe* did not immediately replace the agreeing complementizers *ti/di*, *hi*, etc. The two 'compete' for a while before the Contemporary Welsh situation, in which (in virtually all dialects) only *mi* and *fe* are found. Again, however, these data are compatible with the change being discrete. Suppose that the change was discrete in that it involved the removal of features of the lexical entry for *mi* and *fe* which required them to co-occur with particular forms of the verb. If so, the change would result in *mi* and *fe* spreading immediately to all persons and numbers. However, they will not replace the agreeing complementizers immediately, since the separate lexical entries for these complementizers survive unaffected by the change. This is exactly what seems to have happened. Therefore, as before, a change which is clearly lexical seems to have discrete properties.

Finally, we must conclude that the loss of unmarked SVO entirely from the language has occurred since the end of the eighteenth century. This was linked to a parametric change—namely the loss of the possibility of Nominative Case assignment by AgrS under agreement (Section 7.10). The change results in the obsolescence of the one remaining class of clausal coordination structures, and therefore shows the 'cluster' property associated with parametric change. Although detailed data for this are lacking, there is every reason to believe that the change proceeded in a parametric manner. SVO orders lost ground in performance to VSO orders, which involved less movement in their structural representation (a 'step'). Eventually they were so rare as to be unacquirable, and the Case-assignment parameter changed. This led to the loss of the residual coordination types (a trailing change).

The two parametric changes proposed—namely, the loss of V2 and the loss of Case-assignment under agreement—seem, in so far as it is possible to judge, to exhibit the hypothesized properties of parametric change—namely, the properties of being discrete, of having a number of surface exponents, and of involving obsolescence (Section 2.4). The investigation of them therefore tends to support the notion of parametric change as a useful concept in historical syntax.

Consideration of these various patterns of syntactic change also leads us to conclude that a number of changes which must be viewed as lexical (non-parametric) exhibit discrete patterns of data in much the same way as parametric changes. This should not really be surprising. It is reasonable to assume that most of the features under consideration are binary and discrete. For example, the feature requiring *mi* to co-occur with a first-person-singular verb may be either present or absent, but not 'slightly present'. Syntactic change that involves such features is likely to be discrete, even if it is not considered to involve a parameter. The best example of this is the reanalysis of preverbal subject clitics as complementizers, which results in the sudden introduction of two new syntactic patterns (pronoun-doubling and postverbal conjunctive pronouns), and the sudden obsolescence of another (preverbal conjunctive pronouns) (Section 7.2).

On the other hand, there *are* changes in lexical entries in natural language which are entirely gradual and non-discrete. Changes in lexical semantics often appear to be gradual, as do some changes in the subcategorization frames of verbs. In the present study this also seems to be the case with the weakening of subject pronouns to clitics in late Middle Welsh.

The question then arises as to how the two types of change, discrete and non-discrete, can be kept apart. Clearly the distinction between parametric and non-parametric change will not suffice. One possibility worth pursuing is that change in the lexical entries of functional categories (determiners, complementizers, inflectional markers, and so on) may be discrete, whereas change in the lexical entry of lexical categories (primarily verbs and nouns) may generally be non-discrete.[1] For instance, the preverbal elements in eighteenth-century Welsh may be pronouns (determiners) or complementizers but not some intermediate category. Verbs, on the other hand, may list a number of different subcategorization frames in their lexical entry. Changes in frequency of one or its loss entirely has no effect on the existing possibilities.

It is clear that a number of instances of lexical change in functional categories show patterns of development indistinguishable from those hypothesized for parametric change. There is thus every reason to conflate the two categories into a single category of discrete syntactic change.

Under a minimalist syntactic theory, this is in fact a fairly natural development. Chomsky (1995) has argued that parameters do not have independent existence, rather they are essentially the lexical features of functional categories:

> It has been suggested that parameters of UG relate, not to the computational system, but only to the lexicon. We might take this to mean that each parameter refers to properties of specific elements of the lexicon or to categories of lexical items—canonical government, for example. . . . If substantive elements (verbs, nouns, etc.) are drawn from an invariant universal vocabulary, then only functional elements will be parameterized.   (Chomsky 1995: 131)

In doing so, he reinterprets a number of well-established parameters as features on functional categories. For instance, a positive setting of the V2-parameter is interpreted as a strong DP-feature on C, VSO is interpreted as a weak DP-feature on T (Chomsky 1995: 198–9; cf. also 160).[2]

Under this conception of a parameter, parametric change would be the change in some feature of a functional category. For instance the loss of V2 would be a change in the strength of the DP-feature on the lexical entry for C from strong to weak. An explanation is therefore available for why parametric change and lexical change in the pronoun/complementizer system should exhibit patterns of data that are so similar. They are both specific instances of a more general kind of syntactic change, involving changes in the features of the lexical entries of functional categories.

8.4. CONCLUSION

This study has aimed at presenting a full and coherent account of the development of word order in Welsh from the fourteenth to the nineteenth century.

A re-examination of the testimony of the medieval period and the introduction of previously unstudied material from the modern period has led us to challenge the most widely held view of the development of the 'abnormal sentence'. The development of Welsh syntax remains a complex area, and the results presented here will need to be supplemented and confirmed by further research. Particular emphasis needs to be placed on the further investigation of the complex patterns of data observed during the loss of V2 in the sixteenth century, and of the evidence of non-literary sources in the Modern period. However, I hope that this study has shown that these are both feasible and profitable areas of enquiry.

This study has also attempted to make a contribution to linguistic theory on a more general level. The account of the history of Welsh syntax has been comparative in nature, drawing on parallels with a number of other languages. Where appropriate, the patterns of data found in the history of Welsh have been integrated into this wider picture. Many of these parallels are far from obvious features of language, and investigation of them can provide valuable information about the properties of possible human languages.

Finally, I hope that this study has contributed towards a more articulated account of syntactic change. In doing so, it has extended the number of languages to which a parametric model of change has profitably been applied. At the same time, it has attempted to clarify some problems posed by lexical change to the parametric account of syntactic change. It is only through continued research along these lines that a full account of syntactic change can be developed.

Notes

1. INTRODUCTION

1. These particles are now all often omitted in speech, although their mutation effects remain (see Ball 1987–8; 1988*a*: 67–9).

2. Although not part of the main suggestion, the origin of the mixed sentence is fairly clear. It develops from the loss of the copula in full cleft sentences like that in (i), a type fairly securely attested in Old Welsh (D. Simon Evans 1964: 140–1; Richards 1940).

   (i) ... *is did ciman haci* ...
         is day whole REL+have-2S
       '... it's a whole day that you'll have ... '   (CF 256. 3)

3. See, however, Sections 3.3.5 and 3.6 on the syntactic differences between the two.

4. These contexts are irrelevant for the present discussion since they have manifested dominant VSO throughout the history of Welsh.

5. In the course of this study, it will be seen that there is substantial evidence for a form of the abnormal sentence in non-literary Modern Welsh prior to the twentieth century (see Section 7.10). However, for the moment let us accept the assertion as given.

6. See Section 7.2 (esp. Section 7.2.2), however, where it is argued that apparent instances of SVO in these dialects actually involve an agreeing affirmative complementizer with a postverbal null subject, and are therefore essentially VSO in structure.

7. This statement of word-order possibilities of Old Welsh is open to question. There *is* evidence for preverbal full nominal subjects. However, the evidence is clearly exceedingly debatable, and no hypothesis is likely to stand or fall on the basis of such data alone.

8. There is, however, no reason to connect Middle Welsh narrative prose entirely with the south-east—as the availability of northern Middle Welsh texts in Chapters 3 and 4 of this study demonstrates. The scenario is also curiously inconsistent with the idea that the 'original' rule of British survives in south-east Wales. Since it is the abnormal sentence in its full form which is 'loaned' into literary Middle Welsh from the dialects of the south-east under this scenario, one must surely have to suppose that these dialects developed the full form of the abnormal sentence from the British rule of SVO with pronominal subjects, but then lost it again. Clearly, in that case, the fact that these

dialects have SVO with pronominal subjects is not support for the claim that this was the rule in British.

9. More recently, verb-raising has been motivated by the presence of a strong V-feature on Infl/AgrS (Chomsky 1995: 349).

10. Presumably there is some way to assign Case to the subject of these clauses in the absence of tensed Infl, either through Case-assignment by the (obligatory) coordinating conjunction, or through some default Case-assignment mechanism (cf. Chung and McCloskey 1987 on a similar construction in Irish).

11. This can be recast in a minimalist framework as a weak DP feature of Infl in VSO languages, contrasting with a strong DP feature of Infl in English. In Welsh and other VSO languages raising of the subject to check Case in SpecIP would occur only covertly, whereas this movement would be overt in English (Chomsky 1995: 198–9).

12. I assume an aspectual projection immediately dominating VP, headed by the aspectual particles *yn* 'progressive', *wedi* 'perfective', *ar* 'prospective', *newydd* 'recent perfective', etc. For motivation, see Hendrick (1991).

13. If SpecNegP is an A'-position, then, under Relativized Minimality, A-movement of the subject across it will be legitimate.

14. Roberts (1993*b*: 22) assumes that SpecTP is an A'-position, and therefore rules out the possibility that subjects might raise to it to receive Case. This assumption is required to prevent inversion in affirmative main clauses in English in his analysis. If we wanted to maintain this analysis, it would be necessary to postulate an additional functional projection between AgrSP and TP to which the subject in Welsh could raise to receive case. Alternatively, *ddim* could be analysed as an adverb adjoined to AspSP, and the subject would raise to some specifier position below TP but above AspSP, say SpecNegP. For the sake of simplicity, I shall, however, proceed assuming the structure in (36) and (38).

15. The short movement of subjects to SpecTP in Welsh is problematic in a minimalist framework, which allows Nominative Case to be checked (covertly or overtly) only in SpecAgrSP. If Case is checked covertly in a VSO language, and therefore Case-assignment does not motivate any overt raising, it is not clear what motivates short movement of the subject to SpecTP in these languages. By Procrastinate, the subject should remain in SpecVP. The only possible account seems to involve variation in the strength of the V or DP features of T (cf. Bobaljik and Carnie's 1996 account of subject-raising to SpecTP in Irish; also Chomsky 1995: 216 n. 40), although this does little more than restate the problem.

2. SYNTACTIC CHANGE

1. This has been applied to the history of Welsh. Fife and King (1991: 148) claim that

typologically Middle Welsh is a VSO-language. Fife (1993: 30) further claims that topic-initial languages generally develop into SVO-languages. Therefore, if Middle Welsh had really been topic-initial it should have developed SVO. This line of argumentation, based only on tendencies of historical development, is unconvincing unless supported by detailed empirical evidence from the language under investigation.

2. Lightfoot in general claims degree-o learnability, that is, that information from embedded contexts is not available for parameter-setting by children. He therefore excludes from the discussion subordinate-clause evidence, which would also have shown the OV order.

3. Since a consistent drop in frequency is not the same as random variation in frequency, there may be some explaining to do even here.

4. One presumes that a new construction is introduced by a change in feature specifications for some item in the lexicon—i.e. a form of lexical change. For discussion of some of the difficulties with this see Section 2.3.1.

5. There are plausible phonological and pragmatic reasons why this might happen. For example, phonological erosion of case endings might encourage the use of less ambiguous, unmarked word orders. A plausible pragmatic reason would be a universal tendency towards increased use of subjects as topics in topic-prominent languages. This is a legitimate area for an account of language change, but one which lies outside the scope of the parametric model itself.

6. This seems to leave the way open for the possibility that a Diachronic Reanalysis may not induce a parameter change. If so, there are some Diachronic Reanalyses which in themselves (that is, without the aid of a simultaneous parametric change) alter the set of grammatical structures (although perhaps not the surface strings). Such a development must involve a change in the grammar, but one which is non-parametric. This seems to necessitate an explicit role for something like lexical change in syntax. See Section 2.3.1.

7. It is difficult to see how a Diachronic Reanalysis could lead to a change in frequency of construction. A more typical setting for a change in frequency would be drift in the thematic meaning of a construction—e.g. heavy-element movement rules or left and right dislocation becoming less stylistically or pragmatically marked.

8. It might be argued that this itself is a syntactic change. Presumably, however, the ability of adverbs to appear in sentence-initial (CP-adjoined) position is governed by features in their lexical entries.

9. Again, one wonders why, if adjunction to CP is generally so bad, Middle French not only allows it to happen at all, but even allows it to spread. Presumably the universal availability of left-dislocation constructions must be invoked at this point, allowing the possibility either of parametric variation in whether the option of left dislocation is taken, or more probably, of lexical features on individual adverbs overriding the

prohibition on adjunction to CP. If the latter option were to be chosen, it could be argued that an increase in markedness in the peripheral grammar is eliminated by a reanalysis.

10. I find it hard to accept that this can actually be a Diachronic Reanalysis at all. Two possibilities exist: either SVO order with the subject in AgrP rather than in CP had always been available, in which case this is a step, increased selection of one rather than another structure supplied by the grammar; or, the structure where SVO order involves the subject occupying SpecAgrP is new, in which case some parametric change is required, presumably allowing the [+Agr] feature not to raise to C (see Santorini 1995: 64–7 for this as a possible parametric change in Yiddish), and therefore for SpecCP to be left unoccupied. In fact, I find it hard to see how (logically) a Diachronic Reanalysis that does not lead immediately either to a parametric change or a change in lexical features can exist. Roberts hints at something like this possibility when he states (Roberts 1993*b*: 159) that 'the notion DR may also prove to be epiphenomenal', and 'all DRs may turn out to be instances of Parametric Change'. See Section 2.3.2.

11. This seems to be tantamount to admitting to a parametric change in the distribution of [+Agr], that is:

C may bear feature [+Agr]   Yes
C must bear feature [+Agr]   Yes → No

12. Of course, in this case, one might try to use parameterization of nonfinite Infl, but even then we are dealing only with one possible lexical instantiation of nonfinite Infl. The properties are therefore highly language specific.

13. Arguably it can be rescued by adjoining the adverb to CP, but, since the whole reanalysis was triggered by the need to avoid this, such a possibility seems unlikely.

14. There may, of course, be lexical changes, a possibility that is ignored here.

15. Note that in this case the relationship is not reciprocal. That is, although the construction helps to set the parameter, the parameter does not dictate the presence or absence of the feature. Even if the parameter were set to VO, the separable prefix constructions could be reanalysed.

16. Actually, acceptance of degree-0 learnability is not at all crucial to this example. The frequency of subordinate clauses in children's trigger experience can safely be assumed to be quite low, in which case subordinate word order will have little effect on setting parameters, and will be a trailing feature.

17. In fact, the data may not be so clear-cut. Very few of the texts in Santorini's corpus by individuals give anything like even numbers of both. Of her East Yiddish texts (ignoring court testimony from multiple speakers), no text of reliable sample size lies in the range between 13% and 72%. The picture is also complicated by the development of literary norms in Yiddish in the period under consideration. In literary texts, strongly influenced by a norm, there is no reason to expect theories of *natural* language change to hold.

18. This will be a factor only insofar as children are sensitive to this, paying more attention to speakers from their own social background. It may simply be that this factor reduces to network theory (James Milroy 1992; Leslie Milroy 1987), with children from particular social groups socializing more with children and adults of the same social group. They would therefore be exposed to more data from their speech, and set parameters according to such input data. Stylistic variation, and possibly also a large amount even of social variation, is unconsciously learned rather than acquired, and produced via adaptive rules in the periphery of the grammar.

19. It is, of course, conceivable that a parameter in a given language may have only a single exponent.

3. VERB-SECOND IN MIDDLE WELSH

1. The association of a particular text with a particular geographical area does not necessarily mean that the surviving manuscript versions of that text were written in the same geographical area. Middle Welsh dialect features did survive copying. For instance, although *Kedymdeithyas Amlyn ac Amic* shows late northern dialect features, Hywel Fychan, the scribe of the Red Book of Hergest in which it is found, was probably from south-east Wales. Other texts that Hywel copied in the same manuscript exhibit different dialect allegiances, suggesting that he was a faithful copyist who did not significantly alter the dialect of his exemplar (Peter Wynn Thomas 1992: 298–9; 1993: 42–3). This justifies the use of this text as evidence for northern forms of Middle Welsh. At the other extreme, one of the best cases of a text with a purely northern history is the extension to *Brut y Tywysogyon* in Peniarth 20 providing chronicle entries for the years 1282–1332 (BTy_1 292–302). Both internal evidence (the preoccupation with events in north-east Wales) and palaeographic evidence suggest that this had a continuous link to the north-east (BTy_1, p. xix).

2. The examples in (1) are from southern texts. Parallel examples from northern texts are: preverbal subject: BTy_1 300a. 17; preverbal object: BTy_1 215b. 16; preverbal adverbial adjunct: BTy_1 292a. 4; preverbal adverbial complement: BB_1 47. 13; VP-complement of auxiliary: BB_1 47. 16; preverbal verbnoun: BB_1 91. 17.

3. A number of complementizers are followed by main-clause word order in Middle Welsh—for instance, *kanys* 'since' and *os* 'if + cleft'.

4. However, see also Section 4.2, where it is argued that even these figures overestimate the true extent of V1-clauses in Middle Welsh.

5. For further exemplification of this idea from Middle Welsh tales, see also Poppe (1989: 54–8; 1990: 455–8; 1991*a*: 189–99).

6. See, however, Travis (1991), where it is argued that SVO main clauses in some Germanic languages do not involve movement of the verb to C.

7. Note that IP and VP in German are head-final. Parametric variation in the position of the heads of I and V with respect to their complements and in the possibility of V-to-I raising will mean that the embedded clause order will differ considerably between German and the other V2-languages.

8. In the so-called 'symmetric' V2-languages, Icelandic and Yiddish, matters are more complicated, since V2 is permitted in both main and subordinate clauses. This requires either CP-recursion or topicalization to SpecIP. For full discussion, see Rögnvaldsson and Thráinsson (1990) on Icelandic, and den Besten and Moed-van Walraven (1986) and Diesing (1990) on Yiddish. Santorini (1994) offers a comparison of the two languages.

9. There is also a question surrounding the movement possibilities of nonfinite verbs (verbnouns). Since all V2-movement under this account is to SpecCP, it is expected that only phrasal constituents may occupy the preverbal position. This creates a difficulty, since Middle Welsh verbnouns may move to preverbal position without their complements, as in (If). This problem of Long Head Movement recurs in a number of V2 and non-V2 languages. I shall not dwell on it here. For discussion, see Borsley *et al.* (1996) and Schafer (1994) on Breton, and Rivero (1991, 1993, 1994) on Slavic and Romance. Fife (1986) discusses aspects of VP-topicalization ('*gwneud*-inversion') in Modern Welsh.

10. Adverbs following nominal subjects are very common, see also BTy_1 84a. 8, 89b. 14, 91b. 4, 91b. 26, etc.; BTy_2 16. 18, 22. 26, 26. 25, 70. 5, etc.; BY 7. 24, 14. 11, 14. 15, 15. 9, etc.; *FfBO* 31. 4, 35. 13, 35. 20, 35. 32, etc.; *HGK* 3. 20, 3. 28, 13. 23, 16. 2, etc.; *KAA* 131, 547; *MIG* 210. 13, 219. 33; *Peredur*, 16. 17; *PKM* 17. 11, 21. 9; *SDR* 157; *YCM* 27. 14, 140. 23, 141. 4, 142. 3; *YSG* 157, 525, 608, 766, 910. For this construction with a simple pronominal subject, see Section 5.1.1.

11. A selection of further examples is given below: in topic position: BB_1 22. 4, 24. 11, 35. 2, 48. 14, etc.; *BD* 26. 26, 28. 11, 147. 5, 183. 22; BTy_1 65a. 15, 82b. 12, 86b. 19, 109b. 2, etc.; *ChCC* 69. 32; *KAA* 532, 660; *Owein*, 13, 155; *PKM* 18. 3, 39. 11, 65. 2; *YSG* 662, 887, 1399, 3707; in pre-topic position: BB_1 124. 12, 141. 11, 174. 8, 187. 4, 198. 11; *BD* 29. 15, 149. 13, 182. 24, 184. 34, 185. 23; BTy_1 114a. 11; *ChCC* 61. 6, 63. 3, 67. 1; *CO* 1069; *KAA* 554; *Owein*, 159, 226; *Peredur*, 8. 7, 10. 1, 13. 29; *PKM* 10. 24, 38. 7, 45. 21, 79. 9, 79. 16, 82. 22; *SDR* 1053; *YCM* 21. 8, 114. 23, 140. 12; *YSG* 164, 207, 245, 635, 679, etc.

12. Watkins (1993: 137) does make a distinction between 'predicative' adverbials and 'sentential/connector' adverbials which roughly corresponds to the distinction between argument PPs and adverbs, although he does not investigate their distribution.

13. Further examples with a variety of similar verbs include BB_1 15. 11, 16. 15, 49. 12, 77. 3, 90. 1, 98. 6, 163. 4, 163. 6; *KAA* 53; *PKM* 20. 21, 25. 5, 64. 8; *YSG* 216; and with verbs of motion BB_1 20. 16, 23. 17, 24. 1, 40. 2, etc.; *BM* 7. 6; *Owein*, 193, 200; *Peredur*, 7. 18, 17. 7, 29. 28, 42. 23; *PKM* 12. 26, 41. 19, 41. 21, 55. 20, 57. 5, etc.

14. This, of course, should be ruled out only on the interpretation 'On this [plan of action] the men agreed'. It is fully acceptable with the interpretation 'Thereupon (then) the men agreed'. For a possible exception to the generalization about argument PPs, see *ChCC* 67. 1.

15. Further examples of *hagen* in post-topic position are *BB₁* 70. 7; *BTy₁* 91b. 4, 158a. 22; *BY* 15. 16; *CO* 868, 880, 899, 1027; *KAA* 239, 300; *Peredur*, 32. 23, 35. 15, 58. 10; *PKM* 6. 28; *YCM* 120. 1, 137. 28; and of *heuyt BB₁* 188. 4; *BD* 27. 12, 28. 26, 184. 28; *BTy₁* 206a. 2, 282a. 20; *BY* 10. 10, 52. 8; *HGK* 11. 25; *KAA* 576, 578; *YCM* 26. 9; *YSG* 1548, 2431, 2918. Clause-initial positioning of *heuyt* is an Early Modern Welsh innovation.

16. But see Section 3.3.5, where some apparent exceptions to this are analysed as left-dislocation structures. This will permit grammaticality for sentences such as *Myrdin i Arthur y rodes eur* 'Merlin to Arthur gave gold', and *Myrdin eur a rodes i Arthur* 'Merlin gold gave to Arthur', which are predicted to be ungrammatical under the current constraint.

17. Platzack (1986: 29) also mentions that the adverb *kanske* 'perhaps' causes the verb to appear after second position in Swedish, but he analyses this adverb as instantiating C.

18. There are some possible exceptions to this statement, with two arguments in preverbal position (*ClILl* 64, 133; *PKM* 19. 29), but even here the interpretation is far from secure.

19. Isaac (1996: 59–62), developing an idea of Mac Cana (1973, 1991), has recently argued that all instances of the abnormal sentence are in fact left-dislocation structures. However, there seems to be good reason to maintain the traditional distinction; see the treatment of negation in Section 3.6.

20. Further examples of demonstrative PP adverbs preceding imperatives are *BB₁* 174. 17; *FfBO* 36. 29; *KAA* 85, 136, 309; *YCM* 8. 19, 11. 25, 18. 32; *YSG* 218, 2638, 3172; with other phrasal adverbs *KAA* 87, 619; *Peredur*, 22. 21; *PKM* 13. 5, 14. 29, 63. 3; and with clausal adverbs *ChCC* 67. 10; *CO* 906; *KAA* 226; *Peredur*, 9. 26, 9. 28, 9. 30, 10. 1, 12. 1; *PKM* 13. 3, 15. 2, 15. 12, 15. 16, 63. 25; *SDR* 517.

21. Full agreement occurs with a pronominal object or possessor but not with a full lexical object or possessor:

    (i) *am   Dafydd*   *amdano*   pro/*ef*
         about Dafydd   about-3SM *pro*/him
         'about Dafydd'   'about him'

    (ii) *afalau Dafydd*   *ei*   *afalau* pro/*ef*
         apples Dafydd   3SM-GEN apples *pro*/him
         'Dafydd's apples' 'his apples'

    (iii) *gweld Dafydd*   *ei*   *weld*   pro/*ef*
         see-VN Dafydd   3SM-GEN see-VN *pro*/him
         'seeing Dafydd'   'seeing him'

22. Doubt has been expressed over the grammaticality of this example (Poppe 1990: 453). However, given the other parallel constructions cited in (83), there seems no reason to doubt that this is a straightforward instance of topicalization.

23. If this is true, we would expect that A'-movement of subjects would sometimes result in a non-contrastive reading—i.e. in traditional terms there should be syntactically *mixed* sentences (i.e. with no subject–verb agreement) in Middle Welsh which are pragmatically unmarked for focus. A number of authors have noted such cases as a problem for the traditional abnormal/mixed contrast (D. Simon Evans 1964: 180; D. Simon Evans 1971; Emrys Evans 1958: 5).

24. Note the appearance of this construction in Old Welsh:

    (i) *Grefiat guetig nis   minn Tutbulc   hai   cenetl in ois oisou.*
        title   NEG+3S-ACC needs Tudfwlch and-his kin   in age ages
        'Tudfwlch and his kin shall not need a title evermore.'   (SM 270. 10–11)

    Mac Cana (1973: 95, 113) and Isaac (1996: 12) give this as an example of a *nominativus pendens* construction (i.e. left dislocation). In the light of the discussion in Section 3.6, this seems unlikely.

25. It is commonly assumed for all Celtic languages that the negative marker occupies C; cf. Chung and McCloskey (1987: 184) for Irish.

26. Variation in the form of the object clitic between -*s* and '*i* is conditioned lexically by the host element.

27. Another possibility would be that all the instances of verb-second in Old Welsh poetry are later interpolations into the manuscript traditions of the texts. This seems unlikely on two grounds. First, verb-second orders are not uncommon in Old Welsh poetry— the number of interpolations would therefore have to be rather large. Secondly, the supporting evidence of prose texts, where the manuscripts are in general contemporary, confirms that verb-second structures were available in Old Welsh.

4. VERB-FIRST IN MIDDLE WELSH

1. The statistics give the number of absolute verb-initial affirmative clauses as a percentage of the total number of main clauses. They are, therefore, not strictly comparable with statistics for Middle Welsh such as those given in Section 3.1, since the latter exclude negative clauses, copular clauses, and a number of other clause types. For more on the implications of these differences, see Section 4.4.

2. Clearly there may be language-specific lexical devices which block or interfere with V2—e.g. the adverb-placement rules of Middle Welsh. These might permit limited VSO in a V2-language. This would be the case for verb-initial subsystems of Middle Welsh grammar—e.g. negative main clauses and the periphrastic verbal forms (see Section 4.3).

3. Further examples with a pronominal subject: *BM* 1. 6, 7. 10; *ChCC* 61. 1; *HGK* 20. 9, 20. 11; *PKM* 40. 21, 47. 20; *YCM* 14. 26, 18. 20, 18. 22; *YSG* 182, 3243, 5414, 5467, 5491, 5638, 5650, 5661; with a nominal subject: *ChCC* 59. 21; *HGK* 3. 12, 3. 19, 8. 1, 10. 5, 16. 1; *Peredur*, 11. 28, 31. 18, 46. 16; *SDR* 1067; *YCM* 117. 28, 140. 23; *YSG* 146, 184, 202, 214, 3189, 5442, 5487, 5671, 5675.

4. Further examples: BB_1 25. 13, 42. 14, 49. 7, 85. 4, 96. 15; *FfBO* 53. 27; *HGK* 18. 7; *KAA* 434; *Owein*, 782; *Peredur*, 9. 13, 11. 23, 51. 8; *YCM* 20. 24, 32. 20, 32. 30; *YSG* 527, 695, 1127, 1359, 1640, 1739, 2843, 3115, 3169, 3242, 3253.

5. In Poppe (1989: 45, 1993: 98) and in Morgan Watkins's edition (*YBH*, p. clvii), this and parallel examples in *Breudwyt Ronabwy* and *Kedymdeithyas Amlyn ac Amic* are treated as 'mistakes'. The parallels with other examples make it clear that the use of *a* here is in fact part of a fully productive grammatical pattern.

6. The counter-argument to such a suggestion for German SLF-coordination involves examples like (i), where a quantified DP subject appears in the first conjunct. Given that pronouns and anaphors cannot refer back to quantified DPs, the grammaticality of (i) rules out an analysis with a *pro* subject.

> (i) *Gestern   ging niemand in   den Wald und fing   einen Hasen.*
>   yesterday went no one   into the forest and caught a   hare.
>   'Yesterday no one went into the forest and caught a hare.'   (Kathol 1992: 272)

I know of no data parallel to (i) in Middle Welsh.

7. An Across-the-Board Violation remains, of course, since the verb in C is extracted only from the first conjunct.

8. Presumably this null operator would bind a trace in an adjunct position lower in the clause.

9. The only other examples known to me are the following: *ChCC* 68. 10; *CO* 1075; *HGK* 11. 22; *Peredur*, 50. 15, 53. 2; *PKM* 35. 23, 36. 4.

10. The footnote in Ifor Williams's edition suggests that this is 'a way of starting a sentence that was going out of use' (*PKM*, p. 152, my translation). The other (Red Book) manuscript has *yna y rodet* 'then was given . . .'.

11. For a similar case of null objects in conjoined structures in Norwegian, see Åfarli and Creider (1987). Like Old Icelandic, Norwegian does not otherwise allow null objects.

12. The interpretation of (43*a*) with a *pro*-gap in subject position (i.e. '. . . and he had sent Amilald King of Babylon to make war on Charles . . .') is ruled out by context. It is Fferacud who is subsequently discussed as making war.

13. The situation is different with *bot* 'to be'. See Section 4.3.

14. For discussion of the nature of the material and analysis of some linguistic features of it, see Awbery (1988) and Awbery *et al.* (1985).

15. Watkins actually gives ten instances, but two contain an expletive subject in topic position.

16. Strikingly, in the cases cited by Poppe from *Breuddwyd Maxen*, all instances of V1 with a verb other than *bot* are in conjoined clauses, whereas none of the cases of V1 with *bot* is in a conjoined clause.

17. Watkins (1977–8: 395) and Poppe (1990: 448; 1993: 107) find that the order Pronominal Subject + *a* + Verb is associated with direct speech, a fact which fits uneasily with this claim. Although it appears to be true that in the texts that they investigate the overall frequency of this pattern is considerably higher in dialogue than in narrative, this is only to be expected given the general syntactic differences between direct speech and narrative. Direct speech contains on average fewer constituents per sentence, and in particular more sentences containing only subject, verb, and object. It also contains a far higher proportion of pronouns in general than does narrative. Consequently, if the syntactic rules were identical, there would be far more scope for topicalization of subject pronouns in direct speech than in narrative.

18. Also Brecon Sessions (1577, 1586); Cardigan Sessions (1610 (×2), 1632, 1640, 1647); Pembroke Sessions (1627, 1629, 1634).

19. The percentage would, of course, be higher if imperatives and interrogative were excluded from the total of 174, but Fife's presentation of the data does not allow this to be done easily. Nevertheless, the point remains: the frequency of absolute V1 is much lower than it at first sight appears.

20. The absolute V1 main clause in (50) does, of course, represent a real innovation. See Chapter 6 for full discussion.

5. SUBJECT PRONOUNS AND THE EXPLETIVE CONSTRUCTION

1. For further examples from *Llyfr Blegywryd*, *Ystorya de Carolo Magno*, *Llyfr Gwyn Rhydderch* and *Llyfr yr Ancr*, see Emrys Evans (1958: 26, 28–9). Also *BY* 45. 6; *CO* 880, 899; *YCM* 38. 1; *YSG* 1144 (MS B).

2. For further discussion of the syntax of emphatic reflexives in English, see Napoli (1989: 319–20).

3. The only example known to me from a non-religious text of the sixteenth century is *RhG* ii. 51. 1.

4. This is particularly common in William Salesbury's translation of scripture in *Kynniver Llith a Ban* (1551). Other sixteenth-century examples are DFf 113. 13; *KLlB* 1. 25, 3. 3,

3. 25, 4. 1, 4. 18, etc.; *RhG* i. 97. 7, 103. 16, 124. 17, 126. 5; ii. 51. 12, 79. 9; *TWRP, Y Dioddefaint*, 145, 985, 1012; YAL 281. 9, 286. 45.

5. Other sixteenth-century examples are *TWRP, Yr Enaid a'r Corff*, 44, 153, *Y Dioddefaint*, 994.

6. Another possibility which I shall not pursue here is that one of the subject pronouns is an expletive base-generated in a non-theta-marked position. This is defended for West Flemish subject clitics in Haegeman (1990). The decisive evidence there is the ability of the subject clitic to move around the clause, behaviour which would be difficult to explain if the clitic were an agreement element.

7. Clearly, parallel evidence cannot be tested in Early Modern Welsh because it, unlike West Flemish, licenses preverbal adverbs in adjoined positions in addition to SpecCP.

8. Examples are common in 'Ystori Alexander a Lodwig' (e.g. YAL 279. 30, 280. 30, 280. 39, 282. 43, 283. 28, 283. 35, etc.); cf. also *LlTA* 18. 30, 21. 18, 39. 27, 74. 10.

9. Further examples are *FfBO* 38. 2, 44. 17, 47. 7, 50. 13; *Owein*, 346; *Peredur*, 45. 22; *PKM* 87. 4, 91. 17; *SDR* 406, 632; *YCM* 23. 29, 30. 8, 43. 12, 55. 7, 74. 17, 75. 31, 89. 31, 100. 7, 158. 6, 164. 13.

10. The *gwneuthur* construction is found a number of times in *Ystorya de Carolo Magno*. For an example outside this text, see *KAA* 529. The subjunctive of *gwneuthur* 'to do' is used elsewhere to express a wish, as in *YSG* 1329. On the use of *nyt ef a* for Modern Welsh *na*, see also Morgan (1952: 372).

11. Actually the Icelandic expletive is found in embedded but not inversion contexts (Rögnvaldsson and Thráinsson 1990: 29–31), but this is not surprising given that Icelandic allows embedded verb-second generally.

12. The only exception discussed in the literature is Italian, and even there Belletti claims that Definiteness Effects are observed when the expletive construction is strictly separated from instances of Free Subject Inversion (Belletti 1988: 7–12).

13. The possibility of Nominative Case being left unassigned is clearly a marked case, since it is usually assumed that there should be a one-to-one correspondence between Case-assigners and Case-assignees. However, it may simply be that the Case Filter forces this outcome in most cases, since most DPs have only one way in which to acquire Case (cf. Lasnik 1992: 393).

14. The possibility of Case-assignment to SpecCP by Infl in C is implicit in any proposal that SpecCP can be an A-position (see Section 3.5).

15. In fact, this also has desirable theoretical consequences, since it allows the account to transfer straightforwardly to an analysis with a more fully articulated IP.

16. One line of argumentation, which I shall not pursue here, is that in Icelandic both C and AgrS are Nominative Case assigners, whereas in Middle Welsh all Nominative Case assignment involves AgrS. A similar type of approach, although not explicitly involving Case, is that pursued in Vikner (1995).

17. In Contemporary Spoken Welsh the accusative series of object clitics has been lost (see Watkins 1977).

18. Further examples are BB_1 107. 14, 197. 16; *BSM* 3. 20, 8. 27, 20. 11, 32. 24; BTy_1 89b. 18, 111a. 4, 123a. 5, 127b. 21, 159b. 27, etc.; *RhG* i. 37. 3; *YSG* 48, 52, 372, 546, 675, etc.

19. Further examples are *BY* (MS A) 3. 9, 3. 15, 3. 22, 4. 1, 4. 5, etc.; DE 394. 7, 395. 13, 397. 7, 399. 3, 405. 3, etc.; DFf 82. 2, 90. 9, 91. 2, 91. 18, 97. 14, etc.; *LITA* 11. 11, 14. 1, 14. 16, 15. 6, 15. 27, etc.; *RhG* i. 123. 3, 124. 19; Slander cases, Denbigh Sessions (1604, 1626), Flint Sessions (1622), Montgomery Sessions 1619. Variant forms of the expletive—e.g. *fo* in (57a) and *fe* in (57d)—are found in some of these texts. For further details, see Section 5.2.2.3.

20. I assume a two-layer verbal projection, in which objects are generated in a rightward-projecting specifier of the lower verbal projection (the VP in (59)) and Prepositional Phrases as sisters to the verb itself (cf. Larson 1988).

21. Further examples of replacement of a conjunctive pronoun are *YSG* 1108, 1144, 2320, 2538, 3234, 4897, 5245, 5257. Examples of replacement of a reduplicative pronoun are *YSG* 3356, 4597.

22. Examples are common in the works of Elis Gruffydd, for instance, *CI* 143. 8, 167. 15; DEG 312. 24, 313. 26, 313. 40, 315. 1, 318. 8, etc.; *YT* 13, 236. On the construction in *Castell yr Iechyd*, see Fife (1991: 256–7). Further sixteenth-century examples are *RhG* i. 35. 8; and *TWRP, Yr Enaid a'r Corff*, 124.

23. Further sixteenth-century examples: referential *fo*: *RhG* i. 96. 10, 98. 8, 98. 9, 104. 20; ii. 126. 22, 134. 5, 199. 20, 200. 11, 200. 13, 200. 17, 201. 12; *TWRP, Y Dioddefaint*, 941; expletive *fo*: 1 Kgs. 22. 34 (*GPC* 1270); *PA* 115. 4; Henry Perri, *Eglvryn Phraethineb*, 6 (*GPC* 1270); *RhG* i. 74. 4, 74. 15, 74. 32, (?)98. 20, 104. 28; ii. 53. 4, 125. 28, 126. 5, 126. 17, 127. 33, 132. 17, 133. 20, 133. 22, 133. 27, 134. 8, 137. 17, 137. 21, 198. 10, 198. 21, 198. 26, 200. 32; *TWRP, Y Dioddefaint*, 391, 1015.

24. Datings are due to J. Gwenogvryn Evans (1902: 996).

25. Further examples from the sixteenth century and seventeenth centuries: referential *efe*: *CC* [117]. 17, [117]. 21, [117]. 24; *LITA* 49. 29, 53. 23; *RhG* ii. 82. 22; expletive *efe*: Rondl Davies, *Profiad yr Ysprydion*, 103 (*GPC* 1170).

26. Other sixteenth-century examples: referential *fe*: *DC* 1. 7, 61. 8; *RhG* ii. 80. 13, 82. 5, 83. 7; expletive *fe*: DE 399. 14, 403. 7, 411. 11; DFf 103. 17, 151. 18, 175. 12; Matt.

7: 7 (*GPC* 1267); *PA* 7. 3; *RhG* i. 90. 1, 103. 28; ii. 82. 3; *TWRP, Y Dioddefaint*, 396; YAL 280. 35; *YLH* [8]. 24.

27. Other sixteenth-century examples of *e* as a referential pronoun: *KLlB* 7. 9, 8. 13, 8. 14, 9. 9, 9. 12, etc.; *RhG* ii. 10. 24; of expletive *e*: *DFfEL* 85. 14; *HG* 2. 1, 2. 8, 2. 19, 3. 25, 4. 29, 5. 18, 5. 24; *KLlB* 7. 1, 7. 5, 7. 9, 7. 19, 13. 1, etc.; *RhG* i. 75. 1; ii. 19. 29, 126. 19; YAL 279. 25.

28. Further sixteenth- and seventeenth-century examples are DE 393. 6; *LlTA* 8. 16, 14. 15, 14. 23, 16. 3, 18. 30, 22. 2, 22. 20, etc.; Rees Prichard, *Gwaith*, 1. 21, 88. 15, 129. 7, 129. 16.

29. All of these forms, with the possible exception of *y di*, are attested in literature or in the modern dialects (see Morgan 1952: 453).

6. THE LOSS OF VERB-SECOND

1. This, of course, assumes that the child has identified CP as head-initial in Dutch/ German. This is not a trivial task, given that other XPs, notably IP and VP, are head-final in these languages.

2. *Y(r)* replaces *y(d)* as the form of the particle from the fourteenth century onwards (D. Simon Evans 1964: 169).

3. Other sixteenth-century examples are DE 412. 11; DFf 169. 2, 187a. 15; *RhG* i. 55. 20, 105. 11; ii. 13. 12, 131. 2, 131. 14.

4. It is not entirely clear that this movement takes place even in Middle Welsh (see Section 3.3.3).

5. Other sixteenth-century examples are *RhG* ii. 3. 20, 4. 5, 5. 18; *TWRP, Y Dioddefaint*, 421, 639, 814, 847, 872, 987.

6. Of course, if A'-movement in V2 is lost, the expectation is that all non-subject topicalizations must be lost too. However, the claim here is less strong than this: A'-movement is replaced by A-movement in topicalization structures and is therefore restricted to subjects. Instances of A'-movement must remain in contrastive frontings (the mixed sentence), which remain grammatical in Modern Welsh. Claims about the disappearance of non-subject topicalization must be understood in this spirit. The crucial fact about the constructions under discussion here is that they are used as unmarked structures in Middle Welsh, and therefore cannot be saved by being generated as contrastive frontings in the later period (cf. the discussion of residual V2 in Section 6.5).

7. Further examples are *BY* 13. 3, 40. 2, 40. 12; *BSM* 2. 3, 3. 11, 10. 2; DEG 334. 41; *RhG* i. 15. 10, 19. 19, 72. 22, 73. 31, 75. 23, 104. 6; ii. 49. 10, 49. 12, 138. 26; YAL 283. 14.

8. One exceptional example is *RhG* i. 19. 14.

9. Note that it does survive into the later modern period in literary texts—for instance, in Ellis Wynne, *Gweledigaetheu y Bardd Cwsc* (1703), where it is most probably an imitation of biblical style.

10. Cases of such forms are probably hypercorrections (see Watkins 1991: 348).

7. PRONOUNS AND COMPLEMENTIZERS

1. Other examples from the early interludes are *BDGU* 5. 22, 13. 13; *BLl* 10. 15, 26. 11, 33. 19, 71. 23; CDH 45. 19, 53. 17, 55. 15; FfBD 28. 6, 29. 8; *FfM* 16. 15, 16. 29, 17. 23, 24. 5, 43. 10, 53. 24; IYCA 79. 10, 81. 7, 87. 3, 87. 28, 88. 9; YDG 47. 24, 48. 3.

2. The remaining examples in the corpus are: second pers. sing.: BER 2. 4. 23; BHJ 7. 3. 27; third pers. masc. sing.: *HTN* 24. 33; Slander case, Flint Sessions (1767).

3. It is still necessary to prevent raising of the conjunctive pronoun to SpecAgrSP. One possibility is that the verb in fact raises to C to adjoin to the (clitic) complementizer. Another is that the presence of a subject in SpecAgrSP would interfere with the PF-cliticization process between the complementizer and verb.

4. Further examples are *GBC* 22. 28, 25. 22, 34. 15, 49. 13, 56. 14, etc.

5. Other examples from the earlier eighteenth-century interludes include *BDGU* 5. 17, 32. 20, 34. 24, 34. 27; CDH 55. 17, 89. 14; *FfM* 19. 11, 33. 32; IYCA 88. 9.

6. There are also examples in Thomas Edwards, 'Interliwt Ynghylch Cain ac Abel' (IYCA) (?*c.*1758) and Hugh Jones and John Cadwaladr, *Y Brenin Dafydd a Gwraig Urias (BDGU)* (*c.*1765) (IYCA 79. 10; *BDGU* 24. 19, 57. 5, 57. 7, 88. 2).

7. The remaining examples in the corpus are: second pers. sing.: Slander cases, Flint Sessions (1779, 1782 (×2)), Caernarfon Sessions (1779, 1787, 1797 (×3), 1814, 1825 (×2)); third pers. sing. (pronominal): *StG* 4. 7, 16. 15, 16. 17, 16. 20, 16. 24, 22. 10, etc.; Eist. B1. 113. 15; LUSS A2. 7. 32; BER 9. 5. 10; Slander cases, Anglesey Sessions (1761), Bangor Consistory Court (1782), Caernarfon Sessions (1779 (×6), 1793, 1811 ×8)), Denbigh Sessions (1769), Flint Sessions (1760, 1775, 1794 (×2)); lexical subject: *GN* 43. 33; *StG* 6. 12, 6. 14, 12. 9, 12. 15, 13. 20, etc.; LUSS AI. 3. 7, A2. 6. 26, A4. 6. 13; Slander cases, Bangor Consistory Court (1776), Denbigh Sessions (1774 (×2)), Flint Sessions (1801); first pers. plur.: *CD* 14. 35; *StG* 28. 8; LUSS AI. 2. 18, AI. 3. 1, AI. 3. 2; second pers. plur.: Eist. A3. 34. 30; *GN* 22. 30; Slander cases, Caernarfon Sessions (1825 (×2)); third pers. plur. (pronominal): *StG* 8. 19, 11. 22, 25. 20; LUSS A2. 4. 37, A2. 6. 24.

8. In the column for third-person singular, clauses with the perfective auxiliary *ddaru* are excluded, since these have an ambiguous structure. In this context, *mi* appears in slander

cases from both the north-east (Flint Sessions (1760, 1786 (×2), 1794, 1802, 1812 (×2)) and the north-west (Bangor Consistory Court (1782); Caernarfon Sessions (1774, 1802 (×2), 1803 (×3), 1811, 1814 (×3), 1822, 1825 (×2)). For further discussion of the syntax of *darfod*, see Section 7.5.

9. Further examples are *BDGU* 12. 19, 18. 6, 39. 13, 39. 22, 88. 17; *YDG* 73. 10.

10. The remaining examples in the corpus are: first pers. sing.: *CD* 8. 31, 10. 10, 12. 15, 18. 9, 19. 21, etc.; *CmB* 19. 8; *GN* 23. 16; second pers. sing.: *CD* 13. 18; first pers. plur.: *CD* (?)70. 13, 71. 9; second pers. plur.: BJJ 1. 55. 7; *GN* 4. 22, 22. 1, 23. 1, 35. 31, 51. 33, 63. 7; *PN* 9. 4; third pers. plur.: *CD* 51. 11; BHJ 4. 16. 25, 4. 17. 6; *GN* 46. 29.

11. Further examples are *CmB* 6. 20; *HTN* 18. 4; LUSS A4. 6. 15; *PN* 57. 18; Slander cases, Caernarfon Sessions (1801), Denbigh Sessions (1760 (×2), 1765); *StG* 27. 8, 38. 15; *TChB* 9. 70, 43. 18, 55. 2.

12. Similar examples are BHJ 3. 3. 26, 3. 3. 28; *CD* 16. 5; Slander cases, Flint Sessions (1772).

13. Further examples are Eist. A3. 34. 21, A3. 35. 1, A4. 38. 10, A5. 37. 7, B9. 120. 26, etc.

14. Further examples are LUSS A2. 4. 13, A2. 4. 30, A2. 7. 12, A2. 7. 14, A4. 6. 14.

15. Further examples are Slander cases, Bangor Consistory Court (1791), Caernarfon Sessions (1814).

16. Further examples are *CD* 6. 29, 8. 22, 34. 13, 49. 31, 52. 21, etc.

17. There are nevertheless some difficulties with the data in Ceinwen H. Thomas (1993). The grammatical description states (ii. 44) that the form of the independent pronoun (including the preverbal subject pronoun) is *ti*. However, this conforms neither to the examples given in the grammatical description, nor to the dialect texts given, where the form in the preverbal environment is *di*.

18. There are two examples of *fo* in the *darfod* construction, where its use may be referential, but, as we have seen, this case is ambiguous.

19. Further examples are AJP 1. 4. 7; AMW 1. 33. 31, 2. 22. 33; BER 3. 3. 24; BHJ 6. 5. 9, 6. 5. 11; *CD* 7. 4; *CwyC* 5. 21; *CylC* 171. 30, 175. 39, 175. 42, 176. 4; *DA* 5. 25, 6. 34, 7. 29, 12. 13; GA 53. 25; HHGB 33. 29; *HTN* 4. 5, 4. 16, 9. 2, 9. 37, 9. 38, etc.; LAG 40. 16; LTE A74. 13; *MEW* 3. 44, 15. 28; *PN* 8. 17; *Rhy.* 23. 19, 31. 7, 39. 24, 44. 5; *StG* 6. 27, 7. 2, 7. 8, 8. 27, 12. 20; *TChB* 15. 12; *TD* 25. 10; *YRW* 30. 23.

20. Further examples are *CD* 13. 26, 46. 12, 63. 8, 56. 11, 56. 15, 67. 31; *CmB* 14. 34, 22. 23, 24. 3, 24. 6, 24. 9, 26. 27; *CwyC* 9. 25; Eist. B1. 113. 11, B9. 120. 28; GA 54. 23; *GN* 11. 16, 11. 19, 45. 1; *HTN* 5. 16, 9. 36, 12. 11, 12. 20, 12. 25, etc.; LAG

43. 22; LDT 29. 59; LEE 243. 8; LTE A64. 15, A76. 9; LUSS B2. 1. 18, B2. 1. 19; *PN* 24. 36, 46. 36; *Rhy.* 16. 6, 16. 12, 17. 25, 24. 4; Slander cases, Caernarfon Sessions (1797), Denbigh Sessions (1760, 1776 (×2), 1782 (×2)), Flint Sessions (1779, 1781, 1788 (×2)), Pembroke Sessions (1796 (×4)); *TChB* 29. 11, 45. 4, 49. 21, 51. 20, 51. 22; *TD* 26. 1, 26. 18, 27. 24.

21. Further examples are AMW 2. 24. 19; BER 12. 3. 2; BHJ 6. 6. 10; BJJ 1.52. 12; *CD* 18. 24, 32. 25, 50. 13, 56. 1, 56. 9; *CmB* 8. 2, 25. 4; *CwyC* 23. 26, 33. 18; *CylC* 172. 10, 172. 38, 173. 3, 173. 4, 173. 8, etc.; *DA* 12. 34, 23. 17; Eist. B1. 113. 4, B6. 117. 4; *GN* 45. 22; *HHGB* 35. 23; *HTN* 5. 19, 5. 23, 8. 14, 9. 27, 17. 2, etc.; LDT 35. 16, 45. 7, 45. 15, 48. 23; LEE 248. 26; LJJ 86. 19; LTE A 76. 2; LUSS A2. 5. 1, B2. 2. 9; *PN* 20. 38, 31. 20, 35. 27; Slander cases, Denbigh Sessions (1769, 1775), Flint Sessions (1760, 1783); *StG* 7. 10, 7. 13, 12. 10, 16. 29, 26. 18, 44. 3; *TD* 21. 10; *YRW* 33. 27, 48. 32.

22. In a V2-language like German, Case-assignment is not crucial, since movement of the subject to a preverbal position is A′-movement, hence it is the trace in each conjunct which must be licensed. This condition can be fulfilled even if Case-assignment is exclusively under government.

23. Note the special and perhaps revealing case of John Jones's political works. The earlier one, *Seren tan Gwmwl* (1795), has a high level of *mi* and *fe*, and seems to be adhering to the colloquial norm. In the later work, *Toriad y Dydd* (1797), *mi* is removed entirely and the frequency of *fe* is drastically reduced. In the discussion which followed publication of the first pamphlet, Jones was attacked for the quality of his prose (John James Evans 1928: 154). The linguistic differences between the two pamphlets seem to reflect a conscious move away from colloquial usage towards the VSO norm.

24. Lewis's and Richards's examples of SVO in (early) twentieth-century Welsh (Lewis 1942: 20 and Richards 1938: 106, discussed above, Section 1.3.2) may be seen as a relic of this usage.

8. CONCLUSION

1. Clearly, allowance must be made for the fact that syntactic features linked to phonology, such as the clitic/non-clitic distinction, are likely to be gradual.

2. It is not clear that all parameters can be reformulated in this way. Obvious difficulties seem to arise with the null subject parameter and bounding node parameter.

References

PRIMARY TEXTS CITED

Old and Middle Welsh

Armes Prydein, ed. Ifor Williams and Rachel Bromwich (Dublin: Dublin Institute for Advanced Studies, 1972).

Y Bibyl Ynghymraec, ed. Thomas Jones (Caerdydd: Gwasg Prifysgol Cymru, 1940).

Branwen Uerch Lyr, ed. Derick S. Thomson (Dublin: Dublin Institute for Advanced Studies, 1961).

Breuddwyd Maxen, ed. Ifor Williams (Bangor: Jarvis a Foster, 1908).

Breudwyt Ronabwy, ed. Melville Richards (Caerdydd: Gwasg Prifysgol Cymru, 1948).

Brut Dingestow, ed. Henry Lewis (Caerdydd: Gwasg Prifysgol Cymru, 1942).

Brut y Brenhinedd: Cotton Cleopatra Version, ed. John Jay Parry (Cambridge, Mass.: Mediaeval Academy of America, 1937).

Brut y Brenhinedd: Llanstephan Ms. 1 Version, ed. Brynley F. Roberts (Dublin: Dublin Institute for Advanced Studies, 1971).

Brut y Tywysogyon or The Chronicle of the Princes: Red Book of Hergest Version, ed. Thomas Jones (Cardiff: University of Wales Press, 1955).

Brut y Tywysogyon: Peniarth Ms. 20, ed. Thomas Jones (Caerdydd: Gwasg Prifysgol Cymru, 1941).

'Buchedd Fargred', ed. Melville Richards, *Bulletin of the Board of Celtic Studies*, 9 (1939), 324–34; 10 (1939), 53–9; 13 (1949), 65–71.

Canu Aneirin, ed. Ifor Williams (Caerdydd: Gwasg Prifysgol Cymru, 1938).

Casgliad o Waith Ieuan Deulwyn, ed. Ifor Williams (Bangor: Jarvis a Foster, 1909).

'Catwn a'i Ddehongliad', ed. Ifor Williams, *Bulletin of the Board of Celtic Studies*, 2 (1923), 26–36.

Chwedlau Cymraeg Canol, ed. A. O. H. Jarman (Caerdydd: Gwasg Prifysgol Cymru, 1957).

Chwedlau Odo, ed. Ifor Williams (Wrecsam: Hughes a'i Fab, 1926).

Chwedleu Seith Doethon Rufein, ed. Henry Lewis (Caerdydd: Gwasg Prifysgol Cymru, 1958).

'The Computus Fragment', ed. Ifor Williams, *Bulletin of the Board of Celtic Studies*, 3 (1927), 245–72.

'Y Creawdwr Hollalluog', in *Blodeugerdd Barddas o Ganu Crefyddol Cynnar*, ed. Marged Haycock (Llandybïe: Cyhoeddiadau Barddas, 1994), 3–16. See also 'Naw Englyn y Juvencus'.

Culhwch ac Olwen: An Edition and Study of the Oldest Arthurian Tale, ed. Rachel Bromwich and D. Simon Evans (Cardiff: University of Wales Press, 1992).

Cyfranc Lludd a Llefelys, ed. Brynley F. Roberts (Dublin: Dublin Institute for Advanced Studies, 1975).

Cyfreithiau Hywel Dda yn ôl Llyfr Blegywryd, ed. Stephen J. Williams and J. Enoch Powell (Caerdydd: Gwasg Prifysgol Cymru, 1942).

Cywyddau Dafydd ap Gwilym a'i Gyfoeswyr, ed. Ifor Williams and Thomas Roberts (Caerdydd: Gwasg Prifysgol Cymru, 1935).

Early Welsh Genealogical Tracts, ed. P. C. Bartrum (Cardiff: University of Wales Press, 1966).

Facsimile and Text of the Book of Taliessin, ed. J. Gwenogvryn Evans (Llanbedrog: J. Gwenogvryn Evans, 1910).

Ffordd y Brawd Odrig, ed. Stephen J. Williams (Caerdydd: Gwasg Prifysgol Cymru, 1929).

'Glosau Rhydychen: Mesurau a Phwysau', ed. Ifor Williams, *Bulletin of the Board of Celtic Studies*, 5 (1930), 226–48.

'Gwyrthyeu y Wynvydedic Veir', ed. Gwenan Jones, *Bulletin of the Board of Celtic Studies*, 9 (1938), 144–8, 334–41; 10 (1939), 21–33.

Historia Gruffud vab Kenan, ed. D. Simon Evans (Caerdydd: Gwasg Prifysgol Cymru, 1977).

Historia Peredur vab Efrawc, ed. Glenys Witchard Goetinck (Caerdydd: Gwasg Prifysgol Cymru, 1976).

Kedymdeithyas Amlyn ac Amic, ed. Patricia Williams (Caerdydd: Gwasg Prifysgol Cymru, 1982).

Llawysgrif Hendregadredd, ed. John Morris-Jones and T. H. Parry-Williams (Caerdydd: Gwasg Prifysgol Cymru, 1971).

Llyfr Gwyn Rhydderch, ed. J. Gwenogvryn Evans with introduction by R. M. Jones (Caerdydd: Gwasg Prifysgol Cymru, 1973; new edn. of *The White Book Mabinogion*, ed. J. Gwenogvryn Evans (Pwllheli: J. Gwenogvryn Evans, 1907)).

'Llyma Vabinogi Iessu Grist', ed. Mary Williams, *Revue Celtique*, 33 (1912), 184–248.

'Naw Englyn y Juvencus', ed. Ifor Williams, *Bulletin of the Board of Celtic Studies*, 6 (1932), 205–24. See also 'Y Creawdwr Hollalluog'.

Owein or Chwedyl Iarlles y Ffynnawn, ed. R. L. Thomson (Dublin: Dublin Institute for Advanced Studies, 1968).

Pedeir Keinc y Mabinogi, ed. Ifor Williams (Caerdydd: Gwasg Prifysgol Cymru, 1930).

Pwyll Pendeuic Dyuet, ed. R. L. Thomson (Dublin: Dublin Institute for Advanced Studies, 1957).

'The Surexit Memorandum', ed. John Morris-Jones, *Y Cymmrodor*, 28 (1918), 268–79. See also 'The Welsh Marginalia in the Lichfield Gospels Part II'.

'The Welsh Marginalia in the Lichfield Gospels Part I', ed. Dafydd Jenkins and Morfydd E. Owen, *Cambridge Medieval Celtic Studies*, 5 (1983), 37–66.

'The Welsh Marginalia in the Lichfield Gospels Part II: The "Surexit" Memorandum', ed. Dafydd Jenkins and Morfydd E. Owen, *Cambridge Medieval Celtic Studies*, 7 (1984), 91–120. See also 'The Surexit Memorandum'.

Ystorya Bown de Hamtwn, ed. Morgan Watkins (Caerdydd: Gwasg Prifysgol Cymru, 1958).

Ystorya de Carolo Magno, ed. Stephen J. Williams (Caerdydd: Gwasg Prifysgol Cymru, 1930).

Ystoryaeu Seint Greal, ed. Thomas Jones (Caerdydd: Gwasg Prifysgol Cymru, 1992).

Early Modern Welsh

'An Analysis and Calendar of Early Modern Welsh Defamation Suits' (MSS 16th–19th c.), ed. Richard F. Suggett (SSRC Final Report (HR 6979), 1983).

'Buchedd Collen' (MS 1536), in *RhG* i. 36–41.

Buchedd Sant Martin (MS 1488–9), ed. Evan John Jones (Caerdydd: Gwasg Prifysgol Cymru, 1945).

Casgliad o Hanes-Gerddi Cymraeg (MSS 17th–18th c.), ed. anon. (Caerdydd: Cymdeithas Llen Cymru, 1903).

Clynnog, Morys, *Athravaeth Gristnogavl* (orig. pub. 1568), ed. Louis-Lucien Bonaparte (London: Honourable Society of Cymmrodorion, 1880).

'Cyssegredic Historia Severws Swlpisiws' (MS 1604–12, composed 1574–1604), ed. Thomas Jones, *Bulletin of the Board of Celtic Studies*, 8 (1936), 107–20.

'Darn o'r Ffestival (Liber Ffestialis)' (MS 1550–75), ed. Henry Lewis, *Supplement to the Transactions of the Honourable Society of Cymmrodorion (Session 1923–24)* (Llundain: Cymdeithas y Cymmrodorion, 1925).

'Darnau o'r Efengylau' (MS 1550–75), ed. Henry Lewis, *Y Cymmrodor*, 31 (1921), 193–216.

Gruffydd, Elis, *Castell yr Iechyd* (composed 1540s), ed. S. Minwel Tibbott (Caerdydd: Gwasg Prifysgol Cymru, 1969).

—— 'Disgrifiad Elis Gruffudd o'r Cynadleddau a Fu rhwng Harri VIII a'r Ymherodr Siarl V a rhyngddo a Ffranses I, Brenin Ffrainc yn 1520' (composed 1540s), ed. Thomas Jones, *Bulletin of the Board of Celtic Studies*, 18 (1960), 312–37.

—— *Ystoria Taliesin: The Story of Taliesin* (composed 1540s), ed. Patrick K. Ford (Cardiff: University of Wales Press, 1991).

—— 'Ystorya Erkwlf' (composed 1540s), ed. Thomas Jones, *Bulletin of the Board of Celtic Studies*, 10 (1941), 284–97; 11 (1941–3), 21–30, 85–91.

Hen Gyflwyniadau (orig. pub. 1567–1792), ed. Henry Lewis (Caerdydd: Gwasg Prifysgol Cymru, 1948).

Kyffin, Maurice (Morys), *Deffyniad Ffydd Eglwys Loegr* (orig. pub. 1595), ed. William Prichard Williams (Bangor: Jarvis & Foster, 1908).

Lewys, Huw, *Perl mewn Adfyd* (orig. pub. 1595), ed. W. J. Gruffydd (Caerdydd: Gwasg Prifysgol Cymru, 1929).

Llwyd, Morgan, *Llyfr y Tri Aderyn* (orig. pub. 1653), ed. anon. (Caerdydd: Gwasg Prifysgol Cymru, 1974).

'Mab y Fforestwr' (MS *c*.1600), in *RhG* i. 122–30.

Prichard, Rees, *Gwaith Mr. Rees Prichard* (London: J. Darby, 1672).

Rhyddiaith Gymraeg, i. *Detholion o Lawysgrifau 1488–1609*, ed. T. H. Parry-Williams (Caerdydd: Gwasg Prifysgol Cymru, 1954); ii. *1547–1618*, ed. Thomas Jones (Caerdydd: Gwasg Prifysgol Cymru, 1956).

Robert, Griffith, *Y Drych Cristianogawl* (orig. pub. 1585), ed. D. M. Rogers (Menston, Yorkshire: Scolar Press, 1972).

Salesbury, William, *Kynniver Llith a Ban* (orig. pub. 1567), ed. John Fisher (Cardiff: University of Wales Press, 1931).

Smyth, Roger, *Theater du Mond (Gorsedd y Byd)* (orig. pub. 1615), ed. Thomas Parry (Caerdydd: Gwasg Prifysgol Cymru, 1930).

A Study of Three Welsh Religious Plays (MSS 16th c.), ed. Gwenan Jones (Bala: R. Evans & Son, 1939).

Testament Newydd ein Arglwydd Jesv Christ, trans. William Salesbury (no imprint, [1567]).

Thomas, Oliver, *Car-wr y Cymru* (orig. pub. 1631); *Gweithiau Oliver Thomas ac Evan Roberts*, ed. Merfyn Morgan (Caerdydd: Gwasg Prifysgol Cymru, 1981).

Yny Lhyvyr Hwnn (orig. pub. 1546), ed. John H. Davies (Bangor: Jarvis & Foster, London: J. M. Dent, 1902).

'Ystori Alexander a Lodwig' (MS *c.*1590, composed after 1515?), ed. Thomas Jones and J. E. Caerwyn Williams, *Studia Celtica*, 10–11 (1975–6), 261–304.

'Ystorïau Digrif' (MS 1582), in *RhG* ii. 48–52.

'Ystorïau o Ddyfed' (MS *c.*1588), in *RhG* ii. 78–85.

The eighteenth- and nineteenth-century corpus

'An Analysis and Calendar of Early Modern Welsh Defamation Suits' (MSS 16th–19th c.), ed. Richard F. Suggett (SSRC Final Report (HR 6979), 1983), cases for 1760–1825 only.

Caernarfonshire, misc. letters (Misc.): A: Griffith, Hannah (of Aberdaron, Caerns.). 'Hen Lythyr Caru o Lŷn' (dated 1804), ed. Trefor M. Owen, *Transactions of the Caernarfonshire Historical Society*, 20 (1959), 105–7; B: Letter from William and Alice Griffith (of Drws-y-Coed, Caerns.) to their children, 10 June 1777 (National Library of Wales, MS 16098E).

Davies, Walter (Gwallter Mechain), *Rhyddid: Traethawd a Ennillodd Ariandlws Cymdeithas y Gwyneddigion ar ei Thestun i Eisteddfod Llanelwy . . .* (Llundain: T. Rickaby, 1791), 4–48.

Edwards, Thomas (Twm o'r Nant), *Hanes Bywyd Twm o'r Nant, yr Hwn yn gyffredin à Elwir Twm o'r Nant, Prydydd . . .* (Aberystwyth: S. Williams, 1814; first published 1805).

—— letters (dated 1789, 1799–1806); A: *Hunangofiant a Llythyrau Twm o'r Nant*, ed. Glyn M. Ashton (Caerdydd: Gwasg Prifysgol Cymru, 1948), 53–77; and B: *Adgof uwch Anghof: Llythyrau Lluaws o Brif Enwogion Cymru, Hen a Diweddar*, ed. J. Jones (Myrddin Fardd) (Pen-y-Groes: G. Lewis, 1883), 6–11.

—— *Tri Chryfion Byd, Sef Tylodi, Cariad, ac Angau. Yn y Canlyniad o Hyn, y Dangosir y Modd y mae r Tri yn Gryfion Byd . . .* (n.p.: [?1789]).

Evans, Evan (Ieuan Fardd), letters (dated 1758, 1776–83); 'Llythyrau Evan Evans (Ieuan Fardd) at Ddafydd Jones', ed. Aneirin Lewis, *Llên Cymru*, 1 (1950), 239–58.

Griffiths, Ann, letters (dated 1800s); *Gwaith Ann Griffiths*, ed. Siân Megan (Llandybïe: Gwasg Christopher Davies, 1982), 36–46.

Jones, Hugh (Llangwm), ballads: 1–2. *Dwy o Gerddi Diddanol, Y Gyntaf fel y Digwyddodd i'r Prydydd fod mewn Tŷ Tafarn pan Ddaeth Ysgowl-wraig Flin i Nôl y Gŵr Adre; a'r Ymddiddan a Fu rhyngddynt: ar Lân Medd-dod Mwyn. Yn Ail. Cwynfan Merch Ieuangc gwedi Colli ei Chariad, i'w Chanu ar Galar Dôn* (Trefriw: I. Davies, 1813); 3. *Dwy o Gerddi Newyddion. I. Cerdd Newydd ym Mherthynas y Rhyfel Presennol yn America . . .* [by Hugh Jones]. II. *Cerdd ar Ddyll Ymddiddan rhwng y Mr. Tir a'r Tenant . . .* [anon.] (Gwrecsam: R. Marsh, no date), first ballad only; 4. *Cyngor Difrifol i Gadw Dydd yr Arglwydd* (Llundain: W. Roberts, 1763), 14–19; 5–6. *Dwy o Gerddi Newyddion. Cerdd Newydd o Glod Haeddedigol ir Anrhydeddus Foneddigion Sir Fon . . . Yn Ail Cerdd Dosturus fel yr oedd Gwraig Feichiog yn Trafaelio tros Fynydd yn Sir Faesyfed . . .* (Gwrecsam: R. Marsh, n.d. (composed after 1775)); 7. *Cerdd o Ymddiddan rhwng yr Ofer-ddyn a'r Dafarn-wraig* (Caernarfon: P. Evans, n.d.).

—— *Enterlute Newydd; ar Ddull Ymddiddan rhwng Protestant a Neilltuwr: Gyd ag Ychydig o Hanes Ymrafael Opiniwnau a Fu er Amser Charles I Hyd yn Awr; A Byrr Grybwylliad am Ffalster, Cybydd-dod, a Chydwybod* (Mwythig: T. Wood, 1783).

Jones, John (Jac Glan-y-gors), ballads: 1. *Gwaith Glan y Gors*, ed. Richard Griffith (Carneddog) (Llanuwchllyn: ab Owen, 1905), 17–60, 63–81; 2. *Cerdd o Hanes E. J. a Gwenno Bach. Ar Fesur, Mentra Gwen, yr Hen Ffordd* (n.p.); 3. *Cerdd Betti o Lansantffraid* (Newport: Evan Lewis, n.d. [*c*.1815]).

—— letters (dated 1795–1805): 'Un o Lythyrau Jack Glan y Gors', ed. W. Lloyd Davies, *Bulletin of the Board of Celtic Studies*, 4 (1928), 129–30; and *Gwaith Glan y Gors*, ed. Richard Griffith (Carneddog) (Llanuwchllyn: ab Owen, 1905), 83–92.

——*Seren tan Gwmmwl a Toriad y Dydd* (orig. pub. 1795–7), ed. Thomas Jones (Liverpool: Hugh Evans a'i Feibion, 1923).

Jones, Robert (Rhos-lan), *Drych yr Amseroedd* (orig. pub. 1820), ed. Glyn M. Ashton (Caerdydd: Gwasg Prifysgol Cymru, 1958), pp. xxxi–23.

Jones, Thomas, 'Gair yn ei Amser at Drigolion Cymru gan Ewyllysiwr Da i'w Wlad' (orig. pub. 1798), ed. Frank Price Jones, *Transactions of the Denbighshire Historical Society*, 5 (1956), 35–59.

'Llythyrau Ynglŷn ag Eisteddfodau'r Gwyneddigion' (dated 1789), ed. G. J. Williams, *Llên Cymru*, 1 (1950), 29–47, 113–25. Letters by Jonathan Hughes, Owen Jones (Owain Myfyr), Walter Davies (Gwallter Mechain), Thomas Jones (Corwen), William Owen-Pughe, and William Jones (Llangadfan).

[?Parry, Richard], *Ystori Richard Whittington, yr Hwn a Fu Dair Gwaith yn Arglwydd Maer Llundain. Wedi ei Gosod Allan mewn Interlute* (Caerfyrddin: J. Evans, 1812 (composed 1736)).

Prys, John, almanacs: 1. *Dehonglydd y Sêr neu Almanac Newydd am y Flwyddyn o Oedran y Byd 5713 Crist 1764* (Caerfyrddin: I. Ross, 1763); 2. *Dehonglydd y Sêr, neu Almanac Newydd am y Flwyddyn o Oedran y Byd, 5727 Crist, 1779* . . . (Y Mwythig: Stafford Prys, 1778).

Rhys, Morgan John (ed.), *Y Cylchgrawn Cynmraeg*, issue 2 (Trefecca: J. Daniel, 1793), 119–20; issue 3 (n.p., 1793), 170–80; issue 4 (Carmarthen: no publisher, 1794), 234–7; and ed. Gwyn A. Williams, 'Morgan John Rhys and Volney's Ruins of Empires', *Bulletin of the Board of Celtic Studies*, 20 (1962–4), 58–73.

Richards, William (of Lynn), *Cwyn y Cystuddiedig, a Griddfanau y Carcharorion Dieuog; neu, Ychydig o Hanes Dioddefiadau Diweddar Thomas John a Samuel Griffiths, y rhai gwedi Goddef Gorthrymder Tost, a Chaethiwed Caled, Dros Chwech neu Saith o Fisoedd . . . a Gawsant eu Rhyddhau* . . . (Caerfyrddin: Ioan Evans, 1798), 3–35.

Richmond, Legh, *Crefydd mewn Bwthyn; neu, Hanes Jane Bach, yn Dangos y Buddioldeb o Egwyddori Plant* (Bala: R. Saunderson, 1819), 1–34.

Roberts, Ellis (Y Cowper). *Ail Lythyr Hen Bechadur at ei Gyd Frodyr* . . . (Y Mwythig: J. Eddowes, 1772).

—— ballads: 1. Roberts, Ellis, and Gruffudd, Robert, *Dwy o Gerddi Newyddion. I. O Drymder Galarus am Royal George yr Hon a Suddodd yn ei Harbwr* . . . [by Ellis Roberts]. *II. O Fawl i Ferch* [by Robert Gruffudd] (Trefriw: Dafydd Jones, 1782), first ballad and englynion by Ellis Roberts only; 2. Roberts, Ellis, *Dwy o Gerddi Newyddion. I. I Ddeisyf ar Dduw am Drugaredd, ai Ragluniaeth i'n Porthi y Flwyddyn Ddiweddar Hon Drwy Erfyn Arno Roddi Ei Fendith ar yr Ychydig Liniaeth at Ein Porthi* [by Ellis Roberts]. *II. O Ychydig o Hanes y Fattel a Fu'n Gibraltar y Modd y Cynnorthwyodd Duw Ychydig o Wŷr Brydain ym mhen Llawer o Elynion* [anon.] (Trefriw: Dafydd Jones, 1782), first ballad only; 3–4. Roberts, Ellis, *Dwy o Gerddi Newyddion. I. O Hanes Dychryn Ofnadwy a Fu yn yn* [*sic*] *yr Italia Modd y Darfu i Dduw Singcio Tri Chan o*

Drefydd, a Thair o Drefydd Caerog; ac Nid Oes Yno Ddim ond Llyn o Ddŵr Dî-waelod. II. Ymddiddan Rhwng Gwr Ifangc ai Gariad, Bob yn Ail Penill (Trefriw: Dafydd Jones, 1783); 5. Roberts, Ellis, *Dwy o Gerddi Newyddion. I. Yn Rhoi Byrr Hanes Dynes a Wnaeth Weithred Ofnadwy Ymhlwy Llansantffraid Glyn Conwy, Sef Diheunyddio Ffrwyth ei Brŷ ai Ado Fe Rhwng Bwystfilod y Ddaear* [by Ellis Roberts]. *II. Cerdd ar Ddioddefaint Crist, wedi ei Throi or Groeg ir Cymraeg* [by Sion ap Howell] (Trefriw: Dafydd Jones, 1784), first ballad only; 6. Roberts, Ellis, *Tair o Gerddi Newyddion. I. Ymddiddan Rhwng Gwr Ifangc ai Gariad Bob yn Eil Odl. II. Cwynfan Merch Ifangc am Garu'n Feddal. III. Clôd ir Lord Pased, or plâs Newydd Sir Fôn* (Trefriw: Dafydd Jones, 1783), third ballad only; 7. Roberts, Ellis, *Dwy o Gerddi Newyddion. I. I'n Ceision Gosod Allan am y Llywydd Sydd yn y Nefoedd, ar Gwynfyd ar Hapusrwydd Sydd ir Sawl ai Cafodd* [by Ellis Roberts]. *II. Ymddiddan Rhwng Dŷn a'i Cydwybod, Bob yn Ail Odl* (Trefriw: Dafydd Jones, n.d.), first ballad and englynion by Ellis Roberts only; 8. Roberts, Ellis, *Tair o Ganeuau Newyddion yn Gyntaf, Garol i'w Ganu Nos Basg, ar Susanna, o Waith Ellis Roberts y Cowper, ag mae'n Debygol ma'i Dyma'r Diwaetha a Wnaeth Ef ir Pwrpas Hwnnw. Yna Ail, Cyngor i Ferchaid Ifangc* [by Thomas Edwards]. *Yn Drydydd, Deisyfiad Gwr Ifangc at ei Gariad* [anon.] (Trefriw: no publisher, n.d.), first ballad only; 9. Roberts, Ellis, *Tair o Gerddi Newyddion. Yn Gyntaf, Cerdd er Dwyn ar Gòf i Ddynion Ddyll y Poennau y mae'r Enaid Colledig yn i Ddiodde yn Uffern . . .* [by Hugh Roberts (Llanllyfni)]. *Yn Ail, Dechre Cerdd ar Loath y Part* [*sic*] *y Ffordd Hwyaf o Ymddiddan Rhwng Dynn ai Gydwybod . . .* [by Ellis Roberts]. *Yn Drydydd, Cerd* [*sic*] *iw Channu ar Susan Lygad-ddy neu Black-Eye Susi* [by 'Dyn Gwirion'] (Caerlleon: Elizabeth Adams, n.d.), second ballad only; 10–11. Roberts, Ellis, *Dwy o Gerddi Newyddion, Y Gyntaf ar Ddull o Ymddiddan Rhwng y Prydydd a'r Swedydd, neu Un o'r Philosophyddion, am yr Arwyddion a'r Rhyfeddodau Wybrennol, Sydd y Dyddiau Yma. Yr Ail Gwahoddiad i Gloddio ym Maes yr Efengyl am y Perl Gwerthfawr. O Waith Ellis Roberts Cwper Llanddoged* (Trefryw: Dafydd Jones, 1776); 12–13. Roberts, Ellis, *Dwy o Gerddi Newyddion y Gyntaf Ynghylch Rhyfeddode a Welwyd yn y Cwmmyle, sef Llûn Dyn a Chledde yn ei Law ai Hett yn Dair Gwalc, ai Wyneb at y Dŵyrain; ar Naill Droed o Flaen y Llall, fel Un am Gochwyn: ai Liw oedd yn Gôch. Yn Ail o Gwynfan am Un ar-ddêg o Longwyr y Bermo a Dolgeleey* [*sic*] *Sydd yn Garcharorion yn Ffraingc dan Dwylo eu Gelynion* (Trefriw: Dafydd Jones, 1779); 14–15. Roberts, Ellis, *Dwy o Gerddi Newyddion. I. Ymddiddanion Sion yr Haidd, ai Gyfaill, sef, Morgan Rondol. II. O Ymddiddanion rhwng y Dyn ar Wenol Bob yn Ail Penill* (Trefriw: Dafydd Jones, 1783).

—— *Llyfr Enterlute Newydd wedi Gosod mewn Dull Ymddiddanion rhwng Gras a Natur* (Warrington: William Eyres, 1769).

Thomas, David (Dafydd Ddu Eryri), letters (dated 1796–1816): *Adgof uwch Anghof: Llythyrau Lluaws o Brif Enwogion Cymru, Hen a Diweddar*, ed. J. Jones (Myrddin Fardd) (Pen-y-Groes: G. Lewis, 1883), 18–52.

Thomas, Edward (of Rhydwen, Flintshire), *Cwymp Dyn: gwedi ei Osod Allan ar Ddull Interlude, yn Dangos fel y Bu i'r Sarph Temptio y Wraig Yngardd Eden . . .* (Caerlleon: Read a Huxley, n.d. [c.1767–8]).

US Settlers, letters (LUSS): A: Letters by settlers from Merionethshire (National Library of Wales, MS 2722E): 1. From Hugh and Catherine Thomas (Trenton, Oneida, NY) to their daughter and son-in-law, Mr and Mrs J. W. Zachariah (Gwastad Coed, Dolgellau, Mer.),

25 September 1816; 2. From David Jones (David Shone Harry) (joiner of Albany, NY, formerly of Llwyngwril, Mer.) to his wife, 14 October 1817; 3. From John Richards (of Johnsburg, Warren County, NY, formerly of Llanuwchllyn, Mer.), 3 November 1817; 4. From William Thomas (of Utica, NY, formerly of Rhyd-y-Main, Llanfachraeth, Mer.) to his family, 17 August 1818; 5. From David Richard to his brother, 11 December 1818; B: Letters by and to settlers from Carmarthenshire (National Library of Wales, MS 14873E): 1. From [?Samuel Thomas] to Theophilus Rees (Beulah, Pa.), 28 May 1801; 2. From John D. Evans (Beulah, Pa.) to Theophilus Rees (Seiotha, Oh.), 5 May 1807; 3. Item about Theophilus Rees; 4. From Samuel Thomas; 5. From Samuel Thomas to his brother and sister, 18 December 1797; 6. From Moses David (of Trelech), 4 June 1800; 7. From Samuel Thomas to Theophilus Rees (Beulah, Pa.), 25 June 1800.

Watson, Bishop Richard, *Meddyliau yr Esgob Watson am y Cyfnewidiad Diweddar yn Llywodraeth Ffraingc . . .*, translation of *Thoughts of Bishop Watson on the Recent Change in the Government of France, Religious Freedom and the Rights of the Dissenters* (Caerfyrddin: J. Ross, 1793).

Williams, Mathew, almanacs: 1. *Britannus Merlinus Liberatus: sef, Amgylchiadau Tymhorol ac Wybrennol: neu, Almanac ac Ephemeris o Symmudiadau'r Planedau . . . 1794 . . .* (Caerfyrddin: I. Ross, 1793), 30–4; 2. *Britannus Merlinus Liberatus . . . 1807* (Aberhonddu: G. North, 1806), 2, 21–4; 3. *Britannus Merlinus Liberatus . . . 1811* (Aberhonddu: G. North, 1810), 2, 24–7.

—— *Hanes Holl Grefyddau'r Byd, yn Enwedig y Grefydd Grist'nogol etc.* (Caerfyrddin: I. Daniel, 1799), 30–58.

Other Modern Welsh texts cited

'Y Brenin Llyr' (National Library of Wales, MS Cwrtmawr 212A, MS c.1700–50).

Edwards, Thomas(?), 'Interliwt Ynghylch Cain ac Abel' (composed ?c.1758), ed. G. M. Ashton, *Bulletin of the Board of Celtic Studies*, 13 (1949), 78–89.

Evans, John, letter dated 9 November 1873, ed. anon., *Maritime Wales*, 7 (1983), 152–3.

'Frederick Brenin Denmark' (National Library of Wales, MS Cwrtmawr 490A, MS c.1700–50).

Hughes, Jonathan, 'Enterlute Histori y Dywysoges Genefetha' (National Library of Wales, MS Cwrtmawr 120A, MS 18th c. (composed 1744)).

Jones, Hugh (Llangwm), 'Daeargryn Lisbon' (composed after 1755); *Blodeugerdd Barddas o Gerddi Rhydd y Ddeunawfed Ganrif*, ed. E. G. Millward (Llandybïe: Cyhoeddiadau Barddas, 1991), 66–7.

—— and Cadwaladr, John, *Enterlut, neu Ddanghosiad o'r Modd y Darfu i'r Brenhin Dafydd Odinebu efo Gwraig Urias . . .* (Caerlleon: W. Read a T. Huxley, n.d. [c.1765]).

Parry, Richard, 'Enterlude neu Chwaryddiaeth ar Destyn Odiaethol, yn Dangos Pa Drigolion a Fu'n Preswylo yn y Deyrnas Hon cyn Dyfod Cymru na Saeson Erioed iw Meddiannu, o Wnaethuriad R P' (National Library of Wales, MS 833A, MS 18th c. (composed 1737)).

Roberts, William, *Ffrewyll y Methodistiaid neu Buttein-glwm Siencyn ac Ynfydog* (n.p., n.d. [1745]).

Wynne, Ellis, *Gweledigaetheu y Bardd Cwsc* (orig. pub. 1703), ed. John Morris-Jones (Caerdydd: Gwasg Prifysgol Cymru, 1948).

SECONDARY LITERATURE

Abraham, Werner (1983) (ed.), *On the Formal Syntax of the Westgermania* (Amsterdam: John Benjamins).

—— Kosmeijer, Wim, and Reuland, Eric (1991) (eds.), *Issues in Germanic Syntax* (Berlin: Mouton de Gruyter).

Adams, Marianne (1987), 'From Old French to the Theory of Pro-Drop', *Natural Language and Linguistic Theory*, 5: 1–32.

Åfarli, Tor, and Creider, Chet (1987), 'Nonsubject Pro-Drop in Norwegian', *Linguistic Inquiry*, 18: 339–45.

Aitchison, Jean (1989), 'Spaghetti Junctions and Recurrent Routes', *Lingua*, 77: 151–71.

Andersen, Henning (1973), 'Abductive and Deductive Change', *Language*, 49: 765–93.

Armstrong, John (1987–8), 'On Some Middle Welsh Relative Constructions', *Studia Celtica*, 22–3: 10–28.

Awbery, Gwenllïan Mair (1977), 'A Transformational View of Welsh Relative Clauses', *Bulletin of the Board of Celtic Studies*, 27: 155–206.

—— (1988), 'Slander and Defamation as a Source for Historical Dialectology', in Alan R. Thomas (1988), 164–74.

—— Jones, Ann E., and Suggett, Richard E. (1985), 'Slander and Defamation: A New Source for Historical Dialectology', *Cardiff Working Papers in Welsh Linguistics*, 4: 1–24.

Baker, Mark (1988), *Incorporation: A Theory of Grammatical Function Changing* (Chicago: University of Chicago Press).

—— and Hale, Kenneth (1990), 'Relativized Minimality and Pronoun Incorporation', *Linguistic Inquiry*, 21: 289–97.

Ball, Martin J. (1987–8), 'The Erosion of the Welsh Pre-Sentential Particle System', *Studia Celtica*, 22–3: 134–45.

—— (1988a), 'Variation in Grammar', in Ball (1988b), 58–69.

—— (1988b) (ed.), *The Use of Welsh* (Clevedon: Multilingual Matters).

—— (1993) (ed.), *The Celtic Languages* (London: Routledge).

—— Fife, James, Poppe, Erich, and Rowland, Jenny (1990) (eds.), *Celtic Linguistics: Ieithyddiaeth Geltaidd* (Amsterdam: John Benjamins).

Battye, Adrian, and Roberts, Ian (1995) (eds.), *Clause Structure and Language Change* (New York: Oxford University Press).

Bayer, Samuel (1996), 'The Coordination of Unlike Categories', *Language*, 72: 579–616.

Beekes, Robert, Lubotsky, Alexander, and Weitenberg, Jos (1992) (eds.), *Rekonstruktion und Relative Chronologie. Akten der VIII. Fachtagung der Indogermanischen Gesellschaft* (Innsbruck: Institut für Sprachwissenschaft der Universität Innsbruck).

Belletti, Adriana (1988), 'The Case of Unaccusatives', *Linguistic Inquiry*, 19: 1–34.

Benincà, Paola (1989) (ed.), *Dialect Variation and the Theory of Grammar* (Dordrecht: Foris).

Bobaljik, Jonathan David, and Carnie, Andrew (1996), 'A Minimalist Approach to Some Problems of Irish Word Order', in Borsley and Roberts (1996), 223–40.

Borsley, Robert D. (1986), 'Prepositional Complementizers in Welsh', *Journal of Linguistics*, 22: 67–84.

—— and Roberts, Ian (1996) (eds.), *The Syntax of the Celtic Languages* (Cambridge: Cambridge University Press).

—— Rivero, Maria-Luisa, and Stephens, Janig (1996), 'Long Head Movement in Breton', in Borsley and Roberts (1996), 53–74.

Bowers, John (1993), 'The Syntax of Predication', *Linguistic Inquiry*, 24: 591–636.

Brake, Phylip John (1981), 'Astudiaeth o Seinyddiaeth a Morffoleg Tafodiaith Cwm-ann a'r Cylch', MA dissertation (University of Wales, Lampeter).

Brandi, Luciana, and Cordin, Patrizia (1989), 'Two Italian Dialects and the Null Subject Parameter', in Jaeggli and Safir (1989), 111–42.

Burton, Strang, and Grimshaw, Jane (1992), 'Coordination and VP-Internal Subjects', *Linguistic Inquiry*, 23: 305–13.

Burzio, Luigi (1986), *Italian Syntax: A Government-Binding Approach* (Dordrecht: Reidel).

Byrne, Cyril J., Harry, Margaret, and Ó Siadhail, Pádraig (1992) (eds.), *Celtic Languages and Celtic Peoples: Proceedings of the Second North American Congress of Celtic Studies* (Halifax, Nova Scotia: D'Arcy McGee Chair of Irish Studies, Saint Mary's University).

Cardinaletti, Anna (1990*a*), 'Es, *Pro* and Sentential Arguments in German', *Linguistische Berichte*, 126: 135–64.

—— (1990*b*), 'Subject/Object Asymmetries in German Null-Topic Constructions and the Status of SpecCP', in Mascaró and Nespor (1990), 75–84.

Chen, Matthew Y., and Wang, William S.-Y. (1975), 'Sound Change: Actuation and Implementation', *Language*, 51: 255–81.

Chomsky, Noam (1957), *Syntactic Structures* (The Hague: Mouton).

—— (1980), 'On Cognitive Structures and their Development: A Reply to Piaget', in Piattelli-Palmarini (1980), 35–52.

—— (1981), *Lectures on Government and Binding* (Dordrecht: Foris).

—— (1986*a*), *Barriers* (Cambridge, Mass.: MIT Press).

—— (1986*b*), *Knowledge of Language: Its Nature, Origin, and Use* (New York: Praeger).

—— (1995), *The Minimalist Program* (Cambridge, Mass.: MIT Press).

——and Lasnik, Howard (1993), 'The Theory of Principles and Parameters', in Jacobs *et al.* (1993), 506–69; repr. in Chomsky (1995).

Christensen, Kirsti Koch (1991), 'Agr, Adjunction, and the Structure of Scandinavian Existential Sentences', *Lingua*, 84: 137–58.

Chung, Sandra, and McCloskey, James (1987), 'Government, Barriers, and Small Clauses in Modern Irish', *Linguistic Inquiry*, 18: 173–237.

Clahsen, Harald (1988), 'Parameterized Grammatical Theory and Language Acquisition', in Flynn and O'Neil (1988), 47–75.

—— and Muysken, Pieter (1986), 'The Availability of Universal Grammar to Adult and Child Learners—A Study of the Acquisition of German Word Order', *Second Language Research*, 2: 93–119.

—— and Smolka, Klaus-Dirk (1986), 'Psycholinguistic Evidence and the Description of V-Second Phenomena in German', in Haider and Prinzhorn (1986), 137–67.

Clark, Robin, and Roberts, Ian G. (1993), 'A Computational Model of Language Learnability and Language Change', *Linguistic Inquiry*, 24: 299–345.

Conway, Alan (1961), *The Welsh in America: Letters from the Immigrants* (Minneapolis: University of Minnesota Press).

Currie, Oliver (1997), 'The Chronology and Explanation of the Grammaticalisation of *fe* and *mi* as Preverbal Particles', MS, University of Cambridge.

Davies, David (1926), *The Influence of the French Revolution on Welsh Life and Literature* (Carmarthen: W. Morgan Evans & Son).

De Freitas, Leslie, and Noonan, Máire (1993), 'Head Movement, Agreement, and Negation in Welsh Relatives', *Chicago Linguistics Society*, 27: 49–64.

Den Besten, Hans (1983), 'On the Interaction of Root Transformations and Lexical Deletive Rules', in Abraham (1983), 47–131.

—— and Moed-van Walraven, Corretje (1986), 'The Syntax of Verbs in Yiddish', in Haider and Prinzhorn (1986), 111–35.

Dictionary of Welsh Biography down to 1940 (1959), ed. John Edward Lloyd and R. T. Jenkins (London: Honourable Society of Cymmrodorion).

Diesing, Molly (1990), 'Verb Movement and the Subject Position in Yiddish', *Natural Language and Linguistic Theory*, 8: 41–79.

Dodd, Arthur H. (1955), 'Letters from Welsh Settlers in New York State 1816–1844', *National Library of Wales Journal*, 9: 42–59.

Dougherty, Ray C. (1970), 'A Grammar of Coordinate Conjoined Structures', *Language*, 46: 850–98, 47: 298–339.

Evans, D. Simon (1964), *A Grammar of Middle Welsh* (Dublin: Dublin Institute for Advanced Studies).

—— (1968), 'The Sentence in Early Modern Welsh', *Bulletin of the Board of Celtic Studies*, 22: 311–37.

—— (1971), 'Concord in Middle Welsh', *Studia Celtica*, 6: 42–56.

Evans, Emrys (1958), 'Cystrawen y Rhagenw Personol yn Rhyddiaith Gymraeg y Cyfnod Canol', MA dissertation (University of Wales, Swansea).

—— (1959), 'Y Rhagenw Ategol Dwbl mewn Cymraeg Canol', *Bulletin of the Board of Celtic Studies*, 18: 173–6.

Evans, G. G. (1950), 'Yr Anterliwt Gymraeg', *Llên Cymru*, 1: 83–96, 224–31.

—— (1995), *Elis y Cowper* (Caernarfon: Gwasg Pantycelyn).

Evans, J. Gwenogvryn (1902), *Report on Manuscripts in the Welsh Language*, ii (London: His Majesty's Stationery Office).

Evans, John James (1928), *Dylanwad y Chwyldro Ffrengig ar Lenyddiaeth Cymru* (Lerpwl: Hugh Evans a'i Feibion).

—— (1935), *Morgan John Rhys a'i Amersau* (Caerdydd: Gwasg Prifysgol Cymru).

Falk, Cecilia (1993), 'Non-Referential Subjects and Agreement in the History of Swedish', *Lingua*, 89: 143–80.

Fife, James (1986), 'The Semantics of *Gwneud* Inversions', *Bulletin of the Board of Celtic Studies*, 33: 133–44.

—— (1988), *Functional Syntax: A Case Study in Middle Welsh* (Lublin: Redakcja Wydawnictw Katolickiego Uniwersytetu Lubelskiego).

—— (1991), 'Some Constituent-Order Frequencies in Classical Welsh Prose', in Fife and Poppe (1991), 251–74.

—— (1993), 'Constituent-Order Frequencies in Modern Welsh', *Journal of Celtic Linguistics*, 2: 1–33.

—— and King, Gareth (1991), 'Focus and the Welsh "Abnormal Sentence": A Crosslinguistic Perspective', in Fife and Poppe (1991), 81–154.

—— and Poppe, Erich (1991) (eds.), *Studies in Brythonic Word Order* (Amsterdam: John Benjamins).

Flynn, Suzanne, and O'Neil, Wayne (1988) (eds.), *Linguistic Theory in Second Language Acquisition* (Dordrecht: Kluwer).

Foulkes, Isaac (Llyfrbryf) (1883), 'John Jones o Lanygors', *Y Geninen*, 1: 275–81.

Freidin, Robert (1991) (ed.), *Principles and Parameters in Comparative Grammar* (Cambridge, Mass.: MIT Press).

Gazdar, Gerald (1981), 'Unbounded Dependencies and Coordinate Structure', *Linguistic Inquiry*, 12: 155–84.

Geiriadur Prifysgol Cymru (1950–present), ed. R. J. Thomas (Caerdydd: Gwasg Prifysgol Cymru).

George, K. J. (1990), 'A Comparison of Word-Order in Middle Breton and Middle Cornish', in Ball *et al.* (1990), 225–40.

—— (1991), 'Notes on Word Order in Beunans Meriasek', in Fife and Poppe (1991), 205–50.

Givón, Talmy (1977), 'The Drift from VSO to SVO in Biblical Hebrew: The Pragmatics of Tense-Aspect', in Li (1977), 181–254.

Greene, David (1971), 'Linguistic Considerations in the Dating of Early Welsh Verse', *Studia Celtica*, 6: 1–11.

Haegeman, Liliane (1990), 'Subject Pronouns and Subject Clitics in West Flemish', *Linguistic Review*, 7: 333–63.

—— (1994), *Introduction to Government and Binding Theory* (2nd edn., Oxford: Blackwell).

Haider, Hubert (1986), 'V-Second in German', in Haider and Prinzhorn (1986), 49–76.

—— and Prinzhorn, Martin (1986) (eds.), *Verb Second Phenomena in Germanic Languages* (Dordrecht: Foris).

Hale, Mark (1994), review of Lightfoot (1991), *Language*, 70: 141–52.

Harlow, Stephen (1981), 'Government and Relativisation in Celtic', in Heny (1981), 213–54.

—— (1983), 'Celtic Relatives', *York Papers in Linguistics*, 10: 77–121.

Hawkins, John A. (1983), *Word Order Universals* (New York: Academic Press).

—— (1988) (ed.), *Explaining Language Universals* (Oxford: Blackwell).

Hendrick, Randall (1991), 'The Morphosyntax of Aspect', *Lingua*, 85: 171–210.

Heny, Frank (1981) (ed.), *Binding and Filtering* (London: Croom Helm).

Heycock, Caroline, and Kroch, Anthony (1994), 'Verb Movement and Coordination in a Dynamic Theory of Licensing', *Linguistic Review*, 11: 257–83.

Höhle, Tilman N. (1990), 'Assumptions about Asymmetric Coordination in German', in Mascaró and Nespor (1990), 221–35.

Holmberg, Anders, and Platzack, Christer (1991), 'On the Role of Inflection in Scandinavian Syntax', in Abraham *et al.* (1991), 93–118.

Hopper, Paul J., and Traugott, Elizabeth Closs (1993), *Grammaticalization* (Cambridge: Cambridge University Press).

Howell, Jenkin (1902), 'Neillduolion Ieithyddol Aberdâr', *Y Geninen*, 20: 270–1.

Huang, C. T. James (1984), 'On the Distribution and Reference of Empty Pronouns', *Linguistic Inquiry*, 15: 531–74.

Hughes, Hugh (Tegai) (n.d.), *Gramadeg Cymraeg, sef Ieithiadur Athronyddol: yn yr hwn yr Amlygir Deddfau yr Iaith Gymraeg; yn nghyda Chyfarwyddiadau Helaeth i'w Deall, ei Hysgrifenu, a'i Darllen yn Briodol* (Caernarfon: Peter Evans).

Huws, Daniel (1991), 'Llyfr Gwyn Rhydderch', *Cambridge Medieval Celtic Studies*, 21: 1–37.

Isaac, Graham R. (1996), *The Verb in the Book of Aneirin* (Tübingen: Max Niemeyer).

Jackson, Kenneth (1953), *Language and History in Early Britain* (Edinburgh: Edinburgh University Press).

Jacobs, Joachim, von Stechow, Arnim, Sternefeld, Wolfgang, and Vennemann, Theo (1993) (eds.), *Syntax: Ein Internationales Handbuch Zeitgenössischer Forschung. An International Handbook of Contemporary Research* (Berlin: Mouton de Gruyter).

Jaeggli, Osvaldo, and Safir, Kenneth J. (1989) (eds.), *The Null Subject Parameter* (Dordrecht: Kluwer).

—— and Silva-Corvalan, Carmen (1986) (eds.), *Studies in Romance Linguistics* (Dordrecht: Foris).

Jones, Albert E. (Cynan) (1967), 'Jac Glan-y-Gors 1766–1821: Darlith Deucanmlwyddiant', *Transactions of the Denbighshire Historical Society*, 16: 62–81.

Jones, Charles (1993) (ed.), *Historical Linguistics: Problems and Perspectives* (London: Longman).

Jones, Dafydd Glyn (1988), 'Literary Welsh', in Ball (1988*b*), 125–71.

Jones, J. Ifano (1902), 'Llenyddiaeth Cymru Hanner Ola'r Ddeunawfed Ganrif', *Y Geninen*, 20: 27–31, 189–94.

Jones, John Mendus (1847), *Gramadeg Cymreig Ymarferol: A Practical Welsh Grammar* (Llanidloes: J. Mendus Jones).

Jones, Jonathan (1897), *Cofiant y Parch. Thomas Jones, o Ddinbych* (Dinbych: T. Gee a'i Fab).

Jones, R. Brinley (1979), 'A Brief History of the Welsh Language', in Stephens (1979), 18–31.

Jones, T. Llechid (1932), 'Yr Eurgrawn Cymraeg: A Correction of its Date', *Journal of the Welsh Bibliographical Society*, 4: 358–60.

Jouin, Beatris (1984), *Petite grammaire du breton* (Rennes: Ouest France).

Kathol, Andreas (1992), 'On Coordination and Constituency in German', *Chicago Linguistics Society*, 28: 267–81.

Kayne, Richard S. (1989*a*), 'Facets of Romance Past Participle Agreement', in Benincà (1989), 85–103.

—— (1989*b*), 'Null Subjects and Clitic Climbing', in Jaeggli and Safir (1989), 239–61.

—— (1991), 'Romance Clitics, Verb Movement and PRO', *Linguistic Inquiry*, 22: 647–86.

King, Gareth (1993), *Modern Welsh: A Comprehensive Grammar* (London: Routledge).

Koch, John T. (1991), 'On the Prehistory of Brittonic Syntax', in Fife and Poppe (1991), 1–44.

—— (1992), ' "Gallo-Brittonic" vs. "Insular Celtic": The Inter-Relationship of the Celtic Languages Reconsidered', in Le Menn (1992), 471–95.

Koopman, Hilda, and Sportiche, Dominique (1991), 'The Position of Subjects', *Lingua*, 85: 211–58.

Kroch, Anthony S. (1989), 'Reflexes of Grammar in Patterns of Language Change', *Language Variation and Change*, 1: 199–244.

Laka, Itziar (1990), 'Negation in Syntax: On the Nature of Functional Categories and Projections', doctoral dissertation (MIT, Cambridge, Mass.).

Larson, Richard K. (1988), 'On the Double Object Construction', *Linguistic Inquiry*, 19: 335–91.

Lasnik, Howard (1992), 'Case and Expletives: Notes toward a Parametric Account', *Linguistic Inquiry*, 23: 381–405.

Le Clerc, L. (1908), *Grammaire bretonne du dialecte de Tréguier* (Saint-Brieuc: Imprimerie-Librairie de René Prud'homme).

Le Gléau, René (1973), *Syntaxe du breton moderne* (n.p.: Éditions la Baule).

Le Menn, Gwennolé (1992) (ed.), *Bretagne et pays celtiques: Langues, histoire, civilisation* (Rennes: Presses Universitaires Rennes).

Lehmann, W. P., and Malkiel, Yakov (1968), *Directions for Historical Linguistics* (Austin, Tex.: University of Texas Press).

Lewis, Henry (1931), *Datblygiad yr Iaith Gymraeg* (Caerdydd: Gwasg Prifysgol Cymru, repr. 1983).

—— (1942), *The Sentence in Welsh* (London: Humphrey Milford Amen House).

—— (1950), 'Cystrawennau Canu Aneirin', *Bulletin of the Board of Celtic Studies*, 13: 185–8.

—— and Pedersen, Holger (1937), *A Concise Comparative Celtic Grammar* (Göttingen: Vandenhoeck & Ruprecht).

Li, Charles N. (1977) (ed.), *Mechanisms of Syntactic Change* (Austin, Tex.: University of Texas Press).

Lightfoot, David W. (1979), *Principles of Diachronic Syntax* (Cambridge: Cambridge University Press).

—— (1991), *How to Set Parameters: Arguments from Language Change* (Cambridge, Mass.: MIT Press).

—— (1993), 'Why UG Needs a Learning Theory: Triggering Verb Movement', in Charles Jones (1993), 190–214; repr. in Battye and Roberts (1995), 31–52.

—— (1994), review of Roberts (1993*b*), *Language*, 70: 571–8.

—— (1997), 'Shifting Triggers and Diachronic Reanalyses', in van Kemenade and Vincent (1997), 253–72.

—— and Hornstein, Norbert (1994) (eds.), *Verb Movement* (Cambridge: Cambridge University Press).

Lloyd, D. M. (1937), 'Casgliad o Hen Faledi', *Journal of the Welsh Bibliographical Society*, 5: 93–9.

Lust, Barbara, Suñer, Margarita, and Whitman, John (1994) (eds.), *Syntactic Theory and First Language Acquisition: Cross-Linguistic Perspectives*, i. *Heads, Projections, and Learnability* (Hillsdale, NJ: Lawrence Erlbaum Associates).

Mac Cana, Proinsias (1973), 'Celtic Word-Order and the Welsh Abnormal Sentence', *Ériu*, 24: 90–120.

—— (1979), 'Notes on the "Abnormal Sentence"', *Studia Celtica*, 14–15: 174–93.

—— (1990), 'On the Uses of the Conjunctive Pronouns in Middle Welsh', in Ball *et al.* (1990), 411–33.

—— (1991), 'Further Notes on Constituent Order in Welsh', in Fife and Poppe (1991), 45–80.

McCloskey, James (1991), 'Clause Structure, Ellipsis and Proper Government in Irish', *Lingua*, 85: 259–302.

—— (1996), 'On the Scope of Verb Movement in Irish', *Natural Language and Linguistic Theory*, 14: 47–104.

McCone, Kim R. (1992), 'Relative Chronologie: Keltisch', in Beekes *et al.* (1992), 11–39.

McNally, Louise (1992), 'VP Coordination and the VP-Internal Subject Hypothesis', *Linguistic Inquiry*, 23: 336–41.

Maling, Joan, and Zaenen, Annie (1990) (eds.), *Modern Icelandic Syntax* (San Diego: Academic Press).

Mascaró, Joan, and Nespor, Marina (1990) (eds.), *Grammar in Progress: Glow Essays for Henk van Riemsdijk* (Dordrecht: Foris).

Milroy, James (1992), *Linguistic Variation and Change* (Oxford: Blackwell).

—— (1993), 'On the Social Origins of Language Change', in Charles Jones (1993), 215–36.

Milroy, Leslie (1987), *Language and Social Networks* (Oxford: Blackwell).

Morgan, T. J. (1952), *Y Treigladau a'u Cystrawen* (Caerdydd: Gwasg Prifysgol Cymru).

Morris-Jones, John (1913), *A Welsh Grammar* (Oxford: Oxford University Press).

—— (1921), *An Elementary Welsh Grammar* (Oxford: Oxford University Press).

Ouhalla, Jamal (1994), *Introducing Transformational Grammar* (London: Edward Arnold).

Napoli, Donna Jo (1989), *Predication Theory* (Cambridge: Cambridge University Press).

Perlmutter, David M. (1978), 'Impersonal Passives and the Unaccusative Hypothesis', *Proceedings of the Berkeley Linguistics Society*, 4: 157–89.

Phillips, D. Rhys (1937), 'The "Eurgrawn Cymraeg" of 1770', *Journal of the Welsh Bibliographical Society*, 5: 48–56.

Phillips, Vincent Howell (1955), 'Astudiaeth o Gymraeg Llafar Dyffryn Elái a'r Cyffiniau', MA dissertation (University of Wales, Cardiff).

Piattelli-Palmarini, Massimo (1980) (ed.), *Language and Learning: The Debate between Jean Piaget and Noam Chomsky* (London: Routledge).

Platzack, Christer (1986), 'The Position of the Finite Verb in Swedish', in Haider and Prinzhorn (1986), 27–48.

—— (1987), 'The Scandinavian Languages and the Null Subject Parameter', *Natural Language and Linguistic Theory*, 5: 377–402.

Pollock, Jean-Yves (1989), 'Verb Movement, Universal Grammar, and the Structure of IP', *Linguistic Inquiry*, 20: 365–424.

Poppe, Erich (1989), 'Constituent Ordering in *Breudwyt Maxen Wledic*', *Bulletin of the Board of Celtic Studies*, 36: 43–63.

—— (1990), 'Word-Order Patterns in *Breudwyt Ronabwy*', in Ball *et al.* (1990), 445–60.

—— (1991a), 'Word Order in *Cyfranc Lludd a Llefelys*: Notes on the Pragmatics of Constituent-Ordering in MW Narrative Prose', in Fife and Poppe (1991), 155–204.

—— (1991b), *Untersuchungen zur Wortstellung im Mittelkymrischen* (Hamburg: Helmut Buske).

—— (1993), 'Word Order in Middle Welsh: The Case of *Kedymdeithyas Amlyn ac Amic*', *Bulletin of the Board of Celtic Studies*, 40: 95–117.

—— (1996), 'Convergence and Divergence: The Emergence of a "Future" in the British Languages', *Transactions of the Philological Society*, 94: 119–60.

Press, Ian (1986), *A Grammar of Modern Breton* (Berlin: Mouton de Gruyter).

Radford, Andrew (1988), *Transformational Grammar* (Cambridge: Cambridge University Press).

Raposo, Eduardo (1986), 'On the Null Object in European Portuguese', in Jaeggli and Silva-Corvalan (1986), 373–90.

Reyle, U., and Rohrer, C. (1988) (eds.), *Natural Language Parsing and Linguistic Theories* (Dordrecht: Reidel).

Richards, Melville (1938), *Cystrawen y Frawddeg Gymraeg* (Caerdydd: Gwasg Prifysgol Cymru).

—— (1940), 'Y Frawddeg Gymysg', *Bulletin of the Board of Celtic Studies*, 10: 105–16.

—— (1966), 'Yr Awdur a'i Gyhoedd yn y Ddeunawfed Ganrif', *Journal of the Welsh Bibliographical Society*, 10: 13–26.

Rivero, María-Luisa (1991), 'Long Head Movement and Negation: Serbo-Croatian vs. Slovak and Czech', *Linguistic Review*, 8: 319–51.

—— (1993), 'Long Head Movement vs. V2, and Null Subjects in Old Romance', *Lingua*, 89: 217–45.

—— (1994), 'Clause Structure and V-movement in the Languages of the Balkans', *Natural Language and Linguistic Theory*, 12: 63–120.

Rizzi, Luigi (1982), *Issues in Italian Syntax* (Dordrecht: Foris).

—— (1986), 'On the Status of Subject Clitics in Romance', in Jaeggli and Silva-Corvalan (1986), 391–419.

—— (1990), 'Speculations on Verb Second', in Mascaró and Nespor (1990), 375–86.

—— and Roberts, Ian (1989), 'Complex Inversion in French', *Probus*, 1: 1–30.

Roberts, Ian G. (1985), 'Agreement Parameters and the Development of English Modal Auxiliaries', *Natural Language and Linguistic Theory*, 3: 21–58.

—— (1993*a*), 'A Formal Account of Grammaticalisation in the History of Romance Futures', *Folia Linguistica Historica*, 13: 219–58.

—— (1993*b*), *Verbs in Diachronic Syntax* (Dordrecht: Kluwer).

Rögnvaldsson, Eiríkur, and Thráinsson, Höskuldur (1990), 'On Icelandic Word Order Once More', in Maling and Zaenen (1990), 3–40.

Ross, John Robert (1967), 'Constraints on Variables in Syntax', doctoral dissertation (MIT, Cambridge, Mass.).

Rouveret, Alain (1994), *Syntaxe du gallois* (Paris: CNRS Éditions).

Sadler, Louisa (1988), *Welsh Syntax: A Government-Binding Approach* (London: Croom Helm).

Salmon, David (1937), 'Histories of the French Invasion of Pembrokeshire', *Journal of the Welsh Bibliographical Society*, 5: 41–8.

Santorini, Beatrice (1989), 'The Generalization of the Verb-Second Constraint in the History of Yiddish', doctoral dissertation (University of Pennsylvania).

—— (1992), 'Variation and Change in Yiddish Subordinate Clause Word Order', *Natural Language and Linguistic Theory*, 10: 595–640.

—— (1994), 'Some Similarities and Differences between Icelandic and Yiddish', in Lightfoot and Hornstein (1994), 87–106.

—— (1995), 'Two Types of Verb Second in the History of Yiddish', in Battye and Roberts (1995), 53–79.

Schafer, Robin (1994), 'Nonfinite Predicate Initial Constructions in Breton', doctoral dissertation (University of California, Santa Cruz).

—— (1995), 'Negation and Verb Second in Breton', *Natural Language and Linguistic Theory*, 13: 135–72.

Schmidt, Karl Horst (1990), 'Gallo-Brittonic or Insular Celtic', in Villar (1990), 255–67.

—— (1993), 'Insular Celtic: P and Q Celtic', in Ball (1993), 64–98.

Sells, Peter (1983), 'Relative Clauses in Irish and Welsh', *Yorks Papers in Linguistics*, 10: 159–72.

—— (1987), 'Binding Resumptive Pronouns', *Linguistics and Philosophy*, 10: 261–98.

Shlonsky, Ur (1994), 'Agreement in Comp', *Linguistic Review*, 11: 351–75.

Sigurðsson, Halldór Ármann (1990), 'V1 Declaratives and Verb Raising in Icelandic', in Maling and Zaenen (1990), 41–69.

—— (1993), 'Argument-Drop in Old Icelandic', *Lingua*, 89: 247–80.

Sproat, Richard (1985), 'Welsh Syntax and VSO Structure', *Natural Language and Linguistic Theory*, 3: 173–216.

Stephens, Meic (1979) (ed.), *The Welsh Language Today* (2nd edn., Llandysul: Gomer).

—— (1986) (ed.), *Oxford Companion to the Literature of Wales* (Oxford: Oxford University Press).

Stump, Gregory T. (1984), 'Agreement vs. Incorporation in Breton', *Natural Language and Linguistic Theory*, 2: 289–348.

—— (1989), 'Further Remarks on Breton Verb Agreement: A Reply to Borsley and Stephens', *Natural Language and Linguistic Theory*, 7: 429–71.

Suggett, Richard F. (1983), 'An Analysis and Calendar of Early Modern Welsh Defamation Suits', SSRC Final Report (HR 6979).

Tallerman, Maggie O. (1983), 'Island Constraints in Welsh', *York Papers in Linguistics*, 10: 197–204.

—— (1990), 'Relativization Strategies: NP Accessibility in Welsh', *Journal of Linguistics*, 26: 291–314.

—— (1993), 'Case-Assignment and the Order of Functional Projections in Welsh', MS, University of Durham.

—— (1996), 'Fronting Constructions in Welsh', in Borsley and Roberts (1996), 97–124.

Taraldsen, Knut Tarald (1986), 'On Verb Second and the Functional Content of Syntactic Categories', in Haider and Prinzhorn (1986), 7–25.

Thomas, Alan R. (1988) (ed.), *Methods in Dialectology* (Clevedon: Multilingual Matters).

Thomas, Beth, and Thomas, Peter Wynn (1989), *Cymraeg, Cymrâg, Cymrêg: Cyflwyno'r Tafodieithoedd* (Caerdydd: Gwasg Taf).

Thomas, Ceinwen H. (1974), 'Y Tafodieithegydd a "Chymraeg Cyfoes" ', *Llên Cymru*, 13: 113–52.

—— (1993), *Tafodiaith Nantgarw: Astudiaeth o Gymraeg Llafar Nantgarw yng Nghwm Taf, Morgannwg* (Caerdydd: Gwasg Prifysgol Cymru).

Thomas, David Oswald (1989), *Ymateb i Chwyldro. Response to Revolution* (Cardiff: University of Wales Press).

Thomas, Peter Wynn (1992), 'In Search of Middle Welsh Dialects', in Byrne *et al.* (1992), 287–303.

—— (1993), 'Middle Welsh Dialects: Problems and Perspectives', *Bulletin of the Board of Celtic Studies*, 40: 17–50.

Thorne, David A. (1993), *A Comprehensive Welsh Grammar* (Oxford: Blackwell).

Thráinsson, Höskuldur (1986), 'V1, V2, V3 in Icelandic', in Haider and Prinzhorn (1986), 169–94.

—— (1994), 'Comments on the Paper by Vikner', in Lightfoot and Hornstein (1994), 149–62.

Timberlake, Alan (1977), 'Reanalysis and Actualization in Syntactic Change', in Li (1977), 141–77.

Timm, Lenora A. (1988), 'Relative Clause Formation in Breton', *Word*, 39: 79–107.

—— (1989), 'Word Order in Twentieth-Century Breton', *Natural Language and Linguistic Theory*, 7: 361–78.

—— (1991), 'Discourse Pragmatics of NP-Initial Sentences in Breton', in Fife and Poppe (1991), 275–310.

Tomaselli, Alessandra (1986), 'Das unpersönliche "es"—Eine Analyse im Rahmen der Generativen Grammatik', *Linguistische Berichte*, 102: 171–90.

Traugott, Elizabeth Closs, and Heine, Bernd (1991) (eds.), *Approaches to Grammaticalization* (Amsterdam: John Benjamins).

—— and Smith, Henry (1993), 'Arguments from Language Change' (review of Lightfoot 1991), *Journal of Linguistics*, 29: 431–47.

Travis, Lisa deMena (1991), 'Parameters of Phrase Structure and Verb-Second Phenomena', in Freidin (1991), 339–64.

Trépos, Pierre (n.d.), *Grammaire bretonne* (Rennes: Imprimerie Simon).

Vance, Barbara (1993), 'Verb-First Declaratives Introduced by *et* and the Position of *pro* in Old and Middle French', *Lingua*, 89: 281–314.

Van Kemenade, Ans, and Vincent, Nigel (1997) (eds.), *Parameters of Morphosyntactic Change* (Cambridge: Cambridge University Press).

Vikner, Sten (1994), 'Finite Verb Movement in Scandinavian Embedded Clauses', in Lightfoot and Hornstein (1994), 117–48.

—— (1995), *Verb Movement and Expletive Subjects in the Germanic Languages* (New York: Oxford University Press).

Villar, Francisco (1990) (ed.), *Studia indogermanica et palaeohispanica in honorem A. Tovar et L. Michelena* (Salamanca: Ediciones Universidad de Salamanca).

Warner, Anthony R. (1983), review of Lightfoot (1979), *Journal of Linguistics*, 19: 187–209.

—— (1995), 'Predicting the Progressive Passive: Parametric Change within a Lexicalist Framework', *Language*, 71: 533–57.

Watkin-Jones, A. (1926), 'The Popular Literature of Wales in the Eighteenth Century', *Bulletin of the Board of Celtic Studies*, 3: 178–95.

—— (1928), 'The Interludes of Wales in the Eighteenth Century', *Bulletin of the Board of Celtic Studies*, 4: 103–11.

Watkins, T. Arwyn (1960), 'Cymraeg Canol y/yn Berfenwol', *Bulletin of the Board of Celtic Studies*, 18: 362–72.

—— (1977), 'The Welsh Personal Pronoun', *Word*, 28: 146–65.

—— (1977–8), 'Trefn yn y Frawddeg Gymraeg', *Studia Celtica*, 12–13: 367–95.

—— (1983–4), 'Trefn y Constitwentau Brawddegol yn *Branwen*', *Studia Celtica*, 18–19: 147–57.

—— (1987), 'Constituent Order in the Old Welsh Verbal Sentence', *Bulletin of the Board of Celtic Studies*, 34: 51–60.

—— (1988), *Constituent Order in the Positive Declarative Sentence in the Medieval Welsh Tale 'Kulhwch ac Olwen'* (Innsbruck: Institut für Sprachwissenschaft der Universität Innsbruck).

—— (1991), 'The Function of the Cleft and Non-cleft Constituent Orders in Modern Welsh', in Fife and Poppe (1991), 329–52.

—— (1993), 'Constituent Order in Main/Simple Clauses of *Pwyll Pendeuic Dyuet*', *Language Sciences*, 15: 115–39.

Watkins, T. Arwyn and Mac Cana, Proinsias (1958), 'Cystrawennau'r Cyplad mewn Hen Gymraeg', *Bulletin of the Board of Celtic Studies*, 18: 1–24.

Weinreich, Uriel, Labov, William, and Herzog, Marvin I. (1968), 'Empirical Foundations for a Theory of Language Change', in Lehmann and Malkiel (1968), 97–195.

Weissenborn, Jürgen (1994), 'Constraining the Child's Grammar: Local Well-Formedness in the Development of Verb Movement in German and French', in Lust *et al.* (1994), 215–47.

Williams, Edwin (1977), 'Across-the-Board Rule Application', *Linguistic Inquiry*, 8: 419–23.

—— (1978), 'Across-the-Board Rule Application', *Linguistic Inquiry*, 9: 31–43.

Williams, G. J. (1969), *Agweddau ar Hanes Dysg Gymraeg* (Caerdydd: Gwasg Prifysgol Cymru).

Williams, Stephen J. (1980), *A Welsh Grammar* (Cardiff: University of Wales Press).

Wunderlich, Dieter (1988), 'Some Problems of Coordination in German', in Reyle and Rohrer (1988), 289–316.

Zaenen, Annie (1983), 'On Syntactic Binding', *Linguistic Inquiry*, 14: 469–504.

Index